CW00937597

Naughty

Naughty

Mark Chester

MILO BOOKS

First published in September 2003 by Milo Books

ISBN 1 903854 17 2

Typeset by e-type

Printed and bound in Great Britain by
Creative Print and Design, Ebbw Vale, Gwent

MILO BOOKS LTD
10 Park Street
Lytham
Lancs
FY8 5LU
info@milobooks.com

Contents

Vis Unita Fortior
(United Strength is Stronger)

Motto on the City of Stoke-on-Trent coat of arms.

Opening Words

THIS WAS NO ordinary fixture. Millwall on a Sunday lunch-time. The coaches were arranged for a six o'clock departure from our main boozer, Charley Browns: four vehicles with over 200 boys. Most had spoken of little else for weeks. The excitement was so contagious that some lads decided to join up while enjoying a lock-in with a couple of our lot on a weekend-long session. Charley's was rammed.

A few bevvies then we were away. No-one needed psyching up for this one. We all knew we were heading for hostile territory and the natives definitely weren't friendly. We met up with a couple of vanloads at Euston, then moved on to Bermondsey, and were on their manor while they were still thinking about putting the kettle on for their first cuppa. We plotted up in a boozer called The Fort. The delightful old couple that ran the place were superb. They opened up early for us and the lads appreciated the gesture; everyone watched their language and anyone who wanted a spliff went out into the beer garden. They were so busy they asked some of our lads to help out behind the bar. Trust and hospitality – what more could we ask for? When we left, they stood by the door and said we would be welcome again.

For the next five minutes all that could be heard was the breathing of men on a mission and the sound of 280 lads marching on trainer-clad feet. We were tight and commited; the only slightly unnerving thing was the Bermondsey housewives looking at us with silent malice. If this was what the lads we were looking to fight had to face after a night on the lash, then we were going have our hands full. We turned the corner and there it was nestling in the shadow of a railway bridge: The Tropics.

We fanned out in the street silently. A bottle whooshed through the air, but this wasn't your average empty street weapon. As it hit the wall of the boozer, it exploded – a Molotov cocktail, not normally on the bar list. As flames coated the wall, one of their lads stuck his head out of the door.

'Fucking hell, they're here.'

A second petrol bomb hit the arch above the door and ignited the doorframe, like the gateway to hell. Lads stood on the windowsill putting the glass through with their fists as Millwall tried to barricade the window with a pool table. Even their hardened veterans must have been shocked by the barbarians calling it on outside, and possibly wishing for their own Hadrian's Wall. Sirens screeched up all around us as the old bill arrived.

He was right. Stoke were here. We were visiting for Sunday lunch and we'd brought the roast.

Let's get this straight from the off. This is a book of short stories and factual accounts concerning men and events that have happened in our town over the past forty years. There are many stories like the above, a true account of a visit to Millwall. If all you want to read about is conflict and violence, I suggest you flick to the page of your choice, and then place this book on the shelf with the rest of your collection. Football violence does feature heavily in this story but there is also a life and a culture that surrounds it. To those of us involved, it was something special and that is what we most want to convey.

You might think that because I am writing this book, I'm some kind of top boy or general, a ringleader. Nowhere near. In our society, in Britain, we all have the opportunity, some more than others, to choose what we want to be.

There was a young lad, ten years of age.
Back in the Seventies, 1974 to be precise.
The time of The Grimleys, flared trousers, Wrangler jackets with big eagle patches sewn on the back with Stoke City on them.
Scarves tied round both wrists, as many metal lapel badges as you could fit on your person, Doctor Marten boots as high up your shin as the doctor allowed.
The really trendy Stokie of the day would own a £1.50 white silk Stoke scarf, which would adorn his neck like a proper dresser's tie, with a tight, smart knot.
This young lad went to his first professional football match at the Victoria Ground and stood on a huge open terrace called the Stoke End because he thought that was where all the Stoke fans went. He was wrong.
He was mixed in with a load of Leeds fans, and he saw some fighting.
He saw a lot of things that day, and it opened his mind, and from then on he was obsessed with watching Stoke City.
They won that match 3–0, the opening game of the season.

The next home game, he stood on the Boothen End. It was twenty pence.
This time, instead of watching it swaying and listening aghast from the opposite
end of the ground, he was part of it. That was it.
A habit was formed for the rest of his life.
The Boothen End.

That was my choice, no-one else's. I had seen enough, and with my two schoolmates, Eddy and Gibbo, walked shyly at first into this world of passion and thrills, sadness, disappointment and despair. Emotions that we all share and crave, emotions that, when put together, give you that one big adrenalin buzz. And as we know, adrenalin is addictive.

Some folk, for example the Cambridge University Extreme Sports Club, travel extensively and spend fortunes seeking that buzz, that pushing yourself to your limit, that challenge. Well it's no different dropping off the side of a mountain or riding that perfect wave than travelling to another ground and entering the home enclosure, knowing it will be full of like-minded people whose turn it was that week to defend instead of conquer. This is as good as any night-dive or rally car race, believe me.

I wanted to be like them, the older lads, the ones I would scan the crowd for instead of watching the match, waiting for that big gap to open up and the windmilling to start. I wanted to be like those lads. So there's your answer, just a young lad who wanted something badly enough. No top boy. Everybody's equal round our way.

I'm going to give my best shot at explaining why I chose to become a football hooligan and live the life I've lived. After much discussion between us all, some of the lads have chosen to remain anonymous, and others have shared with me their own upbringings and insecurities and their own particular reasons for being part of our family. Others have chosen to have no part in it at all and everyone respects their decision. To write about such a phenomenon and chart over forty years' history in a little over 140,000 words, I have barely scratched the surface. Even so, our journey takes us through the Fifties and up to the present day. I'm not ashamed to have been what I was, and if I could go back, I would do it all again. I'm sure we all would; the highs have always outweighed the lows.

At first I puzzled how to begin to write such a book, and how to do it in such a way as not to let down any of my friends; after all, it has been a joint effort and all of us have suffered one way or another over the years. The only way, I feel to approach this, is by giving it 100 per cent and baring my soul, sharing everything and exorcising some ghosts in the meantime. On that basis, although my life has not been that spectacular, I have chosen to use my story as the spine of the book, introducing characters from all eras as they have appeared throughout my life.

As for the ridicule and the backlash I might face from the world I come from: simple – when you've all got the bollocks to stand up and say it as it is, then I'll listen to what you have got to say. I've got a story to tell, and I'm going to write it as I'd speak it. And the first thing I would like to say is: we're Stoke City, we're Naughty Forty, and we're game as fuck.

So let's have it.

For Queen, Country and Stoke City

chapter one

As for Me

A S FOR ME, well why don't we start from the beginning? I was conceived on a golf course and born Mark David Chester on 21 September 1964. My parents were second cousins in Llandrindod Wells, in what was then Radnorshire, mid-Wales. Just teenagers when my mother became pregnant, they 'did the right thing' and got married. My father found employment as a steeplejack with Pirelli and headed off to the Persian Gulf to provide for his new family.

The role of motherhood, however, did not come naturally to the self-indulgent, party-going harlot he had married. She preferred entertaining the Italian waiters at a local hotel rather to nurturing her new-born son. Money sent home was squandered, and rumours circulated; it was a small spa town and word got round. Inevitably, I was handed as a toddler to my grandparents, and found some stability.

When I was three, a baby brother arrived. He was spawned out of wedlock to an Italian father, and was afflicted with Downs syndrome. It was the final straw. The embarrassment of my mother's behaviour became too much and my devastated grandfather sold up and put in for a transfer. From the age of thirteen he had worked for Standard Oil, first as a barrel boy, then a wagon driver during the War and on into site management. He ended up in Tunstall, Stoke-on-Trent, and my heartbroken grandmother wept as she traded lush, open fields and valleys for pot kilns and terraced streets.

Initially we found accommodation in a hotel in Hanley, resulting in more depression for an isolated woman who longed for clean air and a garden. Months of searching for a home proved fruitless until a work colleague invited them to meet his family and have a meal. They liked the area, and weeks later they moved into a small, three-bedroom, detached house with garden in Alsager, south Cheshire. And that's where I grew up.

At the local county primary, I met Eddy. He was six months older and at the respective ages of five and five-and-a-half we had our first scrap. It was at the bottom of a hill we called 'the bank', among some reeds and in a ditch. It drew a good crowd of our fellow pupils, though their chants of 'Scrap! Scrap! Scrap!' were dulled somewhat by a spiteful whack with a cricket stump. I could hardly hear my name being shouted anyway, as Eddy was always very popular with the other kids (nobody could ever catch him at British Bulldog). I didn't fare too well but Eddy did stop for a while to let me retrieve my sandal, and gave me time to put it on. Soon after, the fight was broken up by the sound of a whistle, and Eddy and I spent the next twenty minutes facing the wall. Several times during our metamorphosis into manhood, we came close to having a rematch, but I always respected the amount that Eddy had shown me in the ditch. Always thought the stump was a bit harsh, though!

Our school was right in the middle of Radway Green estate and consisted of an old set of council flats converted during the war, with flat roofs and reinforced leaded windows. In this bunker-style building, I met my first mentor, an old-fashioned teacher called Colin Mellor, who loved history and breeding moths. I was petrified of Mr Mellor from the moment I saw him reading from the register. He soon won me over and I was captivated by the way he would stand up on the balls of his feet, and rock up and down, showing meticulously polished brown brogues that finished of his three-piece tweed suit to perfection. Colin Mellor was a military man and it showed. Through him came my fascination with Sir Francis Drake and the ocean.

Eddy and I were ten when we met Gibbo. Our school football team, with me in goal and Eddy as striker (of course), played away at Pikemere Road, a modern, single-storey place. We beat Pikemere Road 5–4 (I saved a penalty, and gave one away, and 'Eddy Hurst' scored a late winner deep into injury time). As we were handing in the bibs, a friend of Gibbo's called George came over to shake my hand; it was his penalty I had saved. He had a huge grin and his head kept nodding as he shook my hand.

'Nice save, Jasper.'

My name must have been shouted out dozens of times that afternoon, yet George had mistaken 'Chester' for 'Jasper'. I had just been given my nickname and Gibbo and George became close friends. In particular Eddy, Gibbo and I were Stoke City mad. Loads of lads of all ages went from our area to watch the Potters, travelling on a knackered old coach that went from Minshulls paper shop on the Radway, but we three would stand out from the rest as addiction set in.

As far as I'm concerned, life with Nan was cool; I've no complaints.

Being the product of a one-night stand was never held against me, even though she was nearing retirement and could ill afford to take on that kind of responsibility and cope with the needs of an ailing and begrudging grandfather. Life with Nan was organised around her husband's work and his alcoholic fallout. If he was on days, life was relaxed and we would spend hours in the kitchen. I would watch her bake cakes, and staring intently at the bowls of chocolate sauce and licking the wooden spoons whose other role was to serve me with Nan's pre-War form of discipline.

If he was on nights, it would be a raised spoon and, 'Shush, grandad's sleeping.' I would be sent to my room to find solace with a tin of crayons and a box of soldiers. I would cut out and make a covered football end out of a grocery box from Liptons supermarket in the village. I would paint some of my soldiers red and others blue and would place them behind the goal in this makeshift stand: blue on one side, red on the other, with open terrace in the middle. No fences, no coppers, just like I saw every week at the matches in the early Seventies.

It was going to go off! Singing under my breath and living the scene, I would place my Airfix German paratroopers, their right arms raised (to deliver a lump of terracing or a dart), smack in the middle of a tight mob. *Packed together in the middle, all jumping up and down, the crowd sways forward, then backward.* The crowd was getting louder and I was in control of a mass brawl as both sets of soldiers charged across no man's land to enter the other's territory. They would fight for as long as my imagination would let them. Anyone watching would have seen a nine-year-old boy playing with his soldiers, but this was in fact the beginning of a journey of bitter feuds, incarceration and life-long bonding.

Imaginary bedroom brawls were no longer enough: this kid needed some real action. My idea was to get as close to the mob in the middle of the Boothen End at Stoke as possible. This was the furnace; all the hard lads stood here. At first we sat on the fence behind the goal, where it was dead easy to look up into 15,000 pairs of clapping hands on the second blast of an air horn, which would be waited on with feverish enthusiasm every time we were awarded a corner or free kick. That unison, those cries of emotion – it got me. *I was doing that. I was part of that clapping and people were nodding at me. I must fit in. Yes! City, City.* This was the best feeling ever. I would shout as loud as I could, always lose my voice, clap until my hands were ringing. And when no-one was looking, I'd cry tears of joy because I was happy. People hugged you in the Boothen End.

The Boothen was invaded regularly in the Seventies but Manchester United were the only fans to take it completely, in 1969, by their satura-

tion tactic of getting in early with hundreds of lads. It proved too much
for the 100 or so proper fighters in the Boothen that day, but would never
be repeated. Tottenham Hotspur and Wolverhampton Wanderers were
two others who rarely failed to show. You could guarantee that within
minutes of the whistle, you would hear their battlecries from deep within
the Boothen. Most mobs, if they were to have a serious go at taking our
end, would get in tight, usually slightly more elevated and to the side of
the home mob. If they had any sense they would also not be too far from
an exit, in case it came on top.

1976 saw Tottenham visit on two successive Saturdays, first in the
league and then the FA Cup. Stoke won both matches and the Tottenham
mob tried to take the Boothen both times. I witnessed a mob run the
length of the pitch and jump in the Boothen for the first time. There were
no more than twenty of them, the majority being black lads who wore
denim dungarees and white Rubettes hats. They dropped into the bottom
right-hand corner, which was already full of Stoke's lads. Undeterred, the
Tottenham mob got in tight and for the next ten minutes it was pure
fighting, Stoke coming on top through sheer numbers. I tried to get as
close as I could and pretty much went where the crowd took me. A tartan
flask emptied its weight all over my head and shoulders and it stank of
piss. That was the end of my involvement; I moved back behind the goal
to the lads off the Minshulls coach. Eddy soon joined me. He and Gibbo
had lost sight of me in the melee, and told the other lads they had seen
me steaming in towards the Tottenham lot.

'Fuckin' hell, nice one Jasp.'

The lads closed in. Some patted me on the back, and I filled out in
stature. 'Cheers lads.' It was obvious that Eddy and G had failed to notice
that both my feet had been at least six inches off the floor throughout.
And I failed ever to tell them.

Some of the Tottenham lads had managed to stay in, and sporadic
outbursts of fighting continued throughout the game. I drew what I saw
that day, scribbled it down on some scrap paper. I was chuffed I had got
some action. Though I wasn't ready yet for a day out at White Hart Lane,
I knew I would never forget the Spurs.

It was the first time I can remember properly looking at her. Standing at
the school gate, she had a perfectly cut, shiny black bob, over-exaggerated
eye-liner and thin, cursing lips from which a cigarette hung, dripping ash.
Her white lacey boob tube was half-full and matched with a miniscule
denim mini-skirt, white clogs and a thoroughly out-of-place silver Rolex

watch, one of a matching his-and-hers set purchased in the Persian Gulf. It was my mother.

Until then, I had never understood why my grandmother had white hair and all the other kids' mums didn't. Now, homeless, penniless, and without a friend in the world, my mother had been driven out of her hometown and, as a parasite moves from one carcass to the next, she had chosen the softest target. My weary grandfather provided her with a flat above a shoe shop in Alsager village, a new start and a chance to fulfil her role as a mother. And I had to move in there too.

She found employment in a little country pub on the outskirts of town called the Plough – and in as many months, had affairs with three men: a local entrepreneur, a well-known motor cross rider and a left-sided midfield player who was a legend in the Stoke team of the time. She ended up getting pregnant by her eighteen-year-old babysitter, who would use her flat to revise for his exams, and within months the tiny flat had the sound of a baby's cry. With her unable to serve behind the bar, and the student on a small grant, this family of four survived on benefits. The flat became a hangout for local dropouts and skint students. My bedroom was a box room above the stairs and along the corridor from everyone else. I became isolated and confusion found a soul to settle in.

To the young graduate's credit, he found a position in a local school as a relief teacher and found a new house. A sky blue Vauxhall Viva laden with boxes and bags took us to a three-bedroomed, flat-roofed home on the Radway Green council estate, a far cry from my grandmother's detached residence on an estate where all the kids had pocket money and had to be in at tea-time. Once again I got the box room.

Academically I began to fall behind the other kids in my class. My mother was told on numerous occasions that I needed to do extra work if I was to achieve anything at school but, short-tempered and utterly unsuited to helping me with homework, she would 'tut' loudly and the book would slam. Her idea of a solution was to make me watch *Sesame Street*: 'Jesus, if he can't learn anything off that …' At the age of ten, a year before my advance into secondary modern education, I was held back a year and attended Offley Road remedial school in Sandbach. While the rest of my friends read *Hobson's Choice*, I began to read about *Peter and Jane*.

I ended up at Alsager comprehensive school, which was reputed to be one of the best in Cheshire, having collected numerous academic and sporting achievements during its history. Over 800 attended, and the disappointment of not being in the same year as Eddy was replaced with delight as I lined up to join my new form, along with Gibbo and George, the Pikemere Road lads that we saw at the match.

As adolescence replaced boyhood epics, the pen replaced my toy soldiers. My interest in football violence was becoming an obsession, and as I was disruptive in class, teachers were happy to section me to the back of the room, where I was left to my own devices. With a workbook, ruler and multi-coloured pen, I drew graphic depictions of crowd scenes, all the time chanting and living a crowd in the back of my throat. I would sketch huge open terraces with stanchions and floodlights, then a stick-man crowd in the colours of their team, mobbing up behind the goal. Twenty-two more stick men would play out an imaginary quarter-final replay, changed to a neutral venue as the result of serious crowd disorder at the previous fixture. Kicking the ball about the park like a dot-to-dot, the underdogs score, and for the next few minutes I jump about inside myself, going berserk on paper, drawing crazed arms in all directions giving the effect of an end exploding after a goal, with thin, straggly toilet rolls arcing across the sky. *Yes!* Now the mob at the other end spotted some action of their own. Fifty red stickmen are in their end, and they want to know. Another massive roar goes up and – as Columbus discovers the New World – my classmates are wondering who has scored. The fifty underdogs are facing an onslaught from 300 bovver boys in blue. The bell goes and it's time to go home.

School wasn't all about sitting at the back of the class having it off big time on the back of a textbook. Certain teachers I liked, usually those who taught geography and my favourite subject, history. All through school I achieved good grades in these two subjects, which led to the year tutor's theory: 'He's a bright boy but is only prepared to work and pay attention if he actually likes the subject and teacher.' As for the disruptive behaviour and fooling about, they couldn't put their fingers on that one. Pretty bloody simple, really. If a child is unsettled and depressed in a home where he spends eighty per cent of his time in a small bedroom on his own, then when out of that environment he's going to want to play and do the things that other kids would do under the supervision of their parents or caring guardians. With school being my time, I chose to let off some steam.

Kev Hollins was my form tutor and a Boothen Ender. Mr Hollins liked me and did everything he possibly could to keep me from being downgraded to another form. He could see, and told me, there was a likeable but misunderstood chap inside. With hindsight, how nice it would have been to explain to him at that time what exactly my problem was and how unhappy I was living with a tyrant who used her husband's profession as a smoke screen of concern. I don't think Mr Hollins was all that daft really; you had only to look at me to see that fish fingers four nights a week were not helping me grow into a strapping young man. He cared and it showed. Weekend field trips were organised to Dovedale and the hills around Derbyshire. It was at these times that he would sit and chat to me about things that I found interesting and ask me what I'd like to do with my life.

'Well I like Sir Francis Drake, and I love the ocean. And when I grow up I want to be a cowboy and live on my own in a little log cabin in the woods.'

A fourteen-year-old boy seeking a life of isolation: Kev Hollins knew that without any guidance and direction, that was where this kid was heading. Sports were one solution for my ever-growing aggression that was now witnessed during most lunch breaks. For one reason or another, somebody would let me down or upset me, the inevitable confrontation would take place and I would be left alone again, the persecuted outcast who trusted no-one unless they followed Stoke City and stood on the Boothen End. In the end I chose basketball; I was over six foot tall at four-teen and the sport was taken seriously in Cheshire. I took to it naturally and soon became the team captain. We didn't win any school titles, but we performed hard and showed pride in ourselves. And Kev Hollins was proud of me.

He had an idea. 'You love history, you love fighting and you love the ocean.' It was agreed there and then: I would seek a career in the Royal Navy. The next step was to join Training Ship Excalibur, the sea cadet unit an hour's bike ride away. I attended the sea cadets twice a week for the next two years, gaining the rate of able seaman. Weekends away sailing in Weymouth and on Winsford Flash and spending time with other kids settled me down for those periods. I was looking forward to leaving school and getting off to sea.

Life in the house, however, was about to get intolerable. Most days after school, I would spend time with Nan before going back 'home', so she was still very much in my life. This came to an end when ill health and years of smoking and drinking brought my grandfather's career to an abrupt end, with a consultant's firm advice that he seek a better climate with plenty of fresh sea air. A small place north of Blackpool called Bispham was their eventual destination. Nan was gone and I was devas-tated. Nan had been brought up a Quaker. She was the third youngest of fourteen kids, her mother died when she was eight and her father, a coal merchant, drank himself to death. She was raised by her sisters and found little affection for herself. As a grandmother she was perfect in every way, but she had grown up in a non-tactile environment and to this day has never hugged me or told me she loves me. Her display of affection would be a little clip around the cheek and an, 'Ooh, you're a bad bugger.' Not a lot of show but better than none.

Reality hit me hard. 'Look you were a bloody mistake, and if it wasn't for your grandmother, you'd have been given away like the other one,' said my mother. Cutting, but still, you listen on. More bad behaviour at school followed. I was caught trying to take Polaroids up Miss Jennings's skirt from under the desk at the front, where she had put me to keep her eye on me. A corridor chase and shocked and angry screaming saw me heading for the stairwell and my escape.

'DON'T YOU DARE, YOUNG MAN.'

I froze. It was Mrs Heady, the head of English, a no-nonsense, by-the-book, north Yorkshire woman from Middlesbrough. She was a sturdy woman and her Teesside accent bellowed through every classroom on that floor. Although I didn't know it at that moment, this was to be a turning point in my life, and Hilary Heady a great friend.

'If he's that disruptive and nobody wants him, I'll have him,' she declared. 'Put him in with me.' The problem was solved, everybody was happy, and I had just been promoted from CSE to O-level English.

When I walked into her classroom for the first time, I was purposely late. The class was in complete silence. Mrs Heady sat at her desk; she didn't raise an eyelid as she stared hard into her writing. The silence continued and I shuffled uncomfortably. One or two of the kids side-glanced over.

'Erm, hello.'

'Yes?' She flew up out of her seat, slamming the pen down on the desk.

'Erm, I'm Mark Chester.'

'And?'

'And I've, er, come here to work.'

'Right, then. I suggest to you, Mister Chester, that you sit down at this desk in front of me, and do some work.'

'Thank you.'

I did exactly as she said. I liked her manner and almost enjoyed being put in my place in front of all those kids. Who the hell did I think I was, anyway, turning up for a lesson late and disrupting the class? *Show some respect.*

At fifteen I left my punk image behind. Perry boys were the fashion down the match: wedge-head haircuts, Lonsdale sweatshirts, faded blue jeans and white Adidas Stan Smith strapover tennis shoes set the likes of Eddy Gibbo and myself apart from the rest of the Alsager teenagers, who were all into Van Halen, Rainbow and motorbikes. We felt a little bit different, that we were part of something that wasn't derived from the music scene. What we were getting into wasn't going to drop out of the charts next week.

Breaking point came in the early autumn, and the new term. Six weeks' summer holiday had gone and with it my freedom. I had been left to my own devices all summer long, camping in the woods, bike rides, everything. I must have stayed out every night; if it wasn't in the woods, it would be in a tent in a friend's back garden. I loved the summer time. Although I was looking forward to seeing everyone again, school meant I was back in the bedroom. Now I was getting a bit older and starting to stand on my own feet, I was fed up of being insecure. I had people like Kev Hollins around me, he thought I was strong, and Ron Tipping, the drum master at the sea cadets, he was always laughing at my jokes. *Bollocks to this sitting around in here every time I step in the house, I'm not creeping round anywhere any more, I'm not going to have to chew my food for ages so I won't make a gulping sound when I swallow. I've just spent a whole summer and seen her no more than a dozen times. So what difference does it make where I live?*

I threw the bag down into the back garden from the first floor window, and climbed out onto the dormer. Steadying myself, I looked down into my oversized shadow cast across the lawn. Within a second I had landed in the arms of my own shadow, which disappeared as I stood up. *Yes!* The house had been empty when I made my flight and I could have walked out of the door. But I needed to make that jump. I needed to feel I had escaped.

The first week I spent in Sylvia Millicent's garden shed. Her son Steven was in primary school with me and Eddy, though 'Milly', as we called him, had chosen the biker lifestyle and had sideburns at thirteen. If I wasn't going to be missed there was no point telling any of the boys' mums, so our robbing spree began. All the lads got at least one thing from their houses: blankets, an old kettle, a deckchair, and most importantly, a sleeping bag. Only three of us knew where my new home was going to be: we had found it by chance on one of our bike rides during the holidays, and had hung out there. A mile or so north of Alsager were some old, overgrown railway sidings that were part of the ordnance factory up until the Sixties, when government cuts had closed part of the factory down. Unless you actually stopped to look, you would never have spotted the disused signal box; after years of neglect, it had been covered up by the vegetation. It was not big inside but that didn't matter – I was used to that. The view from the cobwebbed windows made up my mind. I was having it there and then.

We cleaned up the place between us and I hung my Stoke City rosette on the wall. The next problem: how was I going to get back my books without them seeing me? I had to get into the box room. *No problem, we'll break in.* Milly meant it, and we did. We got in over the dormer and through my bedroom window in the middle of the afternoon. There was no car in the drive and the only window open was the one at the back. I climbed into the window while Milly clung on outside. I could smell the bastards before I saw them – a pair of hairy toes sticking out of the sheets of my bed.

'Who the fuckin' hell's that, Jasp?'

'Oh hello, you must be Mark. I'm, er, Jonathan. I'm at the college. I'm renting this room until I get some proper digs.'

'Proper digs, eh?' That was all I had to say.

I loved my signal box. The toilet out the back was still there, though it did smell a bit, and the sink had running water. For safety reasons, we set up a few booby traps, and made the stairs inaccessible. The only means of getting upstairs was a nylon rope ladder I had pinched from sea cadets. Inside I had an angler's deck chair and a sleeping bag laid out in the foot space beneath the brass levers. The homely feel was completed by my Debbie Harry and Mickey Thomas posters. I have always hated Man United, mainly for the fact that Stoke sold Jimmy Greenhoff to them to find money to replace the Butler Street Stand, which had been blown down in horrific gales on the eve of a Tottenham Hotspur fixture. But Mickey Thomas was my hero. The Welsh Wizard. So I didn't mind having his picture up. My Stoke rosette had been placed over the Red Devil on Mickey's shirt. Poignant really, as Mickey went on to become a legend of our own at the Victoria Ground, and also one of my best mates.

My freedom was shortlived. Cold weather set in and a close shave with a bike gang who decided to use the place for a party left me wondering how I was going to cope. All of a sudden the thrill had gone. I had carried on with my normal routine, attending school every day, working in the classes I enjoyed and drawing in the others, and even keeping up a morning and evening paper round. However, my increasingly grubby nails and greasy wedgehead were the giveaway, and Mrs Heady told me to stay behind after dismissing the class. She wanted to know what was going on.

I made no attempt to lie to her, so desperate was my plight. Immediately Kev Hollins was brought in and informed of my new address. Kev sighed. He had no choice but to inform the school, who would obviously tell the social services. It was a mess, and Kev feared the worse. I sat with my two teachers and listened to them fathom out a resolution. 'If Mark had a permanent address, and the social services agreed that it was a suitable arrangement, their job would in effect be done.' They would not have to place me in care.

The headmaster was informed and after much deliberation, the social services placed me in the care of Mrs Heady. It was made legal with a signature from a third party, and so many pounds a week were paid to the teacher towards my upkeep. It was over, and legally. I never wanted to step inside that house again. I was fifteen and had turned a corner. All I had to do was finish the last few months of education and I was my own man.

I let Mrs Heady down badly. After months of being in her care and untold hours of extra tuition in English language, I was expelled from school just weeks before my final exams. One break-time brawl too many and I had broken Kev Hollins's last promise. The school had had enough. I was still allowed to sit my exams, being met at the gates each morning by the deputy head and escorted in and out of the school grounds. For each exam I sat alone in an office next to the library, under the supervision of a male teacher. History, geography, English language and literature were the four I sat. And I passed them all.

It made no odds. Weeks earlier and against all the advice I had been given by Kev Hollins, I had walked straight past the Navy careers office in Hanley and opened the door of the Army office instead. After everything that I had been through in my childhood, I had such a low opinion of myself that instead of seeking a position with a trade in the Forces – but one I might fail to be selected for – I went straight to the bottom of the pile and volunteered for the infantry, where I was virtually guaranteed a place. I wasn't expecting anything out of school and reckoned the infantry would take just about anybody. In my book, I desperately needed employment, and a home too.

I first had to attend a selection centre at Sutton Coldfield, a chance to have a look at the establishment and for them to have a good look at you. Lads from all over the country were present and some of them looked hard. It became clear immediately at Lichfield station that I had stepped out of Civvy Street and into my first lesson in grown-up life and discipline. A sergeant stood pointing us to some old National Service coaches. As we walked two abreast to our transport, the sergeant lunged forward, grabbing the youth to my side and yanking him out of line.

'What's your name, boy?' he bawled.

The boy next to me, now standing on tiptoes, replied, 'Whittaker, sir.'

'Sir? Sir? Do I look like a fucking sir? I've got three fuck-eyed stripes, son. Look at me when you talk to me. You call me sergeant.'

I looked along the now ashen-faced line and back to Whittaker, who was having the sleeve of his T-shirt pulled over his head.

'How old are you Whittaker?' The sergeant yanked him forward and raised his left arm up towards us.

'Sixteen, sergeant.'

'Sixteen, Whittaker. And the legal age for somebody to be tattooed is eighteen, which means you son are a self-confessed LIAR.'

And with that, Whittaker was escorted back to civvy life.

A couple of times on the journey to Sutton Coldfield I looked around at the vacant expressions, but mostly I just gawped out of the window; it was easier than trying to make conversation. I could not get over the sergeant's onslaught; it left me numb but wide awake.

On arrival at the centre, we were greeted by the commanding officer, who rocked backwards and forwards in his immaculate Sam Brown brogues as he greeted us. Little did I know as I looked at that crisp toecap, polished to a shine you could admire yourself in, how many times I would do that over the next few years. After the induction and being shown to our blocks, the now calmer sergeant took a turn in his character and as he marched us in three ranks, even he found it difficult, even if it only showed in his eyes, not to smile at these contemptibles as we donkey-marched to the cookhouse for our first taste of army cooking.

As I squeezed down my last mouthful of liver and onions, a familiar face appeared in the queue, a lad from Holmes Chapel who used to go to Stoke. I didn't know his name but the only thing missing when I collared him outside was Cilla Black; we were like two long-lost brothers, immediately closing ranks. We forgot all about the itchy blankets and lumpy gravy and chatted about the match and home. Suddenly we were tight.

'Yeah, I'm gonna join the Paras. What about you?'

'Fuck knows, I just want to get in mate.'

After three days of lectures, films and tests, I did get in and was awarded a position as an infantryman in the Staffordshire Regiment, via an intensive leadership and fieldcraft skills course at Shorncliffe Barracks in Kent. The tide was turning and I was about to grow up.

With the help of Kev Hollins and Hilary Headey, I also achieved some reasonable school qualifications, albeit only in the subjects I had decided to work in. The subject I had taught myself in the box room and at the back of the classroom – football hooliganism – carried no diplomas; to succeed in that world, which saturated my emotions, would be a hands-on affair spanning decades. So a small stint in the Army would stiffen me up and prepare me if I was going to succeed in the subject I had studied under the noses of the system so intently. Before that, I had one last attempt as a civvy to gain acknowledgment among the Stoke following, with an opening game of the 1980/81 season at Arsenal.

chapter two

The Clock End

T'HE STREETS AND houses reminded me of the film *Oliver!*
It was a scorching August afternoon at Highbury. Eddy and I had
travelled to our first away game in London on a football special. At
last we had graduated from the members' coaches and their strict sched-
ules to going freelance with all the 'nutters'. The tickets cost £2 each, and
with £5 to spend, we were going to make the most of this one, as it was
my last match before joining up. Around 600 went down on the train,
mainly men. The group we were with arrived at Islington and immediately dissolved into the throng of locals who, I noticed, were dressed with
style and had a cavalier air. Ed and I also noticed that the Stoke lads had
disappeared. We looked at our turnout and, without saying a word,
acknowledged that we stood out – hence the phrase 'scruffy northerner'.
We were clean and tidy and probably cut it with the heads around our
way, but not down here; from the off we felt inferior, and the day would
deteriorate from then on.

Ed and I followed the general direction of the Arsenal supporters. I had
not been to London before and the aggressive, in-your-face manner of the
place had me wishing I had stayed away. Highbury was unlike any other
ground I had attended. It was built inside a row of terraced houses, with
little alleys leading to concealed turnstiles. With no visible floodlights, and
the Highbury Tavern's windows packed with gruff men, the fear and
adrenalin were pumping to an all-time high.

Evading unwanted attention, the two scruffs found the entrance they
were looking for and walked onto the steps of the Clock End. Our relief
at making the Stoke end shattered. From the corner in which we had
entered, we looked across to a small fenced-off section in the middle of
the vast open end. It looked miles away, and the few Stoke fans that had
travelled were barely visible. We both swallowed hard and, with no other

choice, tucked our chins into our chests and made that long journey. It was the most terrifying gauntlet I had yet had to run. Looking back, those cockneys would barely have noticed two such insignificant figures timidly edging their way through the end to what they thought was safety. But as soon as the two adventurers made their objective, they came under the psychological abuse being dealt to their compadres by a surrounding mob of belligerent Londoners.

We were embedded in the heart of the Clock End, surrounded by sarcastic remarks and throat-slitting motions and having cigarette ends flicked at us continually, something that did upset me at that time of my life. I had never been this close to opposing fans before. These weren't matchstick men seen from a distance; these had stale breaths and psychotic glints in their eyes. Instead of punching or kicking us, the Arsenal lads toyed with us, like a cat that has all the time in the world to terrify a mouse before moving in for the kill.

And so the first half continued: 800 Stoke fans immersed in the theatre of hate and most of them dreading the interval and the tea bar below. On forty-four minutes, Lee Chapman opened the scoring for Stoke. As terrified as we all were, we just couldn't help ourselves. 'YES!' Yet the full-on attack everyone expected came in the form of loud hysterics as the Aresenal lads rolled with laughter, mocking our celebrations. Why we went down those steps to the tea bar at half-time, knowing it would be safer on the terraces, I don't know. Neither Ed or myself had enough money to buy anything, but the lure of the unknown was too strong, as always. It was a chilling experience. Throughout the day I had seen dozens of old Stoke faces that normally would be high-spirited and irrepressible. Down in the tea bar, as I stood with my back to a wall, I could pick them all out trying to look inconspicuous and doing it so poorly that they would receive one straight punch in the nose from out of nowhere, and then be left to chew on it. It was nothing short of torture and the cockneys loved it. It was plain to see that Stoke were not ready for this new decade of football violence. Many of the lads still looking and behaving like they were in the Seventies succumbed to the intimidation and moral assassinations that day.

We won 1–0 and somewhat timidly made our way off the Clock End and out into a daylight nightmare with all the promise of a *Warriors*-style escape back to Coney Island. Both of us were glad we were not part of any Stoke mob, as anybody who looked anywhere other than at their feet was persecuted. It was horrendous. We headed towards one of the few policemen in attendance.

'Excuse me please,' I whispered. Eddy waited quietly beside me as the man looked down.

'Yes son, what can I do for you?'

I cringed at the man's loud tone and asked, 'Can you tell me which way it is to the station please?' I think we both wanted him to say, *here we go lads, I'll show you, come with me.* Instead, in an even louder voice and pointing for all to see, he said, 'Well you can go that way and kick your way there, or you can go this way and not get there. It's up to you, lads. You came here.'

Have you ever felt yourself plummeting? I did there and then. Both of us went to pieces. *Fucking hell, even the coppers don't give a fuck down here. Thanks for nothing mate.* We headed in the 'kick your way' direction.

We arrived at Islington station exhausted. Along the way we had witnessed several Stoke fans being turned over and chased off into the warrens that led off the packed, sun-drenched streets. We could only cringe at the thought of what might happen to them. 'Fuckin' hell Ed, this is my worst one so far,' I said. 'Is it for you?' Eddy nodded – and he had been to Millwall in 1978.

Visibly shaken, the 600 Stokies that had made it back waited in subdued silence. There were no police in sight and all were relieved at the sight of our train approaching. With everybody aboard and minutes to departure, Arsenal appeared on the stairway leading to our platform. My head was out of the window watching, and I immediately clocked the main instigator from the Clock End. This fella was in his late teens, with short blond hair and bushy black eyebrows, a scarred face, green Irish eyes and a mental grin, like the Joker. Twenty of Arsenal's lads strolled onto our platform and called it on with more slaggings.

Seconds before the train was about to pull away, someone from our side lost his head and leapt from the train screaming, 'Come on you cockney bastards.' My heart was in my mouth, as I was feet from the action and all of a sudden it looked like Stoke were going to show a bit of form. But the cockneys were in creases, falling about at the sight of the scruffy northerner who had had all day to make his point, and now wanted it when it was time to go.

'You norvern slag, look at the state of you, you sad cant. Coming down here giving it the big one. Look at you, you've got Tesco fackin' trainers on. You're 'avin' a laugh mate.' Destroyed by the blond-haired lad with the Irish eyes.

Less than a week later, I took my country's shilling and enlisted in the British Army. Three days after that, I turned sixteen.

Over 3,000 raw recruits arrived on the same day. It was bedlam. They appeared in all shapes and sizes, speaking in many dialects. Joining the throng at Waterloo Station, I silently followed the directions of four bellowing sergeants and took my seat on a packed troop train. The afternoon sky was heavy and the short journey down to Folkestone, for most, was muted. We were met by more screaming sergeants in a variety of uniforms and were herded onto waiting four-ton trucks and taken with speed to Sir John Moore Barracks, my home for the next ten months.

On arrival, we were told to join a long line being processed as each lad handed in his enlistment papers. The battalion was split into five companies and depending on which part of the infantry you were joining, you were detached to one of: Salamanca, full of cockneys; Arnhem Paras, from all over the country; Corona, the Jocks; Waterloo, the Guards, who were also from all over the place; and my company, Peninsula, the county regiments. The rivalry, although we did not yet realise it, started there.

The word to describe my feelings on the first day is 'shocked'. The pace of it all, the raised voices and incessant four-letter abuse, the itchy blankets and starched sheets, the metal springs and the taste of the tea. *Bromide.* I was placed in Eight Platoon with forty-seven others, divided into twelve-man rooms. Each person had a locker and bed space and had been given an eight-digit number to memorise for the next morning.

My first mistake came on the first evening. Not knowing where I was going, I leaned into an open doorway of an office on the landing, outside our block. Inside sat two men. Timidly I knocked the door, and said, 'Excuse me sir, I'm lost.' The barrage of crude four-letter obscenities that followed had me reeling back. I had just called Sgt Ron Foley 'sir', and he flipped.

'Stand up straight boy. Where are you going?'

Without being given a chance to reply, I was marched to my room and told to do fifty press-ups in front of all the other recruits, so they too would all learn from my mistake.

The first couple of weeks were the worst, getting used to being around people continually. I kept quiet and watched others take prominence among the remaining trainees. In the first fortnight, our platoon's numbers fell from forty-seven to twenty-nine; almost on a daily basis, people were going home to their families. Those that remained became the heart of the platoon, and started to gel. I wanted to get out too for the first three weeks, it felt so daunting at times, but I changed my mind the day we were taken by trucks to an exercise area deep in the Kent countryside. Until then, everything had happened within the confines of the camp and firing ranges.

The platoon NCOs showed us a prepared firing trench and explained how to go about digging one that would be suitable to live in and fight from for an uncertain amount of time. Splitting into sections, our task was to dig our own as quickly as possible. It was hard work and the tree roots that hindered our progress had me cursing like Shane, but it was a team effort, with the incentive of beating the lads in the other sections. The skies darkened above us and mid-afternoon brought a biting wind. Sweat-drenched fatigues turned cold, and the lads' heads began to drop.

'Come on lads, keep digging. War doesn't stop for a downpour,' shouted Sgt Foley from inside his Land Rover. He was right and I found myself agreeing with the man entirely.

'Come on lads, let's get stuck in,' I shouted. 'Then we can have a brew.'

That was the only way any of us could look at it. And we all got to digging at a feverish speed, with dogged determination.

I had been pissed off and completely wet through, yet that night as I washed my kit and mulled over the day's events, I found that it had been the best thing that I had done so far. I felt a sense of achievement, and it had brought the lads closer. It was our first bonding, something that got stronger as the days and tasks got harder.

That was pretty much what Shornecliffe was about. We were pushed to our limits and through it we became a very close-knit bunch who would have gone anywhere and done anything for each other. This achieved, the Army then went on to train us to become human weapons. All became proficient with an array of armoury ranging from nine-millimetre Browning automatic to an eighty-eight-mil Carl Gustav anti-tank weapon – one of my favourites.

The lads in Eight Platoon were mostly from South Wales and were due to serve with the Royal Regiment of Wales. In our room there was Taff from Bridgend, Taff from Barry, Taff from Abertillery and Monkey from Swansea. Monkey was huge and had stood on the North Bank at the Vetchfield as a kid. He had been one of the young Swansea Skins. I found out that he was also an orphan. He became my best mate at Juniors; I could relate to him through the football, and although we followed different teams at least their intitials were the same: SCFC. Fights became part of our daily lives as some weakened and others grew stronger; funny how the ones that are larger than life at the beginning end up doing the chores. Monkey and I soon had the company in order and the lads from Eight Platoon, P Company, were soon getting a repu-tation for being a bit nutty.

After twelve weeks, we all passed off the square, and coveted berets replaced our floppy 'Bill and Ben' bush hats. This was a significant moment for all of us; until you reach this milestone, you are known in the batallion as a 'sprog'. With the beret came another privilege: at last we were allowed out of camp, and down into Folkestone. The curfew was ten o'clock and although this was early for some, it gave us time to sniff out the local girls, who for the last three months had taunted us at night from the woods behind our block. We were all like a dog with two dicks.

Shades was the local disco and was squaddie-friendly. It became the hunting ground for most of the battalion, but with hardly enough women around to satisfy the local lads, let alone us lot, confrontation was inevitable. The first big kick-off was an internal affair between the Guards from Waterloo Company and the Paras from Arnhem. It took place in the Rotunda amusement arcade, along the front, on a Saturday afternoon. The fight had been arranged secretly among themselves, as no whispers had breached the NAAFI, where most people gathered on weekends off. Monkey and I, along with Yan and Pete from Swansea, had decided to seek out the local tattooist. I was going to get my first Stoke City tattoo, and although I knew it was going to hurt, I was buzzing with the anticipation of having my loyalty to my club etched onto my body for life.

The fight took place directly opposite where we were sat in the tattooists. Yan pointed out that some of Arnhem were milling around, looking confrontational. We went to look, losing our places in the queue, and sat on a sea wall, eating our 99s. In the distance a long line of three ranks marched over the pebbled beach. Just by the size of them, we knew they were Guards. We shuffled on our ringside seat; *this was going to be a belter*. It turned out that this brawl was an annual affair instigated by lower-ranked NCOs, part of the rivalry encouraged about camp. It was, however, strictly unofficial, though allegedly observed by one or two money-wagering corporals.

The Guards drew closer, their boots crunching on the shingle. They were led by an older lad from the third term, who halted his mob of six-footers and fell them out. All stood ready to go. The Paras took this as their moment to run charging onto the beach from several exits in the Rotunda. All hell let loose as these sixteen- and seventeen-year-olds fought a determined battle with over 100 on each side. It was just like the match with all the Stokies going berserk. The fight lasted a little over five minutes before locals called the MPs, who swooped on the area and made several arrests. *They're well in the shit*, we all agreed as we returned to the tattooists.

Three days after having my Stoke City tattoo, it was noticed by a snidy lance jack from another platoon. I was reported, charged with a self-inflicted wound, and bollocked severely for being a liar (as if that tattooist didn't know my age!). I lost my lance corporal's tape, which I had received not long after the trench exercise. It suited me though, because I preferred being one of the lads getting fucked about rather than the one dishing it out.

By the time we had reached the third term, our platoon numbered eighteen and all of us were tight and loyal to one another. After all the shit we had been through together, each of us had the utmost respect for the next. Even the sergeants loosened the reins a little and showed their human side. I was happy, enjoying myself, and for the first time in my life had a good body; I was ripped! Class work and exams became more part of our curriculum, and a whole week was set aside on the history of Ireland and the Six Counties. We were shown how the Troubles started, what the intended solutions were and what our role would be while serving a tour. I found the history fascinating, but footage of work and living conditions at one of the camps opened my eyes to what was in store. *Don't like the look of Crossmaglen in South Armagh at all, hope I don't get a posting to that hole*, I thought.

The final six weeks were spent at battle camp up at Otterburn in Northumbria, a desolate place but perfect to put all our skills to practice for our final assessments. Luckily the weather was superb for the whole exercise and Monkey even received a field promotion for some outstanding leadership skills. We all passed with flying colours. It was a very proud moment, and all that was left was to pass out and join the regiment in Gibraltar. I had made it, and decided there and then to extend my service time to nine years instead of six. *Security!*

The night before the passing-out parade, all eighteen of us had a quiet moment in one of the rooms. It was sad that we had been through so much together and learned so much about each other, only to split up and, probably for some, never see each other again. We decided to have one last night out in our club, Shades, and say goodbye to the local fillies.

Shades was packed that night; everyone in town knew the big parade was the next day, and the atmosphere was full of pride and achievement. And all the sad sweethearts were out for their farewell kisses. In the six months we had frequented the club, several flashpoints had arisen with local youths, who pretty much detested us with our money and charm. They hated the fact that the attentions of their women were permanently focused elsewhere and they had chosen our last night to exact their vengeance.

The night started well, all dancing away to Haircut 100 and Tenpole Tudor, but I couldn't help noticing cans of lager being passed round the edge of the dance floor. Shades was an under-eighteens club, and served no alcohol. I pulled Monkey and brought his attention to a gang of older lads who looked to be in their late teens and early twenties. Nobody recognized any of them.

'Monk, these are squaddie bashers. What do you reckon?'

He agreed and pointed out an argument between a local girl and one of these older youths. The atmosphere turned to ice as we counted their numbers and looked for reinforcements. Few had ventured out on the eve of their special day; most had stayed in the blocks bulling their boots. It was down to us eighteen and four second-term Scots Guards from Dundee. The girl being harassed was seeing one of the Scots lads, and her aggressor was a former boyfriend who hated squaddies. We decided to move to the back of the club by the toilets and storeroom. It was more open, and held less threat of anyone getting dragged into a corner and being punished.

The squaddie bashers gave us little time to form our ranks, a good job really because nerves had gripped one or two of us. Their numbers equalled ours but their age gave them the psychological advantage. None of us thought these cigarette-smoking, beer-swilling sloths would last a minute in the boxing ring, while we had spent hours a day doing squat thrusts and sit-ups, but we lacked experience in these situations. As they approached us, a large audience retreated to the edges of the club and watched as they produced clubs, iron bars and a set of nunchakas.

'These aren't that sure, if they need tools,' I shouted. 'Come on, let's give it 'em.'

We met them on the dance floor with mops and buckets grabbed from the storeroom. Thank God we gave as good as we got, as this was the first real head-on brawl I had ever been involved in. The thrill of it all was fantastic, being knocked to the floor by a blow, being saved by a friendly face, and getting back up and running in together. This was Eight Platoon's swansong to each other and we fought like tigers.

Passing out the next day with a bruised liver was the most painfully proud moment of my life up to that point. After a sad farewell to all my friends, I said goodbye to Shornecliffe, and headed back to Stoke for two weeks' leave, before the big step up to the regiment.

chapter three

Joining The Regiment

AFTER THE HARDEST ten months of my life, my two weeks' leave flew by and it was time to join the regiment over in Gibraltar. I was anxious. We had all heard stories back in juniors about the regiments and what went on, especially the initiations. Shornecliffe had been tough but I had really enjoyed it and was going to miss the Welsh lads. All of a sudden I was facing uncertainty again. I scratched my head and mulled it over. *There's something missing.* Too right, I knew what it was. I had been trained and prepared to take on any task given to me, under any conditions, and to respond to those orders in a responsible fashion. I was about to go from being a boy soldier to being a soldier. For the first time in my life, I can honestly say I wasn't scared. I had something that I had to do, and I was well up for it and whatever came with it.

I was posted into C Company, who were separated from the main regiment at the top of the Rock at Lathbury Barracks. We were stationed in the middle of a populated area nearer the docks and nearer Main Street and the nightlife. South Barracks was to be my home for the next nine months until our next posting back to Colchester.

Lathbury was a modern barracks with up-to-date equipment and new accommodation blocks with four-man rooms, but South Barracks was still how it had been in the eighteenth century: grand and on three floors, painted brilliant white, with open corridors leading under arches to the soldiers' accommodation and latrines. It reminded me of the prison block in the film *The Hill* with Sean Connery. I probably felt like he did when I saw it. Nine Platoon were on the third floor, right at the top of the concrete stairway. The sweat was dripping off me by the time I had reached the top and the company commander's office. One beige army issue suitcase with leather binding, one green, army-issue sausage bag with name and last four numbers on, both packed to bursting point, and I was wiped out. The climate had done me in.

The company sergeant major met me at the top of the stairs. The barrage of abuse I received as I stood there in my civvies had my head spinning. I felt nauseous and the sweat turned cold and sent me into a shiver.

'What the hell is this man wearing?' He punched me hard twice in the solar plexus, emptying me of any strength I had left. 'Stoke fucking City!'

He was literally holding me up by the little pin badge I was wearing on my shirt. All I could do was dangle and look up at him; it must have looked pathetic to any soldier looking on. I can't remember another word he said; all I could see was this big mouth in the middle of a pitted, fair complexion and eyes that looked like they belonged some place else: cold, blue and spiteful.

This was CSM 'Chucker' Smith. Not only did he hate Stokies, but his assault had more to it than met the eye. Another Stafford called Charlie Watts, a half-oriental youth from Wolverhampton, had passed out of Shorncliffe four months before me. He and I had not seen eye-to-eye. Unfortunately he was now in Seven Platoon on the ground floor, and had informed all the old sweats that there was a right gobby youth from Stoke joining who thought he was a bit of a hard man and football hooligan. He said I thought I was top boy at Shorncliffe.

I was shown to my bunk, which was at the far end of the open corridor. There were a number of black lads in the regiment and they all shared the same room. It was like a sweatshop in there, radiators on full knacker and blankets covering the windows and the light. Babylon. And my new home. I was about to make up the numbers to eight: seven black men and one white man. Alone again. My bed was in the furthest corner of the room and right opposite the door. Each bed space had been made as private and as comfortable as possible by the lads; they had even hung up blankets as partitions. It was quite homely really, unlike the rooms I had passed on the corridor. They had looked so regimented they were almost depressing.

I was now part of a regiment that had been on a ceremonial posting. Its job was to keep Gibraltar British and keep the Straits ours. The Gibraltans were all British and spoke the language, and the vast majority were happy to do so. Daily life encompassed a number of tasks, from wearing combats and patrolling the border with Spain to wearing your number twos and guarding the Governor's residence on Main Street, where the tourists would come and photograph you every hour on the changing of the guard. It should have been a relaxed posting with plenty of time for sports and socializing with the rest of the lads. It doesn't take me long to pick up on an atmosphere and pretty soon I was aware of one. The only time anybody spoke to me or acknowledged me was during working hours, and that was only when I was being given an order. For the next ten weeks, I ate alone and I was left alone. I knew something was coming, and I had an idea where from. On the middle floor in Eight Platoon were the old sweats. These were lads who had done the full term and were due to get out. Though they had only ever reached the rank of private, they were old boys and had their code, and everyone beneath the rank of sergeant pretty much abided by it, or else. There were four of them.

One Sunday night I was writing a letter on my bunk. The room was quiet and, bar one other person, I was alone. That didn't last for long. I watched the man leave his bunk and head for the door sharpish. It was time. Ten weeks of mental torture and waiting were over as four hooded men entered the room. My initial reaction was to jump up, charge straight in and take my chances. Either way I was going to take a kicking, so I decided to stand and take it like a man. They were already at the bottom of the bed, and the room now was full of lads from all different platoons who crowded in and climbed lockers for better vantage points. I could see they were whipped-up and baying, but I couldn't hear a thing. The bed was flipped in the air and me with it, leaving me sat on the metal springs. A huge cheer went up, and the weight closed in. I saw four white pillowcases cut with eyeholes and tied as hoods, and another four pillow-cases weighted with bars of soap and wrapped as weapons. The men manhandled me face down onto the springs and ripped off my shorts. Seconds later I was being tied to the bed, with bungees similar to the ones used on car roof racks.

That's me fucked. I'm not going anywhere. Right, just take it. Here we go.

The mob surrounding me went crazy as the pillowcases crashed into my buttocks and thighs, one after the other, time after time.

'Yarghhh. You bastards.'

I just had to hang in there; it would stop eventually and I would be accepted then. It did stop and I was exhausted. I had tensed up to take the blows and it had left me like a rag doll. I lifted my head and looked up. There was still a crowd and they were falling about in hysterics. It threw me.

The handful of boot polish was slapped straight up the crack of my arse in one hit. It was freezing and left me stunned. Instinctively I tensed up again. Everything I had left I squeezed into the cheeks of my arse. I must have made more noise than the lot of them as my legs were prised apart.

'You fuckin' bastards. You fuckin' cunts. I'll kill the lot of yer. You fuckin' want it? C'mon, come fucking on.'

It came in the shape of a broom handle. And that's that.

I think I was shitting boot polish for the best part of two weeks but the atmosphere did change. I could even tell that some of the lads who had watched and just joined in for a laugh felt it had gone too far. They kind of respected me for taking it, and keeping my mouth shut. I did keep my mouth shut. Too right, that's the way it goes. But I had not finished. Throughout the ordeal, I could remember only one face, and he had been perched on top of my locker directly above me. He loved it, and was 'God-ing' it, laughing and pointing. Fucking enjoying it.

Two weeks to the day later, I entered Colligan's room and bed-ended him in the same way. Colligan sat dazed and looked up in disbelief as I picked up his bedside table and unleashed it. Army life for me moved on from there. Yet in truth the psychological effect of that incident left me in a mess. I had been presented with a situation where I had ignored my instinct and better judgement in order to fit in. To belong. To do what was expected of me. I had underestimated my situation and accepted the consequences before they had arrived. I had given myself away. For that, I was punished beyond any rule or code, call it what you like.

And from that day on, at the age of seventeen, whenever faced with a situation that was not familiar or along the line that I walked on, my answer would be to steam straight in and worry about it later. Perhaps the lads will now understand those outbursts and rages I occasionally unleashed on some of them over the past two decades; they never really knew why, yet all stayed loyal to me, and for that I thank them.

Life in the regiment became more bearable. During the isolation period, they had all inadvertently shown me their strengths and weak-nesses. I had spent the time watching and analyzing every one of them. I knew who was going to end up being a close mate without them even knowing yet. One was Steve Bloore, a Stoke lad from the Bucknall area near the city centre. Steve was a nineteen-year-old private and was metic-ulous, the kind of soldier that stood out from the rest. He was five-foot eight with an athlete's physique, a kind and approachable face and spoke in a soft and controlled manner. One day he asked if he could borrow my iron. He didn't have to; he had the sharpest creases in the company, and every other man jack owned an iron anyway. It was his way of breaking the ice. Funny that, because he was one of the lads that I knew would become close. Steve went on to be the best friend I have ever had – and he had never been to a football match in his life.

The sprog who everybody couldn't wait to hate was fast becoming a known face in the regiment. It was not long before I met Tonka, one of the Wolverhampton lads. Tonka was in B Company and boxed at light-heavy, the same weight as me. His accent killed me. Tonka was dark and striking, one of those men who, when you know, you know. He was a rum fucker.

When the Fleet came into Gibraltar it was lock up your daughters time. This was when all the fun happened. The Falklands conflict was becoming inevitable, and the Staffords were preparing for war. Each company took its turn on twenty-four-hour standby to go. The lads were buzzing and so was I. As the Task Force gathered momentum, Gib came alive. It was hectic, the mood had purpose. It is claimed you can drink in a different pub 365 days of the year on this natural fortress; the place is heaving with bars but has just a handful of clubs. The matelots had their favourite haunts and the squaddies had theirs. The Buccaneer was the roughest club on the Rock, and the eventual destination for both factions. The entrance was a little reinforced metal door at the bottom of a large fortified wall that surrounded the main part of town. There were no other bars or any lights and signs to attract you, you just knew it was there.

Tonka had worked on the Buccaneer door since knocking out the previous doormen weeks into the Staffords' posting. He had claimed the place for us, in all its glory. No more than two months after my initiation, I got my first door job there with Tonka. The one small room was about the size of a terraced house knocked through. The walls were stone, cold and empty. The décor was minimal but for the fluorescent strips glued around the edge of a small wooden dance floor in the corner at the back of the club, which was about the size of a grand piano and reinforced with lino. The place had obviously been a storeroom. It had one door in and out, held no more than 200 people, and when full the fluorescent strip above the optics turned everybody's drinks green and their eyes psychotic. The sight of drunken sailors and squaddies pawing over Gib Liz, the local whore, who was well into her sixties and had sunk half the fleet, reminded me of the Bar at the End of the Universe in *The Hitchhiker's Guide To The Galaxy*. I was drafted in for back-up for Tonka. It was busy and the mood could go either way but we discussed it and, at the end of the day, this was going to be the last drink some of these boys ever had. Bar smashing up the place, as far as we were concerned they could do what they wanted.

The fleet had been at sea for six weeks on a big naval exercise, and had reached Gib under a whisper of war. Word had got round the ships but it was in the pub where the crews watched TV and read the papers that reality sank in. The Falklands: half the lads didn't know where it was. Lads off the *Coventry*, the *Sheffield*, the *Ardent*, the *Antelope*, the flagship *Invincible* and the *Battleaxe*, all came ashore to discover their fate.

For the next five nights of shore leave, the Buccaneer was packed. Matelots and squaddies drank side by side in an atmosphere of togetherness, a rare sight indeed. One of the sailors was Nige Kenny, an eighteen-year-old radio operator and the only Stokie on HMS *Battleaxe*, a type-22 frigate. Nige got chatting to a couple of lads with familiar accents and made himself comfortable in their presence. War in the Falklands was imminent yet all Nige could talk about was Stoke City and the away games he had been to with the lads back home.

'Think you'd better speak to our mate,' said someone. 'Jasp, here y'ar.'

Nige Kenny was brought over to me at the bar and we drank the rest of the night away as if we had known each other all our lives. Nige later went to sea, disappearing over the horizon with neither of us knowing that our paths would cross again.

It was months later, well after the conflict had been resolved, that I got my first sight of the Royal Navy in action against another fleet. It was a Tuesday night and the USS *Nimitz* had docked after a spell in the Med. We watched it dock; it was an awesome sight as 4,000 US sailors lined the decks dressed in their best whites. Sadly it was the norm for the Staffords to be confined to camp when large numbers of ships were in port. The Yanks were big spenders and loud with it. They piled off that cruiser in their thousands, a multitude of Popeyes looking for Olive, but she wasn't in town. Gib was dead apart for the bars and Duty Free shops, and with all the civvies sat in their flats watching pirate copies of *ET* on Betamax, the Yanks had the place to themselves – except for the Royal Navy. Our lads had limped home from the South Atlantic for minor repairs before their voyage back to Portsmouth.

The block was busy; it was rare that all the lads were in at night. Some smoked and chatted on the balcony or wrote home, while others bulled their boots. The sound of cutlery clattering inside mess tins suddenly stood the company to. Running feet and shouting filled the verandas with soldiers, some still holding books, others draped in towels to cover their nakedness. The sound of banging mess tins was an unofficial call to arms, and everybody knew there was going to be a fight.

Main Street had been rowdy all day. Lads returning from Four Corners and border patrol told us in the cookhouse that the docks were heaving. It was a sunny day too and all those starched tunics looked like white surf flowing along the alleys and stairways. The pubs in Gib were open all day, some for twenty-four hours, and by early evening the stench of stale beer was everywhere. Casualties littered the streets and Navy Land Rovers drove round picking them up, throwing the sunken sailors into the back and taking them back aboard.

Light-hearted banter at the bar of the Horseshoe pub was heading in one direction. All day the Yanks and Brits had drunk happily together, taking snaps, looking at pictures of loved ones and swapping stories. Apart from the drunken state of these men, the day had passed off without incident, but as the tide at sea changes, so did the mood in the Horseshoe. Tonnage was mentioned, number of guns too. A big Texan had been there, seen that, and done it, the lot. As far as he was concerned the United States Navy was the cream of the ocean.

'Where've you fought then, Tex?' came the taunt.

'Well I certainly wasn't on the *Sheffield*, hey boys. Ha ha ha.'

The Texan hadn't even raised his glass to his lips when a bottle crashed over his head. These particular matelots had all lost mates on the *Sheffield*, one of four of our ships sunk during the Falklands conflict. Over 100 seamen erupted spontaneously inside the Horseshoe, and as a fire would rush through a thatched village, the surrounding pubs went up one after the other. Mass streetfighting engulfed the Rock.

We stood on the verandas and looked down the short hill into town. You couldn't see the carnage but you could hear it. From up above, the town looked as peaceful as ever, old and still with that orange glow, but it wasn't hard to form a mental picture of what was going on.

'Who's fighting who?' somebody asked.

Nobody knew which ships were involved but we reckoned our lads must be heavily outnumbered. What happened next was utterly spontaneous. *Fuck the curfew, there's English lads down there and it's going off.* Lads from all three platoons were ready and on the parade square in minutes. Up to 100 from C Company formed three ranks on the square and marched with purpose out of camp and down the hill. It took us a good ten minutes to march down through the winding streets, amongst the flats with their terracotta-tiled roofs. Local families appeared on their small balconies, craning to see what was going on and where we were heading. That became obvious to us as we levelled off onto the main drag into town. It was approximately eight-thirty but already darkness had been drawn in by its neon advocate.

During the whole ten-minute march, not a word was spoken by any of us. I listened intently over my heavy breath and my pounding heart. I heard screams, shouts, glass smashing, sirens, dogs barking. War. The majority in this reinforcement contingent were young bucks and single; nobody over the rank of lance corporal had joined the ranks. To be caught for this kind of insubordination would mean certain jail and loss of privileges and it was too much for a married man to lose his tape.

As we reached the scene, it was impossible to make out what the hell was going on 100 yards in front of us. Missiles littered the air; even a toilet seat was hurled backwards and forwards amongst the warring factions. The Horseshoe was a shell; even the window frames had been pulled out and used as weapons. Policemen and Military Police from both sides had abandoned all formation and were more or less lost in the fight, as were their dogs, which were running wild and out of control. We marched in three ranks, and piled into the mayhem. Within seconds our formation had disbanded and it was a case of every man against Popeye. The Yanks may have had the superior tonnage that night but the English boys were the big guns. The fighting stopped when nobody could fight any more.

Life in the regiment and on Gib wasn't always like that, but every now and then when the Navy were in, you never quite knew what to expect. Months at sea in confined spaces with the same faces were bound to have an effect. Generally, however, life was pretty relaxed. It was the height of summer, the weather was fantastic, and I played basketball and boxed for the company. Boxers' privileges were always nice, a life of tracksuit order with better diets and no drill – well worth a few clips round the earhole.

I fought Wally Walters, a southpaw veteran and Golden Gloves champion at home. Wally was a six-foot-four redhead representing HQ Company, and on paper I didn't stand a chance. Expectations were high and the hall was packed to the rafters with all ranks. The worst thing was having to wait around for the other fights to finish; almost every boxer that returned to the changing rooms had bust lips, a broken nose and swollen eyes.

I came out for the first round as George, my trainer, had told me to and took it straight to him. The first four big punches of the fight were fast and all connected. C Company at ringside were out of their seats.

'Go on!'

'Fuckin' hell, do you think he might do it?'

The sight of the crowd jumping up and down and going berserk reminded me of a football match and I automatically wanted to be a part of it. I took my eyes off my opponent and was rewarded with a sweet left jab right on the nose, breaking it instantly and covering my face in blood. I got a standing count thirty seconds into the fight. My eyes were watering, my ears were ringing and I swallowed blood. I kept out of his way, or he allowed me to, for the rest of the round. The second round was much the same. Wally kept his distance nicely and just picked me off. It was impossible to get near him or read his punches. All I could do was hang in there for pride. Two more standing counts saw the referee stop the fight in favour of HQ Company and Wally raised my glove. Back in the changing rooms it was my turn to get patched up. Two metal prongs were placed up either nostril and banged sharply from the side. 'Better it done now before it has time to set, Chester,' said the butcher who masqueraded as a ringside doctor. Defeat wasn't the hard thing to swallow; I had done myself and the company proud. What bothered me was how difficult it had been to fight a man who fought in that style. Two things I learned from that fight: never take your eyes off your opponent, and sort out that left-handed punch.

I now knocked around with Steve and the lads in Nine Platoon. They were all keen soldiers, enjoying the life but taking it seriously, as they should. I didn't get into much mischief with them – I found that with Lenny. He was in B Company downstairs, a year older than me at eighteen and smaller in build. He was cheeky and a massive Stoke fan. As soon as I saw his face in the Cannon Bar, a pub cluttered with Stoke scarves and memorabilia donated from within the regiment, I knew him. He was one of two young skinheads from the Bentilee council estate, the roughest in Stoke, who went to every game, in their boots and Sta-press. They were a bit similar to me and Ed: enthusiastic and always there, but usually slightly to the side of the action, waiting for scraps. Lenny reminded me of home. If we were both off duty, Saturday afternoons would be our biggest and most anticipated piss-up: the BBC World Service on a transistor radio in the Cannon Bar, listening to the football results and the all-important score.

This was when we would get into trouble. The lads nicknamed us both The Goppers and by the time they arrived for their Saturday night session in town, the Goppers had already been out since midday and could be seen supporting themselves against a bar or stood on a table singing, 'We're by far the greatest team, the world has ever seen.' Army terminology for someone found to be in this state would be 'gopping'.

It was on one of those nights that Lenny and I had got so mindless that we pinched a push bike from outside the officers' mess at the RAF quarters near the airport runway, one of those daft ideas you have when you're prepared to be locked up for theft and drunk-driving rather than pay a £4 taxi fare. Lenny sat in the basket on the front and I began to pedal across the runway and along Main Street. Singing and laughing, we dodged in and out of taxis and revellers.

Minutes from the barracks and right outside the Gibraltar Arms pub, we slowed down to watch as two women and a man failed hopelessly to calm and restrain a thickset, red-headed bloke in a mental fit of rage. At his feet lay two unconscious sailors. Their dozen or so friends were trying in vain to retrieve them and both parties were pleading hopelessly with the man to release his victims. We cycled on.

'Fuck me, he was berserk, Len.'

'That was Trevor Hughes, Jasp.'

I had heard that name before off a Stoke mate called Lippo. He had told me how Trevor had literally squeezed the life out of a doberman dog during an insane fight at a pub in Colchester, during which Trevor's brother had been shot dead (see page 249). Now I had seen him in action – and all that because of a bit of bad language off the sailors in front of the wives.

Our stint in Gibraltar was coming to an end. We were to exchange warm weather endless drinking and lazy days for Colchester and combat exercises in the field in pouring rain. It was spearhead time; we could be deployed anywhere, at any time. As we packed our MFO boxes, the advance party of our successors arrived at South Barracks. They were the Duke of Wellington Regiment, Yorkshire lads, nicknamed the 'Duke of Boots'. It didn't take them long to find the Buccaneer and it was not much longer before the inevitable fight.

The club was open seven nights a week and the Yorkshire lads hit it hard. They had recently finished a tour of Ulster, and as their reward was two years in the sun, they were in the opposite spirits to us. For the first couple of weeks they settled in quietly on the ground floor of the barracks. Seven Platoon had already packed up and gone to Colchester as part of our advance party and the Duke of Boots had taken residence after we had scrubbed the place clean for them. I sat and watched the new arrivals playing football down on the parade square. It was a warm morning, just coming nice, and the lads were playing 'tops' versus 'skins'. I was scanning their arms and chests, looking for tattoos that would reveal their football allegiance. Our lads liked their tattoos but this lot were covered in them, anything from 'The sweetest woman I have ever kissed was another man's wife: My mother!' to huge Chinese carps swimming down a man's calf. It was the picture of a peacock that caught my eye. I had seen that picture before, loads of them. My mind went back to 1974 and my first ever match at the Victoria Ground, when I had gone into the Stoke End by mistake and been surrounded. The man I was staring at was a supporter of Leeds United and he looked like he could do a bit.

We said farewell to our Rock with an all-day pub crawl, paying our respects to all the drinking dens and memories. Inevitably we finished off at the Buccaneer. The Leeds lad I had spied was called Rene, and he was on the piss that night as well. The Bucks was rammed to bursting point.

'Ay up, Tonk. Busy mate?'

'Mayhem mate, too fucking busy.'

He was right, it was uncomfortably busy. I squeezed in at the bar.

'Large vodka please, when you're ready sweetheart.'

'Now then, she'll be ready when she's served me.' His voice was deep and carried weight. It was Rene.

Fuelled with vodka, the question in my head was, *hang on a min, didn't I just say to that barmaid, 'In your own time sweetheart'? So where's he coming from?* It was that mentality that afflicts many of us at times of intoxication. *I've been coming in this club since I got on this rock, and I wasn't even talking to the fella, so he's involved himself in my life for no reason at all. Not only that, he's got an aggressive manner.*

Bang!

I had been practising for months. He was to my right and I slammed one of those peaches that you don't feel connect straight into his chin.

'C'mon.'

He had been held up by the mass of bodies crammed at the bar but was visibly stunned and I followed in with a butt. This time, as I connected with the head, he locked onto my neck and both our footings went as we crashed to the floor. Rene was obviously a mauler; this was his ground. The man was seething: he was in his late twenties, and took this attack from a young sprog as a major insult. A small gap opened up, as they always do, but the bar was so busy that neither of us had room to get on our feet for a proper stand-up.

'One on one, one on fucking one,' was the cry.

To be perfectly honest I would have preferred everybody to join in. I was knackered, and to make it worse my bottom lip was in the Yorkshireman's mouth. I felt the lip tear and tasted blood, which I tried to spit up into his face, get in his eyes, or something, anything. The lip came away and I clapped my hand to it and continued to use my head, as our bodies were locked together. We were both soaking wet, filthy and soaked in blood. Eventually one of us would have to let go, and I had a troopship to catch in the morning, so I didn't fancy spending the night with him. The outcome was a gentleman's draw, though to look at us both, it was obvious who had got the result. We shook hands in the proper fashion and things very quickly got back to being merely rowdy.

I felt both sadness and excitement as the troopship *Sir Bedevere* left for sea. We lined the decks and waved to friends we had made who followed in a small flotilla of boats, sounding off their horns and waving flags. We were going home to Blighty at last; two weeks' leave and a chance to go to the match. I would have had a smile from ear to ear, but the six stitches in my lip felt tight and burstable. So I just gave the Rock a thumbs-up and watched the orange glow that lit up the night sky slowly disappear in the distance.

chapter four

The Glebe

I HATED COLCHESTER. We all hated it. I had been spoilt by my first posting; now gone was the sunshine and endless drinking and in came the rain and draconian opening hours. Garrison life was also an eye-opener. There was too much top brass around to smooch about in tracksuit order, everything was by the double and dress was as ordered – immaculate.

We were now very much part of an active regiment on standby as part of a spearhead battalion that had to be battle-ready and prepared to go anywhere at any time. That thought softened the disappointment at first, and a tour of Armagh was just around the corner, so I thought, *fuck it, just get on with it, you've joined the infantry to soldier, so get the cam cream on.* Regimental security was high at Roman Way Barracks and it was down to the troops themselves to provide it. The perimeter fence started and ended at a single-storey, flat-roofed guardroom that provided the entrance to our camp. There was no other way; if you wanted to go out of camp, you had to sign in and out there. If you failed to do so you were immediately reported as missing. AWOL. No more nipping over the fence for a quick pint at the Gibraltar Arms.

This place was on the same road as the Military Corrective Training Company – the glasshouse – filled with everything from swindlers to murderers, the dregs of army life. Each of the four companies in the regiment would take it in turn to control the camp security for a week. Your weekend leave being cancelled, so one weekend out of every four you were not allowed to go home. End of.

Those three other weekends meant one thing to me: the match. I had been away from the football scene for a considerable amount of time, perhaps only seeing half a dozen games over the 1981/82 season, so I was not fully aware of the transition that had been taking place within the terrace culture.

Eddy introduced me to Jem on my first weekend's leave home. It had been a while and the lads had a different air about them, and this new strut that complemented their designer tracksuits. Jem's well-rehearsed stride was larger than life; he had it off to a tee. He was a solid, six-foot-four thoroughbred of true Anglo-Saxon descent and he said it as it was, never once losing your eye as he looked deep beyond your conversation, almost as if he were choosing your words for you. And keeping you in line. This man had the coldest blue eyes I had ever seen in my life.

'Have you heard of Wilson, Jasp?'

'No, who's he?'

'His old man has the got the Glebe pub in Stoke, and Wilson has been running coaches to the away games.'

'Yeah? Have you lot been on 'em?'

'Too right! It's fucking mental. There's lads from all over the city going on them, all dressers.'

Dressers? That was a new one to me. I was strictly desert boots, faded jeans and C Company sweat-top. It sounded intriguing and I couldn't wait to get on board.

The Glebe is an old, three-storey corner pub in Stoke town centre, next to the Kings Hall and its car park and directly opposite the grave-yard. It was well placed to build the foundations of what was to be Stoke's first organised 'firm'. Wilson was lively and decided to start providing transport, tipping people off by word of mouth. In no time he had amassed fifty lads from all corners of the city for his first trip, to Sheffield United in a cup tie. A few weeks later he had four coaches at Everton. Every game lad in the city began talking about the Glebe coaches; they were bringing warring factions together for the first time, though not without a few of the inevitable disagreements that different tribes encounter when sat at council. All in all, there was no problem that could-n't be sorted and sooner or later the pecking order would be resolved among themselves.

My first trip with them was to Aston Villa. Two coaches were booked and Eddy, Jem and myself took the train up to Stoke early to catch them. Wilson had the back bar of his old man's pub open by nine o'clock and sold warm cans of mild and bitter from under the counter. We entered the pub from the car park at the back, through a private door that turned out to be Wilson's kitchen and then along a small maze of corridors and into the back room.

I could not believe my eyes. The place was packed with evil-looking lads. Some were big, some small, but they all had that time-served look in their eyes. It was obvious that every one of these men, whose ages ranged from seventeen to twenty-five, were going to Birmingham at ten o'clock in the morning for a fight. I liked what I was seeing. There were over 100 game-looking lads here, organised and concealed from unwanted attention, travelling in at an early time to ensure they reached their destination without complications, and from what I was hearing, intending to have a go at the Holte End. Even better: a strategy as well. I decided to watch and listen a while, to see who was who. I knew a couple of the older faces, they had been about when I was a kid, but I didn't know anybody by name. There were a lot of acknowledging nods and winks, but there seemed to be laughter only among the groups that actually came from Stoke and the surrounding Trent Vale, Fenton and Longton areas. Other small groups of threes and fours were from places like Stone, Cheadle and Blythe Bridge, all semi-rural, and they were similar to us Alsager lads. It seemed we would have to wait to be accepted on performances rather than just looking the part.

One man who did look the part was a big, gruff, bull-neck of a character from Trent Vale. He was called Miffer, and just the sight of his big tattooed forearms and the sound of the deepest voice I had ever heard had me staring at him quite openly, not in an offensive way but slightly in awe. A certain kindness in his manner was blatantly apparent but he was not a man to fuck around with. My first impression of Miffer was correct; I was looking at one of the top boys of this era. The man was a full-on character and loved life, especially Stoke City FC and his mates. At nineteen years old, Miffer was in charge of the Glebe mob, and led by example. I was about to see him in action on the first day of meeting him.

We arrived in Aston at eleven-thirty. Both coaches pulled up outside the Aston Villa sports centre and 100 lads spilled onto the street, immediately adopting this new walk with the swinging of arms and flicking of heads. They had adopted their own form of identification and you could tell by the way each individual presented himself how much confidence and status he held among this pack. Other members who took prominence were Ant and Midge Walton, two brothers in their early twenties who came with a small number of Smallthorne lads from over on the east side of the city. Gaz Gwilt was probably the oldest at twenty-five, a tall, well-built lad with appalling eyesight and horrible milk-bottle-round glasses that had been repaired a dozen times. His was a face I remembered from the Boothen in the Seventies. Over the years I could never quite make out whether Gwilty was either one of the gamest lads I had ever met or was that blind he couldn't see who we were fighting until he had caught one in the kisser. Either way, Gwilty stood, and in time was one of the first Stoke lads to get to know me. Along with Gaz was Dalton; I had seen this man in action many times as a kid.

I was made up. I had finally managed to get close to those lads that I had so wanted to be like as a boy. Jem was right, this was mental, you could feel the energy building as confidence jostled with arrogance, the fear of violence from within this pack at any second only heightening the adrenalin that was pumping round my body. What a buzz – and there hadn't been a punch thrown yet.

Our bus driver Terry was the man that Russ Abbott modelled himself on. Terry and his missus Jean were both Teds and were well into their forties. Jean had a bleached blonde beehive and Terry wore drainpipes and winkle pickers, with his tight, curly, black hair ever so slightly quiffed. After taking the coach fare off the lads, Wilson would always make sure that Terry and Jean got a £50 whipround early doors. Terry would use that to treat Jean to an afternoon in a B&B. In return, Terry was prepared to stop the coach anywhere, at any time, to let us get out and fight, even if it was on a dual carriageway. Terry would sit shaking his head and chuckling as he watched us perform.

As the two coaches let us off and then pulled away, we were left together, tight and well into Villa's manor.

'Here y'are, this way innit?'

A hundred lads turned in unison and looked in the direction of a public house across the road. It was ten to twelve, a good time to launch a swift *we're-here-and-we-want-it* attack and hopefully gain the psychological advantage.

'No noise. No fucking noise.'

Miffer was already halfway across the road, accompanied by his lifelong friend Bodie. Bodie never spoke a word to anybody, ever. You did well if you got a nod off the man. Like Miffer, he was a bull-neck. He also had large tattoos on his neck, one of which said, 'AVFC'. Bodie had been a Villa fan as a kid and it looked bizarre to me as he dashed through traffic to take his place at the front of the mob that was about to stage an assault on a Villa pub.

We were all on the move now, breaking into little jogs and admiring ourselves in shop windows. The images that meet your eyes in a window's reflection are essential to a mob on the move. That is your opportunity to see yourself in that pack environment, to see what you look like, how game you are and if you fit in. Vanity is not shelved on match day.

'Straight in! Straight through the doors! Here we go!'

We were strides away, all of us in quick motion, and Miffer was calling the shots. Everything around me was a blur. I was pumping that bad that I started to growl and pull a hideous face.

'Come on Stoke, let's fucking give it 'em.'

The silence could be contained no longer as 100 lads roared in through the double doors. We went in blind, no-one having a clue what was going to meet us, and the thrill of it had me fighting my way to the front, alongside Miffer and Bodie.

'CITY!'

Our grand entrance was witnessed by a total of two barmaids and twelve Villa lads, who were to the right of the bar standing around a pool table. The shock on their faces turned offensive instinctively. I was hurled past the bar and in their direction by sheer weight and had no way of stopping; all I could do was brace myself as a Villa fan stepped forward and smashed his pool cue across my head. The Villa lads were prepared to make a fight of it but they did not stand a chance, and on that basis, they were left alone. Although a few punches already had been thrown by both sets of lads, we had to respect the situation. It's no big deal turning over a handful of game lads just to claim a result; you wouldn't like to be on the receiving end of such a kicking yourself, so why do it?

I had been concussed but it didn't ruin my day. All of a sudden, people were talking to me. Including Miffer. Twelve noon, and we had let them know we had arrived.

'Keep walking. Just keep walking. They'll find us now.'

Miff was at the front with Ant Walton. Ant was a Jekyll and Hyde character, a softly spoken roofer who would not drink on a Friday night and went to bed early so he was focused for the next day's fighting. Ant could flip at any moment. Between them they were leading us towards the ground and the Holte End. It was far too early to even think about going in the ground but the sight of 100 Stoke lads walking around the back of their main end would soon get back to the Villa mob. They would know that we didn't care where we were or who they were. We were just here and we wanted it. Two psychological advantages achieved early doors; I was loving this.

By one o'clock, the streets around the ground were starting to get busy. We finished our second lap of the ground and settled in the Witton Arms, behind the away end. By this time the local police had been deployed for crowd control, and we knew it wouldn't be long before we were spotted and the chance of a row would be more or less over. We got a good couple of hours' drink inside us and, at ten to three, left to make our assault on the Holte End. The feeling now was charged, the alcohol was making us braver for sure but I felt as sober as a judge as we filed out of the pub doors and on to the street. I felt euphoric. All those years sat drawing and playing out the role, and then going to the match as a kid and watching the storming of ends; now finally it was my turn have a go at taking somebody's end. *Arr, this is fucking mad. I hope all the Stoke fans sing, 'We're proud of you,' as we are led round the pitch.* I was close to fulfilling a boyhood dream.

'CITY, CITY.'

'Shut up. Shut fucking up. Dickheads.'

One or two of the lads were cut down immediately by Miff's gruff voice and they sank back well within the ranks, embarrassed by their impetuosity. *Gone are the days of singing in the street,* I thought to myself, as this tight, silent mob of Stokies spread across the road, filling it ten deep. I found myself falling into this new strut I had found that day, and positioned myself on the outside of the mob's formation. The streets were packed solid with Villa supporters all pointing and nodding towards us. I wanted every one of them to see me, and all of a sudden my arms started to swing, not in military fashion but bent and loose, one arm going higher than the other and slightly to the sides. This was my version of the casual strut.

So far we'd had an easy ride but I had memories of Villa Park from the Seventies and I wasn't the only one who knew that sooner or later we would find each other. The mob that had congregated at the turnstiles of the Holte End was huge, but it was hopeless. The police had cordoned off the street completely, making it very difficult for any Villa not sitting in one particular stand to get access to the street we were on.

'Let's just steam straight through the old bill, Miff.' Mad Ant was psyched up and wanting a full-on assault on police lines. 'Even if we don't get through, at least they'll know we want it.'

He had a point, but Ant was mustering only a handful of lads. Most of the expectation was hanging on Miffer and his decision. Then we heard another voice.

'Stand still lads. Where are you lot from?'

Four mounted policemen had followed our rear from the Witton Arms and could see from their elevated observation points that this bunch were about to be naughty boys. They took no nonsense; the West Midlands Police never did. The back ends of the horses banged into us, scattering us all over.

'CITY,' we roared, for the fuck of it. If you can't get the row, make some noise. Get the attention.

'Villa, Villa,' immediately came back at us. More horses cantered in amongst the queuing Villa, breaking their momentum and sending them running up a grass bank. However, Stoke's mob had been split up, and almost immediately everybody reverted to their old habit of being territorial under pressure. We were no different, and the three Alsager lads grabbed each other and darted into the nearest turnstile.

'Fuck it. Jump it, just get over,' Eddy screamed. And that's what we did, straight over, laughing our heads off as we went inside the ground.

'It's mad, innit Jasp? These lot are mental.'

'That Miffer and his mate are. Not sure about our predicament here, lads.'

We immediately stopped chatting about how good it was in case it turned into a nightmare. It had been obvious outside in the street that this newly formed alliance of Stoke men had not seen enough action together yet; they had all split up as soon as the confusion set in. Ourselves and the Stone and Blythe lads had all made it inside the ground; as our numbers were fewer and we were familiar with each other, it was easier to stick together. We were back in the position we used to be in at away games – on our own. Only this time, because we had lost our relative safety in numbers, we found ourselves in a position that could have been slightly beyond our experience.

We sat down on the benched lower tier of the Witton Lane stand. Although we had not made it into the Villa end, it still felt good looking over into the Stoke fans to our left. We could see small pockets of lads off the coaches gathering by the segregation fences, trying to stay discreet as they searched the lower tier to the side of them. These lads must have been gutted to have been thrown in there. That was them scotched until the final whistle, at least. Meanwhile my adrenalin was going through the roof. It was nowhere near over for us, we were still on the hunt. Anything could happen at any moment, and we couldn't wait.

'This is what we want.' Jem was also relishing the thought of having an off so close to such a huge audience of Stoke fans.

'It's not going to go in here, Jem,' said Eddy, staring at the Holte End. 'All their lads will be up there.'

All three of us looked. It was an impressive sight and the mob in the middle looked massive.

'Villa, Villa.'

Throughout the first half, more and more of the Glebe lads appeared in the seats around us. It seemed that not all of them had split up. Gwilty, Dalton and both the Waltons, among thirty or so others, had managed to evade capture by the police. We thirty all of a sudden felt that we were the gamest lads off the Glebe coaches. After all, we were still on show; it was down to us.

Half-time saw the emergence of Miffer, Bodie and Wilson. They'd had a three-on-three in the stand above and were buzzing. 'Villa know we're in here,' said Wilson. He was right. With ten minutes of the game left to play, our mob, now of fifty, was caught napping by the same numbers of Villa. The stewards had barely opened the big, double exit doors for any fans who wanted to leave early when the Villa mob, waiting outside, charged in. These were an older bunch of lads and looked battle-hardened, especially the dozen or so black lads that got well stuck in to Miffer, who stood windmilling like a bear. The shock of the attack had at least twenty of us on the back foot. Some of our lads jumped up onto the pitch to review the situation before running along the touchline to the next aisle, where they jumped back into the stand. This would turn out to be a good flanking exercise.

The Stoke fans behind the goal cheered louder than they had done all match and surged down the terraces, hurling themselves up on to the fences. 'Stokie aggro, Stokie aggro, aggro, aggro.' How long had I waited to hear that.

The fight was thirty seconds old and it was hectic. The Villa lads were giving it everything; we had upset them all day and their onslaught was vicious. It was going off now half on the benches and halfway inside the stand and Villa were getting the result – until the dozen or so lads that had run along the side of the pitch came wellying in from side on. It was enough force at precisely the right time and gave us the edge for a brief moment.

'Get together, get together.' Miffer had blood streaming from both nostrils and was spitting it everywhere as he screamed advice. Stoke charged into the Villa lads, who were now making a fighting retreat back through the exit, which the stewards then managed to force shut. Nobody mentioned steaming back out with the Villa; each man was drained. The fight had lasted only a few seconds over a minute, but it had seemed like an hour. For now, that was enough, and the lads burst out laughing and started hugging each other.

'Did you see that Brummie's face when he fell on the floor!'

The whole mob laughed together, whether they had seen the Brummie or not. This was something they wanted everybody to know they were a part of. The feeling was one of a great bonding amongst fellow warriors.

That was the end of the action that day. We returned to Hanley and a good eighty or so headed to the Roman Candle pub to get pissed and talk about events. The Candle was a bar-disco below street level, with a treacherous set of stairs leading down into it. It was drab and smelt damp, the purple carpet had turned black at the bar, and no matter how pissed you were it was impossible to fall over, as your feet stuck to the floor. One good thing was that it had the theme album from *The Wanderers* on the jukebox. The Candle had become our new HQ for our nights out in Hanley.

'Where are you from mate?'

I had seen this man clocking me through the corner of my eye for most of the day. He was another bruiser, a typical rugby player type.

'Alsager, mate.'

'We've seen your two mates over there before.'

'Yeah, I know, and you haven't seen me. Right?'

'Just asking.'

'I'm on leave.'

I didn't like being questioned. Not by anybody. But the big, curly-haired lump before me, in his navy blue Lacoste jumper, was one of the lads that had run along the pitch. He had been thereabouts all day, and was most of the weight that managed to come to our aid in the Witton stand in that side-on attack.

'On leave? What are you in?'

'I'm in the Army.'

'Army!'

The man startled me as he jumped back in delight and rolled up his sleeve. 'PBA all the way.'

I stared at the initials tattooed on his forearm, then shook my head and frowned.

'PBA all the way?' I asked, as he raised his hands in the air and turned to the group of eight lads he had been stood with around the cigarette machine. On cue, every one of them raised his pint above his head and began to chant aggressively, 'PBA, all the way, fuck the Pope and the IRA.' Over and over and louder and louder. I had to chuckle even though I didn't have a clue what they were on about, but I liked the passion they were putting into whatever it was they were doing.

Packmoor was a tiny mining village in the north east of the city and about four miles from Alsager. It was rough, desolate and had one pub, the Dog and Partridge, and a miners' club, which was packed out on weekends. Other than that, blink and you would miss it. This was the home of the Packmoor Barmy Army – the PBA – who numbered between eight and twelve on a good day. The man introduced himself as Philler, and was immediately referred to by one of his mates as Philler the Beast. These lads became my, Jem and Eddy's first allies in this newly formed Stoke mob.

Philler was their handful, but I soon noticed that they centred on one lad, a tall, fair-haired youth called Modder. He was the founder of the

PBA and made it law that you could only be a member if you lived on Scragg Street, which ran right through the centre of the terraced village. Even in such a small community, you had to be privileged to be a part of the Packmoor Barmy Army.

That weekend's leave had been one of the best of my life. I had loved it.

The rain fell lightly over my kitbag as I leaned against the bus stop at Bank corner in the centre of Alsager. It was five to twelve on the Sunday night, and as always Steve was on time. The gold Honda Civic pulled alongside and I smiled as Steve and Bri Elliot, another soldier in Nine Platoon, gave me the thumbs-up, a sure sign they had both had a shag that weekend.

'Ay up lads. Eraight?'

I threw my kit bag across the back seat and jumped in, sticking my head between them both as I slammed the door.

'Been shagging?'

For the next hour I sat and listened to the sexual exploits of two horny squaddies let loose on weekend leave with a pocket full of money and a bag full of semen. We stopped briefly for fuel at Hilton Park service station, just north of Birmingham. The rain was running down the side of the windows as I looked out into the dismal night. *Fucking hell, I've got to go back to Colchester and a six a.m. start.* We had stopped at Hilton Park the day before on the way to Villa, just a passing halt on the off-chance of there being a coachload of like-mindeds on the way to somewhere else. I smiled at the memory of all the light-fingered Longton lads, who had emptied the services of anything that wasn't worth robbing, just for the crack, such as tubs of mint humbugs, which were used as missiles on the coach in a brief South Stoke/North Stoke encounter. Philler the Beast ended up getting carried away and had to be pulled off a number of the Trentham members.

I sat back and watched Bri and Steve in deep conversation as we pulled away on our journey back down to Essex. Yeah, I wouldn't have minded a shag myself, but I hadn't stopped climaxing all weekend and I hadn't even looked at a bird. Women had not entered the equation once during the whole time I had been with the Glebe lads. There had been a lot of handshakes, slaps on the backs and male bonding, and all I could think about was the next time I could get back to Stoke and do it again.

Battalion life was busy. A massive NATO exercise in Germany was being prepared called Eternal Triangle, and our commanding officer was eager to show that the little sunshine break in Gib hadn't softened his men. After an early morning run and block cleaning every day, we would be out in the field, training hard and preparing. I enjoyed all of this, as did most of the lads. None of us minded getting dirty and wet, nor a week in the trenches dug in in a wood somewhere, training for camouflage and concealment. It was not a lot different to when you were kids building a den.

What pissed me off was the night-time. The blocks that we lived in at Roman Way barracks were grim: sixteen-man rooms, with tiled floors and grey radiators that had to be kept spotless, a difficult task with that amount of men all coming home after a day on the ranges, covered in shit and stinking of gunpowder. Rivalry amongst the ranks started; people were missing loved ones and friends they had just spent a weekend with and now they had to wake up to some hairy squaddie's sweaty arse. At least in Gibraltar, you could accept your situation: miles away from home, at least a week by boat, mail every day, with a return date to look forward to. No frustration. At Colchester however, you were just a four-hour drive away from everything that you loved doing, yet instead of being able to go and do that you were sat around with a load of other sad people, all thinking about home while they cleaned weapons or bulled their drill boots. It seemed to us all that the closer we had come to home, the more homesick we had all become.

Fights were regular events amongst the lower ranks, and I had my share. It was not long before I was a regular visitor to the camp jailhouse, and wearing a red tin helmet with a number on it became more familiar to me than my beret. Trevor Hughes was the Regimental Police corporal in charge of all prisoners when outside of the guardhouse, and depending on how many soldiers were in custody, usually at least six at a time, he would march us all at double time, even to the cookhouse. Trevor had no idea that I knew anything about him. To him I was just a young soldier fighting his way amongst the ranks. He called me 'Stokie', and I would smile and clench my fist. It was only now that I got a close-up look at the man that I had heard so much about. His thickset body, rich red hair and huge hands made him an imposing figure, but it was teeth marks across his nose that I couldn't take my eyes off. *I wonder if he got those off the Doberman.*

By the time I had been to several games on the Glebe coaches, I was familiar with pretty much all of the 100 or so lads that travelled on them. I was becoming particularly friendly with Wilson, and he would pick me up from my drop-off point when I was on weekend leave. Wilson would then take me to Alsager for last orders and a pint with Jem and Eddy, always making sure we were coming on his coach in the morning before he left for another boozer and another promise. That season I travelled to Everton, Villa, Man United and Tottenham with the Glebe.

White Hart Lane was the most frightening. Stoke failed in an attempt to take the Shelf, where Tottenham's lads stood, and they repaid the compliment by coming into the Brick Lane End and dropping down among us at half-time. London for us at this stage was a learning experience and one with the ever-present threat of injury or incarceration. After the final whistle, we came under attack again as we left the ground. We numbered over 100 lads in a crowd of 600 Stokies and made our exit immediately so as not to get caught up with the rest of the crowd and lose our formation. There was no relying on the big man Miffer this day, as he had not travelled, and there was an air of uncertainty among us. It was a red-hot end-of-season match and the sun was in our eyes as we came onto the street. The Tottenham mob numbered no more than fifteen, and in all honesty they didn't even need that. They were all time-served lads well into their thirties, and experienced campaigners in Europe at the time. They hit us with no sound as our first thirty lads reached the street and sent them back into the ground and us scattering all over. Then all fifteen cockneys casually walked back across a narrow street and gave us space to get back together and come out and have a go. Their confidence completely unnerved us, their numbers even more so. They had won the psychological battle hands down and stood back to gloat and take the piss out of these scruffy northern muppets. 'Don't fucking back off from these. C'mon Stoke, get fucking into 'em.'

Bamf was a strapping, seventeen-year-old Viking with tight gold curls and a nine-inch member that he liked to introduce as his 'other tool'. He was a miner's son from Kidsgrove and fancied a shot at becoming a leading member of this new coalition. Credit where it's due, Bamf didn't give a fuck, and without waiting for any back-up, he ran out into the sunshine and waded into the cockneys, followed by Modder and several others. For a brief moment the Tottenham lads had to get stuck in too, and punches were traded, resulting in Bamf being arrested with a broken nose. There was no shouting or bawling or to-ing and fro-ing; the police had the situation quickly under control, which left the Tottenham lads laughing and strolling along beside us as we were escorted to our coaches, and had us feeling a little relieved. There were no more incidents, and after half an hour our coaches were released and were on the way.

'Oi, Wilson. Tell the driver to pull over. We're not leaving Bamf youth.'

Terry pulled the first of the two coaches round and we headed off to retrieve our friend. It wasn't long before we were lost and two streets later we ended up on the Broadwater Farm estate, the scene of some of the worst rioting on mainland Britain ever to be witnessed. It became apparent almost immediately that we had made a wrong turning and a certain uneasiness fell upon the coach as we drove slowly through the tenement flats and high rises.

'Fuck it, just stop the coach. There's no point going any further in. We're lost.'

Wilson was right. Dusk had fallen and the sound of reggae bass boomed from within the estate. I couldn't help thinking to myself that unless we made our presence felt in a calm and positive way, the locals would sense our fear like sharks and we could be in a lot of trouble.

'Look, we can't leave Bamf. We're lost in a fucking nightmare estate, why don't a couple of us go to the nearest pub and see if any of the locals can give us directions. Better us find them than them find us.'

We all knew what would happen if a coach of football hooligans had got lost and stopped off in an area in Stoke such as Bentilee, a sprawling council mess to the south of the city. They would get torn apart by every lunatic on the estate, including his missus. It was decided that Wilson, Jem, Ed and myself would go to find a pub or something and phone a taxi to show us the way to the police station. Within seconds of leaving the coach and crossing the road, we heard shouting from the balconies way up above us.

'Keep walking, don't look up,' someone said.

We all had the same thought: *this is going to go berserk any minute.* My heart was pounding fast, and sweat appeared on my brow. I was worried but couldn't help liking the feeling. I wiped my brow, crossed over the road and headed in the direction of what looked like a community centre. It was a flat-roofed building, part of a row of flats and next to a newsagents and greengrocers. Its two small windows were covered with thick meshing, and just inside the front door I could see a long line of local black youths, all nodding in time to the rhythm of the reggae beat. We all stopped and turned to each other.

'What do you reckon, Ed?'

I looked behind me at the coaches 500 yards away. *This can go either way,* I thought. A hundred lads against the Broadwater Farm estate. It didn't bear thinking about.

'Just ask 'em. If it goes off, it goes off. We're here, aren't we?'

I walked into the doorway and backed out again immediately as a huge rasta loomed before me.

'Members only, guys.' He smiled, shook his locks and jigged a little before pulling his massive bongo dread to one side and peering down. 'You boys looking for someone?'

He was joined by about twenty others of mixed race, but his demeanour remained friendly and a little inquisitive. We were obviously talking to the right man, as nobody questioned his way. We explained our situation from start to finish. They found it amusing that we were football hooligans on a day out, and started telling us about some of their stories of rioting against the local police. It looked like we were going to be all right and our shared hatred of the police was our pass to Go. We left Broadwater Farm with a local boy running alongside and pointing the way for us.

Bamf had already been released. He spotted us first as we pulled up outside the police station on Seven Sisters Road, and milked the moment, strutting up and down waving his hands wide and clapping.

'Cam on, let's 'ave it. Sav'nors are the gav'nors. You know the fackin' rules.'

Bamf's impression of a cockney was piss-poor but he still climbed on board to a hero's welcome, especially from his mates from the Whitehill area of Kidsgrove: Mono, Mickey G, Stinge and the Urchin (who were joined occasionally by their very own Stig of the Dump, Lilley). As I watched them greet their friend at the back of the bus, I could see the pride on their faces. One of their own had got stuck in and nicked for Stoke City, and put the Whitehill boys firmly amid the infrastructure of the Glebe mob.

It was pointless me heading back to Stoke with the lads, as we were off for a nine-week exercise in Canada first thing on the Monday, and I had loads of admin to get through. I was dropped at Kings Cross and stood alone, watching the coaches disappear into the evening sun. I watched silently until they were barely a speck in the distance. My stomach was heavy as I turned and went to look for my platform and the train heading east.

Sitting in the empty carriage I amused myself by reading the graffiti carved into the wooden doors and window frames.

'Hammers kick to kill.'

'Hurry up Arry.'

'You've just met the famous ICF.'

All southern slang and all alien to me, it added to my sadness. All I could think about was where the lads were going to stop off for a drink on the way home, and if they would end up having a mass brawl that would be talked about for years. I hated the thought of missing out.

★

Canada was fantastic. We had a hard and successful exercise alongside the Canadian and French military in the vast training area of Camp Wainwright in Alberta. During a seek-and-destroy exercise miles from any facilities, C Company set up a non-tactical, bivouac-type camp, just inside a treeline set on a ridge overlooking hundreds of miles of open prairie. It was magical, and nigh-on everybody sat in awe, gazing at the sky as the sun went down over the North Pole and the Northern Lights took their place in the heavens.

'I love it here,' said Steve. 'Do you, Jasp?' He sat relaxing at the foot of a tall pine tree, watching me crawling around inside our bivvy, trying to roll out our gonk bags.

'Jasp, aren't these Northern Lights supposed to be one of the Seven Wonders of the World?'

I crawled up out of the bivvy, stood up and followed Steve's thoughts up into the multitude of bright lights that followed one after the other over the Northern Hemisphere.

'Seven Wonders of the World? I'm not sure mate. Fixtures are out in two weeks though.'

Steve laughed. 'Stoke mad, you are. Never right.'

We drifted off that night with our heads sticking out of our shelter, watching the stars. We talked about travelling across America on motorbikes, and figured out how long we both had left to serve before our journey could begin.

'When we get to California, I'm going to find that hotel that the Eagles used to hang out in. I'm gonna find myself a cowgirl, mate.'

Steve had already dropped off. All about me was quiet and dark, and I listened to the night owls calling their chicks home. Then I crawled inside my bag, checked that my general purpose machine gun was facing down towards my feet inside the my sleeping bag, and wondered to myself. *I hope we get a good away fixture, first match. Leeds or Man United will do. Can't wait.* With that I was out for the count.

That night we were hit by freak weather, or so we were assured much later by a Canadian officer detached to our company. Hailstones the size of squash balls hammered us for hours, followed by lashing rain and an ice-cold wind that trashed our positions. Almost every bivvy ended up flooded as the water ran down the pine trees and followed the roots into our kit and sleeping bags. Nobody escaped the drenching and I cannot describe the wind-chill. It was so cold that one soldier, Michael Foot, one of the black lads from Birmingham whose room I had first lived in, was found frozen to a tree, his fingers embossed to the barrel of his self-loading rifle.

Steve was out of his bag and began rallying his friends. 'Come on lads, get it together, quick.'

I was out of my bag too and looked around in the half-light at my comrades fumbling aimlessly with their kitbags. It was hopeless; our spare clothes were already sodden from the previous week, as we had been in the field for days. Every one of us looked like he had jumped into a swimming pool fully-clothed and then been thrown into the middle of nowhere to survive. I shivered as I watched my friend struggling to remove his water container from his shrunken webbing. His fingers were blue and he had limited movement in his hands. Within minutes, casualties started to fall to the floor, ranked soldiers amongst them. It had literally become a life-or-death situation.

'Arghhh! Phew, got it Jasp.' Steve yanked free his water bottle and put it to one side on the forest floor. I didn't move to help him. I was rooted to the spot and starting to pass out. I had never been so cold and wet; the pain in my hands and feet was excruciating. I stared at Steve as he struggled to release one of his mess tins from inside his kidney pouch. He struggled and screamed and cursed, using his teeth to eventually prise free his container and get out his brew kit.

'Tea or coffee mate?'

Steve looked up at me and winced as he pulled out his hexi-burner and saw that all the tea bags stored inside were mush.

'Fuck it, coffee it is then.'

I stood and watched the man as he crawled round on his hands and knees inside the flapping bivouac, looking for the tiniest bit of shelter so he could strike his waxed matches and get the burner alight. I had gone. I can remember drifting in and out of consciousness, and feeling bad about not helping my friend, but that was about all I could do, apart from make a strange chattering sound as I tried to stop my teeth from destroying each other.

'Jasp, here y'are mate.'

The big black mug was handed up to me out of the storm. I looked inside it at the lumps of powdered milk and pine needles floating in black treacle. It was at that point that I thought to myself, *this isn't too bad this, I'll just go peacefully, fuck it.*

Looking back on that night, I often cringe at the thought that I was prepared to give in and pass away without a fight. Other lads in Nine Platoon ended up having to be cas-evacced to the nearest hospital with severe hypothermia and frostbite, so at least I survived it. I'd got my little friend from Bucknall looking after me, and the warm coffee that he had fought tooth and nail to make for us kept me alive. Make no bones about it, I had gone. I definitely owed Steve my life.

After surviving that night and nine weeks in the field, the lads were ready for a piss-up. By the time the exercise had more or less been wrapped, the mood was relaxed. It was admin time, time to wash our kit and read our mail. Steve and I sat in the NAAFI having a beer and marvelling at the facilities the Canadian troops were given to make their time off as 'civilian' as possible. Their NAAFI was like a roadhouse, with neon beer signs, pool tables and a Wurlitzer jukebox, on which I played John Cougar's 'Jack and Diane' over and over. We sat and chatted about normal things, like what name you would call your son and how nice it would be to meet that perfect woman. Steve had a calming influence on me.

The end-of-exercise party was scheduled for the second to last night of our stay. The party was held in an aircraft hangar, where seating for 2,000 soldiers of all ranks was laid out among rows of tables in front of a makeshift stage. It was freezing in there but rumour had it that a dozen strippers had made the six-hour drive from Edmonton especially to entertain us. Dressed in civilian clothes, we packed the place, and in no time the sound of French, English and Canadian laughter filled the air as impromptu comedians, jugglers and sopranos who had volunteered from within the ranks gave it their all. It was like a scene from *It Ain't Half Hot Mum*, the only difference being that we were freezing our bollocks off. Crate after crate of Labbatt's beer were being dished out as fast as it could be drunk, and true to form it was turning into an orgy.

'Where's these strippers? Come on, let's see some tits.'

The lads were getting impatient and the slow hand-clapping and whistles started. Unbeknown to us, the girls had taken a look at their audience from behind the stage and were showing reservations about performing in front of such a mighty show of testosterone. The hangar had certainly started to warm up and got decidedly warmer when the compere informed us that unless we got down off our tables and sat in an orderly manner, we wouldn't be getting a show.

'Boo! Bollocks!'

The place was in uproar. We had been drinking for over three hours and we hadn't seen one pair of tits.

'Shhh. Sit down. Sit down.'

Relative order was restored and the lights went out to deafening applause. The girls were told it would be best all round if they got on and did a quick set before the place got wrecked. Visibly shaken, the first stripper took to the stage to the Stones' 'Brown Sugar'. She was a chunky black girl with huge breasts and an afro hairdo, and was wearing a leopard-skin bikini. She looked about forty years old, and tried to remain professional and focused, staring at the wall at the back of the hangar. You could tell she was going through the motions and she had disappeared from the stage before the end of the first chorus. That's where the night plummeted without recovery.

Her swift departure saw the immediate arrival of Mickey Southall from Wolverhampton, who was bollock-naked and squirting whipped cream all over himself. Mick had lost his chin in a bar-room brawl in Gibraltar with some Dutch merchant seamen; a blow from a pool cue had completely shattered his bottom jaw and left him with just a huge bottom lip. From where we sat he didn't half look like Mick Jagger, who he now impersonated. We were in uproar as two burly security men wrestled him to the floor. Mick locked onto one of them and proceeded to 'shag' his leg, with all three men struggling and slipping in the whipped cream.

Most of the Staffords had been at the back of the hangar, with the French and Canadian lads at the front and to the left and right of the stage. None of us actually saw who it was who threw the chair onto the stage, but it definitely came from the French. The missile bounced off the three struggling men without being noticed by any of them, but that was not the point. We English saw that as an act of aggression, and an unnecessary one at such a time of frivolity. Mickey's impression of Jagger was the best act we had seen all night, and the on-going struggle was hysterical, as Mick had managed to undo a security guard's trousers and had yanked them down to his knees. Everybody could see the funny side, except the French.

Now if squaddies are going to kick off, they are going to kick off, no matter where or when. But the sight of one of your own company sergeant majors having a stand-up with a sergeant major from a foreign army – that's a definite green light. Mickey Southall was not a brilliant soldier but was good for morale and loved by everyone throughout the regiment, and the sergeant major was not having anyone throwing anything at one of his lads. Nobody. He launched himself at his French counterpart and the two men did battle in a flurry of punches and well-aimed kicks for about a minute. The hangar was bedlam as hundreds of squaddies clambered over tables and chairs and headed to the French quarter of the room. We were all paralytic, but even so people were not quite sure whether to join in in case of repercussions. We wanted to steam into the French Army but held back and watched out of respect. I had never seen such high-ranking soldiers having a drunken brawl before but had heard loads of stories; after all, these men had worked their way up from private and they'd had countless fights.

It was difficult to tell who was getting the better of it, as the hangar was still in darkness, but they were getting well stuck into each other when the space around them closed in for a second. We lost sight of the two men as they stumbled into the French lines and fell to the floor. The French swallowed them up, then the French sergeant major regained his stance. None of us could honestly say, but it looked like our sergeant major had been held down to give the other man the advantage. It took our man at least ten seconds to get back to his feet, only to receive another haymaker.

That was it: spontaneous combustion. The place went absolutely berserk as the Englishmen ploughed into the French, using bottles and chairs as weapons. That hatred towards the French made for one of the bloodiest fights I had ever seen, going straight in at number three in my all time top ten army rows. It was broken up ten minutes later by the arrival of the Canadian Mounted Police, all big, stocky lumps with chiselled jaws. On the night these men reminded me of robots; the way they conducted themselves and handled the situation was precision. I thought to myself, *I wonder if every end-of-exercise party ends up like this when the English have been invited.* What a way to say goodbye to Canada.

chapter five

Beginning of the End

OON THE THRILL of the Rockies was a faded memory, and the
doldrums of battalion life once again had me marooned without a
tack to sail on. We were all bored shitless. Steve had been placed back
on an NCO's cadre he had already passed in Gibraltar; it was a kick-in-
the-teeth trick from a CSM who hated all Stokies. He wanted to make
life hell for all of us, and succeeded. Discipline in the regiment disinte-
grated; one or two of the old sweats said it was the worst they had known.
Changing parades for punishment became part of army life. It was a
bastard having to report to the guardroom for inspection every hour, on
the hour, in whatever uniform was designated, throughout your spare
time, but having to do it in World War One uniform with hob-nailed
boots and gaiters – even Trevor Hughes raised an eyebrow at that one.
That's what happened and we endured it.

As pissed off as I was, at least I had something big to look forward to.
The opening fixture of the 1983/84 season was Everton away at
Goodison Park. Rumour had it that Wilson had four coaches going from
the Glebe and it was all anybody was talking about in the pubs up Hanley.
I couldn't help worrying that my turn to be on guard duty would not
come round on that weekend.

I arrived in Alsager late on the Friday night, totally relieved that I had
made it home for the match. We had handed over guard duty to A
Company that tea-time, devastating the Stoke fans among them as we
headed out of the gates in our little gold Honda Civic, windows down
and me shouting, 'Goooo on you rip-roaring Potters,' as we mounted the
kerb and sped off. I was sick with the excitement and anticipation of our
trip to Liverpool.

True enough, Wilson had filled four coaches, in fact he could easily
have taken five, as the convoy of four fifty-six-seaters left Stoke at ten in

the morning, rammed with seventy lads on each. People stood in the aisles while some of the little ones were shoved into the baggage spaces above. Everybody had at least eight cans of beer, and with no toilets on board and little room to move, empty cans were soon being filled and passed towards the skylight. The coach had a real football smell to it.

We lost one of the coaches along the M6; it blew up, covering the northbound carriageway in thick smoke. They were knackered old buses used for taking schoolkids to the baths, and seventy grown men had broken this one's back. The occupants were left walking alongside the M6 with their thumbs out. At least thirty of them got picked up by normal Stoke fans in cars, squeezing the odd little one into the boot.

Two friends from the pre-fabbed Blurton area of the city, Harvey and Mad Weston (our very own Johnny Rotten), pulled up in their works Escort van after spotting the smoke in the distance. They managed to pile nine of the lads in the back, all lying on top of each other like sausage rolls. Alas, less then five miles later, they too ended up with their thumbs out; the weight proved too much for the old Escort and it blew up by the side of the road.

Those of us who did make it pulled off the M62 on the outskirts of Liverpool and stopped for a drink at the Rocket pub. It was half eleven and 200 lads piled off the three coaches and pissed everywhere, the huge sigh of relief and the sound of men aiming onto corrugated sheeting sounded like the Zulu warriors of Rourke's Drift beating their shields. The small stand alongside the pub's bowling green was flooded in seconds. Inside we sat and chatted, waiting for any stragglers to make it off the motorway. For now we were all right, tucked away with little chance of catching a Stanley blade up your back. We were all well aware of the dangers of travelling to Goodison.

Stoke had played at Goodison a couple of seasons before and the lads had seen first hand the capabilities of a pissed-off Evertonian. Keith was a bus driver for PMT – Potteries Motor Traction. He was also a well game football hooligan in his mid-twenties. That day he managed to get a double-decker out of the works yard unnoticed and drove it to the Roman Candle pub in Hanley, where eighty of the original Stoke casuals were waiting with their cans of beers and rolled up newspapers. These lads included Dickie Duds, Bodie, Miffer, and Tim, the eldest of the four McGlochlan brothers. Also on board was Robbie Campbell, the firm rasta. Rob was a chancer who lived it as it happened. Sharp and astute, he rarely missed an opportunity for a bit of action, whatever the stakes and whatever the game. While waiting for his bus to take him from Stoke town centre up to the Candle in Hanley, he noticed that Bourne Sports had a display saying, 'Clearout Sale.' The shop window was full of mannequins in school uniforms and sportswear, each one holding a hockey stick or cricket bat. At the feet of the models, laid out across floor, were a number of rounders bats, with the sign '50p each'. Rob grinned.

As Keith the driver left Hanley to the sound of the lads singing, 'Get on board, get on board, get on board with the double-deckers' (a tune from a popular kids' programme starring a young Patsy Kensit), Rob made his way to the front of the bus and leaned over.

'Where are you getting on the A500, Keith?'

'Stoke roundabout, Rob. Why, what's up?'

'Just need to nip in Bourne Sports for a min.'

The bus pulled up outside the sports shop, and held up the traffic while the rasta sauntered inside. Rob was a mover and cool as fuck; only he could walk as casual as that with an audience of eighty-plus. He caught the attention of a shop assistant and pointed to the window display.

Keith leaned out of his window, peeping his horn impatiently. 'Hurry up Rob. I've got shoppers queuing to get on here.'

Rob left the shop chuckling, carrying the last remaining rounders bats: 'Warriors, come out to play-ay!' The bus was in uproar as he climbed back on and handed out the tools.

Keith pulled up on the Anfield side of Stanley Park. It was one o'clock, and the weather was glorious. The lads piled out of both exits and entered the park; not a word was spoken as this determined mob headed over to the blue half of Liverpool. With no sign of any resistance, they left the park yards from the Stanley pub opposite. Miffer was in command once again.

'Wait here on this side, lads. I'll go and have a look in there.'

The big man crossed the street cautiously, taking Tim and several other bat-wielding Stokies with him. Nobody was sure how many, if any, of Everton's lads would be in the pub and the anticipation had the lads breathing heavily as they patted the palms of their hands with their 50p bats. Miff got on his hands and knees and crawled below the stained glass window, standing on the other side and peering in.

'It's packed with 'em.'

The lads across the street stood ready to do battle immediately as the five men tapped gently on the windows, smiling inside at the unsuspecting scallies. As a dozen curious and surprised faces filled the windows, they were suddenly fired through. Miffer went berserk, showering the unsuspecting locals in shards of glass. Two huge roars went up immediately, one from inside and the other from across the street as the Stoke mob charged over.

The Everton fans in the Stanley reacted immediately and staged a mental breakout, using anything that hadn't been bolted to the floor as a weapon. Everything was hurled back out through the windows, injuring a dozen or so of Stoke's front line. Stoke backed off across the street to regain some ground and grab a quick breather, while missiles littered the street in front of them. Miffer knew that if they waited any longer the scallies would make it out; he could see that they had stirred a hornets' nest, and if the Everton got out, Stoke were going to get badly stung. The big man ran back into the road, picking up a bar stool and launching it back into the mass of bodies inside.

'COME ON.' The Stoke mob did the same, picking up anything that came to hand and returning it through the windows. The same missiles then came back out again as soon as they had been spent.

This could have gone on all day, had it not been for a huge Everton skinhead wearing jeans and a white T-shirt. He attempted to jump out through the window several times, each time being beaten back with a bat or hit with a flying chair. As the tired arms dropped and the momentum slowed, he was out and into us, crazed and windmilling. Everton were out now too, and hand-to-hand fighting continued until the police arrived a minute later. No policeman or Stokie went near that big fella with the white T-shirt.

Stoke had arrived at a reasonable time, with a good tight mob of eighty lads, and they wanted it. Had they turned the corner and headed off along County Road, they would undoubtedly have come under attack from every angle – it's no stroll in the park at Everton. However, that would have meant ignoring the Stanley and its occupants. Turn your back on a scally? I don't think so. Nobody is claiming a result – if anything, towards the end Stoke started to struggle a bit – but they had taken the initiative. In the corresponding fixture Everton stormed all over Stoke town centre, smashing pubs and Mike Lloyds Records. I will always remember one of their lads stood at the bottom of the Stoke end wearing a mohair jumper, and flashing his Stanley blade over to us. Everton took the piss that day.

In the Rocket pub, our day was going to plan. It was early, we had arrived unnoticed and the beer was flowing. I sat down at the back of the pub by some French doors that opened out to the bowling green. I was joined by half a dozen fifteen-year-olds from Trent Vale, or 'Vegas', as they lovingly referred to it. Podge, Ada, Goggsy, Nomad, Spiv and Cossack

were all as wild as jayhawks and were all nurtured by the big man himself;
to Cossack, Miffer was the father he had never known. He even resembled the big man in many ways, down to the bull neck and copious
tattoos.

Cossack deserves a special mention. A game lad from humble begin-
nings, he gave his loyalty to what would become the Naughty Forty as no
other. Belonging is everything to Cossack, a family man with two sons,
two lurchers, and an owl, and who is a locally renowned breeder of working dogs. When not out with the firm, he would be with his dogs,
persecuting the countryside with a cold-blooded killer instinct apparent
at every match. This man was a predator, famed for an unstoppable left
hook that at times left his opponents as stiff as the many vermin he
disposed of. Everything was a trophy to Cossack; if his victim had not
been stuffed and placed on his mantelpiece or wall, there would be a scar
or a bust knuckle to boast of. Big in stature, big in heart, you always felt
loved with Cossack, and his impressions, facial expressions and body-
popping graced many a coach ride or night in the cells

These youngsters were the newly formed Trent Vale Game Casuals,
the TVGC, and had an air of arrogance as they chatted nonchalantly
about the previous night's annihilation of some local doorman who had
dared to call them kids. The lads also took turns to ask me about the
army and the rows I'd had around the world. While chatting, I couldn't
help noticing a sad-looking boy of about the same age as the lads I was
with. I didn't know his name but had seen him on every trip with the
lads. He was always alone. I felt sorry for him, just one of those gut feelings that you get.

Philler the Beast had turned up for the coach that morning in a mess;
he and his best mate Soss had been in an all-night lock-in at the miners'
welfare club in Packmoor, and he had turned up drinking Tia Maria neat
from the bottle. He had been loud and aggressive from the moment he
slumped out of his taxi at the Glebe. Because of the state of the big man,
most of his drunken drool fell on deaf ears.

His attentions turned to the lonely young figure looking out at the
bowling green, somewhat distant and lost in his thoughts. I clocked
Philler clocking him, and watched as the big man demanded that the
youngster went to the bar and fetched him a drink. The boy didn't budge;
Philler could have been talking in backslang for all he cared, he wasn't
moving. Pretty much everyone in the pub was watching Philler now, and
it was becoming a bit of a scene. Philler saw the youngster's refusal as lack
of respect but I was starting to have enough of this.

'Do you know that lad?' I asked the Vegas boys.

Ada said he had been in school with the youth, and he'd had a sad life. I was mortified when he went on to tell me that the boy's mother had died the previous night, yet he had still come for the match. I looked over at the boy and snarled at his tortured soul. Here was a young man who took sanctuary amongst the arms of strangers and all for the love of Stoke City Football Club and its unique following, the family that you've never had.

'Twat him,' I shouted to the young lad.

The Beast spun round, snarling. 'Who fuckin' said that?' He looked mean and horrible, his huge neck and head turning purple with rage.

'I fucking did.' I was up out of my seat, regrettably smashing my pint pot on the table and offering the Beast the naughty end. I had been impetuous with the glass, and had no intention of using it on anyone, so I launched it into the wall beside me.

'Leave the lad alone Philler.'

All of a sudden the landlord wanted us gone. There was a ten-minute delay to our departure as Philler and I went onto the car park together to sort out our differences. Thankfully that was done verbally, and in over twenty years of friendship the Beast and I have not had a cross word since. As for ridicule and bullying, it was totally unacceptable within our ranks – everybody was there for each other – and it stopped from that day on.

Our three coachloads headed off, intending to use the same approach as the season before: park up at Anfield and head through the park. Along the route, each of the coaches received incoming fire from an air rifle, and we arrived with shattered windows and stiff necks from ducking down. The sniper must have been shooting from a vehicle, as the coach I was in came under attack several times at different sets of traffic lights. Terry the driver, as always, sat shaking his head, unfazed.

None of us waited for the coaches to stop; everyone piled out of the rear exits in traffic as we approached the park. We were fed up of being shot at like sitting ducks and decided being a moving target was a better option. Immediately we started to get split up. As the main bulk of lads headed through the park, numbering a little over 100 now, we were greeted by a large police presence entering at our intended exit. We scattered again, charging over bowling greens and running blind for any way out. Stoke's mob was decimated; suddenly it was every man for himself.

I ended up in the company of Brasso and Piko, two mates that had made a pact never to leave each other's side, no matter what. Piko was the youngest member of the PBA and whenever he turned up for a match was greeted with a collective rendition of, 'Cuando, cuando, cuando, cuando.' He had been a champion ballroom dancer as a kid and had appeared on the *Benny Hill Show* with his sister, dancing to the 'Cuando' song as Benny fell about on stage. Those that didn't see the programme were promptly told by Philler, and Piko has had to live live with that tune ever since.

We got to the ground at half past two and immediately bumped into other small groups of shaken Stoke lads, some sporting black eyes and ripped jumpers. It was a frightening place but at least nobody had been slashed − yet. Justifiably we were all feeling uneasy, and decided not to stand around in a mob of twenty but to split into twos and threes and attempt to mingle in. Entering the ground would have been a safer bet but this was more fun; the adrenalin was peaking. We three headed into a bookies and pretended to look at some form sheets, while really we scanned the street outside through the open door.

In the bookies was a scruffy geezer in his fifties; he was short with tight black curly hair, and wore a grey pinstriped suit jacket on top of black corduroy trousers. He looked like a proper Paddy, and after a once-over we paid him scant attention. In the street, thousands of Evertonians streamed towards their turnstiles, anxious not to miss the first kick of the season. We stayed where we were, scanning for the arrival of any friendly faces. That was beginning to seem like an improbability, as a quick check of a watch showed it was five to three.

The whole time we had spent sussing the situation on the street outside, the scruffy geezer next to us had been sussing us and had moved in close, positioning himself in the bookie's doorway. He flicked through a pile of old betting slips that Brasso noticed he had scooped up off the floor. Something about this fella didn't add up. Unease gripped all three of us, a quick eye-to-eye acknowledgement went three ways and we made our decision. *Come on, let's fuck off.*

Almost at the instant of stepping towards the door, it happened. Thirty Stoke had at last got it together and bowled into view, roaring, 'Come on,' to anybody that might want it. It was instant panic as the majority of Everton fans scattered. That was our cue and we leapt past the scruff and darted towards our lines. Stoke's little show sounded impressive but fell short of a curtain call, as I was not the only one running towards the Stoke ranks; several hundred scallies of all descriptions were charging in the same direction, screaming abuse and throwing pies.

I was relatively safe, as the police response was swift. Not so for Brasso and Piko; they were having a nightmare. As we had fled the doorway, the scruff had pulled out a bread knife and lunged at us, catching Piko's coat and snagging it with its serated edge. Piko had retaliated immediately and caught the fella with a backhander under his nose. These two were then on their own, on the street and scared. The young friends who had made a pact to never leave each other during a row were being put to the test now.

'Fucking hell, he's still coming Brass.'

Nobody in the street behind the Gwladys End batted an eye at the sight of a knife-wielding man tearing out of Stanley Racing and taking up the pursuit of the two friends. Caught up in the mass confusion of the Stoke mob's arrival, they headed against the tide, bobbing and weaving in and out of the baying scousers. They had to get to the Park End quick. The maniac followed them doggedly, bumping and barging past his own in his attempt to get within stabbing distance. The sight of the Blue House pub in front sent the lads into a mad dash; they knew they had to get past that to reach the away end and potential safety.

Running full-on but with the man and his knife making ground, Brasso went over on his ankle yards from the Park End turnstiles. He crashed to the floor at speed, losing a layer of skin from his chin. Piko had made it, and cried, 'Thank fuck!' as he turned to his friend, but his relief turned to horror as he realised what had happened.

'Nooo. Fucking nooo.'

Brasso was on his feet again, with the man seconds away, the bread knife released from inside his jacket. This madman was about to satisfy his lust for blood. Brasso was off again, his will to live keeping him just ahead of the cold steel. He ran screaming into the face of his mate, who had removed his coat and began to flail it at the attacker, beating him back like a lion-tamer. It worked, and both the lads got into some precious space, instantly becoming the aggressors. Police action was swift, as there were plenty about awaiting the arrival of the small mob who had turned up late, but the Betting Shop Butcher was not about to be taken in easily. The Stoke fans still outside even expressed some admiration at his determination to escape the police. He was eventually wrestled to the floor and jumped on by at least ten officers in a front garden 100 yards away. The two friends laughed with relief, and shook each others hands. *Fucking scousers.*

Minutes after kick-off, they joined the rest of the Glebe lads in the bottom left (as you view the pitch) corner of the Park End. Two hundred congregated along a segregation fence, staring over at the young scouse mob in the enclosure below the Main Stand. Stoke knew that Everton's more established faces would be in the seats above, but they were a young mob themselves and looking to make an impression on a big stage. Anything that resembled fair game was eyed up.

An hour into the match, Everton opened the scoring and the place erupted. Stoke fans cursed through their teeth as the jubilant

Evertonians in the enclosure piled onto the fences and sarcastically beckoned us to join them. As their roar faded to applause, the pin to a smoke canister was pulled and deployed over the fences under the cover of a full-on charge from the Park End. Stoke fans were already climbing over when the canister hit the fence of the enclosure and dropped kindly down onto the terracing among the baiting scallies. With no inkling of the impending chaos, they rallied to meet Stoke's assault.

I think everyone in the ground heard the dull thud that preceded the thick mass of green smoke. Within seconds the scousers had disappeared, then the whole Main Stand vanished from view. Even the invading Stokies had to climb back down, coughing and covered in green dye. Goodison was awash with green for at least five minutes, and the game was temporarily abandoned while police restored order. For the remainder of the game, our terracing came under ceaseless fire as coins rained from above and the side – all coppers, we noticed.

We pissed Everton's lads off that day; they thought we were cheeky fuckers, like we didn't have the right to come and have a go or something. Nobody had ever thrown a smoke bomb at them in their own backyard and they didn't like it. Stoke's new young mob was starting to get it together, and showing some panache.

Outside the ground, the Merseyside Police took a different approach to the Stoke fans and stood brandishing their infamous straight sticks. These were five-foot willow poles and something I have only ever seen at Goodison. They did a good job of boxing us off and any intended Everton attack was averted, though we did sustain the odd swipe of willow from the odd Everton-supporting policeman.

The three Glebe coaches left Stanley Park with a dozen or so others that soon lost sight of each other in the heavy traffic. The lads on Terry's coach requested another lap of Stanley Park on the off-chance of catching a farewell row and came under attack again, not from a sniper this time but from several young burglars who had dropped their stolen TV to argue among themselves. When they saw our bus, they all stopped bickering and hurled parts of the bust-up TV at our windows. We'd had enough, and the decision on the coach was unanimous: 'Let's fuck off up Hanley!'

The first of the three overladen coaches blew up a mile past Knutsford services, and left a stream of eighty pissed-off Stokies trudging back to Knutsford and a chance that one of the others had pulled in. Travelling back from a fixture in the Midlands was a steady stream of coaches and vans carrying Liverpool fans, who were pretty soon swopping hand gestures with the walking Stoke. Imagine the Stoke delight when a Transit van pulled onto the hard shoulder opposite and fifteen scouse lads jumped out and ran up the bank for a piss. 'They're lads, they are.'

All of the men stood taking a leak were in their late thirties and looked the part. One or two of them even nodded over as they did up their flies. You could see that they were trying to figure out who we might be. *Shall we show them?* It took only one to lead and within seconds twenty Stoke were darting through the speeding traffic and heading for the central reservation.

'Oi Mickey. We're Stoke. Do you want it?'

Anything that came to hand – bricks, hubcaps, old registration plates – were lobbed over at the hysterical scousers, who couldn't contain their amusement at these ranting nutters jumping up and down like cavemen in the cental reservation of the M6. The scousers sped off in uproar, peeping their horn and baring a backside through the rear window. The Stoke lads burst out laughing at the big white hairy arse being slapped by several pairs of hands. 'Yeah and I bet there's another dozen hands going through his pockets,' someone quipped.

They darted back over to their mates. Little did they know what had been going on at Knutsford while they had been entertaining themselves. Terry's coach had arrived twenty minutes earlier and the lads had piled off into the toilets and café. A couple decided to nip over the bridge and have a little shufti about to see if they could find a bit of mischief.

Mischief they found, almost immediately. A coachload of Huddersfield's lads had stopped and were stood around eating Cornish pasties and reading the *Pink Final* for the scores. The two Stokies strolled through the Huddersfield and discreetly counted their numbers before deciding to go back and tell the others.

As they turned to head up the bridge staircase, one pastie-eating Yorkshireman stepped forward and, with a mouthful of pastry, questioned the two friends.

'Ey ar lads, who are ...'

BANG. A perfectly timed rabbit punch had the man sinking to his knees, before keeling over and smashing his head onto the concrete with a sickening thud.

'Leg it!'

The lads tore up the steps and took flight across the footbridge with thirty or so Huddersfield fans in close pursuit. 'Kill the little cunts. Who are they?'

As the stairway down loomed before them, the pair ran blind off the top, hurling themselves so as to gain an extra couple of yards on their assailants. To their relief, congregated at the bottom of the stairs were most of the lads. 'They're here,' came the shout from the youngsters as they landed among their bemused fellow men.

The thirty or so Huddersfield lads poured like ants over the top of the stairway, all in full flight and screaming like banshees. Our two little mates had obviously upset them. Stoke sprung into action, immediately unleashing anything they were holding. Cans, bottles and brollies were all thrown and stayed the Yorkshiremen's charge. The battle that ensued was short and bloody. Huddersfield went toe-to-toe halfway down the stairs but were beaten into retreat by the superior numbers howling into them. Stoke got them on the back foot as they slugged it out on the glass-panelled footbridge. What that must have looked like to any motorist passing under beggars belief.

Huddersfield's numbers swelled as the rest of their coach arrived and things turned even uglier as knives appeared on both sides. In the midst of the swirling melee, blood was drawn, which was the cue for the dispersal of anyone with anything to hide. The fight stopped immediately and police spent the next few minutes searching for witnesses amongst the parked-up motorists. Some of the lads ran for over two miles across fields to Knutsford town centre, from where they caught taxis to the Roman Candle.

Hanley was packed to the rafters, as usual. Ten of us sat upstairs in Leadbellys Wine Bar, a favourite haunt of the football lads on a Saturday night. In amazement we watched the return bout of a long-running feud between some women off the Bentilee estate and their local rivals from Abbey Hulton. They slugged it out in the bar downstairs. 'I tell yer what. If I do decide to settle down, it won't be with any bird from round here,' said one of the lads, and I couldn't agree more. We had gone to Leadbellys to chill a while before hitting the madness of the Candle and its occupants, but the ongoing ruckus downstairs had us finishing our pints and getting off; when the old bill arrived it was odds-on they would turn their attention to us rather than the warring women.

The scenario we encountered as we approached the Candle was apocalyptic. Bodies were strewn across the road, women were screaming and, even worse, some of our lads were taking a hiding. When Miffer and twenty or so others had arrived, they had been confronted inside by a coachload of miners from County Durham who had been on a picket line and had stopped for a drink on their way home. Nobody knows to this day what sparked that incident off, but with two sets of highly charged individuals saturated in alcohol, one set not being of native descent – need I say more? The fight had gone on below street level for ten minutes before eventually spilling onto the street. I wasn't there so I don't know for sure, but it sounds like Stoke made a 'tactical retreat' up a dodgy set of stairs to get into some space in the street outside.

I don't remember who or what hit me but it came from the side and it hurt. The fight had escalated around us and we were drawn in without realising. I hit the floor on my right shoulder and slid across the wet tarmac, resting underneath a double-decker bus between front and back wheels. I was left dazed and staring up at the axle of a bus. My heart was in my mouth as the axle started to rotate; the bus was pulling away to flee the mayhem, and I was lying underneath it. I froze.

'Oi, I thought you were a squaddie, not a mechanic.'

I was dragged by my feet from a messy fate and lay looking up into the toothless grin of Miffer. 'Thank God, Miff. Cheers mate.' I staggered, shaken, back to Leadbellys.

chapter six

AWOL

SUNDAY NIGHT AND the depression of heading back to camp had me leaning inside the bus shelter, finishing off the previous weekend's 'Stoke City FC' graffiti with a two-pence piece. Steve was late, only twenty minutes or so but it was unlike him. Finally his car pulled up and I jumped in the back. I could feel something was wrong immediately, and decided to wait and be spoken to before saying anything other than, 'Ay up.'

We pulled off with a screech and a joint 'ay up' back. Bri went to sleep, or at least he pretended to. I had lived in the same room as him for months and knew that when he was really asleep he snored and blew bubbles from the corner of his mouth. I sat back. The silence felt awkward. I started to worry that my friends had read the national Sunday papers and been disgusted at the banner headline 'THE LOUTS ARE BACK!' that had screamed off the back page of the *News of the World* after the events at Everton. I decided to sit it out and watch Steve's reflection in the rear view mirror. His eyes looked troubled, and he gripped the steering wheel with sweaty palms. Then it dawned on me. He was to start the NCO's cadre that morning; another six weeks of being beasted by Chucker Smith, the Stoke-hating bastard of a sergeant major. I knew how much he dreaded having to do it all again. I felt sorry for my little friend.

Bri woke up as we pulled into Colchester railway station. It was half past four in the morning, and still dark. 'Right, come on Jasp, we'll catch a taxi from here.'

I watched in confusion as Bri unloaded our bags from the boot and beckoned a taxi. I looked at Steve. 'I've made my mind up, Jasp. I'm going. Bri's only got six months of his nine-stretch to do, and you need to keep your nose clean, mate. Don't worry, I've got a friend from school, Bucko, he's on the run from young offenders. We've got something sorted.'

I gave my mate a hug and told him that if I wasn't on guard, I would be home for the Man United match the following Saturday. I assured him that I would get a whipround off the lads from the match and get it to him and Bucko. Then Steve was gone. I shook my head.

'Fuck me, I should have gone with him Bri.'

'That's exactly why he didn't say anything. He knew you'd go. He just wanted to get you back down here before he went, Jasp. You can't afford any more mither. It's not just Chucker who's got it in for you mate. The RSM has as well.'

Those three letters struck a bolt of lightning through me. Terry Ellison, or 'ET' as we called him, was another high-ranking non-commissioned officer who took great delight in giving me pain.

'Yeah, you're right Bri. Come on, let's get back to camp before we're reported AWOL.'

Manchester United's Red Army had rampaged through Stoke several times throughout the Sixties and Seventies. There's no denying that. Their huge numbers were always a key factor, of course. That was one reason why all Stoke fans hate Man Utd, who they refer to as 'shit fans'. Taking Jimmy Greenhoff was another reason, as were the glory hunters who attach themselves to the club. If you are from Salford or Greater Manchester, fair enough, but Milton Keynes?

The day of our game started early, with the back bar of the Glebe being opened to the right faces. Whenever the Mancs had come to town previously, they had met resistence from small pockets of unorganised chancers who would use hit and run tactics on solitary vans or coaches, but Stoke had rarely had the chance to stand and have it with big numbers. Word had it that this day was to change all that. By ten-thirty, reports were coming back to the Glebe that fighting had broken out outside several town centre pubs as Mancs were attacked in vicious fistfights with lads from the Neck End making their way to the Glebe. It had gone round all the Potteries that a call to arms had been requested, and large numbers were expected to gather to defend Stoke town centre early. The request was upheld, and I met a lot of older faces not known to me before.

They included Mickey Moonshine, Sammy Boon and Decker. Moonshine was one of the Hughes brothers (including my Army mate Trevor and the formidable 'Coddy' – see Chapter 20) and was a small, round-faced fellow who spent his whole life whizzing his bollocks off on amphetamines and partying around the clock. Mick was a man of few words who communicated through his darting eyes and infectious smile.

I couldn't help but like him immediately. Sammy was a striking-looking character off the Bentilee estate who held great status amongst his community. His gypsy features conveyed an air of charm and made him a firm favourite with the girls up Hanley. Behind the looks was a full-bore nutter, Stoke City to the core. Decker was from Trent Vegas and one of Miff's mentors. He was big and decked people.

By eleven o'clock, Stoke were out of the Glebe and on the streets hunting for Mancs. It took less than five minutes. It was not hard finding them but we were not interested in any of their shirt boys, who were everywhere in town. Hands up, one or two did get a cuff as we passed by, but that was the risk they ran. After all, it was Man U, and when they had rampaged through Stoke and other towns there had always been plenty of shirt boys joining in.

Our information had arrived at the Glebe via Acko, Stoke's attempt at cloning Catweasel and Old Man Steptoe together. He reported that the Phoenix was their base and their numbers were 200-plus. The Phoenix is slightly off the main drag of town, on a long, narrow, one-way street. During the short walk through town Stoke's numbers swelled from 200 to 300, all up-for-it lads. A couple of young Manc scouts must have spotted us because they were out and filling the street 100 yards away well before we had come into view. The Manc army roared and charged full throttle towards us, hurling bottles and pool balls.

'Stand. Fucking stand Stoke.' Decker ran ten yards ahead and turned to face us, his arms stretched wide open. 'Don't run from these,' he commanded.

Our nervous edge ebbed slightly as other Stoke moved forward too. Decker's action had prevented a panic and now Stoke roared out too.

'COME ON.'

There was still a good thirty yards of no man's land left and United were making ground at speed, their weapons now spent and intent on a good punch-up. Then the two sides came together in one almighty clash. Around 500 men stood toe-to-toe for more than five minutes before police arrived to quell the disorder. It was brutal and many of our lads ended up with slash wounds. One, little Harry from Castle, had such a thick, purple-red stripe across the side of his face that he ended up with an appalling complex and would cover his scar with his sleeve when he talked to you. Harry knew some of the Liverpool scallies and went on robbing sprees across Europe with them. He went with Winder and Spike to Heysel and I think it pushed our mate over the top, watching the events of that night. On his return to Stoke, he made a wire noose at work, and minutes before we were due to pick him up for our annual trip to Blackpool, he hanged himself in his bedroom. It had all got too much for him. Little Harry R.I.P.

Several of the Alsager lads were heavily involved in the fighting. They had taken the opposite route to most of the Glebe lads and had run for over a mile to get to the Phoenix at roughly the time it would have been due to explode. They arrived as the mayhem was at fever pitch and volleyed in side-on, with plenty of unsuspecting targets to choose from. Jem was on top form as usual and unleashed four well-aimed punches to send four individuals sprawling. That was as good as it got, as the Mancs soon swallowed the fighting friends up in a frenzied counter-attack.

Fighting continued throughout the day as vans were sought out and turned over and the occupants chased off. Around the ground, the Mancs came under continued attack and outside the supporters club Pak Man and the Cockney Reds fought a running battle with Ringdan, a staunch proddy from Scotland whose family had come down to work in the pits. He had a real problem with Man U and his little crew of fifteen, including several of the few black lads that followed Stoke at the time, gave an outstanding performance under overwhelming odds.

After the game, thousands of United supporters waited in the sun in a blocked-off street in front of the train station. They stood around idly waiting for their trains back to Piccadilly. It was well over an hour after the game had finished. Most of the ambushes from the graveyard had subsided and the Mancs relaxed, some playing football with an empty beer can while the cops seemed happy to observe.

'Manchester, la la la, Manchester, la la la.'

Like an alarm clock raises you from a deep slumber, the Mancs and police were all up and on their toes as they turned to greet the sight of a mob over 200-strong marching towards them.

'United! United! United!'

The roar from around the station was deafening as the Mancs hailed their returning warriors, and the police lines opened like a parting wave to let them through. Officers even smiled and nodded as the arrivals poured past them. Once the police lines had been breached, however, a roar went up to the sheer dismay of the smiling Mancs.

'Come on!'

This mob, led by Decker, Miff and Moonshine, had walked for an hour through the backstreets of Stoke and Shelton to reach the station undetected. A full sixty minutes of pumped-up tension was released on the authority of the police. They flipped and scattered the fleeing Mancs everywhere, before being baton-charged by mounted police officers, who were immediately deployed from their position in front of the North

Staffs Hotel. Stoke were chased all the way back into the town centre pubs; anyone caught took a severe whack from the disgruntled officers. We had pissed them off, getting behind their lines and causing havoc. Nineteen Stoke fans were arrested that day and for the second week running we were headline news, with a picture in the papers of an unconscious United fan lying in a gutter. On the pavement next to him were a pair of brilliant white Adidas Trimm Trab trainers belonging to Philler the Beast. He had thoroughly enjoyed his day out.

Jem was also one of the nineteen arrested, and he appeared in court at Fenton magistrates a fortnight later. He had been charged with assault on persons unknown after being arrested following the Phoenix battle. There were no witnesses to his crime, but the blood streaming from an eye wound and his bruised knuckles saw him yanked into a van and kept in until the next morning. Jem chose myself and Eddy as his witnesses and I was granted a day's leave to attend court. We sat beforehand with the defending solicitor, got our story right and were told to stick to it and answer any questions honestly. Well I was up for that, as my grandmother had raised me to be honest and tell the truth, as had the Army. A perfect witness.

I was still eighteen and had never been in trouble so had never been in a court of law. I found it a little daunting when my name was called out by the court usher, and everyone in the corridor turned to look. I got my bearings as soon as I was shown to the witness stand, acknowledged the magistrate respectfully, and looked over to Jem, who was sat with his solicitor and looking anxiously over at me, his saving grace. The initial questions were put to me by the defence brief. He more or less put the words in my mouth for me and it looked like the little nods amongst the magistrates were going in our favour. Jem had told his brief that he had stumbled into the fight after getting off a bus and in my mind that was the truth and I had to stick to it.

No sooner had the defending solicitor thanked me for taking the time to attend than the prosecution was up out of his seat, throwing his papers across his desk. He laughed out loud and the courtroom suddenly turned stifling. For the next ten minutes I endured a barrage of accusations of conspiracy and lies. Finally he approached the witness stand and, with his last question, put it to me that we had indeed headed to the Phoenix public house to look for the Manchester United fans drinking in there.

'You knowingly walked into the lions' den, didn't you Mr Chester?'

He had completely bamboozled me, and I answered truthfully: 'Yes.'

Jem's solicitor dropped his face into the palms of his hands and I felt a hot, prickly sensation on the back of my neck. I didn't need telling; he had caught me out. Eddy was relieved of his witness duty, as the damage had already been done. Jem received a third conviction for football-related violence and a £140 fine plus costs. Needless to say, he didn't rely on me in court ever again, but I apologised and chipped in for his fine. My lesson that day: think before you speak.

That night after the Man U game, Bri picked me up in his Triumph Dolomite and drove me to a secret rendevous with Steve and Bucko. We left Hanley and headed south-east out of the city towards the Peak District, uncharted territory for me coming off the Cheshire Plain. Our destination was a dense forest on the shore of Knypersley reservoir. It was pitch black and eerie. We pulled up alongside an open stretch of the shore, and waited. I sat in the passenger seat with the window down straining my ears and cursing my lack of night vision. It felt bitterly cold. Neither Brian nor I spoke a word for what must have been over half an hour as we sat in the darkness, waiting on our fugitive friends to appear. The hoot of an owl came out of the thick forest three times in succession, and Bri let out a sigh of relief. I jumped out to greet my little friend. It was so dark and dense in the woodland that we had to hold hands in single file as Bucko led the way. He knew these woods well, as it was not the first time he had absconded from a young offenders institution. Their camp was a rickety woodcutter's hut, about a mile inside the forest boundary. Although old and long forgotten, it was an ideal holdout for any desperado. I liked it immediately. It had one fair-sized room with log burner and stove and a tap with running water out back; what more would you need? The four of us settled down in the cozy cabin and drank neat vodka.

It was great to see Steve, who I had missed. He had always seemed to keep an eye on me round camp. He once spent three nights cleaning a corporal's buckles and boots to stop him grassing me up for butting him in the dinner queue. That day at the match I had told the lads of my friend's plight, and without hesitation their hands went in their pockets. Steve and Bucko were chuffed to bits with the £160 I gave them, and so was I.

Brian and I arrived back at Roman Way Barracks on the Monday morning with barely twenty minutes to parade. Neither of us had spoken on the way back but we both knew what the other was thinking about: going AWOL. By eleven-thirty that morning, we were on opposite sides of the classroom, paying little attention to an explanation of the working parts of an M16 Armalite assault rifle. Plans were being made to shelve the reliable SLR and the Armalite was being looked at as a possible replacement. *So fucking what?* I looked at Bri for the fourth time in a minute; his glazed stare caught mine and we both smiled. We both knew, immediately, what the other was thinking. Brian's slight nod of his head, was all I needed. *That's it, we're off. We're going AWOL.*

For the next six weeks of my life I too became a fugitive, carefree and wild. All four of us lived together in that shack. We had Steve's Honda Civic and Bucko's Honda 400cc motorcycle at our disposal and a twelve-gauge shotgun, origin unknown. I celebrated my nineteenth birthday on the run in the woods, hiding not only from the military but also from the Staffordshire police force as well. On reflection, the immaturity of my actions feels almost embarrassing, yet at the time it felt like being a member of the James Gang, sitting out the winter in the Hole in the Wall, safe from the trail of any Pinkerton Agents that might be seeking us out. It was a great adventure while it lasted.

As much as I enjoyed being an outlaw, it soon became apparent that it would be too risky for me to go down the match. It left me with a dilemma: remain a fugitive in the woods until finally captured and not be able to see the lads, or give myself up, do some time and get back to the buzz of the football. One day Steve put it to me straight as we walked along the bank of the reservoir.

'You might as well go back, Jasp. We know you're missing your football and the lads.'

He was right, though in the end it was a joint decision by all of us, with no disappointment or malice. Nothing in the world was more important to me than being able to go to Stoke, and like a junkie who needs a fix, I promised myself one last fixture before handing myself in. That game was not for another nine days but I had to see them out, as the fixture was West Ham at home.

For a person like me to miss a game like West Ham through choice would be the first sign of brain malfunction. It is a massive fixture in any hooligan's book, though everyone awaited the arrival of the infamous Inter-City Firm and its colourful East End characters with some trepidation. West Ham had always come to Stoke, not necessarily in massive numbers but always for a ruck. As a kid I remembered many of the classic encounters of both supporters in and around the graveyard and terraced streets.

In the fourth year at school, Eddy and I had caught the Stoke-bound train at Alsager when the Hammers were in town. If I remember correctly it was Phil Parkes's first game for West Ham as a million-pound goalkeeper and was to be screened on *Match Of The Day*. As soon as we sat down in the first of three carriages we caught the sound of cockney slang, something to do with Stoke-on-Trent, and then rolls of laughter. Our attention was brought to no more than six southerners, all aged around twenty. Neither of us could take our stare from these Londoners, who had obviously travelled up via Crewe, and were sat as bold as brass, paying no attention to the budding schoolboy hooligans sat opposite and hanging on their every word. They oozed confidence, and Eddy and I admired and feared them at the same time.

We left the station and followed along ten yards behind them. Neither of us knew what we would do if they turned around and said something, but we had to follow. Our trail didn't last long, as the London lads entered the first pub they came to – the Roebuck. We hung around outside on the post office car park for twenty minutes, collecting a couple more arrivals from the station, not that we had any delusions of getting it on, we just felt compelled to wait and watch what might happen. Nothing did happen, and we headed a little deflated into Stoke.

'I thought those West Ham were supposed to be berserk,' muttered Eddy, kicking the pavement. There were loads of Stoke fans in that pub but nearly all would have been normal supporters. We assumed the lads off the train must also be in that category.

'Perhaps they weren't ICF then, Ed.'

We headed to the ground and entered the Boothen, standing as always at the bottom to the left of the goal. It was a near full house again this day, the Boothen was packed to the rafters, and the atmosphere as always was electric. Phil Parkes looked impressive between the sticks but inevitably received a huge chorus of, 'What a waste of money.' He chuckled and gave us a smile. Smiles and two-fingered salutes were presented back, but I already was beyond all that. My eyes were firmly held on the Stoke End and the West Ham mob in the middle of it. They looked like matchsticks but were definitely grown-up matchsticks; there were no kids in their crowd, just men. Gruff-looking men.

Within two minutes of the referee starting the game, the expected happened. No more than five bodies away from me, the terracing opened up leaving a small gap. The cry of 'ICF' came from within it and I realised that the six young men stood trading punches back-to-back were the lads off the train. I have never forgotten the events that followed. It is one of those lasting memories that we all carry from childhood and from time to time fondly recollect. As game or as suicidal those cockney lads were, there was only ever going to be one outcome against such odds and they were beaten savagely over the fence and down into the moat that separated the Boothen from the pitch. Stewards and police aided them up onto the playing surface and attempted to escort them round the pitch and back into the Stoke End, as was the rule in those days. The cheeky cockneys revelled in being acknowledged as lunatics and walked casually along with a swagger and nonchalant disdain. Then they all raised both arms in the air, clenched their fists, they crossed their wrists in the Hammers sign and hissed out, 'ICF.'

This met with a storm of abuse from the Boothen as hot Bovril and coins showered down. The cockneys laughed and played it up, but the six Hammers didn't laugh for long, as for some bizarre reason the police escorting them decided against walking them around the pitch and instructed stewards to open up the gates of the Boothen Paddock.

'Paddock sort 'em out. Paddock, Paddock, sort 'em out.'

The Paddock Mob was originally formed among people who for one reason or another had got into trouble in the Boothen and had been banned from entering it. Isolated from their mates on the other side of the fence, these lads gained a fearsome reputation, and a lot of inter-mingling took place among lads from parts of the city that normally would pass each other by. As the West Ham lads prepared to leave the scene and return to their own ranks, I think everyone in the Boothen stood speechless that they were actually being allowed to walk through the Paddock. It was only a matter of seconds coming, and only the police and the cockneys were blind to it. My last sight of those six lads was of them disappearing into a swarm of seething heathens. Coppers helmets were thrown from the Paddock onto the pitch as they too took a sickening beating. The whole thing looked in slow motion to me, and does to this day. Help did arrive, and dogs were brought in to quell the attack. In no more than a minute the cockneys were gone and the police had retreated onto the side of the pitch. I remained rooted to the spot, staring at the fifty or so Boothen exiles, as they stood solid, arms raised in defiance and roared, 'The Paddock, the Paddock.' I wanted to be in the Paddock Mob. So did Ed, as he turned and said, 'Those West Ham were berserk.'

The morning of the much-anticipated game arrived and I was like a kid at Christmas. Brian took me up to the Roman Candle on the back of Bucko's motorbike. I had declared my intentions to the lads the night before: 'Right, if I manage not to get nicked in Stoke, I'll have a last night out in Hanley, then hand myself in on Sunday to the police. Then I'll just get my head down.'

The Candle was packed shortly after opening, with 100 lads making short work of their first pints before leaping onto a couple of buses and heading into Stoke town centre. The excitement among us as we sat on the top deck, giggling and simulating our who-wants-it expressions, must have had us looking like a bunch of schoolkids on a day out to the zoo rather than a small bunch of mercenaries intent on eradicating an unwanted junta. Nevertheless, foolplay is part of any day out with the football lads; you can relive your boyish escapades all day long, and then in an explosive moment of sheer madness you can catapult yourself from childhood to boyhood hero warrior slaying the invading forces, and returning home heroes yourselves. And all that on a belly full of beer and a shag to round off your night. Fantastic.

We arrived in Stoke at 11.15 and it had already gone off twice. West Ham had arrived early with a couple of mobs of small sizes. Estimates from the lads that had bumped into them were of no more than fifteen or twenty in each group. They added that all the lads in the second group looked decidedly younger than their colleagues. For the moment, both mobs had disappeared.

It stayed that way for most of the morning and early afternoon. Several false alarms, mainly off young Acko, had us moving from pub to pub, and the longer the anticipation and excitement escalated, the more the nerves crept in: 'These fucking cockneys are up to something.' It was agreed that we had stayed in town long enough, and that we should get up by the ground. It was two o'clock.

As we approached the ground, we split into two groups of fifty. One mob moved through the market and headed past the police station while others scoured the graveyard. They both met outside the Victoria pub opposite the away end. I was getting nervous and had it in my head that every copper on every street corner was looking for me. The rushes going through my body at this time were volcanic.

Our mob observed each of the four routes leading to us, and where West Ham had to get to. We resembled a family of meerkats on the hunt. Less than 100 yards away, slightly out of our vision and feet from the Boothen Paddock turnstiles, was the Stoke City Supporters' Club. This held about 400 people and was usually full of old beer monsters from the Seventies. Outside it was an ideal spot to monitor both the away end and Boothen turnstiles at the same time. This was usually the meeting place for the Walton brothers and their little crew from Smallthorne.

That's where it started and where the roar came from. We charged immediately, giving out a huge roar of our own, and seconds later were witnessing an encounter between about forty older shirt lads, the Waltons, and West Ham's so-called Under-Fives (their junior hooligans). It was difficult to put a number to them but there looked to be about twenty.

The young West Ham lads, many in suede jackets, were brash and oozing confidence and had been more than holding their own, but were backed into the doorway of the Supporters' Club by the swelling numbers. Walton was going mad and having a real tussle with a black lad with a five-pronged afro comb, which he jabbed at Walton's face every time he closed in. Seconds later, the Stoke mob was scattered by a line of charging police officers, who waded in with leather batons. Soon we were all back out on Campbell Road, moving hastily towards the away end and a possible nibble at the Under-Fives again, as they were being escorted through.

On the corner of the away end, Stoke's mob charged the escort and brief exchanges took place. West Ham kept their composure but did look relieved to be placed safely amongst their own fans. The Stoke mob retreated onto the car park at the back of the Victoria pub, and fell into a furious conversation.

'Did you see what they were wearing?'

'How game was Walton, the loon.'

It was quickly pointed out by several people that while we were swapping fashion tips and exchanging opinions, there was an older, more dangerous firm of ICF still unaccounted for. Everybody came to their senses and marched out of the car park and crossed over towards the away end again. There were ten minutes to kick-off.

Five hundred gathered outside the Stoke End turnstiles, many of them shirt boys and pissheads off the estates. The casuals numbered around 100 and it was decided that seventy would stay with the main bulk of Stoke to defend that part of the ground, while the other thirty would head in the direction those Under-Fives had appeared from. From there they could patrol the back of the Boothen End and on past the Butler Street Stand, bringing them round to arrive on the far side of the West Ham turnstiles. No opposition was found around the ground and the thirty split again. Ten went back over to stand in the Boothen Paddock, in the section close to the West Ham fans, while the other twenty went in the Butler Street Paddock, again in the section closest to the away support.

West Ham's following numbered around 1,200 and they all looked aggressive. The small mob of Stoke yards away in the Butler Street remained silent and observed. The silence erupted into full-bore hysteria as the Stoke and West Ham players took to the field.

'City, City.'

The hearts of the twenty Stoke in the Butler Street sank at the sight of the Paddock opposite opening up into a pitched battle. They had made the wrong decision and were missing out on a chance to defend their ground. About a dozen West Ham had gone in the Boothen Paddock opposite and were fighting like crazy from the bottom of the terrace. The audience in the Butler were not captivated for long, as seconds later Brasso spotted another fifteen Hammers coming up the tunnel from the refreshment bar below. These London lads were a part of the older firm that until now had been only a secondhand report. Stoke flew down the terraces and into the tunnel to face the fronting West Ham. The Hammers stood tight together, not shouting the odds but with arms wide open and smirking as if to say, *Well, do you want it or don't you?*

The decision was unanimous as the twenty Stoke casuals all produced Vics bottles filled with olbas oil and sprayed them, before charging down into a furious fistfight. The ensuing battle lasted for about a minute as the two sides ran riot in front of the refreshment kiosk. Neither side gave an inch in the confined passage. Stewards and police were quick to react and soon took over. A small number of stewards who had witnessed the brawl from the terracing above the tunnel pointed out main instigators to the police, though all issued vigorous denials. Though the fighting stopped, a large argument took its place and the police lost patience and arrested six lads from each group. The twelve were taken out of the Butler Street Paddock and walked along the ash track surrounding the pitch. They were being led to the police control box in the opposite corner of the ground, which took them past the Hammers behind the goal. The London fans spat and hurled abuse at the Stoke lads and cheered and clapped their own.

'Cam on you Irons. Facking give it the norvern mankeys.'

Brasso was one of the six Stoke nicked, along with two others from Alsager. They were separated and put into individual holding cells, as were the West Ham lads. Things were still lively inside the ground, with pockets of West Ham being sorted out and skirmishes taking place. More and more Stoke fans were being brought down into the holding cells, and the police decided that at half-time they would relieve the congestion by taking the first party of prisoners down to Stoke police station for processing. All twelve Stoke and West Ham fans were taken, placed in the back of a waiting van and cuffed to the seat. They were then left unattended for several minutes. As soon as the back door of the van was slammed, the verbals erupted from both sides, with threats being hurled to and fro until a cockney voice silenced them.

'Oi, listen, this is getting us facking nowhere.'

The van fell silent. He was right. Brasso stared at the geezer speaking. He was in his mid-twenties and sported a tight black curly perm, shaved slightly at the sides, a pale complexion, piercing eyes and a crescent-shaped scar circling his left eye. Brass had seen this man while following England on several occasions. The Stoke lads listened as the West Ham fan hatched a simple plot. 'Say you were all drawn in, you were fleeing and you've been arrested by mistake.'

At Stoke police station they were separated again and taken for interviews. By this time the game had finished and both sets of supporters had taken to the dark streets. Fighting broke out within minutes when Stoke fans heading into town crossed paths with some Hammers seeking their friends who had been arrested earlier. A vicious streetfight took place immediately outside the doors of the police station. Again the police dragged fighting fans off the road and marched them to the cells. With such an influx of prisoners, one of the police officers got confused and forgot to lock a segregation gate, behind which were several other Stoke fans arrested inside the ground during the second half. These Stoke lads saw this as an ideal opportunity to attack several West Ham lads in the corridor waiting to be fingerprinted. Again mayhem reigned as officers dashed back to separate the bust-up.

Brasso, who had peeped through the eyehole in his cell to catch a glimpse of the fighting, was relieved when the door finally opened and he was taken for questioning. He was sat before a sergeant in uniform holding a pile of eleven statements. With no representation from a solicitor, the interview commenced. The sergeant read through question after question and Brasso answered as had the others. The interview was terminated and a flushed sergeant told the young man, 'Son, the sun's shining out of your arse today.' Those Stoke and West Ham lads arrested all adhered to the unwritten rule of keeping it tight and saying fuck-all. Brasso was back in the Roman Candle and on the piss by ten o'clock, celebrating the end of another visit by the notorious ICF.

chapter seven

The Glasshouse

I HANDED MYSELF in the next afternoon at Alsager police station. The three bobbies that manned this part-time station had being doing their utmost to track me down during my time on the run and I could tell they were pissed off that I had walked in instead of them enjoying some smalltown glory and recognition at the bar of the local pub. Sad bastards.

I was cuffed and driven to Congleton police station, where I thought I would get my head down for a couple of hours before the Army came to get me. Wrong. I was detained by Congleton CID for forty-eight hours, during which they questioned me over just about every burglary that had taken place in Stoke-on-Trent during the period I had been absent without leave. They would not accept that I had been surviving off money collected at Stoke games. It goes to show that coppers are not likely to understand that kind of friendship; I have some great mates who served in the Forces and went on to finish their careers in the police, and not one of them stuck it out for the pension. Tittle-tattle and suspicion rule the roost.

After the CID had finished their quizzing, I was locked up again and told that the Army had been informed of my 'capture' (*I handed myself in, dickhead!*) and that a unit of Regimental Police had been given the go-ahead to collect me. The fella was speaking to me as though he had co-ordinated the whole operation and was due to receive a commendation. I looked down under the interview desk, smirking at the man's cheap brown brogues with plastic soles. And he wanted me to take him seriously!

My cell door opened at 6.30 a.m. the next day and a uniformed bobby stepped inside. I was awake and stood up to face him.

'Right, come on Mister Chester. Sergeant Major Smith has arrived to escort you back to Colchester.'

I froze on the spot; the life drained out of my body at the sound of that name. My initial reaction was to sit back down on the wooden bench, on the basis that Smith would almost certainly beat me. I was in the throes of refusing to move when Trevor Hughes's face appeared in the cell doorway.

'Eh up, Stokie.'

The relief I felt at seeing my mate's face nearly brought me to tears. Trev had travelled up to collect me with a dog handler in a Land Rover. I was formally released into his custody and bade farewell to Congleton nick.

As much as Trev loved me, he had to handcuff me for the journey back down to Colchester, and I was put in the back of the jeep with an alsatian for company. Trev made light of the situation and even asked me what had happened against West Ham the previous day, but all the same I knew I was in deep shit. I spent the first night behind bars awaiting Adjutant's Orders the next morning. The adjutant is a captain in charge of any disciplinary matters within the regiment. The thought of that was bad enough, but marching me there from the guardhouse would be Terry Ellison and Chucker Smith, my regimental and company sergeant majors. It was a long night as I lay staring at the solid metal door. All I could think of was our little hut and the lads brewing up on the stove while Bucko played his acoustic guitar. That got me through.

I did not get the beating I expected that morning off Chucker and ET but the bollocking was of the highest standard. I didn't know where my head was as they screamed abuse into both ears at the same time. The adjutant told me in no uncertain terms that I was a disgrace to the British Army and an embarrassment to the regiment. He asked me where privates Bloore and Elliott were hiding out, and I told him that we had split up weeks before and I was uncertain where they might be. He didn't look surprised at my reply and sentenced me to eighteen days' imprisonment, which meant I would be released from gaol the morning that the regiment departed for exercise Eternal Triangle in Germany. Two weeks in the trenches on top of eighteen days in the slammer. Result.

Life in the prison gaol was different now that I was a convicted prisoner. I had to wear the red tin helmet at all times with fatigues and, because I was classed as a runner, had no laces in my boots. Every morning at 6 a.m. the door to my cell would open and Terry Ellison would come in. I would be stood to attention, my bedding folded into a block and my kit laid out in Bristol fashion on my mattress. Prison regulations stated that when spoken to as a prisoner by an officer, you would state your name, rank and number, followed by the section of the crime that you had committed. This I did every morning, with my feet six inches off the floor and my adam's apple in the palm of Terry Ellison's hand. Throughout, as I coughed and spluttered for breath, I stared over his shoulder at the cell door where Trevor would be grimacing and nodding slowly, as if to tell me, *go on Jasp, keep in there son.* There were another nine soldiers on the run from the regiment, all from different companies but pretty much all as pissed-off with the petty rules that ravaged the blocks. One called Mason, from the same platoon as me, had been captured a week before my arrival and was being released for the military exercise as well. He was of Hispanic descent, came from the Newtown area of Birmingham and had a drink problem. We spent an hour together every night, when we were allowed to write our letters and relax. One evening, Mason said, 'Why don't we put in for a church visit? At least it will get us out of this place for an hour.' I had never been much of a churchgoer but I agreed; any way of getting out of this place was worth a go.

The next morning we went through the usual routine of being throttled and having our beds turned over and kit trashed and, by the book, we were asked if there were any complaints or requests. Inevitably there were no complaints from any of the ten serving prisoners, but two requests were put in to visit the chapel. ET looked deep into my eyes and grunted on hearing my request. He left the cell without answering.

Neither myself or Mason thought we were being clever about asking to visit the chapel, but at 3 a.m., as both our cell doors were flung open, we regretted the whole thing. Both Terry Ellison and Chucker Smith were stood in best kit, with a party of regimental police ready to escort us to the regimental chaplain, who was waiting to take a service for me and Mason. We had two minutes to get out of bed, make it and get into our best number-twos. None of the RPs forced to get out of their beds looked impressed as they double-marched us from the guardhouse across a blustery parade square and over to the camp church. For the next hour, Mason and myself knelt in an empty church, saying prayers and singing hymns with the solitary vicar. There were no more requests for the rest of our stay in the camp gaol. Exercise Eternal Triangle, however, was a belter, a full-on, two-week NATO exercise with the Yanks playing the role of the baddies. The weather was appalling and the lack of food and rest hit hard, but it was the best exercise I ever went on. It was also great to see the lads. I had not seen or heard from my friends on the run for almost six weeks, and nearing the end of the exercise in Germany I began to wonder how they had been getting on in the winter. The regiment arrived back weary but in good spirits; a week of cleaning kit and then long week-end's leave followed for those entitled. People were whistling while they cleaned their equipment, bored no more; it's amazing what a battle in the fields and woods does for morale. My own jovial mood did not last long as I was informed that I was once again on Adjutant's Orders first thing in the morning. My gut feeling told me that some-thing was wrong. I was double-marched by ET into the adjutant's office and slammed my tabs in front of his desk. I stood to attention and waited. The captain sat behind his desk reading a long letter and not once acknowledging my presence. After about five minutes, he put the letter down on his desk and barely looked up.

'Ah Chester. I take it you want to be a pallbearer at young Bloore's funeral?'

The bottom of my world fell out with that one sentence and I began to sway. He went on to tell me that he was going to grant me compas-sionate leave to see Steve, who was on a life support machine at Bucknall hospital. He said I didn't deserve this privilege but because of my appalling record of going AWOL he was going to grant it, as I would probably run away again anyway.

The way that captain broke that news to me was inhumane, and if you're reading this, you wanker, how does 'fuck you' sound?

The news also hit the block hard. Feelings ran high and Chucker bore the brunt of the whispers. Money was collected in for my train fare home, and I was gone. I arrived at Stoke that afternoon and headed by taxi straight to the North Staffs Royal Infirmary. In my haste to get to Steve's bed in time, I had got the hospitals confused and had headed in the wrong direction. I was informed at the North Staffs that Steve had been a patient with them in the initial stages of his illness but had been transferred to Bucknall as his condition deteriorated.

Six weeks ago when I had left those lads in the woods, Steve had been the picture of health, and I could not understand what type of illness had hit him so severely. The staff nurse apologised for not explaining properly. 'Sorry Mark, but your friend has tried to end his life by drinking some form of poison.' I crumpled.

The taxi journey from the City General to my mate lying in Bucknall took over thirty minutes in rush-hour traffic. I don't remember a minute of it. All I can tell you is that I arrived at 4.15pm, and one of the best friends I have ever had died in a coma at 3.50. I was twenty-five minutes too late to say goodbye. Steve was nineteen.

I had nowhere else to turn other than the lads from the match. They were devastated for me – they all knew how much Steve had meant to

me – and decided to cheer me up the only way they knew how, on a trip
to Villa Park two days later.

In the months following the previous season's day out at Villa, the lads had
started to get it together. They were gelling into a unit, with trust and
loyalty being the spine around which they were structured. Prominent faces
had started coming to the fore, but the basis was still the same: we were all
equal, nobody called the shots and we kept it tight. My place in this firm at
that stage was, according to the lads, 'that mad, army-trained bastard' who
would go on the run for the match and was completely manic.

Two coaches left the Glebe early and headed south along the M6. The
lads were all aware of my loss and had all offered their condolences before
leaving. I was told to hang on by Dalton. He was an ex-squaddie himself,
having served in the 3rd Royal Tank Regiment for six years. He knew
exactly where my head was that morning, and pulled me to one side.

'Listen Jasp, you don't need to be with all those loons on the coaches
with your head in bits. Come with me.'

Dalton had commandeered Ant Walton's Ford Escort XR2 along with
Ant, his brother Midge and Philler the Beast. I was chuffed that someone
cared. Up until then I was holding my sadness deep inside and it was
weighing me down. Ender instructed Ant to head into Birmingham city
centre rather than Aston. He felt that a few quiet beers might help me
settle down. We ended up drinking in the Hippodrome and shared our
favourite memories from the past.

I sat back after a couple of pints and analysed the four men I was with.
Dalton was in his mid-twenties and an experienced campaigner with the
Stoke lads. I could tell he was trying to nurture me through a difficult
time. All four of them must have been itching to get to the rest of the lads
but they were taking time out of their day to make somebody else's
richer. It meant a lot.

We joined the rest of the lads at a pub opposite the Villa leisure centre.
It was half past two, and we were late. I walked up to Jem and Eddy with
a resurgence of purpose. They informed us we had missed nothing. The
majority of our lads had tickets for the game and would be standing with
the Stoke crowd behind one goal. Twelve were ticketless and remained in
the pub, supping and watching through the windows as Stoke's mob of
100 was escorted slowly by mounted police and doghandlers towards
their section of the ground.

I was one of those twelve, and with Jem, Eddy and George, the mate
from school who had given me my nickname, I discussed how we were

going to get into the ground. Both Walton brothers, Ant and Midge, and their mate Stevie King, who had turned up for this match with a packed lunch, were in favour of taking our chances in the Holte End. It sounded a good idea to me. I would have pretty much gone anywhere as long as I was going to get a row. It was a unanimous decision and we all scored our pints and moved out onto the streets. It was a cold November day and already turning grey.

As planned, we headed for the Holte End turnstiles. We had decided to get in at the bottom near to the corner flag and take our chances. I can speak only for myself, but the huge mob of black lads being escorted towards us from the park to our left had me shaking. All of a sudden I was questioning my role. I turned to Dalton, who had seen that the best way to avoid being detected by both lads and police was to pay straight into the lower tier of the Witton Stand – the same as last year, only this time nearer the Holte End of the ground.

I pulled Dalton to one side as we queued up to use the urinal inside the Witton Stand. 'Dalton, my arse started to go a bit outside there.'

'Mine too mate,' he replied, 'but there was no point us lot getting battered out there where nobody can see. At least we're in the ground now. If it goes off in here, our lot up there will love it. And at least now all the shirt boys will have something to talk about down the pit on Monday.'

I suppose that made sense. I took my seat next to Jem and Eddy but through the first half I hardly watched the game at all. I could think only of my mate Steve. I kept on torturing myself, thinking it was my fault for handing myself in. *If I hadn't have done that, he would still be alive today. He would never have taken poison if I'd still been with him.*

'Half time Jasp, do you want a brew?'

I snapped back together. 'Yeah, nice one, loads of sugar.'

The second half started with a quality goal by Mark Chamberlain right in front of the Holte End. He silenced them and ran, arms outstretched, towards the twelve celebrating figures who were now climbing onto the pitch to receive their goal-scoring hero. The Holte End went berserk at such cheek and audacity.

'GET THOSE CUNTS OFF OUR FUCKING PITCH.'

I really was on an emotional rollercoaster, one minute shivering and shitting myself, then filled with remorse, and now on Aston Villa's pitch, hugging a hero and screaming, 'Bastard!' at the top of my voice – and crying at the same time. I could have gone any way at any moment. I was fucked.

We spent the remainder of the second half collecting the coins that rained down on us. All twelve of us expected to be either ejected from the ground or at least escorted to the rest of our fans. Neither happened, and we wallowed in the respect and attention which was being directed over from the Stoke fans behind their goal. 'Stokies here, Stokies there, Stokies every fucking where, na na na na na na na na na.' I had loved that chant as a kid. We knew that such attention would come with a price, and Ant and Midge were on it.

'I tell you what, our youth,' said Ant. 'These cunts will be straight in here as soon as those fuckin' gates are opened. Guaranteed.'

Midge smiled and rubbed his hands. 'Let 'em come, Ant. I'm Stoke City and I'm going nowhere.' Midge, as always, stood up and down on his tiptoes, chuckling and muttering to himself under his breath. He was the second youngest of five, and kind-natured. Tall, with dark features, he had a chiselled jaw similar to Desperate Dan's. Six days out of the seven you would find it hard to believe, but spend a Saturday with him at the match and you would definitely fit him into any twelve-seater minibus of quality lads for an important away fixture. This Walton wanted it.

Ant's prediction came true within minutes. 'Eh ar, they're here,' he muttered. Surprisingly, the seething mob we expected was only nine-strong. This little crew were all white and in their thirties and had left their Holte End to come straight inside through the nearest exit. We were at least one block of seats further along, making their approach a drawn-out affair as they climbed over and through the empty seats in an attempt to fan out around us and close in for the kill.

We rose, making no attempt to move forward to meet them. Instead we waited until the Villa line had properly formed in front of us and kept it tight until they were a couple of seats away. In effect, we had let Villa walk straight into us, and with no noise both sides plunged into each other, fists swinging. It must have made great viewing as both Villa and Stoke supporters applauded from either end of the ground.

We had the edge in numbers, and with the greatest respect to the Villa lads, they came unstuck. Stoke were bang up for this little beano and beat them into a retreat right out of their ground, along with five or six stewards who tried to break it up. Villa disappeared into the darkness and the stewards jumped a turnstile back into the ground. We now backed away into the darkness ourselves and stood silently at the top of the green bank opposite the main Holte End exit, which was still waiting to be opened. Nobody needed to ask anything; we all knew that as soon as those doors were opened, we were going straight through them and onto the terraces. The sound of bolts being undone finally had us running silently down the bank, across the tarmacced forecourt and up to the opening doors. With a roar of, 'Come on, we're fucking Stoke,' we charged past the startled

The author with Mark Bentley (right), a former Grenadier Guard and one of our biggest guns. Mark tragically died after being struck by a train in 2001, on the same day that Miffer (below) passed away.

Stoke legend Mark 'Miffer' Smith in the early stages of his fight against cancer. Sadly this was one of the very few fights the big man lost.

Tony the Axe Man received his nickname for undisclosed reasons. He was one of those who put Stoke's firm on the map in the Seventies.

AWOL from the Staffordshire Regiment, 1983: myself, Steve and Brian when we holed up in the woods. The union flag is covering our car.

The author passing out at Shornecliffe with Swansea lads Monkey (left) and Pete Mizen (right).

Luton's firm come out to play outside Kenilworth Road as we turn up to infiltrate their main stand.

Here we go: most of the Luton lads start to back off as we pile in but they generally put up ferocious opposition in several encounters with Stoke.

More action from Luton away in 1984 as lads clash on a ramp. Pitch invasions and toe-to-toe brawls around town were a feature of our clashes with the MIGs.

Smoke bomb kid's tears

☐ SOCCER'S back . . . and a young fan is the first victim of the louts. A smoke bomb goes off on the terraces at Goodison Park and a tearful fan tries to escape. Police moved in as trouble flared after Everton's goal against Stoke.

Picture: JAMES CLARKE

A trip from the Glebe pub to Everton in 1983 and our smoke bomb on the terraces made the headlines.

In the cells in Northampton after our battle with Man City at Rothersthorpe service station in 1984. That's Cossack right at the front and me towards the back with the beard and evil grin.

The author in Pompey's ground at midday, pissed off and with hours to go to kick-off. The Naughty Forty were born on this day in 1985.

The shattered windscreen of our van after Hampshire Police had stopped a fight between us and the 6.57 on that fateful Portsmouth trip.

Stoke City Under-Fives take it to Huddersfield in a typical street encounter

Hunting for the Zulus at St Andrews in 1992: myself (looking worse for wear), Robbie and Ged.

Stoke leave The Fort in Bermondsey and head for Millwall's Tropics pub.

The Tropics has been trashed and torched, curtains billowing through the smashed windows, and the N40 head for the New Den.

Lee Carter, our very own Tasmanian Devil and the gamest of lads. He was stabbed to death in a vigilante attack on a druggie's house.

Some of the Under-Fives before an Anglo-Italian fixture in Padova.

stewards and up onto the terraces, looking for suitable opponents and windmilling in their direction. Hundreds of Villa fans fled back in panic, opening up that huge gap that I had longed to see while following Stoke away as a kid. Now I was stood in the middle of one, doing the same as my contemporaries, and lapping it up.

'Come on. Who wants it, eh? We're Stoke fucking City, come on.'

We couldn't hear any of it, but the Stoke end was going absolutely berserk.

'Go on! Stokie aggro, Stokie aggro.'

Our heroics were shortlived, as the weight of Villa's numbers had us scrambling to get back out onto the street and find some space. All twelve of us made it safely out and decided to stand and have it again. A couple of hundred Villa had chased us out of their end, but most of them had been pissed-off and well-up-for-it shirt boys, with only thirty or so casuals of mixed races. It was this thirty that were prepared to carry on the fight till the end, and now followed us out. They filled the double doorway three-deep and charged out roaring, 'Villa!'

Stoke backed off slightly, giving Villa what they thought was the edge. Then the pin to a smoke canister was pulled and the charging Villa were hit with an explosion that could be heard from inside the ground. Panic engulfed the Villa mob and Stoke chuckled at the sight of the confused Brummies disappearing in a dense green cloud of smoke.

'Now!'

We ran blind into the smoke, throwing wild punches at anyone trapped in there. We made it back inside the gates of the Holte End, coughing and spluttering but hanging on to every moment. To us, it didn't get much better than this. The view from the other end again was one of pandemonium as Villa fans fled the mayhem, and the claret and blue was now awash with green. As the fumes lifted up into the night sky and disappeared, the cheering Stoke fans saw their mates now being run back down the steps by a mass of seething bodies. Many admitted later that as much as they enjoyed the show, they did not envy our predicament and were glad that they were where they were. They were right. It was on top, of the highest order. We felt we were literally running for our lives, as the mob now chasing us was 100-strong and fuming.

In our minds as we tore alongside the Witton Stand was the idea of getting to the Stoke turnstiles, from which our lot would now surely be piling out. They would know that we needed help and it gave us hope. As fit as I was at the time, my lungs were bursting and ready to explode, and a side glance told me that some of my mates were struggling. We weren't going to make it. I slowed and looked over my shoulder. Villa were a good twenty yards behind us still. We had enough space to make a quick stand of it and hopefully grab a breather. I stopped running and grabbed Philler.

'Stand Jimmy, let's try and get into some space.'

We both stopped and turned. 'Come on then, let's have it.'

The others stopped too and Stoke held firm and waited for Villa's front line to arrive. In less than ten seconds, both sides were punching and kicking, with Stoke immediately being put on the back foot again.

As the chase continued on, Villa's numbers started to dwindle, and another quick glance told me they were back down to about thirty again. I decided to try to stand again, right by the Witton Arms pub at the end of the street from which our lads were shortly due to appear. We had nearly made it. We turned together again and made another stand of it, this time holding the line for a little longer. This encounter was toe-to-toe, and we picked up several injuries. They broke us again and we turned and fled on past the Witton Arms.

'Oi lads, stop, for fuck's sake. I can't go on.'

Philler was in a bad way, vomiting as he bent over a car bonnet. He had been dropped to the floor with a flying kung fu kick and then volleyed on the way back up. It had completely knocked the wind out of him and the look in his eyes told me he wasn't going on. We had to make a final stand and hope for the reinforcements to arrive, though it was starting to bother me that they had not appeared. Villa's lads were yards away and loving the sight before them. They knew they had got us and slowed down to gloat over their superior numbers and our dire situation. I looked around and noticed that on the street opposite was a canopied fruit and veg stall, with a light bulb illuminating all the potential missiles.

'Here, get these.'

We seized the opportunity and tooled up with an array of offensive melons, pumpkins and cabbages. Villa, sensing the balance might be shifting, made a full-on assault in the hope of reaching us before the barrage began. Too late; we weren't hanging around and let loose, dropping several of their front line. My melon was aimed at the youth who had previously drop-kicked the Beast; this time he was making a beeline for me and screamed as he closed in. I flung that melon with all the venom of a man possessed, straight at his contorted face. He was quick, I'll give him that, and reflexively ducked the missile. As it lost height but gained momentum, it crashed into his mate's bollocks, sending the lad a full 360 degrees to the floor. Those Villa lads must have had a laugh about that one over the years.

We had managed to slow down Villa briefly but could not stop them coming, and now took to more hand-to-hand fighting. This lasted no more than a minute, until the sound of screeching brakes and sliding doors told us that the party was over. I was nicked for the first time in my life, for fighting at a football match with people who wanted to fight with me.

Nine of the fighting Stokies were arrested at the scene and manhandled into the back of two black marias. Each one was handcuffed to the seats and told to shut the fuck up or they would be battered. I could see Villa's boys outside, through the tinted windows. Some were arguing with the police but none was arrested. The police were only interested in nicking us.

The reason our cavalry had not arrived became clear as the back doors of my van were forced open by a raging mob. It was the lads. The police had attempted to keep all Stoke supporters inside the ground to prevent an escalation of the trouble, but the lads charged at a bolted door several times in numbers until they managed to force it off its hinges. They ran out into the darkness and rampaged in all directions. It was too late for us though, as we sat in the back of the open van laughing at the sight of them being beaten back by a flurry of police batons. Our day was over; we were heading for the cells and a charge of Section Five. I wasn't bothered. It had been an emotional rollercoaster and a day I will never forget. I have since met the Villa lads present that day and we laugh about it often. Respect to Harold, Fordy and Terry the Doctor for times shared and for looking after some of ours while sharing the same prison landing.

I was released from the cells in Birmingham that night and travelled back to Stoke. I had not been told how long my compassionate leave was to last and I hadn't bothered to ask. I had no intentions of ringing them now or even informing them of my latest misdemeanour. As far as I was concerned, I was sent home to see Steve before he passed on, had missed the opportunity to see him and so convinced myself that, now he was no longer with us, my leave would be extended until after the funeral, surely.

I bedded down for the next week on Jem's settee, spending long periods with his youngest brother Stan, who was about to leave school and join the Grenadier Guards. I encouraged him to do it, and enjoy it, but prepared him for a few of the pitfalls, without going into too much detail about my own initiation. I also spent much of that week in the Alsager Arms watching the world through the bottom of a pint pot. My outlook, and certainly my attitude, was beginning to change. A butterfly sheds its cocoon and brightly flies off to find its mate. I did the opposite: I shed the happy-go-lucky skin of a kid who wanted only to be involved in lighthearted mischief and banter with his mates, and became very disillusioned.

In my eyes, authority was now the enemy and anyone in a position to use it over me became the potential target of a rage beginning to build inside me. A rage that has afflicted me to this day.

The next fixture was, to the lads, a run-of-the-mill game that held little prospect of a major row, even though it was a Midlands derby at home to Nottingham Forest. Plans were to meet for a casual drink and see what the day brought. Little did I know that the consequences of this day would change my life.

I travelled up to Stoke by train early and alone. It had just turned eleven and I walked the streets looking for signs of life. I missed the arrival of forty Forest lads, a mixture of young and old, who headed into the Sea Lion pub and settled down unchallenged. The Sea Lion would have been classed as one of our pubs in those days, so they had taken the initiative and got in early. It has always been unclear what happened there that morning, as none of the lads was present to witness it, but shortly after their arrival, a fight broke out between them and some local drinkers. One man was thrown through a window into the street. Forest's mob quickly dispersed, leaving small clusters of them roaming unfamiliar streets.

Blissfully unaware of impending danger, I caught sight of some familiar faces several hundred yards from me on London Road, which heads out of the town centre and along to Trent Vegas. I headed across the road and walked along up to the five skulking figures. Their behaviour seemed odd as they darted in and out of terraced doorways. *These are well onto something here,* I thought, and picked up the pace. I darted into one of the doorways and looked into the toothless grin of Miff. He was with Gwilty and two other prominent faces of the time. I also caught sight of their unsuspecting prey. Miff's eyes lit up.

'These have just kicked it off in the Sea Lion. A local youth has been thrown through a window. They've come for it, Jasp.'

We were like five bloodthirsty lions watching a family of gazelles cautiously making their way to water. The prey were four of Forest's lads, all in their late teens, who had been part of their earlier mob but had obviously been split up from the rest and were looking for some form of refuge. Little did they know that the further they headed uphill towards Penkhull Bank, and away from Stoke, the closer they were coming to an uncertain fate. The steep terraced street was empty, on a fresh November morning, and the four Forest lads were walking up it oblivious.

We quickly decided that if they crossed the next intersection and carried along up the hill, we would hit them, quick, hard and decisively in the narrow road. They were obviously disorientated and stopped to turn back. *Shit, we've lost the chance, they'll see us now and have the advantage of the hill.* We darted behind parked cars and watched through the rear windows as they changed their minds and switched direction again.

We seized the moment and charged from our hiding places. The four startled Forest lads had no chance to run as we were already on top, grabbing them and sending kicks and punches into the flailing recipients. They fought back doggedly, as every man has to when faced with such a situation, and even gained a little ground. We had not been that clever with our planned attack, as none of us had noticed that a terraced house yards in front of the Nottingham lads was being gutted. They managed to grab weapons from a skip and turned to greet us with a new wind. They hit us with lumps of timber and broken masonry. We stood and staved them off using the extra man to our advantage.

As the fight degenerated, a craft knife appeared from the jacket of one of the Forest lads. He slashed at Gwilty and sliced off his ear. That, along with a street full of curious residents, triggered a sharp exit from both parties. First blood to Forest.

They had certainly come to Stoke for a row that day and over the next few hours fought several small, hard battles with similar numbers of Stoke. The police did not have their fingers on the button all afternoon; had the numbers been bigger, there would have been anarchy. Night arrived at four-thirty and as the crowds left the ground it was turning into a shitty evening, pitch black and raining hard. Forest left the ground with their original number of forty again and found no resistance in the rain-drenched streets as they walked to the railway station. As they approached the station, they looked confused. Some began to argue as they stepped on each other's heels. Heading out of the railway tunnel and preparing to turn left, they were met by two police officers, who for some reason presumed they were Stoke and ushered them away from the station and along Leek Road.

Forest did as they were told and walked on. Not one of them was aware of the nine dark figures that had stalked them closely from leaving the ground, even when they passed within touching distance of us hidden in the bushes along the walled boundary of the graveyard. Now Stoke silently closed in and fell alongside their rear ranks. We walked with them for thirty yards or so until they had cleared the main road and junction and had drawn level with the Post Office car park. The weather was atrocious and a biting wind made it difficult to hear. We were in among them and could see their hesitation at carrying on into the darkness.

Nine clenched fists hit their unsuspecting targets from the dark void that surrounded them. They panicked, not knowing who or what numbers were facing them, and we had them scattering into the main road and over the wall into the car park to their left. It was at that point they realised the numbers that were routing them, and charged back, enveloping us in a buffalo-horn pincer movement and making escape near-impossible.

The hysterical screams of a man with his throat cut open pierced the night. The fighting petered out as everybody watched the young man stagger around with blood flowing from a gaping wound to the side of his neck and face. Immediately the surrounding Forest fans grabbed two approaching policemen and pointed in my direction.

'It was him.'

I was advised immediately by a couple of ours to 'fucking leg it', but why should I run off and get nicked further along the road for a crime I didn't commit? I was still looking at the lad I had punched yet he was pointing with the rest of them. I chose not to run away but to stay and face the consequences. I was man enough to place myself there, so here we go. I was arrested, and fifty minutes later I was behind a desk being interviewed by two CID officers on a possible charge of attempted murder.

The injured Forest fan had been one of the four that had been fighting in the streets of Penkhull earlier in the day. He was thereabouts when Gwilty had his ear cut off and after being stitched ended up in the North Staffs, lying in the next bed to one of their victims. Rumour has it, though unsubstantiated, that a Stanley knife was dropped by one of those Forest lads in that first bloody encounter and that it was the same blade used on them. Ironic, because none of us had felt that we had to tool up for this fixture.

While I was being interviewed in Stoke nick, the Army was informed. A team of the Army's Special Investigation Branch was assigned to the case and smashed open my locker at camp to search my belongings. I was bailed into their custody two hours later, and taken back down to Colchester under a heavy cloud. The regiment was outraged and I was once again placed under lock and key to await their decision. Trevor didn't hold much hope for me this time and bluntly told me to expect the worst. After two days of being locked in solitary confinement, I was climbing the walls of my cell. I had counted every brick 1,000 times and started to fear the worst. *What if he dies?*

My fears turned to a mixture of relief and sadness when I was both told of my imminent release and informed that another serving soldier had admitted to the offence and had been escorted to Stoke to face charges over the slashing. He was a close friend at the time, and I think he came forward out of loyalty to me rather than out of remorse for his victim. Although exonerated, I was still scum, and the scourge of the 1st Staffordshire Regiment. I was living on borrowed time.

My life around the camp was now spent mainly on RPs – restriction of privileges. Every spare minute I would be cleaning, peeling spuds or washing dishes, under the watchful eye of Trevor Hughes. Home became a distant memory. How I missed the match, and everything that went with it. I was a problem soldier with nobody to talk to about it. As far as the Army was concerned, I could rot.

New Year came and I was released back into the regiment, being placed into B Company and away from old mates like Mickey Southall and Colligan. I was now serving in Seven Platoon, which was full of lads from the Black Country, Tipton, Dudley and similar areas. If that was the Establishment's attempt to isolate me or get my back up, it failed. I met some of the maddest lads I have ever come across and was in stitches from the moment I was shown to my new billet. Gone were the coarse army issue blankets and the sad blue heavy curtains; I stood speechless at the sixteen bed spaces all decked out in fine, Laura Ashley flowered bedspreads and matching curtains. I had never seen a bunk like it, and I walked in to be greeted by Tolley from Walsall, who strolled over in a very casual manner. He was in full uniform but wore his beret in a peculiar fashion, almost like a floppy pancake, with the cap badge not an inch above his left eye, as required, but pulled over the lobe of his left ear. Tolley formally introduced himself with a little skip as he slid his left foot to attention and raised a three fingered salute, followed by a huge rasping noise from the corner of his lips, and shouted, 'Troops,' in a camp, high-pitched voice.

I had just met the founder member of the NFI crew and this was their domain. NFI stood for 'no fucking interest', and all inhabitants of this room refused outside of working hours to wear anything, sleep in anything or talk about anything military. They were all totally fucked-off with the shit that was going on in the regiment and had decided to make a stand. I bought my new bedspread and matching lampshade the following Saturday.

I soon became a prominent face amongst the NFI crew, and we made light of any situation the Army could throw at us. Some NCOs and a couple of officers actually liked what the crew did for morale; among the blocks, they were like in-house entertainment for some. Such officers were all aware that these disgruntled men were good and proficient soldiers once switched on. They hoped that the forthcoming tour of South Armagh would have the lads back to their best.

The maddest thing about being moved over to B Company was that I was no longer going to be stationed at Bessbrook Mill with the rest of C Company. B Company had got Crossmaglen, and the dreaded 'subs' that had frightened the life out of me whilst studying the history of Ulster at Shornecliffe were shortly to become a reality. The 1st Staffordshire Regiment left for its tour of duty on St Valentine's Day 1984. We flew out from RAF Stanford in Norfolk and transferred at Aldergrove from a troop plane to Chinook helicopters. From there we were dispatched to our stations. I will never forget the noise and smell of the Chinooks, the laughter from both co-pilot and pilot as we came under fire from a light machine gun on our approach, and the look on those Grenadier Guards' faces as they knelt with kit alongside the helipad, waiting to fill our seats and head home to Blighty. I remember looking at them and immediately thinking the same: *I can't wait to go home.*

Serving in Armagh, and especially down south in Bandit Country, was the highlight of my time in the Army, and I'm very proud to say that there were no more shenanigans. Everybody, the NFI crew included, fell immediately into the role of combat soldier. It was tense, frightening at times, but overall it gave me something that up until now had only been promised: action. That was something I had been getting regularly with the lads off the Glebe coaches but not with the Army. For the first time I can remember, I felt secure, doing the job I wanted to do.

A tour of Crossmaglen for the three platoons that made up B company consisted of a week on sanger (lookout posts in the corners of the camp) duty, watching and logging all goings-on around the clock, until being relieved and going on street patrols, which were more dangerous, as you never knew whether a pram or phone box was booby-trapped or a passing vehicle might open fire. After a week of that, you went on country patrols, where you would be taken out by chopper and dropped off in the arse-end of nowhere, to march back for twelve or fifteen miles, logging CB radio aerials or anything that might be of interest to Intelligence regarding the surrounding farm buildings and barns, which were often used for storage and training by the Provisionals. Because of the intensity, tours of South Armagh lasted only for four months. During our time there it was lively, with several attempted mortar and pipe-bomb attacks on our base, several shootings, and one fatality, which hit us hard.

Living conditions were the hardest part of XMG (Army shorthand for

Crossmaglen). We were piled in like sardines. Twenty-six men would share bunks four-high, in narrow, submarine-like passages that all opened to an octagonal room that was the hub of the platoon's activity. I don't think any of us saw complete darkness, or slept in the quiet, for the whole tour. Living in these conditions and under that much strain, it was only going to be a matter of time before somebody exploded.

It came in the canteen at the end of a three-day OP, in which I had spent the whole time with three others sat in a hedge watching a farm along the Dundalk Road, which ran along the border. Intelligence had received information that this farm was being used as an illegal crossing point for gunrunners. We arrived back cold, wet and hungry, but I had other things on my mind. England had played France in a football friendly international at the Parc des Princes in Paris and I knew Stoke had sent a few of the lads over: Mono, Woody, and several others. I was dying to catch the news on TV to see how England had got on and if I could spot any Stoke flags inside the ground. I ordered my brew and waited for the late news to come on. *Come on England.*

The canteen had filled up with a dozen or so people, who huddled round the small portable TV fixed on a shelf up in a corner of the room. As the news headlines were aired, the England result came second to the outrageous reports of rioting English supporters leaving a trail of destruction across our neighbour's capital city. Most of the lads present had a chuckle, as hatred of the French ran deep through our regiment. The newscaster went on to report concerns that the following Saturday's Five Nations rugby fixture between France and England could be placed under jeopardy as a consequence. With that news, the atmosphere in the canteen changed, and Corporal Vernon, a huge rugby fanatic from Hanley, voiced his opinion.

'They should be locked up, the fucking lot of them.'

I took no notice, as film footage of the fighting inside the stadium was being aired. I automatically moved towards the TV, as if preparing to get involved myself.

'Fucking go on lads!'

I could hardly contain my delight: right there on the screen were Mono and Woody, fighting like fuck with a heavier mob of French youths. They were being beaten backwards down an aisle but were still windmilling away. That was enough for me, even though the incident had taken place hours before and the pair of them were probably robbing the ferry's Duty Free shop by now. My head flipped.

'Oi, dickhead.' Vernon was up out of his seat and over, shoving his pitted face into mine. My face went back into his immediately and we locked on like two stags, frothing abuse through clenched teeth. Vernon saw this as insubordination of the highest degree; *how dare I front him up.* He piled one of his big heavy fists into my nose, breaking it once more and covering us both in splatters of blood.

I'm not sure where my head went. I no longer saw Vern as a senior rank, and couldn't place myself with him in that shitty canteen. I was elsewhere; maybe on the steps of the Parc des Princes with the lads, I'm not sure, but Vernon to me was one of them, whoever 'them' might have been. I flew straight back in with a butt, attempting to bite his nose as well. We had a brief stand-up, a bloody affair until the others broke it up. We both came to our senses and shook hands.

'Let's put it down to the stress.'

I took the man's outstretched hand and shook it. 'Okay Vern.'

The next morning Vernon and I shook hands again, both apologised and laughed at the thick lips and swollen nose. It was behind us – or so we thought.

'Chester, Vernon, the RSM wants to see both of you. You're being flown over to Bessbrook this afternoon.'

Neither of us said a word; I couldn't have found a word to express how I felt at that moment anyway. Getting a story together to cover our tracks would have been a help, but the Army were onto that, and Vern and I travelled independently to Bessbrook Mill, meeting back up in the corridor of the RSM's office. We had two armed Military Police officers supervising our every move. Vern looked gaunt and nervous. Me, I had been here before.

Terry Ellison had always looked a hard bastard, but today as he sat staring at the pair of us being double-marched before him, he looked fearsome. We silently awaited his inquisition. I felt a trickle of cold sweat rolling down the back of my spine. Then he spoke, very softly.

'Corporal Vernon, can you explain to me how you received those injuries to your face?'

Vern began to stutter and I felt sick. 'Well sir, I gained my injuries while on the op with Chester, sir, I fell through a bramble bush, sir.'

Ellison nodded quietly, and looked into my face.

'Private Chester, how did you receive your injuries?'

'Well sir, I was walking through …'

Ellison cut me dead halfway through my sentence. He turned to Vern again.

'*Lance* Corporal Vernon, again I'd like you to explain how you got your injuries.'

He had demoted Vern right there in front of me, taking his much-earned second tape. I was shocked, and riddled with guilt. To his credit, Vern took that massive disappointment and carried on with his original story. But he was married with a kid and I couldn't let him do it. Losing a stripe like that would affect his pay, his overseas allowance, everything. I piped up before he landed himself in deeper shit.

'It was me, sir.'

That was all Terry Ellison had been waiting for. With a wry smile, he sat back in his chair and dismissed Lance Corporal Vernon from the room. I won't harp on about the bollocking and what happened next; it was the usual Ellison-style degradation. But in a mouthful of abuse, my army career was over. I was choppered out of Northern Ireland two days later, with less than a fortnight of the tour to complete, and was back in the guard room at Roman Way Barracks.

It took me less than a week to hand in all my uniforms and equipment, and sign all the necessary paper work. The Army had given me an SNLR – services no longer required. The red leather binder handed to me on my release contained all my assessments, grades and exam results awarded since joining Junior Leaders at the age of fifteen. Every soldier departing the service receives one of these binders. They are to be used to further yourself in your life and to present to any future employer.

Stamped on each of the fourteen pages, in big red letters, were the words: 'DISCHARGED THROUGH MISCONDUCT.'

I had been released from the British Army a couple of months before my twentieth birthday, straight from an active stint in Ulster. I had £1,800 to my name, with little prospect of finding a skilled job. They had taken me as a boy and wrapped me up inside their establishment, providing work, food and accommodation; they even set up your bank account for you, into which they paid your wages. Everything was taken care of. All I knew about banking and money was that every so many weeks I would have time off and loads of beer money to piss up the wall. They were very clever at teaching us how to ghost-walk through a parched forest, or cut someone's nervous system at the neck, but that was all it ever was. Hardly any of the lads I had served with even knew how to write out a cheque properly.

I came out into Civvy Street after four years and had no problem walking into any bar, anywhere, and seeing what happened. In that respect I was fearless. But put me in a boutique where I was wanting to buy a pair of jeans, and have a sales assistant approach me and ask if I would like to try anything on, and I'd start sweating and head for the door, regardless of how much money I had in my pocket. Civilian life was alien to me as an adult, and now I was thrown on the bones of my arse straight into the middle of it.

On the advice of the Army, I pleaded guilty to my brushes with the law at football, to make it easier for them. They didn't want to be sending me, or the representing officer, away from the regiment for any other unnecessary court appearances. *Chester, you're guilty and that's that.* For the incident at Villa I was fined £60 plus £20 costs. Although another man was convicted for the Forest incident, I was still charged with assault on persons unknown, on my admission that I had punched one of their lads outside the post office. For this I received a £140 fine plus costs.

With hindsight, I was really a kid when I entered the Army. Perhaps if I had joined at eighteen after giving civvy life a try, I might have settled in more. Unfortunately an apprenticeship at Rolls-Royce or Radway Green, where most of my schoolmates ended up, was out of the question due to my desperation to flee that house and the hand that ruled it. I had followed my fate and this was where it had brought me. I left the Armed Forces a fitter, wiser man, totally prepared to take on the challenges of the culture I had studied so hard as a child during those years in that box room. Right or wrong, I was physically and mentally ready to be a committed football hooligan.

section two

The Naughty Forty

chapter eight

The Flying Squad

THE DRINKING BINGE I embarked on when I reached Civvy
Street lasted for six weeks, and I loved every minute of it. Eventually
my money began to dwindle and I fell, as most unskilled workers do
in Stoke, into the slip house of a local bone china factory. It was the lowest
and dirtiest job in the factory, and paid the least wages, but I didn't care.
I saw the manual labour as a good daily workout and the wages easily
covered my football costs, which were now guaranteed every Saturday,
home or away.

Now in full-time employment, I needed a place to stay on a more
permanent basis. I had been sleeping on couches and living out of a bag.
Wilson helped out, finding me several places to stay over the years, from
living behind his settee in the terraced streets of Burslem to sharing his
mansion on a hill. Little did I know that I was about to spend the next
fifteen years of my life still living out of a bag.

Fighting became the main ingredient in my life. Stoke's lads were
active at the football, and pub and club life in Hanley always held the
chance of a flavoursome night out. Hanley is classed as the centre of
Stoke-on-Trent, a city formed from the amalgamation of the 'six towns':
Burslem, Fenton, Hanley, Longton, Stoke-upon-Trent and Tunstall.
Putting myself in that environment continuously, it was not long before I
was in trouble with the law again. I was arrested three months after leaving the Army for fighting with the police outside a nightclub. Eddie had
already been nicked for his part in a gang fight inside the place, and it
carried on in the streets. Several Alsager lads made a daring attempt to
release Eddy from the back of a parked police van but police reinforcements arrived, catching us in their headlights and roaring their engines to
a very impressive screech. They scattered seven of us into the waiting arms
of their colleagues, and that was that. Wilful obstruction: fined £80.

Coming clean with the slip house chargehand to get a morning off work for court got me nowhere. The snidy bastard had it in for me from that day on but I wasn't going to take sly comments or laughter off this little ten-men-went-to-mow who had worked on a pot bank all his life, so I opened a slip gate while he was inspecting some shower trays, drenching him in freezing clay from head to toe. Hysterical, I walked off the factory, not bothering to get my cards or even look back. I didn't give a fuck; Stoke were away at Luton on Saturday. *Luton away!*

Ask any of the Stoke lads who served on the Glebe coaches during the early to mid Eighties which was their favourite away fixture and some will say Swansea, others Man U or Birmingham, but most will say Luton Town. Over the three times we went there over two seasons, Luton provided the platform from which we left behind that odd-coachload-of-nutters-from-all-over-the-City reputation. Luton's young but already established MIG (Men in Gear) firm gave us some of the best fighting we had encountered so far and speeded our maturation into a tightly knit firm of veterans.

Most other teams with hooligan followings had adopted names: Birmingham City had the Zulu Warriors, Leeds had the Service Crew and even Luton had the MIGs, but Stoke's mob were still named after a town-centre pub. So on the way to our end-of-season clash at Kenilworth Road in 1984, a discussion took place at the back of one of two packed coaches between several Alsager lads, some of the PBA and the Whitehill lads, all from the north of the city. We needed a name.

The discussion kept us entertained for most of the journey down, with some quality attempts at portraying us as a bunch of ruthless cutthroats. But nothing thought of seemed to sum up who we were or what we were about. That would not happen until two years later. It was, however, decided unanimously that from that day on, us lads from the north of Stoke at least would be known as the Stoke City Flying Squad, and Luton were to be our first scalp.

Two coaches, as always, had left the Glebe nice and early for Bedfordshire. It was a muggy day for the time of year, but spirits were high and the lads were focused. By opening time we were in the Northamptonshire countryside, enjoying traditional cask ale on special offer in an old coaching house. Most of the locals warmed to these 'city folk' visitors and shared in the laughter as Mad Martin Hallam necked a yard of cider and black before collapsing under a table. I don't know what it is about the countryside, but Stoke lads always seem to get excited by it, almost uncontrollably. Coming from the country myself, I don't share their thrill but it's mad to watch.

The landlord's welcoming nature deserted him at the sight of his prized stuffed fox leaving its plaque above the grand fireplace and being replaced by a brolly. His cigarette machine disappearing out of the back door left him with no choice and he called the police. To head off a potentially early end to our day, Wilson acted fast and reclaimed any missing items off the lads, including an assortment of ornaments, ashtrays and place mats. I scratched my head at it all. Petty theft was something that had to be worked on; in my eyes it lowered the tone of the firm. 'Come on, let's fuck off to Luton,' I said, but such a good time was had by all in the countryside that both coaches arrived at the ground twenty minutes after kick-off.

The forecourt was deserted as we ambled off the coaches and stared at the locked turnstiles. We had been shut out. The game sounded like it was end-to-end, and the sound of chanting Stoke fans soon stirred us into action.

'This is fucking brilliant, no old bill to stop us. Lets get up their end and kick the gates in.'

Miff was striding towards a narrow alley that ran along the side of their ground and brought us out at the back of Luton's end. Every man followed suit, falling into little huddles of glee at the lack of police presence and the contemplation of some naughty action. Even in the street outside their end, there was no sign of any authority, just a couple of Asian kids playing in the road on their bikes. The children stopped and watched curiously as we congregated in front of the main double doors to the stand. We numbered a little over 100, with ages ranging from fifteen to twenty-six, all dressed in casual fashion and all dead set on gaining entry to Luton's end – and taking it.

Fryer was the first to notice how the old gate hinges were rusted, so the door looked like it could be booted through if enough charged it together. Thirty of the lads stood back and, with an almighty effort, ran into the doors, all drop-kicking it together and sending a cloud of dust over their prized tracksuit tops. The Asian kids had swelled in numbers and a dozen of them stood in a garden, clapping and cheering, as Stoke's firm prepared to charge at the doors once more. Then with a huge bang followed by a loud crack of timber, the doors fell inside, sending up another cloud of dust.

Stoke charged straight through it, screaming, 'COME ON.'

On the other side of the dust cloud were two sets of metal steps leading up to the top of Luton's terrace. We were literally yards from a potentially explosive situation and, with such a huge element of surprise, had a good chance of running them onto their own pitch. The stairs were wide enough to take four men abreast and as the leaders charged up they could see the top of the away end and the Stoke following. It spurred them on, and they screamed louder.

The noise they made was too much of a giveaway; had they rushed in silently, they would have achieved their aim. Storming an end of this magnitude was a new experience for most of the Stoke lads present and much of the noise they made as they charged into Luton's end was a collective reassurance. They were basically letting everybody know that that they were still there and committed. Sneaking about in threes and fours and infiltrating ends was, for us, still two or three seasons away.

The storming of this end came to an abrupt halt as police with vicious alsatians filled the gantry at the top of each set of stairs. Each man on the front lines faced odds of four-to-one of being savaged by a dog if he carried on. They obviously weren't gambling men; seeing enough, they all turned and fled down the steps and back into the streets. We turned left and headed towards the main stand with renewed momentum. Cries of 'Smash the next door in' were heard. Several officers hastily followed and radioed to colleagues for assistance but we were determined to gain entry by any means.

'Over here, come on.'

A fire escape was scaled by a dozen lads who kicked through a flimsy door and ran screaming into the top tier of the main stand, hoping that this might be the right section for Luton's casuals. The wind left their sails as they realised they had entered a family and disabled section. The twelve men made apologetic gestures to the shocked Luton fans, then turned and humbly left the scene. Outside, the police had started to arrive in numbers and were shepherding our mob towards the away end turnstiles. Fifteen of the lads had other ideas, and managed to slip away.

The Stoke mob entered the open away terraces minutes before the interval, fanning out across the away end to speak to friends from work or old schoolmates who had travelled on the supporters' coaches. Conversation was fast and frantic, as the antics from outside were relayed to curious, nodding Stokies.

'Ah man, you'd have loved it. We smashed their gates in and nearly made it right onto those terraces. It would have gone mental, if it wasn't for the dogs …'

These tales would be passed from workbench to workbench in dozens of factories throughout the city, building the reputation of this new Stoke mob.

'Has anybody seen Miff?'

Slammy was one of the Trentham lads, a bull-neck bastard even bigger than Miff. He stood solid on the terrace, eating a pie, the crumbs and dripping gravy smearing his red and black Fila tracksuit top. Between mouthfuls, he inquired into reports that Miff had been nicked for punching one of the coppers that had followed them out of Luton's end. Nobody knew where the big man was, and he was presumed missing in action. Slammy complained that his pie was 'shit' and headed off into the crowd, seeking more information on his mate.

A large mob of MIGs congregated in the bottom tier of Luton's main stand in the second half. It grew to over 200 and looked an impressive mixture of ages and races. The atmosphere grew increasingly tense as both mobs taunted each other. Stoke began to climb over the fences in an attempt to draw Luton onto the pitch and then laughed and gesticulated at the MIGs' half-hearted response.

With fifteen minutes of the game remaining, the fifteen Stoke who had slipped police notice outside reappeared. They had gone to a boozer for a drink and on their return caught a steward leaving the ground through an exit. They pounced immediately, darting in past the bemused man, who made little attempt to stop them. Unknowingly, they had walked right into the middle of Luton's mob.

The sight of Speg and some of the Stafford and Stone lads strolling through that bottom tier, completely unaware that they were heading for a certain kicking, had us in shock. Everybody had forgotten that this little mob were still about and active. Luton wasted no time, turning in bulk and charging into the shocked Stokies. Luton were ruthless and those fifteen lads who were ambling along a stretch of seats in an effort to get close to their mates in the Stoke end got absolutely battered.

Not giving up – in truth, having no choice – the lads made a fight of it, and people started spilling out of the stand and onto the pitch to escape the battle. It was nothing short of torture for the Stoke fans watching; it seemed to go on for ages, and the worse thing was that you could see a punch coming that was going to deck one your friends before he'd had time to recover from the previous one.

It was too much. Casuals and shirt boys alike clambered over the fences and dropped down onto the pitch. Luton responded immediately by jumping out of their end and, for the next ten minutes, a full-scale riot took place. It was complete mayhem as everybody fought everybody else. There must have been almost a dozen small skirmishes taking place simultaneously all over the pitch and without a prominent police presence.

The carnage continued outside. I don't think order was restored for well over an hour as hundreds of people fought running battles in Luton town centre, until eventually running out of steam. As the police finally got the Stoke fans back to their waiting coaches, we found Terry sat with a wry smile on his face.

'Seen who's on the back seat?'

There with a can of lager and a huge grin was Miffer. He had knocked out a copper in the first incident and ended up being chased through the narrow back streets. He thought he was sure to get locked up for this one, until two of the little Asian kids popped up out of a terraced garden and beckoned the gasping man into their house. Their parents ushered Miff up three flights of stairs and hid him in their loft for over an hour, even giving him a cup of tea and some dunkers.

After such an eventful end to the season, the lads spent the entire summer longing for the fixtures to arrive. Who would be the first to receive a visit from the Flying Squad in the 1984/85 season? It was inevitable really: Luton Town away. We were delighted, especially now we knew where the MIGs would be inside the ground. All the talk of was of how we were going to get into that lower tier of seats and avenge the brutal attack inflicted on our lads. Wilson had an idea on this one, and made arrangements to secure a big enough pub to house the three coachloads of Stoke casuals, just on the outskirts of Luton. They arrived at ten-thirty, and were ushered by a hand-rubbing landlord into his large snooker room at the back of his listed building.

Off the street and out of sight, the Stoke mob settled down to some heavy drinking. Wilson did his rounds as always with notebook and pen, collecting enough money for 100 seat tickets. He left by taxi and headed to the ground. Stoke were in Luton unnoticed, and about to purchase as many tickets as possible for the stand above the seats where Luton's boys would sit. Cocksure Wilson fronted up a deal with the ticket office manager and purchased 100 seats for his party of young lads' and dads' football teams who were 'due to play in a local tournament' the next day. Such was the effectiveness of the blag that he received twenty of the tickets as complimentary, something that must have slipped his mind in the excitement, as the good fortune certainly wasn't shared with the lads. Like the song says: 'Wilson is a conman/He wears a conman's hat/Oh he makes his money on his coaches/And he is a proper twat. Oi!' The lads had been supping for a couple of hours and wanted to get into the town centre, so the tickets were quickly handed out, instructions with directions were issued, and whatever happened on the streets, Stoke were guaranteed to have a good number of lads in their stand by kick-off. *Right, let's hit the town.*

Within minutes of the mob filtering out along the main drag of town, several coaches passed by full of drunken loons from Bentilee. Such was their disappointment at missing the fun the season before that Sammy Boone had brought along a large contingent of some of the worst beer monsters you could ever have the misfortune to bump into. They looked appalling as they rolled by, opening the cracks of their arses and rubbing them onto the coach windows. Animals, but loveable all the same.

We saw them get stuck in traffic about half a mile ahead, and as expected the lot of them piled from the coach exits and onto the streets. Stoke's casuals picked up their pace; the mob in front, as game as they were, were not the firm that we wanted to represent Stoke on the advance into Luton's manor. The Bentilee lads disappeared around a corner, leaving us with only audio contact.

A horrible roar went up, followed by the sound of things breaking. They had reached Luton's main shopping area and begun to rampage, and it sounded bad. We jogged to catch up. Shock brought us to a halt as we scanned the devastation. The beer monsters had gone through the main street like a herd of buffalo, overturning cars and smashing windows. A sack of spuds had been hurled through one window. Even the Mayor of Luton, who was due to make a presentation at the game, had been targeted, along with his wife; their Bentley lay overturned onto its roof, while a chorus of 'Who's the slag in black and green?' was sung to the hysterical local dignitary. This mindless act later saw a letter of apology sent from a very embarrassed Mayor of Stoke-on-Trent, who branded the perpetrators a minority of people from an under-privileged area that needed addressing!

The loonies disappeared into Luton's terraced back streets and left us casuals facing an angry mob of locals and MIGs, who came streaming from several pubs further along the main street. A vicious battle took place and once again disorder reigned for twenty minutes as young men knocked lumps out of each other with little concern for their own personal safety, in a classic Eighties-style football riot.

Most of Stoke's firm then split into small groups to make their way to Kenilworth Road, following the sound of police sirens or the roar of fighting in the streets ahead. Outside the ground, the excited conversations were of small, ten-on-ten affairs, with neither side budging. It seemed that everyone had seen some action and all they wanted to do now was get in the ground and take Luton's seats. This was done quietly and calmly as 100 lads quietly took their seats above the unsuspecting MIGs.

Stoke's following was over 3,000 strong and they packed the section of the open terraced enclosure. As in the previous season, Luton's mob formed in the seats beside them and started baying. Every Stoke supporter and hooligan alike could see that Stoke had a mob in the seats above Luton, yet not one of them gave it away with a daft wave or acknowledgment. It was kept tight, and the lads above could see it. This only added to their confidence and determination. They sat on and waited, undetected.

The Mayor and his still-shaken lady made their presentations, and the game got underway with an early opener from Stoke. The Stoke fans went mental, piling up onto the fences and celebrating in an aggressive manner before the furious MIGs, but still ignoring the seats above. Staying still and not celebrating drove the lads upstairs insane but was vital to their plan. They left their seats and headed down to congregate together above their intended victims. Every man looked down silently at the Luton firm, which was again around 200 strong. As the celebrations petered out, both sets of supporters reverted to staring at one another through the fences. Now it was time.

Speg from Stafford is one of the smallest members of Stoke's firm and usually gets hurt in combat. Having had his nose broken in the fight with the MIGs the previous season, he was bent on revenge and was the first to drop over the stand. As we followed, the Stoke fans behind their goal went crazy. This threw the MIGs; they didn't know what was happening. They were hit in an ambush inside their own stadium and routed in seconds. Hundreds of Luton fled the onslaught. With no other choice, many of the MIGs exited their section of the ground and ran across the entire width of the pitch, scrambling over into the safety of the opposite stand. The game was held up for several minutes as police restored order, while the Flying Squad remained tightly compacted into the first end that they had taken properly together.

Speg got his revenge but received another broken nose from the same black lad that had punched him the year before. This fella appeared again as a pissed-off mob of over 100 MIGs steamed back into the ground ten minutes before the end of the game. They had come to take their end back before we left. This fight was the hardest of the day, although it lasted only a couple of minutes, with another pitch invasion bringing the game to a premature end. The battle carried out onto the streets again with neither side moving.

chapter nine

The Battle of the Mill

EVEN AS PUNK rocker kids, we were the minority in Alsager and disliked by all the local hard lads. As a twenty-year-old football casual, nothing had changed. No longer did we get chased and scolded but violence and confrontation were looming.

The Alsager Arms became the HQ for the Stoke City Flying Squad, and Friday nights would see a solid congregation from all over Stoke making the short train journey over the border into Cheshire. The Arms became a lads-only venue packed to the rafters with beer-swilling men, from teenage wannabes to older 'war veterans'. It was an old-fashioned pub with a good selection of traditional ales, once described as 'one of the best beer houses in England', with a sub-note that read, 'Caution, locals can be hostile', something that was quoted by us for years.

I had been working at the Armitage Shanks pot bank with Wilson for about four months and it was mundane and boring. I had several run-ins with the floor manager, to the point where we had a tussle in front of a floor full of workers. The only good things were the continual football conversations with Wilson, who thought and talked of little else but his coaches and the up-coming trips, and the money I was earning to feed my own footie habit.

The summer fell kind for us that year and I made the most of my freedom. I bumped into several old school pals who had just served their apprenticeships and moved into full-time employment and saw how differently we had all turned out, and how tight they were with their money. In the Army the lads were all the same: nobody quibbled about going to the bar, nobody slyed off with a bird without saying anything, and most importantly, no matter how much of a state you got in or which gutter you were picked out of, you always ended up back in your own pit, with your clothes folded by your bed and, if needed, your spew mopped up as well. Those were the standards I lived by, and the civvies I was meeting were falling well short of them.

Six months into civilian life, I was finding it increasingly hard to converse with anybody apart from the lads from down the match. I had become hopelessly narrow-minded, making life even harder for myself. Packing my bag and escaping crossed my mind several times.

I am proud to say I am an Alsager lad. 'Alsager, Stoke-on-Trent,' is the first thing I say to anybody who asks where I am from. On the other hand, Alsager does not like me, and to this day I can feel a cold undercurrent at the bar of any of the local pubs I seldom visit.

Throughout school, I was seen as being different by most of the other students. At that age it's easier to categorise someone and place them aside rather than take the time to unravel their epidermis and feel their pain. For me, fighting lads who were three or four years older was the norm, and the fact that I always got half a result made them hate me all the more. The only real ally I had throughout those years was Vinny Brown, my schoolyard hero and friend. Vinny was a massive Stoke fan and stood in the Paddock. He knew I was that cheeky little bastard that everyone loved to chase, but Vinny had been the same. He was also one of the hardest youths in town, and a proud hooligan. I suppose I was his little apprentice, from the age of seven until leaving school. What I'm saying is, he was there, and I appreciated it.

The first flashpoint between the locals and me came on a Saturday night in autumn. The usual mob of Stoke lads had come down by train and met in the Arms bar, filling it with talk of the match. By eight o'clock, all buoyant, we were discussing our options. 'Right, we can either stay in the Arms and then go back to Maggot's farm for a party, or we can get a drink till one at the Mill Country Club. Or,' I went on, 'there's an eighteenth birthday party at Rode Heath village hall. I'm not invited, but I know the girl whose party it is and I'm sure she won't mind us coming.'

A village hall party didn't tickle most of the lads' fancy, so only twelve of us made the two-mile cross-country walk to Rode Heath. Laden with cans and bottles of cider, we entered the corrugated building, which housed around 100 pissed-up teenagers and a sprinkling of the local rough nuts. Pretty much everybody was too drunk to pay attention to the uninvited guests, so we found a space in the cloakroom and slid into the mood.

The word must have spread to the two local pubs that 'Jasper's here with that Stoke lot', so they took it upon themselves to remove us from the party and their village. Without warning, the cloakroom filled with locals, all dressed in their denims and boots – they were a very fashionable bunch. Their numbers were roughly the same as ours, though the majority were several years older. Their spokesman, a bulldog I remembered from school called Hodgey, stood forward and offered me straight out, no messing. It was as plain as day that a one-on-one would last as long as a conventional conflict would have during the Cold War before someone pressed the button. A flash of reluctance crossed my mind, as within their ranks was Slug Harris. Slug was a monster and had been one of the hardest lads in our year. I liked him a lot. Many times as kids, Eddy, Gibbo and myself would go to Gresty Road at Crewe when Stoke weren't playing; it was a good place to try out our new 'skills' on lesser opponents, as Crewe languished in the lower regions and played the likes of Scunthorpe and Halifax. It was against Halifax that me, a fourteen-year-old punk, and Slug the heavy rocker went into their end on our own and made a good effort of offering out fifty or so unperturbed Yorkshiremen. I didn't want to fight him this night.

BANG.

The confined room seemed to explode as a distress flare was fired point blank into the middle of the Rode Heath gang. Everybody bar the firer was stunned as the flare bounced from wall to wall, deafening us with a high-pitched, numbing sound. The locals stood no chance as the lads who considered themselves to be my true friends glassed them with bottles and pint glasses. Pure adrenalin and the will to survive got those village lads out of there yet they still made a stand of it on the car park outside and a mental set-to took place, basically for as long as we wanted it to, as there was little chance of any police intervention around this neck of the woods. The lads with me were time-served hooligans who relished opportunities like this one; seldom did you get the luxury of a twenty-minute, all-out war at the match. This was heaven.

As the fighting became more intense, a wooden fence was destroyed by one of Stoke's numbers, and the fight took an even uglier turn as the stumps were handed out and brandished at the windmilling Slug. CRACK! Even I felt that one. Slug had been smashed over the head in a side-on attack that left him staggering. Only brute strength was keeping him up as another blow crashed across his knee, and he fell into a hedge alongside the road. Slug's friends staged a brave rescue attempt but met with the same punishment.

The different levels of experience had been there for all to see that night. For all their bottle, Slug, Hodgey and their mates had been punished for their inhospitality. I wasn't exactly over the moon with it all but I wasn't about to kick off with the lads that had just stood my corner. If anything, I learned that the people who cared about me were not the people I should really call my own. I was being driven deeper into the care of the hooligan world.

The Mill Country Club was exactly what it said: a disused mill converted into a country club and hotel on the outskirts of Alsager, a mile or so down a winding, private drive. The owner had recently put on a Friday disco, with a late bar until one o'clock, and it became popular with local businessmen and self-styled entrepeneurs, men that had been leaving my old school when I was in the third year. They knew me, and I could remember what they used to behave like before they inherited the family business; not much differently to us, if the truth be told. But they didn't cut it in the Paddock, or up town, so they retreated back over the border to become smalltown big faces.

Several weeks after the battle with Slug and his lads, smalltown talk hyped it up that Jasper and the Stoke lads were going to try to take over the area for themselves and that the Mill was their next target. When thirty turned up one Friday for one of the lads' birthdays, we made up our minds: tonight we were all going to the Mill. The building was on three floors. Its rooms were ramshackle, with low hanging beams, and nearly all had big open fireplaces. The hotel reception was on the first level, with a lobby and seating area inside a double set of glass-panelled doors. Down a single winding staircase was the restaurant, and below that, on the stone-floored cellar, was the disco. The capacity was roughly 300, with four local hardmen door staff, all burly forty-year-olds.

We knew we would not get in if we all turned up together, so we staggered our arrivals: two at a time, with the odd one or two sleazing onto the arm of a single woman. It was 9.30 p.m. and the night was crisp, as I sat in the back seat of Turney's burgundy Chrysler Alpine. I had decided to hang on and go in last. In the front seats were the Urchin and Stinge, two of the Whitehill casuals. They were raging potheads, and sat sucking on a hookah pipe, chuckling about Eddie's white Pierre Cardin slip-ons with gold buckles. Through the smoke, I sat looking at the Mill, and its three floors with little orange table lamps filling the windows. Softly in the background, I could hear Paul Young's 'Wherever I Lay My Hat' being played. It reminded me of Steve and Gib. We were joined by Gaggioli, a fresh hit was prepared, and the three of them spent the next twenty minutes in hysterics at the sight of me coughing my guts out off half a toke. While we were laughing on the car park, the rest of the lads had penetrated the club and started to settle in for the night. Some headed directly down into the disco to have a look at the talent, while others chose to stand at the bar on the middle floor. On this floor were the ladies' and gents' toilets. As usual the club was heaving. I can only surmise that the Stoke lads had been spotted as soon as they started to congregate at the restaurant bar. There were sixteen in this group, all in their late teens and dressed in their smartest football attire. It wouldn't have been hard to spot them.

The attack came without warning in the gents' toilets. Three of the lads went for a slash together and were followed straight in by several older local lads. Worlock was still painting the porcelain when the question was scowled into his face.

'You're one of Jasper's lads, aren't you?'

Worlock turned and was met with a vicious butt, splitting the skin across his cheekbone. He was then flung through a cubicle door, his head crashing into the cistern. 'Fucking come on then!' The adjacent cubicle was exited by two of the lads, and a confined punch-up took place to the sound of dull thuds and crashing doors. Soaked in piss and blood, both sets fought their way out of the toilets and into some space in the oak-panelled restaurant.

The yells from the fighting men could be heard from over at the bar. 'Come on Stoke. Worlock's just been battered.' That was all it took; the whole place detonated into fights on all three floors. Pretty much the whole of the Alsager lot and the doormen headed for anybody who did not look familiar and waded in. Stoke stood and had it toe-to-toe. There was little room to move, and any exit was blocked by hysterical, fleeing women.

Gag had poured a shot of brandy into the hookah and my second hit had me warming all over and giggling uncontrollably. I looked up through the smoke and gazed out of the window at the Mill and its pretty little orange lights. Through the windows in the shadowy orange haze, I could see dozens of panic-stricken shadows, running and flailing about. A second look showed me fighting men, slugging it out on a spindled staircase. My jaw dropped. In every window on every floor, I could see a Wild West-style brawl that showed no signs of ending.

'It's fucking going off!'

I scared the shit out of my three friends, who sat motionless with expressions of pure shock. Because we were having a smoke, we had parked well away from the building, but as we jumped out and ran nearer we could hear dull thuds, screams, the smashing of bar stools into optics and the cracking of wood.

A door on the ground floor leading out onto the car park was smashed off its hinges and ten of the lads exploded through it. They could see nothing on the car park as they had been blinded by CS gas. They fell onto the tarmac, coughing and spluttering but at the same time screaming to each other to get round to the front entrance.

We were heading across the car park and up to the main entrance. The sight that met us was incredible. The locals had obviously chosen to take on the Stoke lot when they were sure they had split up. The lads on the bottom floor had met with some tough fighting with larger numbers and had eventually had to let off the gas as a means of getting out and into some space. However the reason for their frantic attempt to get back in through the front door was the fact that the Stoke lads drinking in the restaurant were now hopelessly outnumbered and fighting a battle on two fronts. The noise coming out was horrific.

As the four potheads arrived, so did three packed marias, something you never saw anywhere in Alsager at night. We headed off into some nearby fields. I looked back; the scene was insane. The whole of the wooden frame housing the front doors had been pulled out of the wall, leaving it looking like a cave entrance. Using these lumps of wood as battering rams, the Stokies made their assault on the inside of the club, unaware they were about to be arrested. Sickened to the pit of my stomach, I walked with the others away from the sirens and blue flashing lights.

Order was eventually restored and a fleet of vans ferried the arrested to Congleton, six miles away. It had been an extremely violent and bloody affair and not much of a happy birthday for our friend, who ended up with six stitches in a head wound. Women could be heard screaming at their boyfriends for getting involved, and all the bollocks that goes with it. Police officers stood round questioning potential witnesses, and comforting the injured. And, as always, the grass had to step forward. It was one of the original aggressors. He discreetly pulled a police sergeant to one side and informed him who it was that had brought these type of people to our village. I overheard that information from a nearby hedge and knew it was time to hit the road.

Tragically, that night had been the breaking point for the owner of the Mill. Life had not been too kind to him of late, and the thought of another possible closure of his hotel became too much. Shortly after the incident, he put a shotgun in his mouth and ended his life.

I had not played a major role in the Battle of the Mill. Nevertheless, such had been the seriousness of the fighting that by four o'clock in the morning, I was being driven along the A34 in dense fog towards Manchester Airport. I arrived in Malaga, Spain, later that afternoon, with the grand total of £50 and a return ticket to sell. My small Head bag was rammed with wet clothes and had already begun to start smelling.

The bus station in Torremolinos was my initial destination. From there, I could take the local bus that travelled along the coast road and as close to Gibraltar as I could get. An airport taxi would have caused too much of a dent in my fifty nicker, so I headed off down the hill towards the San Miguel factory and walked the couple of miles into Torremolinos. In no more than an hour, I was combing the resort's streets looking for a fluorescent sign that said 'noche dia'; that was as much information as I had managed to glean off the half a dozen people I had stopped to ask the way to the bus station.

I was half expecting the place to be overrun with British but it was late September, the weather had turned cold and most of the people I could see were Spanish and not in a rush to get anywhere. I don't know how many times I must have walked past it, but I finally clocked the huge 'Noche Dias' twenty-four-hour chemist sign, in big fuck-off red and green lights, in the reflection of a bus window.

'How much is a single ticket to La Linea de la Frontera, por favor?'

'Pardon?'

'Single. One-way. How much please?' *Ah fuck this, I'm getting on, tough. If he doesn't understand a word I say, I can't pay, can I?* I tutted loudly and walked off. Having travelled all day on a bellyful of vodka, with no food other than the in-flight swill and no water, I was dehydrated, knackered and starting to get pissed off.

'It's that one you want mate.'

It was not the dialect I wanted to hear, but it was English. A Brummie pointed to a double-carriaged bus.

'You change at Estapona, and it's two hundred pesetas.'

'Cheers mate, nice one.'

'No probs mate. Oh and by the way, be careful in La Linea at night, especially if you're on your own.'

'Yeah will do, cheers.'

I boarded the bus he had pointed to. *Be careful at night, especially if you're on your own.* I started mumbling to myself. *I'm Stoke City. Fucking Spanish, where were they in the war, eh?*

Not long after leaving Torremolinos, I started to calm down. The bus was empty and I had the back seat. Soon it was dusk and the coast had that purple haze. Trawlers were heading home with the day's catch and every now and then I'd see an old Spaniard dipping his weary feet into the refreshing ocean. *This'll do me.* I felt a smile pushing its way up. I pulled my Walkman from inside my jacket, placed the two little black sponges into my ear holes, and listened to the Eagles' 'Take it to the Limit'. I was content.

Marbella looked like just a road, nothing special, with a few bits of totty knocking about the shops and the odd flash car. It flashed past in seconds. I decided to get something to eat at Estapona, as I would have a good twenty minutes before my connection was due and I was starting to feel vacant and look a bit gormless. The smell hit me before I saw it: a little tapas bar at the back of the bus station. The espresso machine was boiling away and I could detect paella cooking in the pan. I kicked away the peanut shells, drew up a stool and pointed to a huge plate of tuna and potato salad, which I ate off a little two-pronged fork with a couple of fingers of bread, washed down with a small glass of Vino Tinto.

Again the bus was empty, and I sat at the back once more; there's nothing worse than having to spend a journey with a complete stranger sat behind you. I like to see everything, good or bad. Sabinillias was the darkest stop en route. It looked shady, and the small groups of local lads hanging around looked even shadier. The sound of the hydraulic door opening brought my attention to the middle of the bus. Two gypsies were boarding through the exit, and the driver made no attempt to stop them. They were both in their late twenties, wearing scruffy 'Starsky' jumpers with tight jeans and faded slip-on shoes, which tickled me briefly as I remembered the pair of white Pierre Cardin slip-ons with gold buckles that Eddy had purchased for £45 in the sales and still gets slaughtered for to this day. Both had greasy long black hair, thick moustaches and stank of spirits and tobacco.

With an empty bus to choose from, they came and sat two seats in front of me, on the opposite side of the aisle. *Here we go. These two fucking want it.* I scanned under the seats looking for a discarded beer bottle or anything I could use as a tool. I was well aware of the locals' need to carry a blade; a number of the older lads carried knife wounds from a beach battle in Ibiza in 1982. The Falklands War was on at the time, local support for the Malvinas was heavy and fights took place daily with the small number of ex-pats who worked in and around the bars of San Antonio. A well-known character from Stoke who went on to become one of the city's few black councillors received a six-inch knife wound in one street battle, leaving his neck gaping and his voice croaky for the rest of his life. Instinctively I sat forward, resting my arms on the handrail.

The Spaniards muttered to each other. One sat with his back to me, purposely shielded from my view, while his mate kneeled up on his seat, his back resting against the window. Let's not call it paranoia, but awareness definitely kicked in as the Spaniard shielding himself reached into his jeans pocket, while his mate made it clear to me that he was aware that I was aware. We locked eyes. Then the Mill and the reason I was on this coach piled back into my thoughts as a packet of Rizlas appeared from his pocket. I sat back but continued to watch as the Spaniard emptied a cigarette into the palm of his hand and fluffed it up with his fingers. The faces of both men lit up as they huddled around the flame from the lighter. Either I was strung out and hallucinating or I was riding with Lucifer and his best mate this night.

I love that smell; it gets me. One thing about the Spanish: they send the shit over to us lot and keep the best hash for themselves. This stuff smelt delightful. I could see it fluffing up as he sprinkled it into his cupped palm. In one swift movement the two Rizlas were placed onto the hash in the palm of his other hand, and his wrists turned full circle, producing a ready-rolled joint. I had never seen anybody roll a joint like that before.

Gibraltar was imposing as I got my first look at it from the Spanish side. I had spent ten months there with the Staffords, stationed on a rock that sticks up out of the ocean, and you have to see it from afar to understand it. I felt better, positive. Things were not all that bad all of a sudden. I could see where I was going. Gibraltar had become my rock of hope.

I could not believe the amount of smoke, and the stink that was coming from the pair; one minute I'm looking at the devil and his disciple, the next I'm sat next to Cheech and Chong. These two didn't give a fuck. I liked that. I had to laugh.

'San Roque, next stop.'

The two hash heads rose from their seats. *Right you bastards, this is where you're going to jump me, is it?* They stood in the aisle facing the driver and suddenly did not look too stoned. I stood up as the driver pulled to the side of the unlit road.

'Tomar. Here, here, tomar.'

The gypsy held something towards me. His hands were dried and chapped and had ink marks in nondescript patterns across the fingers and knuckles. Normally if someone handed me a joint with two tokes left on it, I'd tell them, 'The ashtray's there mate.' But this time I appreciated the gesture.

'Gracias.'

La Linea de la Frontera had probably been a grand, prosperous town in its day, but as the coach pulled into the main square I could see how dilapidated and rundown the buildings had become. Gibraltar was an 800-yard stroll away but I had spent many times observing this place through a pair of binoculars and I wanted to see what exactly it was the Brummie was warning me about. There was a smell of burning horse chestnuts, and families walked arm in arm round and round the square, picking up conversations where last left. The local nutter was also there, an old bloke who had fallen from grace, walking bare-footed, hands clasped behind his back, mumbling and then shouting 'dos' at the top of his voice. I liked it here.

After a good half hour of observing, I moved on. I fancied a beer. An open-fronted wooden bar, painted green, caught my eye. It was empty but for a couple of conscripted Spanish soldiers, who looked about seventeen. A cat licked round the tables, and an old woman swept up behind the bar. *This'll do me.* I chose a stool at the bar and gave the lady my cheeky grin as she leaned on her brush. I chose a tap that said 'Cruzcampo' and pointed.

'Uno, por favor.'

Four Cruzcampos later, I decided to find somewhere to sleep. It had turned midnight, I had been up for thirty-six hours and I was gone. Not wanting to waste money on a hotel this late at night, I walked towards the border. I reached the beach on the Spanish side and paused for thought. There was Gib standing in front of me, all lit up, as a gentle wind blew through the rigging of nearby yachts. I dropped my bag into a beached fishing vessel and rolled in. I plumped up my bag for a pillow, covered myself with my jacket, and placed my headphones on.

Mine had been a spur of the moment decision. I had run away but didn't really know what from. I checked my passport was in my pocket, and rummaged round to find a comfy spot. Gib looked even bigger now I was lying down; it reminded me of when I was a kid at Christmas watching *Jason And The Argonauts*, when Neptune rose out of the water and separated the two continents. On my own and happy, I had reached my destination. The Eagles were back on and I listened to 'There's a New Kid in Town'. The night was fresh but not freezing, the lavanta cloud that sat on top of the Rock kept the warmth in and I must have dropped off to sleep.

It was not the cold setting in that woke me, but the chill that went through me had me gasping for breath. The sound of muffled voices carried across the water. *It must be the fishermen and I'm in their boat.* Phew, only fishermen. I sank back inside myself, for a brief moment I thought I was in trouble there. I was cold now, and pulled my arms inside my sweatshirt and hugged myself. I was dying for a piss, but it kept me warm holding it in. Just as the thought of taking a leak pushed me to get up out of the boat, the sound of someone having one close by froze me again.

My night vision wasn't good as I had woken up looking at the orange runway lights glowing in darkness. I strained to hear if it was a human or a dog marking his manor. The small click of a lighter and the harsh smell of tobacco answered my question. Whoever it was had taken a piss on the boat I was lying in. More voices, this time from a boat, hailed their accomplice on the beach. Through a missing piece of decking I saw a sixteen-foot rib being rowed in by two men. The geezer who had lit up his smoke was directing six other Spaniards, who formed a chain from the water and across the beach. Almost immediately I knew I could be in serious trouble if any of them spotted me.

Fuckin' hell, they're drug smuggling.

There was little I could do but sit it out and hope I wasn't found. I was half buzzing as well, and eager to see what was going on. The floor of the rib was stacked with binliners that were passed off quickly and silently and disappeared up the beach. These lads had this off to a tee. As the last one was handed off, a short muffled discussion took place and several cases of Marlboro cigarettes were taken from the bag and handed back onto the rib.

Whatever the deal was that went down, the smoking smuggler didn't like it. I could not tell what was said, but each word was accompanied by a blow from a telescopic cosh. His victim fell down onto one knee, trying to shield his head from the slow, deliberate blows. His attacker was enjoying it, I could tell. He was obviously in charge as nobody made any attempt to stop his prolonged attack. The victim's limp body was carried away with the binliners. I sat and waited for morning.

Seeing that man beaten to within an inch of his life opened my eyes to what the Brummie had told me the previous day in Torremolinos. It was the most sickening act of violence I had ever seen. I crossed over the border into Gib at first light and headed straight to Main Street, to an old knife shop I knew. Without hesitation, I chose a sturdy lock knife with a bone handle and slipped it into my pocket.

For the next decade of my life I would stay on the road, continually travelling and seeking out the next adventure. They were great times. I revelled in personal freedom after the inhibiting discipline of the Army. Choices were now mine, all mine. I could rampage on the terraces or lie on a beach. I could buy a lock knife or read a book. However, my adventures along roads that spanned several continents are not relevant to the rest of this book – besides, many would have to be omitted for legal reasons. However, there was one thing that would attract me home every now and then – when the urge became irresistible. Certain cup games, derbies or grudge matches would find me either hitching or, if I was flush, flying back home to England. And some of these occasions were momentous.

chapter ten

Birth of the Naughty Forty

T'HE CHELSEA HEADHUNTERS were at the top of any list of hooligan firms in the mid–Eighties and our fixture at Stamford Bridge in December 1984 was much anticipated. A full coach of fifty-six left Stoke at 9 a.m. headed for the capital. So why were we disappointed? It was not the numbers, it was the ages. Only nine on the coach were over the age of twenty. We fell way short on experience and one or two of the lads started questioning the capabilities of the juniors. Indeed the youngest was only twelve: Martin Hallam, who went on to be the firm streaker!

I noticed that the coach had an air of anxiety, even though Wilson had crammed on 400 out-of-date cans of bitter from his old man's pub and these were flying out at fifty pence each. I sat with the boys that were the target of the older heads' scrutiny.

'What's up lads?'

'Everybody seems a bit a pissed off, J.'

'They are but nobody is pissed off with anyone on here. So don't worry about it, let's just get to Chelsea and give it our best, yeah? Keep it tight.'

And so we carried along with our journey south, discussing courses of action if the situation became worse than we were already expecting. That's part and parcel of this kind of a day out: the not knowing, the what ifs, the just in cases. *Superb*. Being in a battered old Stoniers bus with no toilet on board and Wilson's stale ale was beginning to have the lads cross-legged, and requests for a piss stop could be heard from the back of the coach.

'Terry, next services mate, the lads are dying for a slash.'

Terry pulled off the M1 onto Rothersthorpe services in

Northamptonshire. We were met on the slip road by two marshals in their thirties, wearing yellow fluorescent jackets. They directed us to pull over and climbed aboard.

'Good morning,' the man said to Terry. 'Have you booked a reservation for your party to stop off at these services today?'

Wilson explained that we had not intended to pull over. 'We just need a piss mate, not any food or anything.' The men could hardly expect Terry to back his bus onto the motorway, so they agreed that as long as we didn't go inside the service area, we could pull over by the petrol pumps near the exit, and use the wash room there.

'Nice one mate.'

The services were packed out and coaches and vans lined the car park nearest to the entance. One coach in particular caught everyone's attention, and as Terry slowly continued onward, the lads filled the windows down the right-hand side of the vehicle. Every man on that coach stared intently at the words MAINLINE written in Christmas spray along the windows of a modern double-decker, parked yards away. Congregated outside it, some wearing paper *Manchester Evening News* hats, were an older bunch of Manchester City's Mainline Firm, with a large proportion of West Indian descent. The Mancs held our stare as they tried to figure out who we were. They smirked when they read 'Stoniers of Tunstall, Stoke-on-Trent' on the rear end of the bus. They must have seen us as less of a threat than someone like Leeds, and strutted towards us laughing and offering us on. *After all, who the fuck are Stoke?*

Inside our coach, the confinement was about to blow. Some shouted, 'Fuck the scruffs, lets get to Chelsea,' while others yelled, 'These want it, let's go.' I looked out at fifteen or so Mancs that had left their mates and were yards away, running with purpose under the roof canopy of the petrol station. Terry was unaware of the situation he was about to pull up in.

'Fuck it Terry, drive on mate.'

I couldn't see the point in this one, not when the fruit was riper elsewhere. But it was too late; the emergency exit at the back of our coach had been popped and the lads had started to jump off. There was no other choice.

'Terry, stop the coach. This is it. Come on you Manc bastards, we're Stoke City. Who wants it?'

Our coachload of kids piled off that bus and steamed into those fifteen Manc frontrunners with venom, dropping some and running others. The remaining Mainline, who until this point had thought that they were going to take the piss, headed forward to meet us as we ran towards their coach. The next eight minutes was a riot in the true sense of the word, with running and brick battles ravaging the car park and service area. There were bodies strewn everywhere as men from both sides picked themselves up and charged back into each other.

At one stage, after about five minutes of hard-fought action, the Mancs retreated under a barrage of bricks and Walls ice cream bins inside a huge set of glass doors, in which landed a huge slab of concrete. As the door mechanism jammed, it kept opening and shutting uncontrollably. The Mancs staged a breakout and piled back onto the car park. More brawling took place, with little four-on-fours everywhere. During one of these, I fought off some black lads in their late twenties but in the corner of my eye I could see that one of our lads had been overpowered and needed help. Shaking off my opponents, I turned and ran to the aid of Brasso. He was well in the shit. He had been caught straying too far from his own lines and was being pinned down by two younger black faces and a tall scruffy white lad with long black curly hair and an acne-covered face who was wearing a blue and white pinstriped Lacoste cagoule. As his accomplices tore into Brasso and pulled his jacket over his head, the white lad pulled out a craft knife and slashed him twice across his back. Seeing their victim was no longer helpless, the trio beat a retreat and the bleeding Brasso was back among his own ranks and wanting more action.

The scene on the whole of that service station was shocking. The best part of 100 men fought ferociously hand-to-hand. People were driving away from the pumps without paying for their petrol to get away. Most shocking of all was the sight of Spudder and Spooner slugging it out on the back seat of the Mancs' coach, and actually getting the better of superior numbers. It was too difficult to choose what to look at next. So I just piled back in.

After what seemed an eternity, the police arrived in a Jaguar and attempted to get between the warring factions by driving through them repeatedly. The fighting simply resumed as soon as the police reversed through another outbreak. It was gripping stuff. Cue the arrival of another police car and a brainwave. The officer from the passenger seat of the back-up car forced his way onto our coach and demanded that Terry drive off towards the slip road to the M1. Terry did as he was told, and was then ordered to stop 100 yards away, just out of our sight. As the policeman had planned, we thought our transport was leaving for Chelsea without us. The tide turned, and the retreating Stoke were picked off as they scrambled to gain entry to their coach. Our back window went through with a fire extinguisher, ending the hostilities for the day.

Both sets of supporters were rounded up and taken to separate police stations. A total of ninety-six were arrested and one Manchester City fan was admitted to hospital with cracked ribs, courtesy of the Walls ice cream company and its concrete bin. The Stoke lads were ferried to Mere Way police station in Northampton, where fifty-five were placed in two holding cells while the twelve-year-old waif was kept separate in an interview room. Individually fingerprinted and processed, all were then locked back up together in the two cramped cells, where some played cards and others marvelled at Cossack's body-popping. Pissed off that they hadn't made it to the Bridge, the lads made do with this home entertainment for the next nine hours.

The chief inspector entered looking grim-faced. The cells fell silent as he informed us that a Manchester City supporter was in a grave condition and it looked like an investigation into his injuries would take place. The inspector waited to see our concern and remorse. He was disgusted and left the cell shaking his head as a collective roar filled the station's corridors.

'SO FUCKING WHAT?'

Several hours later, a desk sergeant informed us through the bars that we would shortly be released. They were going to take us out four at a time and put us on a new coach sent down to pick us up. I was in the last four to be released, and it became immediately apparent why it had been such a long drawn out affair. Two uniformed officers escorted me, Ada, Cossack and Podge along a corridor into an interview room at the end. Along that corridor were six offices, and in three of the doorways were plain clothes CID. In the other three doorways were the two black lads and the tall scruffy lad who had slashed Brasso. As if that wasn't bad enough, we last four were called out once more and taken through the process again. An hour later, Ada from Vegas and myself were charged and released on bail to appear at Northampton magistrates a week later. We were eventually all fined.

As we were about to leave Northampton, the chief inspector appeared at the front of the coach. He told us we were no longer welcome in the county of Northamptonshire and that individually we were a bunch of insecure idiots and collectively a bunch of savage animals. I think he had a point. We left for Stoke singing, 'Feed the world, let them know it's Christmas time,' at the tops of our voices, relieved to be going home but pissed off that a chance to have a go with the Headhunters had been ruined.

Another game I made it back for was an excursions from the Alsager Arms to a Milk Cup match at Wrexham on a Tuesday night. Three van loads and five car loads met at midday and sat drinking in the back bar all afternoon until somebody remembered it was 5.30 p.m. and we were late for the match. The convoy embarked on a *Wacky Races* surge along the A-roads of Cheshire. In an attempt to get there first, myself and seven others were crammed into a big purple Marina (minus the furry dice). Our only competition was a white Ford Capri, with six passengers heading down-hill at considerable speed towards a roundabout that by luck had no other approaching traffic. Neck and neck and with us on the outside we had three choices: left, straight across or to the unthinkable right.

We chose the unthinkable. As we span in slow motion, the shouts of 'No!' could have been heard from the middle of Stoke. The look on the faces of the lads in the Capri as we careered on two wheels around that bend was one of sheer shock. Ours was one of sheer terror. In spite of this momentary feeling of panic, the race went on up the hill and beyond. With the Marina past the chequered flag first, we all met up at The Turf, a pub we knew was the haunt of Wrexham's lads.

By now it was dark, and although the game had started our frayed nerves demanded a few large vodkas. As the other lads were ordering up, I booked my place in the van for the return journey, while Miffer pulled our driver to one side and dampened his jubilation by pointing out that he had just gambled five of the top boys for the sake of the race, with a firm that was small enough as it was, and to never volunteer to drive again.

There was no visible police presence on the dimly lit streets, and the noise of the Wrexham kop was enticing. A hundred Stoke lads fumbled in their pockets for notes and coins as they queued silently outside the four still-open turnstiles to the kop. I was one of the first to pay in and noticed immediately that thirty excited faces peered down at us from the stand. I looked into the eyes of a Welshman who silently acknowledged our sortie, and with finger on lip pointed down to the bottom of their end, as if to say, 'We'll meet you there.' Seeing that as a gentleman's gesture, myself, Tony Acko, Piko and Philler led the way in. Call me naïve but I honestly perceived that message as a 'come on lads and we'll fight it out'. Wrexham saw it differently. Our attempt to infiltrate their terracing was met with a brutal attack before I'd even had a chance to put the ticket stub in my pocket.

The attack came from a heavy mob of fifty and although they could-n't all put the boot in, the weight was crushing, as those of us through were pinned back into the turnstiles. I was saved by the big man, Miffer, who fortunately for me had chosen the same entry and was paying his money as I was slammed back inside. Miffer, seeing me bent backwards over the turnstile facing up to a determined eviction, grabbed a handful of my demi-wave 'shocking but fashionable at the time' hair and pulled me out like a cork from a bottle. Trading places, he followed through and with a hate-filled bitterness began trading blows with his mate's attackers. The same action was repeated at the other three entries. We were pulled out and into the safety of the firm, slightly shaken and winded, while our replacements continued our defiant message: *we've come to fight amd if you won't let us in we'll fight you through the turnstiles.* Police and stewards now arrived, leaving Wrexham taunting us as we stood in the open street.

The night took a more personal tone now. We all felt that that gesture had been a sporting invite for a decent fight rather than an ambush. In their haste Wrexham had denied themselves what could have been a classic Eighties-style football ruck with all the trimmings. Our objective now was to find the biggest set of double doors that we could, kick off the hinges and storm the place properly, instead of faffing about with false invites. We found the double doors at the back of their end which we proceeded to kick at, only these doors didn't succumb and the noise brought the unwanted attention of the North Wales Police. They told us we were naughty boys and very kindly escorted us on to the terraces of the away end without paying, which levelled it up for me in a way, as I had already paid once and seen fuck-all apart from a size-ten trainer and tattooed knuckles.

Throughout the game masses of Stoke fans who had witnessed the Wrexham surge volunteered their accounts of how they saw a long line of people hurriedly running down their terracing and heading for the corner. They described how jubilant the Welsh were as they regained the height and position in their kop and celebrated a victory over the English invaders. It properly pissed everyone off and it was decided that another attempt at taking the kop was paramount before the game had ended.

With Keith Birchin scoring the only goal of the game, it was starting to look like Stoke would win for the first time in twenty-eight consecutive matches. Hardly satisfied with the result, the Stokies that had made the failed attempt on Wrexham's kop filed discreetly off the away end terracing, and congregated on the concourse below. No exits were open yet, so they charged a double door with ease and hit the streets, with one direction in mind.

Wrexham had turned out a big mob of over 150 lads for this one and they had the same idea as us. They were coming to meet us. The Stoke lads headed towards Crispin Lane and down onto Grosvenor Road. An assault on the kop had been averted by a strong police presence so the plan now was to get into their town centre through the bus station. Stoke could tell there was a mob on the move in front of them by the sight of scurrying police officers and the revving of police vans. The Stoke lads picked up their speed and jogged onward.

As Stoke turned a corner to their right, the Wrexham firm could be seen in the street being driven back into town itself to the Ragman pub from where they had come. The Stoke mob fanned out, filling the street, and two huge roars went up, visibly startling the officers in front of us. Without haste the police drew their batons: this was going to be no-nonsense tactics. With no more than twenty yards between both sets of rivals the thin blue line held firm for several minutes. A little in front of us was Ritchie Campbell, a small black lad distantly related to the legendary Rob Campbell. Being small – he resembled Butch from *Sooty And Sweep* – and with a little helping hand he was through the open legs of a defiant copper and bouncing tall in no man's land just feet from the Wrexham Frontline.

Ritchie was on his own and that was as far as any of us got, although receiving a couple of punches and a kick up the arse from the Taffies. It was only seconds later that he was being forcibly dragged back and whipped in a revenge attack from the gloating copper he had nutmegged. He avoided a nicking and was soon back with the firm.

It was a stand-off after all that, and definitely a night of what-should-have-beens. My intention is not to knock the Wrexham lads for their impetuous actions; we have all been there at least once in our time. Bollockings were given out and their failings acknowledged. It's more about the big man, and him getting me out of another tight scrape. Cheers Miff.

The Naughty Forty were born on an August 1985 trip to Portsmouth. Until then, Stoke's casual firm had not been known by any particular name, unlike many other mobs that had developed around the same time. Three vans were arranged for the lengthy trip: two leaving at teatime on Friday via Oxford, for a night on the piss with Bamber Gascoigne and his college pals, and the third departing after the clubs later that night. By 8 a.m., after a lot of pissing about, nicking students' bikes and getting lost between Oxford and Portsmouth, all three vans reached their destination outside the legendary HMS *Victory*. Whilst some of the lads cleaned themselves up in the public toilets, others walked around the *Victory*. The rest of us spotted a nearby licensee cleaning up outside his boozer and before we knew it he had agreed to admit us into the back room for a few quiet early beers. Soon all forty of us were stationed in the back bar, supping lager, cider or Guinness with rum and black chasers. To get us into the swing of things, Frankie Goes To Hollywood's 'Two Tribes' was played on the jukebox.

By official opening time, most of the lads were pissed, having topped up from the previous night's drinking. We were also disorientated time-wise and thought it was much later than it actually was. This was probably why we left in a rush to make our presence known closer to the ground, heading for the Fratton Arms, which we believed was Pompey's pub. We drove towards Fratton Park and were dropped off in a side street a few hundred yards from the Arms. The vans were then left out of the way close to a park at the back of the ground. The rest of us continued on foot to the pub and a possible encounter with the 6.57 Crew. We were full of confidence and beer and relishing the opportunity to mix it with an already established and rated firm on their own manor.

This fell completely flat when, rather than being greeted by the 6.57, we met a large group of local constabulary. Without discussion they rounded us up and pushed us towards the ground. We were being shep-herded onto the deserted terraces three hours to kick-off. Gutted. Some of the lads did manage to evade capture but we feared for their safety once word got around that Stoke were in town. However, apart from two of the lads being attacked in Pompey's paddock, nothing else happened either before or during the game, apart from us suffering a 3-0 thrashing.

After the game was a different matter. By now we had sobered up, having not touched a drop for over five hours. Our heads were back on and we were determined to make something of the day. This started to look unlikely once again, though, as the tight cordon of Hampshire Police clung on to us like leeches. They marched the three drivers to our vans and then placed our group with them, along with the supporters' coaches awaiting an escort out of town. This achieved, our group of outcasts were all considered to be safely removed from any potential incidents with the local hooligans. The police had won and we had only pubs on the jour-ney home to look forward to and, scraping the barrel, maybe the chance of a ruck in some arse-end town.

Imagine our delight at the sight of a fat bobby stood in the middle of the road, beckoning our three vans out of the escort. Confused, but happy to oblige, we duly pulled off, and with no police with us, journeyed up the road. This was better. Before we had travelled 500 yards we were again stopped, but this time because of traffic congestion, not police interven-tion. The vans were claustrophobic and over-heating with anticipation. We were back on a knife-edge, the day firmly in our own hands.

To our right, only a few yards away, was a four-foot-high stone wall with a privet hedge on top. On the other side was a park. The sight of thirty 6.57 ambling disappointedly along in single file brought cheesy grins to our faces. We were stuck in traffic and out of sight of these lads, who you could see had already written their day off. We could almost hear them say, 'Well, that's another firm who haven't shown up.' We couldn't let them think that, could we?

By now, each van contained between twelve and fifteen highly charged and previously frustrated emotional nutcases waiting for the signal from the lead van before they could explode onto the streets. Still unaware of Stoke's stalking eyes, Pompey started to exit the park and draw level with our vans. Amazingly they still failed to spot us, which heightened the expectation in the vans. The anticipation was torture.

Less than twenty yards from their hidden surprise, Pompey were joined by two spotters on BMX bikes, another distraction for them. We watched them receive a blank report and had to stifle our laughter.

'Now!'

Like a scene from *The Sweeney*, our explosive arrival had Pompey jumping out of their skins and running hell for leather for the first twenty yards. The BMX bikes were heaved into our path in an attempt to collapse our front line and they made a determined stand at the next junction, under the canopy of a huge sycamore tree. Thirty of them bounced in unison, awaiting our impact, which came in the form of one of the BMX bikes flying back into them. Then roughly equal sides engaged in an old-fashioned punch-up.

The noise alerted the police, who were several hundred yards away with the escort. The fight lasted as long as it took for the first dog handlers to arrive with their vicious charges. As both sides fought on with drop-kicks, punches and headbutts, the first alsatian was going berserk, but was ignored until it was let of its leash, at which everyone dispersed sharply. The yardage back to the vans was covered in record time as no-one fancied being its next snack, and the vans filled faster than they had emptied. The cops, however, were just beginning. They proceeded to give our van one of the worst beatings I have ever witnessed on an inanimate object. It was like being trapped inside a giant's drum kit as their batons crashed into the windows and sides. The only reason I can think that the police then allowed us on our way was to avoid being classed as hooligans themselves.

With no windscreen left, the lead van limped out of Portsmouth. We were relieved but so cold we had to huddle together for warmth.

'That was a naughty little row, that was,' said Podge, leaning over from the front seat. 'How many of us were in that street?'

'Forty,' replied Spegg.

Podge rubbed his brow, laughed and shook his head. 'Yeah, the Naughty Forty.'

That's how we got our name. And those lads present that day are the original and only true members of the infamous Naughty Forty.

chapter eleven

Finbar

IF YOU WERE single or one of the many lads who had no existing family, Christmas fell hard. Those of us in that category always had one event in mind over the festive period: the Boxing Day fixture. Home or away, this was our Christmas Day with the family. Everybody turned out for this one, usually sporting new knitwear and smelling like Pepe le Pew.

1986 saw me hitchhiking from Spain via Switzerland and returning home laden with presents on the day before Christmas Eve. My grotto for this year was one of Wilson's vacant student houses in the backstreets of Shelton. I was sharing the place with Animal, one of the younger Alsager lads, and by eight o'clock that evening, albeit without the permission of Animal's parents, we had furnished the place with the essential TV, video and hi-fi. *Merry Christmas, Mr and Mrs Braddock!* I thought, as we emptied their fridge and cupboards and drove off in Animal's van.

Christmas Eve in Hanley was vibrant and I was sick with excitement as I shook the Deets brothers' hands on the door of Leadbelly's and walked in. I had not seen the likes of Modder and Stiko and the rest of the PBA lads for over a year, and was delighted to see them all congregated at the top of the cast iron spiral staircase that took me up to the first floor and the presence of over 100 of the N40. After dozens of exchanges of goodwill, I sat down with a large vodka and chatted to Lippo about Boxing Day's fixture. Sheffield United at home was not the biggest match on our calendar but all the same offered a good chance of some yuletide commotion.

Within an hour, I was joining the festive singing. Vodka and emotion had grabbed me and at three o'clock, when the pubs closed to prepare for the night-time invasion, I took to the streets of Hanley wearing a chef's hat I had pinched on the way out. In marker pen on the front I had written 'FULL PSYCHO' and on the back 'NO REASON'. Apt words to describe the upcoming absurdities.

Every pub in Hanley had now shed its load and over 2,000 people descended on Fountain Square. People work hard in the Potteries and celebrate hard too. The atmosphere was one of unity, as the girls off the pot banks snogged enthusiastically under the mistletoe with anybody who wanted it. The focal point of this gathering was the fountains; as Rolf Harris once said, 'Kids and water, they love it!' Inevitably it wasn't long before someone was in it.

The police had two marias parked discreetly towards the back of the square, nicely enough out of the way to prevent any unecessary tension with the revellers. It could have been the fact that the cops were having to sit around on Christmas Eve watching everybody else having a good time, who knows, but the twelve police officers that entered the scene were not in the festive spirit one bit. Most people exited the fountains on seeing them arrive, acknowledging that someone could get hurt if they slipped or trod on a broken glass. The crowd parted and made way for the officers.

One over-intoxicated reveller, as always, decided to grab the moment and stripped off his clothes, dancing round the fountains and refusing to come out. He was taking the mickey out of the two officers, neither of whom wanted to get soaking wet halfway through a shift. But one of them had to, so in he went, to the delight of the crowd. I was bent over double with tears streaming down my face. The naked reveller was a slippery customer, and the crowd roared again as both coppers were dragged into the slapstick. Never had I seen such an uproar on such a massive scale.

As dry reinforcements aided in the capture of the yuletide streaker, things got decisively out of hand. The man was roughly cuffed and unceremoniously dragged through the crowd towards the waiting maria. I had never seen an atmosphere turn as cold as quickly. A policeman's helmet flew through the air, igniting a mass public show of disapproval. This was not a football riot; this was again the oppressed citizens of Stoke-on-Trent venting their spleen on the Establishment. For the next sixty minutes, the Christmas spirit was literally out of the bottle as hundreds of people went absolutely berserk. Shops were ransacked, police vans attacked and overturned, and reinforcements were deployed to stop the disorder.

I was as incensed as everybody else and played my part in the riot, assaulting two police officers, one arresting a man who was lying face down in the doorway of Millets and the other who came to his aid. That authoritarian lack of tolerance ended up with twelve people arrested and five police officers in hospital. I was convicted of police assault again and I decided it was time to hit the road once more. California was calling and The Eagles were 'taking me to the limit' one more time.

One thing that kept Stoke a tight firm in my absence was that there was never a vacuum for pretenders or chancers to exploit. As young lads rose through the ranks, there has always been mutual respect. The perfect example of this was Finbar. He plays the game of a gormless thug to perfection, belying a sharp and astute nature that most people miss. He does not often exercise his dry humour but when he does, his timing is usually superb. For years his boyish nature, bright red cheeks and fat bottom lip gave him the appearance to some of a fourteen-stone Labrador puppy. We all knew him as a game lad whose loyalty was never in question. As he has grown into the man we always knew he was, he has become one of Stoke's most respected lads. The chubby cheeks of adolescence gave way to a couple of extra inches in height and his new, lean look was accompanied by an air of authority as he graduated from protégé to top boy. Here's what he has to say:

WE TALKED ABOUT it on the school playground a few days before: me, Jack, Andy T and Tuck. We were fourteen years of age and had been to a few home games together, standing on the Boothen End. Walsall was to be our first away adventure The plan was to catch the 8.20 a.m. train from Alsager to Stoke. We arrived together, full of anticipation and excitement but also with some apprehension. A small group of casual Stoke lads stood on the platform. We boarded the train to Walsall with wry smiles on our faces. We were on the way. I looked at my watch every five minutes of the hour-long train ride. Walsall is a bleak place at the best of times, but when you are fourteen years old and haven't a clue where you are going, it becomes daunting. Sod it, let's get into the town centre.

Before long we came across a pub with a Stoke couple and a few lads standing outside. We ordered four pints of lager before sitting in the corner. More and more Stoke lads came in as we swilled beer. The Old Bill eventually ordered the landlord to stop serving, as they were about to escort the Stoke fans to the ground. We were taken out of the pub to be greeted by police, dogs, horses and vans. I remember feeling part of something and proud to be among a group who were about to be put on show over the next mile or so to the ground.

Fellows Park was nothing short of a shed, with no roof on the away end. We took our places behind the goal and noticed a tighter group of Stoke fans parallel with the halfway line taunting Walsall's mob, who were segregated by a six-foot fence and gap to the other side. We believed that we were ready for the next challenge and so took our place among the rest of our lads. The arrival of both teams was greeted with shouting, taunting and coin-throwing from both sets of supporters. The game continued to the backdrop of to-ing and fro-ing as both groups made attempts to get at each other. I was hooked.

My fun met an abrupt end when two coppers grabbed me, one twisting my arm behind my back. I was then dragged down the terracing to be informed that I had been arrested for throwing coins and inciting the Walsall fans to fight. As I was marched around the pitch, on full show to the Stoke crowd, my initial embarrassment turned to pride as applause rang in my ears.

As I looked up into the crowd I saw a couple of lads from Alsager who I knew to be some of Stoke's top boys. One of them said, 'Ay up,' and gave me a clenched fist salute. I no longer gave a fuck about any charges; I felt so proud to be noticed by them. Luckily enough I wasn't charged, which made it all the more worthwhile. It was the first of many run-ins with the police during my years of following Stoke. Little did I realise I would shortly be hurled into the ranks of the Naughty Forty.

That clenched fist salute Finbar received was off me. I saw something in the boy that had me turning back the pages of time and remembering those boyhood feelings and the wanting, just wanting. I took a final glance at the boy as all the heads stood laughing and applauding his unceremonious departure from the ground.

Of all the young potentials I had listened to and looked out for over the years, none had reached as deep inside as Finbar. Looking at him in his size-eleven, brilliant-white Hi-tech trainers and distasteful colour coordination, I knew I was in for a full-time job but I had just found my first real apprentice. The fact that Finbar hailed from the Linley area of Alsager was a contributing factor, and at the age of fifteen Finbar was introduced to the N40.

His first game away with us was to be Hull City. I had arranged to pick him up at seven o'clock but spent the Friday night totally wasted at a party and rolled out into the sunshine at ten to seven. Being on a bender with several of the lads since Wednesday had left me pale, gaunt, smelly and completely uninterested in the thought of travelling to Hull in a van full of farting lads. *Oh shit. What about Finbar and his inauguration to the firm.* I couldn't let the lad down. He would have been like a kid at Christmas all week.

Finbar was sat on his garden wall with Stan, his neighbour and fellow hooligan, when I turned up ten minutes late. His towering frame jumped up and with a huge smile and a raised thumb, he ambled towards the car. He looked the floppiest six foot three lad I had ever seen, and I chuckled as he approached. Even though I was that much off my head, I still think I could see puppeteer's strings holding him up.

Finbar leaned on the roof of the car with his long arm and smiled down through the open window at me with his red cheeks full of toast. I explained to him that he was being taken to the Kings Hall car park in Stoke, where I would introduce him to the right people to talk to on his journey to Hull. The look of hurt on his face as I explained that I was too exhausted to travel, resembled a puppy that had been scolded. But that was my decision, so he'd have to live with it. Finbar climbed into the empty van and in the seat behind where the Silver Fox would be driving. I nodded to him as I explained to the lads that I wasn't going, but I wanted the youngster looking after all day. His name was asked, and seventeen time-served hooligans plus one headed to Humberside.

Fifteen minutes after collapsing into my bed, guilt had me up from my pit and dialling Wilson's number. He was still up too, and I told him that I had let the lad down, and did he fancy driving up to Hull with me? He agreed, and an hour later, we were heading east with speed along the M62.

What concerned me was recollection of the time Stoke had arrived early in Hull several years before and managed to cadge an early beer off a landlord bottling up outside his pub. It was called the Silver Cod, and the eighteen Stoke lads entered it with no fear of being battered. The landlord told them there would be no bother if they drank there as long as they were quiet and stayed in the poolroom at the back. For two hours the lads played pool and listened to the jukebox.

Why they ignored the warnings I don't know, but they were told twice by a young Hull lad who popped his head in the back bar that very soon the pub would not be safe for them. They chose to stay and played on. Several minutes later, a heavy mob of Hull flew straight into the back bar and into our lads. It was carnage. The Hull mob came across determined resistance, with every pool ball, cue, glass, bottle, ashtray and stool being used but eventually the visitors were forced to escape through the windows and onto the car park. Gwilty, with his coat pulled over his head, was the first to jump through but caught in the wire meshing and hung suspended like a fly until the next Stoke lad carried him through with his weight.

It is fair to say that Stoke got battered in the Cod that day and nobody escaped injury. Chrissy Sawley, a much-loved and respected lad, lost his right eye during the initial stages, when the pub went up in an explosion of hatred. But no malice was borne by Chris himself or by any of us towards the Hull lads; that is the risk that every one of us takes. Chrissy maintained his stature in Stoke's firm but his appearances became less frequent as he slipped into depression and he finally took his own life. He left a huge hole in our firm and is fondly remembered for his soft voice and gentle nature. A quiet man. Chrissy Sawley R.I.P.

That visit was still in my mind as Wilson and I arrived in Hull just after midday and drove round the ground several times looking for signs of either set of lads. We found thirty of our lot camped up in a back street boozer half a mile from the ground, congregated round the pool table playing 'killer', but there was no sign of Finbar.

I shouted over to Millsy, who was just about to take his shot. 'Where's the young 'un?'

Missing his shot, he looked up. 'Where the fucking hell did you find him J? He's driven us insane on the way up here.'

My heart sank. Millsy was one of the main faces and I thought the worst. 'Why, he's not a pain in the arse, is he?'

'No, not that, he's not a bad lad, Jasp. But he just keeps on with his persistent questioning. He's asked every fucker in the van about ten times what their best row was, and how many times had they been nicked. You haven't grown him, have you J?'

The lads fell about and I went outside to a nearby park, where Finbar had been placed as a lookout. *Have I grown him? Why, do I go on a bit?* I wondered. Finbar's thirst for knowledge in this subject was insatiable and never waned. He would openly move from person to person, firing questions, and even if you couldn't be bothered responding at the time, you would eventually find yourself taking a trip back down memory lane just for him.

In time, we could not believe how game this kid was. He came as a surprise package and ended being a frontline heavyweight with the looks of a baby-faced assassin. By the early Nineties, Finbar was an established face in Stoke-on-Trent, a loveable character who made people chuckle when they read of his latest exploits in the local paper. *Finbar again, what's he like? The nutter.*

In 1991, Stoke played at Swansea and a small but tidy firm made the journey down. Swansea had never travelled up to us but down at the Vetch, as all the old heads from the early Eighties remember, they like a fight. The Swansea Jacks pub was filled at opening time with seventy lads. It was chosen for a reason: the previous year, Tony the Axe Man and his lot from the Battle Wagon got turned over in there quite viciously, sustaining several injuries. This season the lads had come to put that right.

A twelve-foot St George's Cross was raised in the main window. It said

'LONGTON S.O.T.' Two scouts, Bert the Meerkat and Meakin, were told to find Swansea, and report back. This they did but were not replaced outside the pub. Swansea must have been observing the goings on at the Jacks, because several minutes later twenty of them appeared at the windows, tooled up with everything from dustbins, lumps of wood and house bricks, which all went in on the window showing the flag.

The attack was over before the last shard of glass had reached the floor and they were gone, nowhere to be seen. Twenty Stoke did spill out onto the street but the majority just took another swig of their pints. Even the landlord shrugged it off as normal.

'Keep it tight in here, if the scouts don't find them, they'll be back, guaranteed,' someone said. Sure enough, the excited scouts arrived back with the news that they had spotted a pub in town called the Garibaldi full of a tidy mob of Swansea's more established older lads. The pints were scored and seventy determined men filled the streets outside the Jacks and waited on directions.

'Through this alley, turn right onto the next long street, and it's three hundred yards further up, dead in front.' The Meerkat zipped up his jacket once more and moved on, satisfied with a job well done.

'Nice one Bert. Let's do it then.'

The Garibaldi lay ahead. The street was quiet, with lots of parked cars but few civilians to get caught up in the trouble. The Stoke firm walked in close formation, making it look smaller than it was, to make themselves less obvious to several SPG vans that had pulled up outside the Garibaldi and were monitoring the Swansea hooligans. Drinking in the street were twenty to thirty Swansea boys who, along with the police, paid little attention to the Stoke mob snaking forward. Hardly believing their free rein, the pumped-up Stoke firm got to within fifty yards and fanned out across the road, immediately finding the eyes of the locals in front.

'No noise. Keep walking. Here we go.'

How we got to within that distance without being seen is beyond any of us but it added to the roll of excitement, along with the shocked faces on both parties. Panic spread through the Swansea ranks as they called through the open door of the Garibaldi to bolster their thin line. Cue the deployment of the South Wales Police who, relishing the opportunity to at last crack an Englishman over the head, flew out of their vans and formed a hurried line between the pub and Stoke.

'Keep going lads, keep going.'

Stoke were less than ten yards away now and beyond any reasoning. Revenge was their mission. The police line was met head on and breached in seconds. Oh boy, had they underestimated this little crew. The first to make it through the police line was Finbar. He was left standing in the doorway of the pub mixing it with five of Swansea's boys. Finbar, legs apart and locked, stood hurling his huge fists into the darkness as bottles, stools and pool balls smashed all around him and the door frame from deep inside the Garibaldi. Nobody wanted to go there with the big lump. He was in his element until brought down savagely with a rugby tackle from behind, leaving him sprawled on the floor and taking a severe beating by the SPG, who had been drafted in from Cardiff for this one.

Such was the ferocity of the attack that Finbar first thought that he had been caught by some of Swansea's lads, and half-expected a blade. Then he looked up and saw several uniforms, wielding several truncheons. Bastards. Curling up in a ball, Finbar could see the Stoke lads as they fought their way through the police to get into the Swansea pub. This battle was now being fought on just one front, and between two foes.

'You English cunts. You're nicked mate.'

As the battle continued, the sound of more sirens approaching confirmed Finbar's fate. He was well and truly nicked, but when was the beating going to stop? He had been dragged and thrown onto the floor of one of the vans and still three officers were piling into him, continually screaming anti-English abuse. The kicking stopped as the door to the van was flung open and two more Stokies landed inside. Podge and the Silver Fox had also breached the police line and, like Finbar, received a kicking for it.

As Stoke claimed another victory, the three friends were taken to gaol, with one fat copper leaning on Finbar's neck with his knee, nearly suffocating him and popping out a contact lens. Joined at the nick by four more of the lads, the tactics continued, with over-exuberant body searches. Finbar was caught in possession of a thumbnail of dope and the police added a 'possession of controlled substance' charge to his violent disorder.

The beatings dished out to the seven Stoke lads nicked had been way over the mark. Finbar, with bruised ribs and arms, a bloodied nose and cut lip, demanded to be examined by a doctor. The doctor's report confirmed his injuries but the police played him for the young naïve he was.

'You drop the doctor's report on us and we'll drop the possession charge on you. Fair?'

Finbar agreed and got a severe bollocking off Podge in the cells. 'Fucking hell Finbar, you could have sued the bastards for thousands and you'd have only got a caution for a spliff's worth of dope.'

All seven men were charged with offences including violent disorder, affray, assault and criminal damage. They all pleaded not guilty, and the trial was set down for eight days at Swansea Crown. That was until on the fourth night, Swansea and Cardiff had one of their derbies that as always ended up in full-scale war. When a rather sullen judge took his stand that following morning, it didn't look good, so halfway through their trial the lads took the advice of their barristers and changed their pleas to guilty.

Suprisingly, the Cardiff riot had not gone as much against them as first thought, and each of them was passed down the maximum amount of community service given 240 hours each, and they were told that they were no longer welcome in the country of Wales.

Many times during my self-imposed isolation abroad I would think back about home, the football and the younger lads like Finbar. I would chuckle to myself as I matched upcoming fixtures with past exploits and wondered whether it would be as good this time. Sometimes I would fret that the firm had started to fall apart and could be turned over at home by the likes of Sheffield Wednesday. Unbeknown to me, my anxieties were unfounded. Another birth had taken place and a new breed of young football hooligans had attached themselves to Stoke City. The next section of this book is devoted to them, and was put together by one of their lads. They called themselves the Under-Fives.

section three

The Under-Fives

By Marcus

chapter twelve

Schooligans

S TAFFORD IS A conservative county town of 60,000 people about fifteen miles south of Stoke-on-Trent. Unlike Stoke, with its solid working class identity, Stafford is a place without meaning, a dormitory town providing safe sanctuary for commuters amid its ring of detached housing estates with front and back lawns, driveways and garages all only a bottle's throw from the countryside. It was from these estates in the north end of the town that Stoke's Under-Fives began.

By 1985, football hooliganism and the culture associated with it had reached its zenith and nadir simultaneously. It had become as overexposed in the media as break-dancing a couple of years before. As a consequence, every brat in suburbia wanted to be associated with it, and when everybody gets involved in a scene, it's usually over. The overnight proliferation of kiddie casuals nauseated many, notably lads from the council estates at the south end of town who were the first to put Stafford on the hooligan map in the early 1980s. These lads saw the culture as their preserve and these estates bred Stafford's first casuals, who modelled themselves on the scally look of Liverpool, just an hour away by train. Anyone in a Pringle jumper and a pair of Trimm Trab at that end of the town supported either Liverpool or Everton. To the bewilderment of anyone travelling through Stafford on the train, they deployed enough white paint to undercoat the Forth Bridge and painted 'EVERTON' everywhere, transforming Rickerscote into what became known as the 'Everton estate' in letters six feet high. Not a park wall, garage door or gable end backing onto the railway line escaped the application of Dulux for half a mile.

Following the media attention given to Millwall's televised riot at Luton in 1985, a couple of thirteen-year-old lads decided that the Stoke v Millwall one o'clock clash the following season was an ideal opportunity to enjoy some hooligan voyeurism. It was not affiliation to Stoke

City that motivated them (one supported Hull City and the other Tottenham) but the convenience of a local bus service dropping them right outside the old Victoria Ground and within 200 yards of some of London's most notorious hooligans. At the bus stop they found half a dozen others from Graham Balfour High School who had the same idea, and when they boarded, they encountered another handful of fellow pupils already on the top deck.

Following an uneventful, police-saturated, scoreless draw, the dozen youths waited in Stoke town centre for the bus home. They soon attracted sideways glances from tough-looking young men in the black leather jackets, paisley shirts and baggy jeans of the day, but were too naïve to notice. Before they knew it, they were confronted from one direction by six casually dressed older lads. From the other direction, fifteen more lads were coming down the main road from the Talbot public house.

'Where's yer fucking boys, Mel-wall,' someone barked at them in a Potteries accent.

They had been mistaken for Londoners and seemed to face instant annihilation. Then back up the hill, beyond those still streaming out of the pub, an impish figure in a brown leather-and-suede jacket could be seen running, waving his arms and shouting inaudibly. As he approached his words became clearer: 'Eh lads, it's me brother!' This eighteen-year-old was the sibling of one of the Stafford youths and had been one of four from the north end of the town who helped to cement the Naughty Forty.

It transpired that Stoke's boys were as excited by the Stafford lad's presence as the youngsters were frightened; they had believed the young lads were Millwall scouts who would lead them into the sort of action that would be rare at home that year in Division Two. Their intention was never to harm them, just to scare them. When it became clear that the newcomers were not Millwall, the youngsters witnessed how when one straw blows away, hooligans immediately cling to another. A lanky lad with bleached blond hair, wearing brightly checked baggy trousers, hurried into the huddle with spurious gossip that Millwall were going to pull the emergency cord on their train at Wedgwood, outside the city, and head back into town. How he obtained such information among the old men in the bookies from which he had just emerged, and before the invention of mobile phones, is beyond the capacity of even a Stephen Hawking.

The youngsters were indulged for half an hour and soaked up the attention. To an observer it would have seemed that Stoke's boys were more interested in the youngsters than vice versa, but that was only because the older lads asked questions while the youngsters spoke only when spoken to, half in fear and half in awe. All that held breath had to burst somewhere, and it did. On the bus home, the elation was like that of kids who had met their footballing heroes rather than a bunch of fans who happen to wear certain clothes and charge around city centres in gangs. All the way home, they renounced their childhood football teams and found justifications for supporting Stoke that were so tortuous they would have made half the Irish football team blush, ranging from 'I used to go to Stoke with my grandad' to 'All the cups and saucers in my house are from the Potteries, you know.'

They could not wait to get back for more. In the meantime, they would have to make do with tales from the older Stafford lad who saved their bacon. At this point they could experience away games only vicariously, and the next two home games, Crystal Palace and Brighton, did little to heighten the allure, since there were more budding Under-Fives in the ground than members of Stoke's firm, who declined to turn up for such hooligan non-events. By the time Stoke played their next home game, against Huddersfield, the seminal Under-Fives' numbers were waning from a peak of twenty, after word had gone around school, to eight.

This kernel would have probably rotted altogether but for the events ten minutes into the game in the Boothen Road Paddock. The Stafford lads were at the bottom corner of the terracing against the railings that began the segregation from the away end. There was a conspiratorial burble on the stale-ale breath of the paddock. Although only about twenty dressed lads were on duty this Saturday, most of those that stood in this part of the ground enjoyed 'a bit o' good-natured' scrapping, and something was in the offing. Everybody turned their backs on the game to face the entrance tunnels of the paddock. Then one or two turned to watch the game again. The murmuring died down. False alarm? About a minute later, everybody turned their backs to the game again. Another red herring. They resumed watching the game. Then out of nowhere the whole paddock erupted: 'Come on!'

The corner emptied as everyone crammed up the terracing, leaving those massive gaps in the crowd that were the hallmark of trouble to these kids when they saw it on television; the only thing missing was Barry Davies's, 'Sadly I have to report a disturbance in the crowd.' The youngsters did not miss their chance; they ran into the fracas, squeezing under sweaty armpits and between beer guts to get involved as 'Stokie aggro, Stokie aggro' and 'Paddock, paddock, sort 'em out' reverberated around the Victoria Ground.

When the youngsters found the action they discovered the twenty

Stoke lads making short work of thirty Huddersfield. The Yorkshire mob were pressed up against the barriers near the players' tunnel, having been chased through the paddock, and the police were forming a protective circle around them. Inside the circle was our saviour from the Millwall game, exchanging blows with one of the Yorkshiremen. That showed he was more than just a storyteller.

The rest of that season saw the youngsters stalking the older lads. They would follow about thirty yards behind, up and down terraced streets and alleyways around Stoke, arriving to witness the aftermath of aggro before the hoolivan arrived. After one of these games, the youngsters noticed that a few of Stoke's key lads had stopped on a street corner to chat with a lithe character about six feet tall. As they passed, they over-heard him being addressed as 'Jasp'. They had never seen him before but his name had long been legendary. As soon as they got round the corner they stopped and erupted in excited chatter: 'That was Jasper!' Jasper: the man about whose antics they had heard so much before his going into exile on Gibraltar. Now here he was, though only home for the week-end, apparently.

One of the youngsters had seen Jasper before but didn't recognise him without his permed hair and moustache. Back in the summer of 1984, at twelve years old, the youngster had lent his older brother some of his birthday money on condition he could follow him up to Hanley to watch what promised to be a gargantuan battle between black and white youths. With the football season over, Stoke City's casuals had decamped from Stoke town to Hanley city centre on Saturday afternoons, with nothing to do but drink. Their presence in and around the Market Tavern and French Horn pubs meant they were invading territory occupied the rest of the year by other groups. As Stoke stood drinking in the sunshine on one side of the square, large numbers of black lads in tracksuits would be break-dancing to ghettoblasters on the other. Over the weeks each side rubbed the other up the wrong way, until a line of police had to be deployed one Saturday to stop them tearing each other to pieces. It was the week follow-ing this that the youngster watched Stoke's firm from afar.

There was a large firm out at first but this seemed almost to have evap-orated by the time the pubs closed at half-past three. It had just started raining when he ran into about twenty-five Stoke. They had just run forty blacks lads down to Leadbelly's pub and were on their way back up into the centre. The rain became torrential and the firm took shelter beneath a jeweller's canopy. The youngster positioned himself among a huddle of shoppers under a veranda opposite. He was like a juevenile private eye, never once taking his gaze from the quarry.

A good 100 or more black lads were marching down the street adjacent to the jeweller's. They were dressed for the wet conditions, many
sporting Lacoste anoraks with the hoods up ready for business. Somehow
they knew exactly where the Stoke lads were and were bouncing like
Zebedees in anticipation. As they reached the corner of the jeweller's, the
youngster wanted to shout over, as in a pantomime, 'They're behind you,'
but he couldn't string a coherent sentence together.

There was no roar. They didn't make any noise whatsoever as they
piled round the corner straight into Stoke, allowing their sovereign-
ringed fists to do the talking. One lad had his upper torso pushed straight
through the plate glass window of the jeweller's as the blacks charged,
pinning Stoke's meagre-looking numbers up against the glass. Stoke ran
about thirty feet into the road and were all over the place leaving one
character who'd had no choice but to fight. He was with his girlfriend,
who screamed as she tried to claw off the guys who were kicking him on
the floor. As the guy on the floor's head fast came to resemble a blanched
tomato tears of frustration welled up in the youngster's eyes because he
was powerless to help and it was his instinct to do so. He felt terrified; he
wished he hadn't come. It might not have been so bad only the very
people he would look to for protection in this situation were being
trounced and seemed to be just as afraid.

Then came the shout that sounded three billion decibels higher than it
was in the surreal nature of the muted street: 'Fokeeen staaand Stowwwk!'
The tall guy with permed hair threw an open sports bag down onto the
street. Stoke's mob crowded round it as he distributed rounders bats to half
the mob before leading twenty-three Stoke charging back into the blacks.
Every one to a man roared, 'Fokeeen coome ooonnn!' It was an amazing
sound. Bats that didn't connect with the opposition were smashing even
more of the jeweller's window and at one point both sides stopped fighting for about three seconds to see if there was anything worth having.
Apparently a few items were liberated during the mayhem. It was a heroic
last stand but more and more blacks were arriving all the time. They were
still standing to fight in spite of the bats because of the confidence their
huge numbers gave them, not to mention there were a good few big and
handy lads amongst them. In the end Stoke, many of them sporting bloody
noses, had no choice but to run once and for all. They abandoned their bats,
which clunked as they hit the concrete and rolled along the gutter. The bats
had 'Alsager Comprehensive' embossed on their handles.

With all that violence the youngster felt shivery as he made his way
past seemingly endless lines of black lads sheltering from the rain now that
victory was theirs. Many of them chatted in Wolverhampton or

Birmingham accents; there must have been out-of-towners amongst the mob, as it was improbable that there were enough blacks in Stoke-on-Trent to muster a firm of that size.

The youngster was wandering round Hanley bus station desperately seeking a service back to Stafford when he heard his name being shouted. His brother was beckoning him from a bus. The feeling of relief on boarding the vehicle was like climbing into a bubble bath after a million-mile march. This feeling of safety was to be short lived for the youngster and the ten other lads who'd boarded, including the purveyor of rounders bats. The bus was crawling through busy Saturday traffic and so marooned amongst the huge mob of black lads roaming the town. Everybody had to crouch down beneath the windows and hide or they would have been smashed to pieces. The bus was going to Stoke where all alighted and went their separate ways.

That wasn't actually the first time this youngster had seen Jasper, just the first time he had seen him and known who he was. The very first time would have been about three months before on a Saturday in April. Stoke were playing Liverpool at the Victoria Ground. On this occasion too the youngster had made his own way up to the Potteries for what was to be a cherished experience for him. The casual culture was probably more magical for twelve-year-olds than for the older lads involved because its glamour was exaggerated by inaccessibility. This casual style was reputed to have germinated in the city of Liverpool, so standing in the queue for the Boothen End that afternoon and watching their firm bowl past was to him like getting front row seats at a Milan catwalk. As the sound of clicking turnstiles filled the spring air he marvelled at the trooping of 200 Adidas Munchen trainers, blue ones and red, and the multifarious Lacoste jumpers and T-shirts. It was not that he had never seen people dressed like this before, just that he'd never seen so many and, apart from the Stoke lads on occasional visits to the Victoria Ground, this was the first proper football firm he'd ever seen.

This was probably the birth of Thatcher's children. The youngster was already coveting designer labels and embracing materialism. Indeed, the whole casual movement could be said to reflect Thatcher's elitist philosophy. Though there were specialist mobs back then, television footage suggests that Seventies football hooliganism was a more universal pastime, with most of the scarf-wearing crowd up for a bit and everybody between fifteen and twenty-five wearing the compulsory Docs, flares, denim or leather jackets. By the mid Eighties, when hooliganism had apparently reached its worst, there were probably far fewer people involved but they had undoubtedly become more clinical.

Not long into the match, the 'Stokie aggro' chant bellowed out from the Boothen End and heads could be seen bobbing up and down, up to no good, on the corner of the Butler Street Paddock near the away end. Stoke unbelievably beat a Liverpool team who were cruising to yet another title. The atmosphere was superb and, with Stoke about fifteen minutes away from a momentous victory, the Boothen Paddock was start-ing to party. On the Boothen End side of the tunnel the metal lattice fence was bending as the whole terracing tried to scale it at once. No-one got over, as a line of police dog handlers was waiting to savage the first encroacher. The youngster decided that was the place to be and rushed out of the big exit gates at the bottom corner of the Boothen. He got into Boothen Road only to discover the gates to the paddock still locked. The street was empty but for two other characters also waiting for them to open.

One of these was a tall guy with permed hair. He had a Head bag over his shoulder with the handles of several bats protruding from one end. That's how easy it was in the early Eighties; you could roam around foot-ball grounds with a bag full of bats. It wasn't until later that the youngster found out that this was the legendary Jasper. The guy with Jasper, who was wearing a purple, blue and silver hooped Ellesse bubble coat and a pair of those brown Adidas golfing shoes, was from Stafford and knew the youngster. 'What the fuck are you doing here?' he asked the youngster. He was too hyped up to wait for a reply and vanity took precedence over concern: 'Did ye see us kickin' it off in the Butler?' It came as no surprise that this pair were responsible for the aggro during the match; they didn't call this particular lad Mad Shaun for nothing. Within an hour, Shaun had been arrested for decking one of Liverpool's lads outside the Roebuck pub. He was only sixteen.

It wasn't just antics such as these that secured him the sobriquet Mad Shaun — that and 'Virgil', owing to an uncanny resemblance to the *Thunderbirds* character. Shaun was a little different. He was not only a hooligan but an artist, reflecting the interesting types the scene attracted in the early Eighties. Violence is, after all, a powerful form of expression. Back then hooligans were setting fashion trends and ushering in the foreign labels everybody now takes for granted. At away games Shaun would wander off with a camera, taking pictures of rubbish bins, winos or the pick-and-mix shelves in Blackburn market, to use later in a montage. He would stroll back regally surveying the architecture of the new surroundings away games offered. Back in the pub, he would only drink orange juice. Perhaps it was the colourings and E-numbers in this that drove him so wild, as the lack of Dutch courage certainly wasn't evident when the opposition's firm turned up. After any incident a hyper-active Shaun would be bouncing around and laughing.

One tale about the arty Shaun was when he went round one of the lads' house in Trent Vale and told him he would go out and get a video for them to watch, his treat. On his return the lad was sat in the dark eagerly awaiting the surprise screening. After ten minutes of watching a German conceptualist movie featuring a round dot in the centre of the screen, he made his excuses and went off to bed, leaving Shaun no doubt chuckling to himself. Shaun retired from the football scene back in 1986 and concentrated on doing his own thing. He now has a Masters degree in art, drinks whiskey by the bottle and instead of prowling round football grounds he terrorizes the middle classes of Glasgow.

By the beginning of the 1986 season, the Stafford lads had been augmented by half a dozen from Trent Vale, an area from which most of Stoke's hardcore hooligans came at that time. They jokingly called themselves the TVGC (Trent Vale Game Casuals). From the opening game of the season, it was apparent that these young lads had graduated from watching to trying to get involved. Just like starting term with a new school uniform, they were kitted out in the latest designer clothes by Ciao, Classic Nouveau and Pop 84, worn with baggy jeans, Reebok trainers and baseball caps.

The first game was against newly relegated Birmingham City, a real firm at last after a year starved in Division Two. The bus into Stoke passed the compound behind the away end and the youths on the top deck crammed into any available seat space on that side to see the 100 or so Birmingham already penned in. Then one of them shouted, 'Fucking hell.' At least 100 more were being herded into the enclosure at the gate on the corner, and they were all casuals. That was obviously Birmingham's firm for the day they thought.

They were wrong. As soon as they got off the bus in town, unfamiliar faces were bowling past. They were shrapnel from a rumpus just moments before. Soon there would be little punch-ups between twos and threes going off all over the place as the fragments of this particular Brummie firm tried to make their escape out of town. About fifteen of them fought with an equal number of Stoke by the bus shelters outside Woolworths on London Road and forced shoppers to stop in their tracks. Birmingham were already fleeing when a riot van skidded up. The pavement was littered in wooden sticks that some of the Brummies had been wielding.

Now the police knew Birmingham were in town, it wasn't long before it seemed they had rounded them all up, though not before several more mini brawls. For about half an hour peace reigned and Stoke's lads retired to the pubs, while about a dozen Under-Fives had congregated on London Road. Half were inside the Wrights pie shop when they noticed a mob of about fifty lads, many dressed in dungarees, come out of a side street and walk past the Talbot pub, only to disappear up the next street, leaving about ten to carry on diagonally up Penkhull Bank. They headed off to alert the lads drinking in the Talbot, munching their steak pies as they went. Birmingham had evidently already been spotted, as about fifty guys were streaming out of the Talbot. Half were dressed lads, the others drinkers up for a row. One of Stoke's top lads whistled up to the ten Brummies. They turned without hesitation, spreading out across the road and bouncing down the hill. *Lambs to the slaughter*, thought the young-sters, who were now at the front ready to impress, some still munching away. With the numbers stacked so firmly in Stoke's favour, this seemed the perfect initiation, but as the two mobs came within twenty yards of each other, the other forty Brummies appeared from a side street where they had been hiding.

Birmingham had raided a newsagent's backyard and its crates of empty milk bottles. These were augmented with bricks and other weaponry picked up in that derelict part of town. Bats were waved and a few of their black lads, of whom there were many, revealed blades from inside their long coats. Their roar went up – 'Zooloo, Zooloo' – followed by a thun-dering 'Come on' as Birmingham charged down the hill. The milk bottles seemed to be dropping from the clouds, as they could hardly be seen against the grey sky. The young lads had noted such terms as 'military precision' in press reports on hooliganism before, but *air strikes*?

Stoke's firm were confused not only by the shower of the bricks and glass but by the apparition of Stoke's very own 'old man Steptoe' gurning as he led Birmingham's dungaree-wearing mob. Steptoe, although a prominent figure in Stoke's firm, was actually a Birmingham fan. Some people saw his actions that afternoon as treachery but most of the main lads appreciated his use of influence to ensure that Birmingham made contact with Stoke's firm.

The biggest problem for Stoke was that the rash youngsters were at the front and had spread themselves across the street. The main lads could not see the wood for the trees and, of course, the Under-Fives were no longer so game. One panicked as a flare fired from a gun whizzed inches by his face and the others needed no convincing; they turned and ran. This caused the older lads, whose only comprehension was of missiles raining down onto the street, to turn and run as well in the confusion. One of the older Trent Vale lads was livid as he carried on forward alone. He screamed at the firm as they passed him in the opposite direction: 'Fucking stand Stoke.' Then he did a flying kick straight into the chest of a Brummie and, as he came back down, punched him straight in the face. A few other Birmingham had to face the terror of this ferocious suicide casual.

There are no eyewitnesses to anything further as people disappeared into side streets or round cars that had screeched to an emergency brake with bottles crashing on their bonnets. There would have been an eyewitness had he not been knocked unconscious: Bozzeye had been in the Talbot toilets when the 'off' began and, on returning to an empty bar that moments before had been full, popped his head out to see where everybody had gone. Seen through his bottle-bottom glasses, the 100 people rampaging through the street probably looked like pensioners doing there Saturday shopping. This would explain why he never saw the outstretched arm of a Brummie who smashed him over the head with a beer bottle. (But then Bozzeye was more often seen lying on the tarmac than actually walking on it. It was not that he couldn't handle himself; he just had a glass jaw. There was always a five-second delay before it registered that he had been struck. First he would stand straight, staring ahead, and then he would do his 'truffle shuffle': two steps forward, two steps back before falling on his arse, legs in the air.)

Birmingham had brought a massive firm and Stoke were still in Division Two stupor, out of the habit of conjuring up big mobs for home games. However, Stoke spirits were eased a little when the Boothen Road Paddock got to take out its frustration on forty Birmingham who very gamely went into Stoke's lair just before kick off. They got as far as the snack bar. The whole Paddock tried to squeeze into the dark exit tunnels to get at them and when there are so many trying to get involved in such a confined area, it is only those at the front who get to do any fighting. This would not have eased the Brummies' fear as hundreds of drunken Stokies scrambled to get at them. Plastic cups of boiling tea and Bovril flew as fists and feet entwined in the snack-bar twilight. The Brummies put up a respectable fight until the police managed to restore order.

At the corner of Birmingham's end was a large firm of black lads. Some were from Stafford and were old school friends of both Under-Five and N40 lads from the same town. A lot of those on the corner were dancing to music on Walkmans and staring hypnotically at the Paddock instead of the pitch. Occasionally they would run fingers across their throats, indicating what they were going to do to Stoke after the match. The party atmosphere indicated a firm that knows it has got a result and that its numbers are invincible.

Thirty Stoke hung back in the Boothen Paddock snack bar for ten minutes until the crowd had dispersed. They hoped that by the time they had left, the Birmingham lads not on the train would have been let out. They especially wanted an encounter with the Zulus from the Penkhull Bank incident, who this time would be on flat ground and deprived of at least some of the weapons they loved so much. As Stoke passed the compound they walked the walk but were no doubt glad of the metal railings between them and the massive Birmingham mob. In the ground it's difficult to gauge the size of an away firm; even in a sparsely populated away end, a firm never looks as impressive as when on the street. Stoke were now confronted with the enormity of Birmingham's mob. The Under-Fives tagged not far behind and each felt particularly self-conscious as they nervously walked past a line of casuals twenty yards long and half a dozen deep. Stoke's thirty lads, though among the country's finest, looked laughable in comparison with these numbers. The Brummies were not saying anything but smiling insouciantly through the bars.

After about quarter of an hour, a Stoke firm that was continually moved on by the police gave up the ghost and went off to various pubs in the city. All that was left were the youngsters, sat on the steps of a bank waiting for their bus. As is often the case, within minutes of Stoke's mob dispersing forty Birmingham came through the main street. The youngsters were petrified. This was exacerbated by the fact that among this mob were the throat-cutting gesturers from inside the ground. One Walkman-wearing black lad spotted them and made a beeline in their direction, with an evil smile on his face. The youngsters were frozen to the spot with fear and looking imploringly at the solitary police officer conveniently stood in front of them. As Walkman passed the foot of the steps, he winked and laughed before moving on. Once again the youngsters had got away with murder because of their age. It was frustrating enough for them to have to sit and watch these guys bowl straight through town unopposed, especially as an equal number of solid Stoke lads had been right there just five minutes before.

Stoke went some way to settling the score the following August, when the two teams met for the first game of that season at St Andrews. On a day that soared into the eighties, and without the baggage of the youngsters, twenty of Stoke's top lads ran seventy Birmingham under a railway bridge. Stoke realised that although outnumbered they could take advantage of the darkness under the bridge and the acoustics there to make twenty sound like a regiment, and they spread out across the road roaring as they charged.

As they emerged into the daylight, the fleeing Birmingham could be heard shrieking, 'There's only twenty of them.' By then the score had been settled. Stoke have never been caught out by Birmingham since.

The liability of the youngsters was reinforced at Oldham a few weeks after the Birmingham home game. About ten young lads travelled on the train along with about thirty N40. This was an honour for the youngsters, who were still at school, and was their first away game. All went into town on a double-decker bus. Again they felt cocksure and protected with Stoke's firm behind them, and were the first off the bus. Oldham appeared almost immediately. The disadvantage of being downhill was crucial again; some of the youngsters flapped and ran, causing a repeat of the Birmingham episode. Bozzeye and a lad from Trent Vale rescued one Stafford lad from the clutches of ten Oldham boys; the decisive blow coming from a half-ender thrown into an Oldham lad's face, knocking him unconscious.

At the next home game, the irritation of the older lads with the youngsters was tangible, especially as forty of Stoke's best lads had run riot around Oldham the year before. Yet for some reason they put up with it; they were a firm with a youth policy.

Stoke did manage to secure one good result around this time. At a home match with Millwall, fifteen of Stoke's top lads stayed behind in Charlie Brown's for last orders and so did not arrive at the ground until ten minutes in. Outside the gates to the enclosure behind the away end is a fork in the road, and on this fork sat a burger van where the lads often congregated before and after matches. With the walk down to the ground and all that beer, everybody had an appetite, so each took a minute to themselves to wolf down the only bit of food they might see that grey, drizzly afternoon.

The streets were desertd but for a couple of police on the corner by the Victoria pub. The roaring and clapping of the crowd in the ground seemed surreal on the empty street; there was a hallucinatory quality to it. Suddenly, as if scripted, a minibus appeared from off set. It was Millwall. People deliberately looked away from the van, which had now slowed down so that its cargo could have a good look at Stoke as they passed. The Stoke lads were talking through the corners of their mouths and trying not to be seen moving their lips: 'Don't look at the van. Make 'em think we've shit it.' Sure enough, the van parked up a little further down the road and about fifteen Millwall bounced confidently across to the burger van. It was equal numbers, as good as.

These are the situations football hooligans love. Forget stories about

500 of us and 700 of them; all that happens in those situations is chaos as the hangers-on start running at the slightest thing and the lads that do want to fight feel unsure about all those people round them who they don't know. If you want to run around making a noise then 500 is great, but if you want to get stuck in then situations like this are what it's all about, with nobody to get in the way, just two consenting firms going for it. That's the ethos of the Naughty Forty, a regular thirty to sixty lads all bonded through shared experiences and a cumulative trust. It is no good going into one of the most dangerous situations of your life with some bloke you've never met before.

Millwall bounced across and Stoke roared straight into them. Millwall's confidence instantly ebbed. Firstly, they had underestimated Stoke, and secondly, Stoke had a weapon that was physically devastating to one of Millwall's firm and psychologically devastating to the rest. His name was Miffer. Miffer was six foot tall and the width of two men. He charged in and punched the most distinguishable member of the Millwall crew, a well-built black guy of about six foot three. The guy was staggering all over the road until he found sanctuary with the two coppers outside the Victoria. They had to stand either side, holding him up by the arms, to prevent him hitting the deck. The ferocity of Stoke's response and the spectacle of their figurehead being disposed of with such apparent ease instilled panic among Millwall, who fled down a nearby terraced street.

Fifteen Under-Fives were in the paddock that afternoon, captivated by the site of Millwall rising out of their seats roaring the 'Lions' on and performing their prolonged and haunting rendition of 'Miiiilll …waalll', the volume of this monstrous drone being out of all proportion to their meagre following.

Fifteen minutes into the game, the crowd in the Paddock began pushing up the terracing towards the exit tunnel and roaring. It was too packed for the youngsters to make headway and many of them climbed up the security fencing at the front to get a view. The surging continued for a couple of minutes until word reached the front: 'They're trying to nick Miffer.' He had been identified from the police control box for the devastating punch he had unleashed outside. It took several policemen to eventually seize him. He was still struggling with them in the segregation area between the Paddock and the away end and the police had to form a line to prevent others storming in to rescue him.

Millwall were regarded as the ultimate test, and away at the Den the previous season Stoke had encountered a south London firm befitting their ferocious reputation. Only twenty or thirty N40 travelled down by train on a January morning. Whilst drinking at the Cockney Pride in Piccadilly the decision was made to abandon the whole adventure, as all agreed it would be suicide to even travel through Bermondsey on a bus with such meagre numbers. The idea now was to salvage the day by enjoying a pub crawl around central London. Shortly after this decision had been made a few Stoke lads who were at this time living in London and several others from cockney clubs but who had associations with Stoke arrived. They were shortly followed by another mob, the Trentham lads. Of course, their arrival reopened the debate on whether or not to travel to south-east London. When twenty older boys who had been at it throughout the Seventies came through the door, all ideas of a day at Madam Tussaud's went out the window and Operation Millwall was back on. With seventy good lads, all of whom had ultimate faith in one another, it was felt they might be able to hold their own.

At about 2.30 Stoke took the tube to Elephant and Castle then very nervously shuffled rather than marched all the way down New Kent and then Old Kent Road, passing the Thomas A'Becket pub. They had miscal-culated the journey time on foot and so didn't arrive at The Den until ten past three. When they arrived a small number of Millwall lads appeared throwing bricks but they soon disappeared. 70 Stoke arrived at a dilapidated ground to find all the turnstiles locked. They rocked the exit gates in an attempt to pull them down and almost succeeded when the police arrived. They were escorted through the back of the main home terracing and into the corner of the away end where they joined about 200 scarf fans. On spotting that Stoke now had a firm in the ground Millwall lads began moving across the side terracing to stand by the fence separating them from the away end. To the Stoke lads that day it seemed that the whole of what could have been no more than a 6,000 gate was all boys. There were hundreds of blokes in black leather jackets giving out cutthroat signs and throwing coins. Some were climbing to the top of the railings to spit towards the Stoke lads.

Stoke were held in the ground for twenty minutes after the game which they won 3-2. This scoreline didn't help matters and bottles being thrown from outside were smashing on the roof above the Stoke fans. The longer Stoke had to wait the more Millwall's tactics of intimidation were taking their toll on everybody's nerves. When the lads were eventually taken out of the ground they were surprised to find the streets empty and eerily quiet. Not far down the road a cockney accent piped up in the middle of the Stoke lads' escort: 'Yer've got a right fackin' firm 'ere, ain't ya? How ya getting' back then?'

A few of the lads replied that they were on the tube, to which he replied, 'Yeah? I think we're gettin the tube too.' Then he disappeared. Seventy Stoke continued to be escorted to New Cross Gate station. It wasn't like the escorts at Stoke where the police keep everybody on the pavement and so Stoke were able to spread out across the street. There wasn't much conversation going on; everybody was anxious and nervously psyching themselves up for an impending attack from Millwall. The only noise in the dark streets was of police dogs barking. These dogs and the police vans were all at the back of the firm and so Stoke would be free to charge if anybody confronted them. Sure enough, at a T-junction on the main road outside the station, up to forty older Millwall came bouncing into the road. One of the Naughty Forty threw a milk bottle then everybody charged. A few punches were exchanged before the Londoners backed off. They seemed a little taken aback at Stoke's appetite. Stoke stayed tightly together and walked slowly towards Millwall when the police, who had been very sloppy until now, waded in. At this point a bloke was walking past with his Staffordshire bull terrier which joined in the spirit of the occasion by attacking a police Alsatian. After a few seconds of snogging one another the Alsatian retreated. This eased the tension a little with people laughing at last and reading the situation as an omen that it was perhaps to be Staffordshire's day after all.

While Stoke were held on the platform a big mob of Millwall could be heard charging in the street outside as they tried to get into the station. Once the police had finally pushed Stoke onto a train, which runs over ground this far out of central London, everybody began relaxing a little and were evidently relieved they had come away from Millwall unscathed. How were they to know fifty Millwall had managed to sneak onto the carriage at the back of the train. At Tower Bridge Stoke got off the train as they only had a couple of police escorting them. A massive roar erupted behind as fifty Millwall charged down the platform. For a few minutes it went crazy with a toe to toe, blow for blow battle. Backing Millwall off at New Cross Gate had only served to rile them. It was a freezing day and Stoke were a little unnerved at the sight of a bloke at the front of Millwall's mob with nothing but a white shirt on. For this alone he deserved the accolade of either the gamest or stupidest man in England, but he had to go three further in making this point. Three times he was knocked on his arse only to bounce straight up and back into Stoke wearing a snarling face. At one point they were getting the better of Stoke until a lad at the front led by example and everyone again piled into Millwall.

Eventually a large number of police stormed down the stairs onto the platform and split the two mobs up. This was only a temporary deterrent to Millwall though, as it was only a few moments before they were charging through the police to get at Stoke. The police had to be quite severe in the end to force them back on the train. In tandem with this the police drove a large number of Stoke's mob up the stairs and out of Tower Bridge station. Whilst they were going up the stairs one of Millwall's lads was shouting from the train, 'Yer good Stoke, yer facking good.' About thirty Stoke managed to get back onto the train before the doors shut. As the two mobs bounced out of their respective carriages at the next stop it was apparent that Millwall's numbers had diminished as well. Again they flew into one another. This ruck would last only as long as it takes for a tube train to board its passengers, then both firms were scrambling through the electric doors into their carriages at either end of the train before they shut. None of the Stoke contingent wanted to be stranded in this part of London, especially with Millwall lads of this calibre knocking about. As the home team Millwall definitely had the advantage as Stoke were having to keep one eye on the doors all the time while they were fighting. The fact that Millwall didn't have that concern was reflected in their numbers, which got smaller at every subsequent stop. It's certainly doubtful that they were getting scared as those who were left seemed to become more aggressive the more their numbers declined. At every stop on the way into central London 30 Stoke and an ever decreasing number of Millwall got off to continue their battle for the 30 seconds it took before the train left again. The dozen Millwall who were left in the final confrontation were just as rabid as when they'd been fifty strong.

A couple of weeks later, one of the Naughty Forty was back in London on a shopping trip with his girlfriend. As they arrived on the concourse at Euston, he saw to his horror hundreds of Millwall boys about to board trains for a fourth-round cup match at Aston Villa. It soon became apparent that all those he had been rowing with on the tube from hell were at the heart of this gathering. His girlfriend, who wanted to catch the bargains at the sales, impatiently tugged his arm to extricate him from the *Woman's Health* magazine he was suddenly pretending to read in John Menzies. He had believed that the most frightening day of his life was behind him; now it seemed it was going to haunt him forever. Still, none of this stopped him returning to Millwall with Stoke on future occasions.

Portsmouth away in August 1985 had been where the N40 got their name, and our home game against them at the latter end of that season was eagerly awaited. Pompey had been certainties for promotion for the second season in a row but floundered in the final weeks. The home fixture was pencilled in for March but the Stoke team went down with the flu, and by the time it took place, on a Tuesday night in mid-April, Portsmouth had slumped and their following had been depleted.

They brought about forty lads up to Stoke. Put in the ground early, they could be seen from outside standing in the windows of the Stoke End snack bar. The sight of them tantalized Stoke's firm as a budgie would a cat. Now, Stoke City were as generous with their facilities as they were with points. With the money accumulated from successes in the 1970s, they had built an impressive new stand behind the north goal – and then allocated it to away supporters. They even named it the Stoke End, bafflingly. Stoke fans were allowed to sit in the seats above the terracing, and if the away supporters did not fill the end, then Stoke fans would sit to the east and away supporters to the west. It was not unusual for Stokies with spare complimentary tickets for the Stoke End to sell them outside for as little as £1.

On this occasion it was necessary to have a ticket to access the Stoke End seats. Forty of our boys solicited every passing fan for Stoke End tickets so as to get a pop at the smug-looking Pompey in the windows. About half secured tickets with ease, causing those without to become even more rabid. About six of the youngsters had managed to purchase these tickets whilst some of Stoke's top boys were deprived. The youngsters were reluctant to part with them. They wanted to go up and watch as much as the lads wanted to go in and fight. It wouldn't be a situation you would be able to see from other parts of the ground as everybody knew the action would take place at half time down in the snack bar. The matey tone towards the youngsters evolved into lucrative offers of a fiver for a ticket that would have cost them no more than a pound. Finally the older lads were getting angry:

'What the fuck are you gonna do up there? Give us your fucking ticket.'

The youngsters had to surrender their tickets and mooch miserably round to the Boothen Road Paddock. They spent the whole game staring up at the Stoke End seats. Half time was agonizing for them as they strained their ears in case the roar could be heard rising out of the exit tunnels from the Stoke End snack bar. As it happened the heavy police presence in the Stoke End prevented any aggro that night.

Now though, on a blistering September day, Pompey arrived and were more proactive. Before the game they caused some nuisance using CS gas in minor scuffles. Stoke were well aware of their presence. Stoke City had been performing as badly as usual and as a result most of the lads didn't even bother with the game. Many made the most of the weather and lay in a park drinking cans of beer and bottles of vodka they had stolen from an off-licence.

After the game, Stoke town was deserted of lads. The youngsters had heard tales about the gassings and could not believe Stoke had decided to give up and go home. Suddenly, about thirty unfamiliar blokes came up the main street towards the Talbot and Bull and Bush pubs. They were shouting in loud Hampshire accents and making their presence known. They looked more like beer monsters than casuals and had the faces of brawlers, with broken noses and lumps of scar tissue. About half a dozen youngsters were in the street; the rest were inside the Silver Coin amusement arcade playing the machines. Those that were on the street froze. Out of a side street several big Stokies appeared, guys in there mid to late twenties. They were immediately trading punches with those at the front of the Pompey mob. One of the Portsmouth blokes ran into the biggest of the Stokies and struck him with a plank of wood. The Stoke lad absorbed the impact before chucking a punch that made the young spectators across the road flinch. The recipient's head flew back and his legs wobbled before his huge weight crashed onto the pavement.

There was no roaring as such, just the predictable shouts of 'Come on' or 'Let's have it'. There was no roar that is until the bookies on the corner suddenly emptied. Thirty of Stoke's main lads had been hiding there behind the frosted glass expecting Pompey to come this way. Both mobs flew into one another. There were brawls going on all over the street like in a cowboy movie as more Pompey and Stoke arrived. It was real violence, no weapons just fists, and there was no place for prancing youngsters. All they could do was look at one another. *Fuckin' hell.*

The melee parted as a riot van accelerated into it. After the van had passed it was like the changing of partners at a ball. Everybody resumed rucking, only with different opponents. The initial dispersal had widened the fighting area. As far as the eye could see, people were launching flying kicks whilst others were doubled up throwing handbag punches as their T-shirts were pulled over their heads. By now there were new duels with lads struggling to escape arrest and police running in all directions looking for anybody to hit with their truncheons. When the riot van U-turned and sped back through the street, a policeman smashed a Stoke lad's head into the side as it passed.

By now the sound of iron on tarmac was getting louder as two police horses galloped into the brawl. Even these only parted the rowing temporarily. Eventually the police managed to control the situation by which time everybody must have been exhausted. As the police escorted

Portsmouth off down Liverpool Road there seemed to be at least twice as many as the initial thirty, and these additions were all casuals.

By November, Stoke City were performing so badly that the home game with Derby attracted a gate of only 12,000. Four thousand of these were Derby; four thousand people you would never have known existed until you got into the ground, so invisible was Derby's firm that day. It was another of those occasions where Stoke's boys were hustling for Stoke End tickets outside. Derby filled about 1,500 of the seats available and Stoke's fifty or so lads sat to the east of them with about 1,000 other Stoke fans.

The Boothen Paddock was packed nearest the away end. Half a dozen police had gone into the crowd here to remove somebody. The youngsters had heard tales of momentous battles between Stoke fans and police, but until now they had remained only myths. Today though was to be a flashback to the Victoria Ground's infamous past. The crowd surged onto the officers. The Boothen chanted the obligatory, 'Paddock, Paddock, sort 'em out.' About fifteen reinforcements came running in through the segregation from the police station on the corner. The battle went on for about ten minutes and only stopped when Derby scored. It was not the goal itself that distracted the Paddock but the spectacle of rowing in the Stoke End seats, again not witnessed for a year or two.

Though Derby had been invisible all day they had secreted themselves amongst the Stoke section of seats. As soon as they rose to celebrate the goal it went off. It was a drizzly, misty day and the floodlights were on. The Stoke End seats seemed dark and shadowy, like looking into a cave lit only by exit signs and the yellow jackets of stewards and police. These jackets disappeared behind seats as they fell trying to restore order amongst boxing silhouettes.

The fighting continued throughout half-time, with rain now driving diagonally against the twilight of the Stoke End Stand. The announcements on the Tannoy system were a bizarre accompaniment to the violence: 'And today's City club draw prize-winner is Mrs Kate Allen from Abbey Hulton. Congratulations Kate,' as injured blokes were being helped down the gangways by stewards; 'Tickets for Wednesday's game are available at the Boothen Road office...,' as the dog handlers charged across a section of seats. By the second half peace had been restored. Stoke lost 2–0 and were near the bottom of the table.

Proceedings at the away match in April were similar apart from fifty Stoke running Derby outside the ground on the corner of the away end.

Stoke returned the compliment from the Victoria Ground with about a dozen lads sat in Derby's Poplar Stand. With a similar number of Derby a cheering Baseball Ground was treated to five minutes of rucking in an otherwise empty section of seating near the away end. The seating was steep, with most of the action taking place in the gangway and an occasional body rolling down the steps. Ultimately it was a complete mish-mash of arms and legs at the face of the exit tunnel before the police arrived and arrested the Stoke lads. The incident was even reported on *Grandstand*.

By February of 1987 Stoke City were on an unusually good run of form. Automatic promotion to the top flight seemed almost assured. Stoke had to play two mid-week FA Cup replays, both at home, against Grimsby. They drew the first before finally beating Grimsby 6-0. This earned them the right to play Division Three Cardiff City at the Victoria Ground on the Saturday in the fourth round.

A big firm turned out in sunshine more associated with late April. When a team is doing well you automatically get big firms, because hooligans are football fans as well, let's not forget, and the idea of meeting Cardiff's Soul Crew was especially attractive. They were in vogue at this time amongst the hooligan aficionados, partly because hooliganism among the big teams in the top flight had been largely suppressed by the police and it only seemed to be bigger clubs in the less well-policed lower leagues that found the freedom to maraud in a way worthy of the papers. Cardiff and Wolves seemed to be chief amongst these. Cardiff brought about 2,000 supporters to the Victoria Ground though none among that number made any attempt to engage Stoke's couple of hundred lads.

Now that the team was doing well, Stoke fans had started to become a little arrogant and were convinced that beating a Third Division team was a formality. Of course, pessimism is never far from the surface when you have a miserable history and everybody was devastated when Cardiff took the lead. In those days the FA Cup was still the most important thing in the world, especially when it was your only hope of playing a top club. When Stoke eventually scored their second and winning goal, the party was back on.

The lads, who stood in the more sparsely populated Butler Street Paddock for this encounter, celebrated by doing pile-ons on top of one another, like primary school kids. One had fallen in the surge toward the fencing and was being mock-kicked and stamped upon. This was a ruse to coax the police in. The law seemed apprehensive to get bogged down in the Butler Street where it was obvious that there was a thin line between high spirits and riotous behaviour. So many of the usual suspects unusually turning up in the Butler Street had thrown the police. Their attentions were now divided between here and the always volatile Boothen Paddock. Indeed, there had already been scuffles between fans and police over there and this meant the police could probably not afford to commit resources elsewhere. The sight of the Butler Street erupting would inevitably have excited the Boothen to do the same.

The firm had stood in the Butler Street Paddock for this game in the hope of storming the Cardiff end. Such a scheme would have been impossible from the Boothen Paddock with the police control box in between. Indeed, just before kick off Stoke had charged into the section of segregation and past two poor stewards who had no choice but to let them through the gate and into the Cardiff end. The Cardiff fans congregated in the centre, behind the goal, made no moves to confront Stoke. The police had already been galvanized by the sight of Stoke breaching the segregation and so managed to intercept them before they got beyond the corner of the away terracing. Things passed off peacefully that day, though it may have been a different matter had Stoke lost.

The game was merely a footnote to the momentous events to follow that Saturday night. Stoke's mob went into Hanley drinking, and by closing time most had either gone home or on to nightclubs, leaving about a dozen handy lads in Leadbelly's. Rumour had it that two coachloads of Coventry City lads were drinking in pubs near the bus station; Coventry were on their way back from Old Trafford, where they had knocked Man Utd out of the cup. Having the nerve to drink in Hanley was bad enough but knocking Man Utd out of the cup whilst Stoke were still in it was even more offensive. Half the allure of the cup for the Stoke fans was the prospect of drawing Man Utd.

Stoke could easily have ignored the interlopers but these particular characters positively thrived on such situations. As they left Leadbelly's, they spotted half a dozen Coventry on a street corner. Stoke bounced across the street and Coventry were off. About six Stoke chased them until they were reunited with approximately 100 others. The other six Stoke jogged up to join the first. As Coventry's mob came forward Stoke huddled in a taxi rank psyching one another up, spittle flying as they clenched fists to one another.

'Who are we? We're Stoke City.'

'Come on.'

'Let's get it together.'

They spread out in a line across the street and ran towards Coventry.

Every Stoke man was fighting for his life and almost as soon as they ran in for their first flurry of punches they had to start backing off. The weight of numbers rolled over them like a giant boulder and one of them had no choice but to spray a canister of CS gas across the line of Coventry. Stoke backed off from its effects, though some could not extricate themselves from the scuffles and suffered along with Coventry.

Coventry were now in confusion as Stoke kept running in to hit a few before backing off again. One Stoke lad was knocked over by a taxi but managed to scrape himself up and continue with the mayhem. Another person who was evidently in pain and hobbling in and out of the ruck was the lad who had been used as a beanbag in the Butler Street Paddock earlier. This was Cockney Darren. He moaned for weeks after about the injuries he sustained.

Two police officers had arrived almost immediately and had drawn their truncheons, only to have them snatched by two of Stoke's more audacious characters, who used them to back off Coventry. It took about thirty police to restore order and a dozen or so were arrested, including five Stoke. Although two vans were used to transport the prisoners to Hanley station there were characters from both cities in each. They all had their hands cuffed in front of them. One of the Stoke lads had a large block of draw in his jeans pocket, and asked the Coventry lad next to him if he would do the decent thing and reach into that pocket to dispose of it. This he did with great dexterity, dropping the draw beneath a seat. When the Stoke lad got to hand over his belongings at the charge desk, he discovered that the Coventry fan had rather less honourably but just as dexterously taken £40 out of his pocket too.

Another person in for a shock at the station was the lad who had been hit by the taxi. The police were adamant he had discharged the CS gas and confiscated all his clothing for forensic examination before bailing him. He had no spare cash for a taxi and had to walk home through Stoke the next morning in a white paper suit.

News of the ruck travelled around the city, so by the fifth-round draw on Monday dinner-time everyone was delighted to hear Coventry City's name drawn out of the hat. But the anticipated sequel to Hanley never materialized. Coventry brought 8,000 of a 31,000 sellout crowd, and short of creating a spectacle of song and colour inside the ground that was a privilege to behold, no-one would have known they were in the city. Stoke did succeed in steaming the away end again from the Butler Street. One bloke fell over while breaching the segregation gate and was trampled over by the bloodthirsty mob. After the police pushed Stoke back he was treated for a broken leg in a tiny bit of segregation between the two sets of fans. When you are injured like that, all you want is painkillers and peace, not 8,000 unsympathetic Coventry fans singing abuse as you are stretchered off behind the goal in front of them.

Because of the big crowd there were more police on duty and so available to deal with both paddocks simultaneously. They had to as well. About twenty minutes into the game both paddocks were surging backwards and forwards, upwards and downwards. Police helmets were swallowed up by the crowd as their owners fell to the concrete. The whole ground cheered every time a trophy helmet was lobbed over the fence and bounced along the asphalt at the pitch's edge. The Coventry fans were really getting into the spirit of things. They were alternately chanting, 'Go on Stoke, go on Stoke, go on Stoke, go on Stoke,' and echoing the Boothen End.

In those days the gap between top-flight and on-form football teams in the old Division Two was not that wide and so once you reached the fifth round of the cup everybody thought that it was their year. As it transpired it was Coventry's name on the cup and but for a tricky third round clash with Third Division Bolton they won it in style too. After that every tie was away from home and they disposed of a tissue of on-form teams: Man Utd; Stoke; Sheffield Wednesday; Leeds and Tottenham in a classic final. Having said that, Stoke, who generally rise to big occasions, can feel aggrieved at their 1–0 defeat. They arguably should have had two penalties, one of which was a blatant foul. On top of this there was a ball running across an unguarded Coventry goal line that just couldn`t be reached by centimetres and a header just past the post in the dying minutes that had the whole ground, including Coventry fans, convinced had gone in. Mickey Ginn, Coventry's moustachioed super sub, was the man who inflicted the devastating blow on Stoke midway through the second half. This game was probably the biggest occasion at the Victoria Ground in at least the last quarter of a century.

There is nothing worse than watching another team's supporters celebrating as they continue on the road to Wembley, leaving you behind. That was possibly the only occasion that Stoke fans, lads included, could be seen with tears of frustration and jealousy in their eyes, as 8,000 Coventry fans stood in a bank of sky blue hats, banners and balloons to sing the Sky Blues' anthem. It was a spectacular sight. Of course, when they sang *Que Sera, Sera*, it was not just maintaining protocol for the cup; you could tell they believed it. There is a powerful aura that emanates from football fans carried along by the momentum of destiny. As for Stoke City? Well, they had already seen a fifteen-match unbeaten run end the week before at the Hawthorns when West Brom put four past them.

This was to continue, with Stoke ending the season somewhere around mid-table. The Coventry game saw the end of the best period Stoke City had until Lou Macari took them to the play-offs for the Premiership in 1996.

The following pre-season, 1987/88, the youngsters, still in their mid-teens, were about fifteen in number when, on a rainy Friday night before a pre-season friendly at home to Derby County, a dozen strangers appeared in town. They were in the same spot where the youngsters had been accosted on their first visit against Millwall. The initial reaction was that these lads were Derby and everyone was buzzing at the thought of a row with lads of their own age, so they took it to them. It transpired that they were not Derby but local lads from Newcastle, down in Stoke to settle a score with the Trent Vale youths, some of whom were in the Under-Fives number that night. A couple of the Stafford lads went over and began to calm the situation down, suggesting that they should all get together on a match day and, although they may have had issues with the Trent Vale lads in the past, they could see the potential.

By the time Stoke played their first home game that season, against Middlesbrough, there were about twenty lads in town from Newcastle, the same number from Stafford and Trent Vale and another twenty from other parts of the City. Some Asians had just opened Hustlers, a pool hall on the first floor of an old building overlooking a junction that away supporters had to cross from the station to the ground. This was to be the headquarters of Stoke's Under-Fives, many of whom could not get served in the pubs. (Everybody tried to get served in Charlie Browns, which was Stoke's main pub, but all failed except, ironically, the smallest and youngest looking member of the group. He had just been drinking coke in a café and was still chewing on ice cubes when he entered the bar. The landlord adhered to the formalities and asked, 'Are you eighteen?' The youngster replied, 'Ice cubes.' He had thought that the landlord had asked what he was eating. This totally fazed the landlord, who served him a pint of lager as fast as he could to get away from the little nutcase.) From the outside, Hustlers looked derelict, but behind its blacked-out windows would always be about twenty lads, chatting on the window sill, their eyes scanning the street.

By coincidence, on the day that the Under-Fives finally became a mob that could be taken seriously for its numbers, even establishing their own haunt, fifty Middlesbrough appeared. They crossed the junction tentatively, pushing up close to one another for some security, their heads swivelling in all directions looking for danger. Their mistake was that they were only looking at eye level. How were they to know that sixty eager Under-Fives had spotted them from the first floor of a ramshackle building less than twenty yards away. The Middlesbrough firm were dressed in baggy jeans, moccasins and brightly coloured T-shirts. They all looked mid twenties to mid thirties. A fair few moustaches and curly mullets amongst them as well as the archetypal pie men.

As the Boro lads crossed the junction and out of sight the Under-Fives piled out down the stairs with the swagger of seasoned campaigners. They were no doubt full of confidence that their experience of inter-estate, teenage gang warfare, could easily be translated to inter-city football hooliganism. Some of the lads caught one another's gloating, dilated eyes and smiled. It was a tacit acknowledgement to one another: *At last. We've got our own firm.*

The entrance to Hustlers was on an adjoining side street. The sixty or so Under-Fives scrambled round the back of the building and across a small gravel car park at the rear, just off the street where Boro's lads had passed. The Under-Fives caught a view of the backs of their firm as they passed the entrance to the car park. As the Under-Fives bounced round the corner, they were no more than ten feet behind the Boro, who were now spread out in the street. Their north-eastern accents were audible. There was lots of laughter amongst them. They were oblivious to the mob that had suddenly appeared like a shark's fin out of water behind them. None of the youngsters needed any prompting. In unison, as if by instinct, the roar went up: 'Come on!'

Before even a foot had made a forward motion amongst the Under-Fives, the Boro mob were gone. The terror of being hit like that just when they were complacently laughing and joking must have been enormous. Instead of continuing towards the ground they bolted off west up a side street. This street bends to such a degree that neither mob could actually see the other for those important first three seconds. As far as Boro were concerned, there could have been 1,000 blade-wielding maniacs pursuing them.

So it seemed like the Under-Fives' inaugural battle was won and against proper hooligans as well. Won, that was, until one of Boro's pie men at the back of the firm lost his footing. Scrambling to his feet, he caught a glimpse of the Under-Fives and ran to catch up with his compadres who were spread out across the road, running for their lives. 'They're only bairns,' he shouted. 'Stand Boro, they're only fuckin' bairns.' Boro stopped running. They turned and faced the Under-Fives about forty feet away. Both mobs seemed completely flummoxed at first and the Under-Fives' confidence quickly drained. It was like the local pub team playing Brazil and scoring in the opening minute. Now for the hard work.

Boro were evidently still shaken from their ordeal. They seemed aimless for ten seconds, arguing with one another until a few collected themselves and bounced towards the Under-Fives. Of course, it only took one or two youths to back off to enthuse the Boro lads. They charged roaring down the street at the Under-Fives, who duly scarpered. The Under-Fives did regroup and have another go back but the age difference was a determining factor. None of the teenagers was psychotic enough to tangle with a moustachioed, mulleted Boro monster in his mid-thirties.

Down by the ground Boro ran into a heavily outnumbered Naughty Forty. Stoke stood their ground until reinforcements arrived. Though still outnumbered Stoke had a worried-looking Boro backing off.

Any West Ham fans reading this account may understandably be fuming at the acquisition of one of their gang names, the Under-Fives, which originally referred to their younger element. The assumption of this name was not a deliberate theft. The older lads had jokingly acknowledged the youngsters as such from day one. The likes of Miffer would walk past the youngsters and wink, 'Ay up, Under-Fives.' West Ham have long been a benchmark by which other teams compare themselves and so the youngsters of most teams are defined as Under-Fives, in the same way as all vacuum cleaners are known as Hoovers. Stoke's youngsters, however, actually ended up calling their firm the Under-Fives, though they did try to differentiate themselves around 1988 with the tag UFAS (Under-Fives Action Service). They even had their own song, customising the chant of German hooligans during the 1988 European Championships – 'Deutschland! Hooligan! Deutschland! Hooligan!' – so that it became, 'UFAS! Hooligan! UFAS! Hooligan!' It was quite an eerie sound when it went off but in spite of this, the original term stuck. People in Staffordshire who knew nothing about hooligan culture also got to know this gang of youths as the Under-Fives. It gained its own momentum.

chapter thirteen

Big Boys?

T'WO MONTHS LATER, newly-relegated Aston Villa visited. Hustlers was a busy place that afternoon. Again rival casuals were spotted from the window and again the Under-Fives took them by surprise. Forty Villa lads backed off until they realised that these were kids, not Stoke's proper firm, but within forty yards of being steamed from a side street by the Under-Fives, they had to endure a potentially worse attack from the opposite side of the road as Stoke's main firm roared out of Charlie Brown's. The main firm had been tipped off by the Under-Fives, who realised they were out of their depth. Luckily for the Villa lads, a riot van skidded up, dog handlers arrived and Stoke were forced up between the market and a Woolworths store; Stoke market was the most popular bolthole for lads trying to shrug off the police.

The Under-Fives were then treated to some classic slapstick. About thirty youngsters were hanging around in the main street outside Hustlers when, on the opposite pavement, a solitary youth came speed-walking out of town, his eyes fixed straight ahead. Everybody looked in his direction. *Was he a Villa lad split from the mob or just an eccentric?* His ears must have had eyes in them. Suddenly his speed walk became a sprint. There was no danger that anybody would be too sadistic to this loner but his sprint was retarded by people running across the road and drop-kicking him as he went. He kept bouncing off Bourne Sports' elastic windows then zig-zagging like a rugby player with the ball before being bounced off the glass by yet another kick.

Among this mob was a character called Bakes. Now Bakes was never noted for his appetite for aggro; in fact, he was a notorious runner. After one ruck in a pub, the landlord found him upstairs hiding in the living quarters. Despite this, he was a true football lad by virtue of his lifestyle and outrageous antics; vandalism, scally behaviour and a merciless sense of humour were his *forte*. Bakes, an even skinnier version of West Ham manager Glenn Roeder, is also one of England's finest actors; with the latest clothes and choreographed swagger, anybody who didn't know him well would be convinced he was a rough lad. In the wake of each running episode, he would have the piss taken out of him all the way home, either on the double decker back to Stafford or on the train from away games. On leaving the lads, he would always bitterly state, 'We'll see. Next week. We'll see.'

Seeing the defenceless Villa loner, Bakes seized the moment. *Was everybody going to see? Was this the week?* He sprinted off after the Villa lad. 'Go on Bakes!' went the roar. Everyone was howling. People could be heard shouting up towards Hustlers windows, 'Quick, come and have a look at this.' It got better. When Bakes finally caught up with the Villa lad, outside a cheap boutique, he struck a punch to the side of his head. The Villa lad now had a twenty-yard breathing space between himself and the giggling Under-Fives and instead of carrying on running, he turned and steamed into Bakes. They were like a pair of mating octopuses as they fell into a display trolley of dresses on the pavement. The trolley began rolling down the pavement, dresses billowing, as the pair wrestled. The Villa lad re-emerged and ran off. Bakes, who everyone presumed must have been unconscious amongst the dresses, emerged a few moments later, when he was sure his foe was gone. He did not have even the dignity of saying he hadn't run, as an angry woman came from the shop and chased him up the street, shouting, 'Yer little wanker.'

The most outrageous incident of the afternoon was twenty Stoke standing up to around 200 Villa. A few Under-Fives had been drinking cans of beer in the back streets when they spotted the huge Villa firm heading up Liverpool Road from the Star and Phoenix pubs. The Under-Fives then ran into about a dozen older lads who they implored to wait for reinforcements. They didn't even afford the youngsters the grace of an audience but bowled into Liverpool Road, spread out and waited for Villa to come on to them. The youngsters felt obliged to go along with them. It seemed as though the street was a conveyor belt beneath the Stoke lads' feet, only they were walking in the wrong direction. The tunnel of terraced houses and pubs became narrower as Villa's mob rushed towards them as if down the zoom lens of a camera. Eyes couldn't accommodate all the angles of danger. There were a hundred coming head-on, another fifty coming from left and right and all pushing against one another as they squeezed around parked cars to get onto the road. It was like a nightmare with evil spirits coming out of the walls.

As the line at the front of this mob halted to bounce and clap their hands, the momentum of those behind drove them into Stoke, whether they wanted to know or not. Broken glass ricocheted behind Stoke's meagre numbers as flying Newcastle Brown bottles over-reached their targets. For a second the lads were aware of the pool cues, half-broken bottles and ashtrays but as the mob rushed onto them, their vistas narrowed until each was staring into the eyes of just one rival. Though they could see only one pair of eyes, they felt the blows and kicks of many more as they became submerged.

The average lad often sees his fearful self reflected in his adversary. Dilated pupils stare back. Many a times there is a tacit pact made and the two will pass one another by or back off from each other. Others, however, are seeing people off with one devastating punch. Others, not as effective but equally as game, are trading blow for blow. Lads who get bogged down in these situations become the victims of hyena packs, and this is where lads with wider vision become invaluable. Those who are bouncing but not necessarily getting stuck in succeed in bluffing and pre-occupying the hyenas, thus preventing the game lads from getting really bad beatings. One of Stoke's top boys suffered one of these hyena attacks. A youngster who was understandably moving away from the affray saw him on the floor with three Villa laying into him. The youngster felt obliged to try to help and put his head down and ran back up the street. By the time he looked up again, two of the Villa were crawling by their fingernails up the Stokie's jeans while he pummelled the one still just about on his feet.

One Stafford Under-Five, just turned sixteen, had actually entered the mob of the big hitters and had run in ahead of everybody else. He decked a lad but was then swallowed up by Villa's mob. As they pushed forward he was lost from sight. This was what inspired the heroics from many of Stoke's lads that day. To rescue the youngster, they had to battle into the thick of Villa's firm. Those in the rescue party arrived just in time to prevent him from being thrown through a window. The lad later recalled being bounced off the window three times and hearing Birmingham accents shouting, 'Kill him.' One of those that dragged him to safety had to kick the glass door of a shop through in order to alert the frightened owner and get the unconscious lad to safety. He was eventually taken to North Staffs General Hospital in an ambulance.

As if the situation was not bad enough, another mob of Villa came from behind. They had been drinking in the Bull and Bush. Luckily about thirty Stoke lads from the Talbot were on their way and intercepted them. These two mobs had a square go in a separate ruck within twenty yards of the first.

Just as in a football match when a player makes a dummy run and takes a defender out with him, similar things happen in a ruck. In this instance one of the Under-Fives, fifteen years old and a mere bouncer, was sucker-punched. He had bounced off the kerb towards a couple of blokes who backed off and he couldn't believe how easy this hooliganism lark was. But he had been lined up from the side. A pool ball smashed straight into his cheekbone.

By now the police had become involved and a helmet bounced along the gutter. They had previously seemed happy to merely cordon the road off and watch, perhaps wanting to see Stoke's firm take a kicking or simply because they were awaiting reinforcements. One of the lads experienced a freeze-frame moment as he made eye contact with a policeman. The officer took off his helmet and tucked it under his arm before taking giant strides through the battleground in his direction. The lad bolted off believing once out of sight he would be safe. It wasn't to be. This was to be the beginning of a chase up and down hilly terraced streets, down alleyways and across waste ground. At one point he was on the verge of giving in; he was out of breath and so hid in a bush to recuperate. The copper ran past and probably ended up somewhere out of Staffordshire Polices jurisdiction.

Stoke fought Villa to a standstill. Draws under these circumstances are the credentials that really define a firm as significant and it is this quality that most defines Stoke's hooligans. Larger teams turn up at away games with 200 lads and take them to all the wrong places; Stoke turn up with thirty, always make an appearance in town and will stand and fight despite the odds. This was certainly true of Stoke throughout the 1980s and early 90s, though in later years Stoke have become synonymous with larger mobs.

The bottom corner of the Boothen End where the lads now congregated (owing to a membership scheme in other parts of the ground) looked like a scene from a Pink Panther movie after a bomb had exploded: shirts hanging off backs, black eyes, hair standing on end and people so exhausted that they gave up the pretence of outward appearances. The lad who had tried the pool ball for size looked like the Elephant Man by half-time. Throughout the game, older lads would pay visits and fail to contain their laughter at the lump on the side of his face; no doubt it made them feel better about the £80 shirts they had just had ripped or bloodied. The fate of the hospitalised youngster was the main topic of debate, and everyone was relieved to see him, helped along by his older brother, coming into the ground at half-time. He had discharged himself from the hospital, not wanting to miss out on anything, but was obviously concussed and in great pain. Even so, he was able to raise a brief smile at the 'Elephant Man's' face.

After the match it was a balmy tea-time in both senses. It was the day before the clocks went back and so there was about an hour of daylight left. The sun was setting beyond the high rise flats on Penkhull Hill, in the distance a typical autumn mist was developing, muffling the sounds of children playing in its cloak. This may seem a superfluous attention to detail but minds remember or romanticize these things on momentous occasions. The adrenalin motivates all senses and so perceptions become acute. Beneath the flats and the then reddening sky is a steep hill serving as Stoke town's main car park, on London Road. A number of Villa had parked vans here. These vehicles received much of the wrath inspired by the hospitalisation of the youngster and every one identified as a visitor's was smashed to pieces. Bakes helped put the embarrassment of the early afternoon behind him by going for the world record number of wind-screens smashed by one man in five minutes. People down on London Road looked up and cheered as thirty lads rolled a van over. Fifteen blokes were crossing London Road towards the car park. From that distance there was no way Stoke could have identified them as Villa until they stopped dead in their tracks and stared up the hill with open mouths. It was their van! Half of those on the hill all had the same idea at once. Lads instinctively flew down the hill at Villa while the other half were too preoccupied with vandalism. The Villa fled in the direction they had just come from.

Just as before the match, Stoke were now all split up: sixty on a hill smashing up vans; forty down at the bottom laughing at the fleeing Villa; another fifty 100 yards down London Road in the town. This fifty were scattered, pretending to wait for buses or lifts, so as not to be moved on by the police. Others would have just been moving around in groups of half a dozen looking for someone to take revenge on. The worst thing for Stoke was that the police had now arrived on the car park and were chas-ing lads in all directions to make arrests. Just as this was happening the fifteen Villa lads reappeared at the front of another 200 Villa who roared into town. Stoke's disparate cells had no choice but to run. Twenty lads did confront Villa opposite the Wheatseaf pub but managed only a token punch or kick before having to run. Among these twenty were the same stalwarts from Liverpool Road before the game but understandably they had no heart to attempt something so suicidal again.

The Stafford Under-Fives were relieved to be back in the safety of suburbia. On Saturday nights, those who did not have girlfriends would meet up at the local shops and discuss the day's events. About a dozen were present on this occasion when one of the lads went off to see his sweetheart. Five minutes later he was back, with excitement and mischief written on his face. 'You'll never guess lads. Them fucking vans are only parked outside the Crispin.' The lads rushed round to the pub on the A34 to see two Transit vans without a shard of glass in them. They were happy to leave it at that – twelve youths against thirty angry blokes isn't sensible – but when one of the Villa lads came out of the pub to retrieve something, leaning through the void that was once a window, much guffawing emanated from the youths. He turned and shrugged his shoulders, seeing the funny side, until one of the obnoxious brats remarked, 'Hey mate, we're the lads who smashed your vans up on the hill in Stoke.'

'Oh?' said the Brummie, before rushing back to the pub. Half a dozen blokes came out of the pub wearing wry smiles. 'Alright boys?' They were looking forward to this. The kerb was torn up where the youngsters stood so a couple hurled pieces of concrete towards Villa, who at first backed off, but as more lads came out the youngsters ran. One of them taunted Villa by doing a body-pop and moon walk before he ran off. He tried to be doubly clever and, instead of running, hid in a leylandii hedge until the Villa lads had passed. He emerged at the wrong time, just as another group came along.

'Ay up lads, we've got the body-popper.'

Wallop! Blood poured from the youngster's nose. Now he ran. All those in the Crispin must have joined in what was to become a two-hour pursuit of the Under-Fives across an area a mile square. It soon became apparent that most of the cars parked outside the Crispin belonged to Villa fans. The youngsters had to jump hedgerows and run through back gardens. Some even knocked on doors for their safety. Every time the lads settled somewhere they thought was safe, a car would skid up and four or five Villa would jump out. Even in the darkest corner of a field about a mile away from the original incident, car headlights suddenly beamed on the youths as Villa sped and wheel-spun through the mud towards them. Their paranoia was unabated until daylight; all were convinced that every slamming car door or cruising engine outside their homes was the precursor to a firm of furious Villa fans storming into their living rooms.

That Monday the lads were astonished to find that it was not the Saturday mayhem in Stoke making the headlines but their game of hide-and-seek in Stafford. It turned out that the Villa lot had attacked an innocent guy on his way out for the night, had given him a kicking and mugged him as well. A few of the Villa lads had been picked up on a security camera at the local off-licence and at their next home game their victim was taken to Villa park and successfully picked out his attacker from the crowd, courtesy of the CCTV cameras.

Villa away at the end of March could not come fast enough and up to 200 lads got the ten o'clock train at Stoke station. Everyone got off at Stafford for a drink and the Under-Fives could not have been prouder, marching down their town's main street with this army of hooligans. Back at Stafford station, the police tried to split them into two groups. Once half had boarded the train, the police started to shut the doors, leaving the rest on the platform. Those on the train threw punches through the open windows in an attempt to get the police off the door handles, while those on the platform pushed forward. A young policewoman caught between fists on one side and a surging crowd on the other was knocked down. Just as everybody succeeded in rushing onto the train one of her legs slipped between the platform and the carriage. The whistle had already been blown. Luckily she was pulled out just in time.

From Witton Station, the police escorted Stoke to the away end. A few broke away and went hunting along Witton Lane, while forty went on the rampage around Villa Park. Anyone coming out of a pub who looked like a casual was whacked. In one melee a Stoke lad pulled a Stanley knife and was quickly grabbed by a police officer. The Villa fan who had been his target came to his aid by telling the policeman that nothing had gone on. Luckily the Stoke lad had managed to chuck the blade; unluckily he had had a pile of Under-Fives calling cards in his jacket pocket when he was searched. The previous night he had borrowed the cards to show the older lads in a Stoke pub and had forgotten he still had them. He was arrested, along with at least a 100 other Stoke City fans that day.

Most of Stoke's lads sat in the Witton Lane Stand, separated from the Villa fans by a black iron fence and a vacant section. During the game, the Stoke lads rose and charged across the seats in the direction of their own fans in the Trinity Road End. Villa had somehow fired a CS gas canister into the Stoke section. Meanwhile, a couple of fifteen-year-olds, knackered after drinking through the previous night and now trying to get some sleep at the back of the Trinity Road terracing, were confronted by two Villa lads. The Villa boys had been in the away end throughout the game.

'Come on Stoke, let's have it.'

The youngsters looked at one another in horror and declined on three counts: two of Villa's top boys would obviously have battered them; they were absolutely shattered; and (the reason later given to their mates) they were right under the police control box. Once the Villa lads felt they had secured their tiny victory, they could not say enough good things about Stoke. They had actually been among those that had tried to throw the young Under-Five through a window in Stoke. 'Fucking superb' was how they described Stoke's outnumbered stand that day. 'Fair play to your lads, you were fucking mad.' They said Stoke were the only firm to give them any competition in the Second Division that season.

Outside was a tense affair. There were a large number of Villa in Witton Lane and both sets of lads intermingled. The houses along this street were boarded up and the reverberations of a low-hovering helicopter served to heighten the eerie atmosphere. Nobody was speaking. Everyone was watching the guy next to him through the corner of his eye. Stoke seemed concerned about being gassed again and were waiting for an opportunity to re-group. Villa had a big mob of about several hundred in number. They were top of Division Two at the time and cruising towards promotion. On top of this hooliganism was experiencing a post-Heysel renaissance, as shown in the European Championships in Germany that summer.

About thirty Stoke steamed into a big gathering of Villa. There was only enough time for a flurry of punches before the police dogs moved in. Stoke have not played Villa since.

The first encounter with Man City in four years came at Maine Road in September 1987. At 9 a.m., 150 lads were gathered at Stoke station, including forty Under-Fives. One of the older lads was going around the platform asking people if they had £1 to give his mate for the train. Everybody was happy to contribute and it only required a dozen dona-tions, but they did not stop there. Once they had acquired about £100, they disappeared back into Stoke for the weekend of their lives. Meanwhile everyone else boarded and disembarked at Stockport.

When 150 maniacs cram into a pub it is easy for those under-age to mingle in and have a few pints. The management dare not say anything; they just want everyone's money and then to get them out with the mini-mum of hassle. The youngsters had already had a few cans of lager; add to this two or three pints and their share of giant bottles of white wine flying around the pub and you had some pretty pissed teenagers. About fifteen Stockport lads arrived and the young lads, full of drunken bravado, wanted to get into them but it turned out they were familiar with Stoke's mob and even contemplated joining them into Manchester. Stoke planned to get double-decker buses to evade the police but in the end everybody was too pissed to deal with the logistics, so they all swayed back to the railway station.

From the minute the mob piled off at Piccadilly, everybody was expecting to be hit, though the police were everywhere, trying to get Stoke onto coaches. A couple of Under-Fives broke away, as the larger one of the two needed to use a lavatory; in his particular predicament, a wall would never do. Unfortunately his torture was compounded by the arrival of ten Man City before he had a chance to reach his destination. The Under-Fives had no alternative. The smaller of the two bowled straight into them, landing an impressive punch. The two then managed to hold their own as the rest set about them. The bigger of the pair, a red-headed lad, later described the misery of fighting for his life while nursing a turtle's head. This red-headed lad had the physique of an ox and at only thirteen had been the toast of Stoke after getting involved in a ten-on-ten ruck with some Sunderland monsters. He bounced in and walloped one bloke and the guy knew he'd been hit, though the youngster didn't have much of an appetite for taking a punch in return. When the temporarily dazed Mackem struck back, the precocious hooligan disappeared into the darkness. Still, many a main lad would have been tempted to do the same.

The Man City lads ran off once the police arrived and the two youngsters claimed to have been the victims of an attempted mugging. They then had to catch up to Stoke's mob, who had refused to board the coaches. The police were pissed off that they would have to walk two miles escorting a bunch of drunks to Maine Road but they finally waved off the coaches. Then the rain began. It absolutely lashed down as the firm trudged, surrounded by vans and horses, along the dual carriageway to Moss Side. The grey concrete high rises and walkways of the since-demolished Hulme estate looked really intimidating on either side, like something from Eastern Europe. As the mob turned into the terraced streets of Moss Side for the ground, they passed a chip shop with about thirty, mainly black, lads outside. They looked agog at the size of Stoke's firm and seemed ill-prepared. Stoke bowled around Maine Road in small groups but nothing came of it.

Stoke City were in their usual position somewhere in the bottom of the league and the total away following was poor – about 1,000 in the away terracing on the Kippax and another 1,000 in the benches behind the goal. This was where the lads went. Everyone was so pissed and soaked that they stripped to the waist and hung their clothes over the backs of the benches to dry. The boys didn't usually sing; it was beneath them. They just stood looking superior. On this occasion, though, the only way to escape pneumonia was to keep active. They conga-danced, sang, 'Let's all have a disco,' and roared across the end when a small group of Man City jumped up amongst the Stoke scarf fans to celebrate the first of their four goals.

Mostly they spent the game singing, 'You got ran by Millwall, you got ran by Millwall, na na na na.' Testimony to the visit of the Londoners in midweek were eight-inch by four-inch flyers pasted on the benches picturing a lion and some clichéd slogan about what Millwall's mob would do to you. Rumour had it that Millwall had taken a big mob a few days earlier and turned City over. The fact that the Kippax just stared ahead and made no retort may indicate the truth. Apart from ripping up a wooden fence at the back of the away end and trying to get the lawn mower started, that was it for that encounter with Man City. A washout.

That Christmas bank holiday, Man City brought 8,000 to Stoke and there was quite a lot of fighting with City fans making their way from cars and vans on the Michelin car park south of the Victoria Ground. The mounted police, elevated above the throng, flew like spectres in all directions. Confirmation of serious aggro was an ambulance struggling through the crowd, lights flashing. Such a sight always sobers people up temporarily, though there was an amusing element to this occasion: one of Stoke's top lads had had one of his testicles kicked into his stomach ('high-balling' as it is known). Perhaps men find such things amusing only because they are too frightening to confront seriously.

It seemed that having your testicles kicked into your solar plexus was becoming the latest badge of honour. Earlier that morning, another of the main lads had suffered the same fate at the boot of a seven-foot Man City lad in the town centre. Twenty Stoke had been spread out along the pavement outside the Wheatsheaf when forty Man City came walking through town. City were well aware that these twenty were Stoke's boys but didn't seem keen to kick it off; perhaps they were worried that more Stoke would appear and probably they had not expected to run into any opposition at 10 a.m. Anyway they carried on up towards the Bull and Bush, with the Stoke marching after them. City then turned, spread out across the street and bounced towards Stoke, who steamed straight into them. A few of the lads were backing off from the aforementioned seven-footer until one finally laid a few on him but at the expense of his manhood. As he doubled up, Stoke charged past for a final assault and chased the City down Liverpool Road.

After the game, on a dark drizzly tea-time, about 500 frustrated Stoke lads patrolled the town centre. About 200 were dressers, the rest just maniacs who had been at it since the early Seventies. These blokes always turn out whenever Mancs or Scousers come to town. There was a disturbing aura of hatred whenever Mancs came to Stoke and everybody would turn out. As Stoke's mob rounded the bend by the market another mob of about 200 came over the crossroads by the graveyard (scene of the infamous row between Stoke and West Ham already described in this book). Both mobs made a massive roar as they steamed towards one another but it was too good to be true – the other 200 were Stoke as well. Now 700 Stokies from all age groups were marching down to the ground for Man City. Their escort back to the station was due. The police had no choice. They must have sent every horse and vehicle into the mob and at pretty high speeds too. Seven hundred people trying to run down a narrow terraced street in the dark is a panicky affair indeed.

The following season saw Man City visit on Boxing Day. They were top of the old Division Two and their 12,000 following – half of the total gate – reflected this. Because of their huge numbers, some of Man City's lads made the mistake of thinking themselves safe to walk around town in small groups. They weren't. Such as these were being picked off and battered all afternoon. What was most striking about this particular encounter was that Man City were at the height of their inflatable banana fetish and, it being Christmas, thousands had decided to come in fancy dress as well. All that could be seen around the ground were massive yellow bananas floating above the crowds. There were so many Man City that they couldn't queue in the compound behind the Stoke End without hundreds having to wait in Boothen Road and round the Victoria pub on the corner as well. This wasn't a good place to be when a firm of 200 Stoke descended on the ground and charged into the fancy dress party. Those in fancy dress stood and fought and were quickly joined by others but in the end they were backing off into the compound, despite having Superman and the Incredible Hulk with them.

Coachload after coachload of City made their way up Boothen Road and there were running battles all over the place, with the Mancs giving a good account of themselves. Inside the ground, Stoke fans were setting fire to inflatable bananas they had confiscated, and there was plenty of boasting in the bottom corner of the Boothen End, the most memorable being, 'I've just had a fight with a lion outside and won.'

Within a week of the City game, Stoke played Liverpool at the Victoria Ground in the third round of the FA cup. At about 1 p.m., forty Liverpool were hanging about at the bottom of Hill Street on London Road. As about ten of the N40 appeared by the Wheatsheaf, Scouse accents could be heard shouting to one another: 'Here y'are lads. Der here, der fuckin' here.' So occupied were they that they did not notice another dozen appear behind them. Among these was one of the now recovered high-ball victims from the Man City game. They flew straight in at the rear and panicked the Scousers, who ran in all directions into oncoming traffic. The Wheatsheaf ten, augmented now by ten more, steamed the disarrayed Scousers head-on and Liverpool were running down the centre of a busy London Road. Most of them managed to turn left at the right moment and run for the safety of the ground but an unfortunate dozen or so were forced back across the road from the direction they had just come. They ran up a grass verge and onto a shopping parade, where they ran the gauntlet of kicks and punches from the more and more Stoke now appearing from everywhere.

Some people argued that the Liverpool team of 1988 was the finest ever. They narrowly missed doing the double that season, losing in the cup final to Wimbledon. They had no right to be in that final. Stoke City outplayed Liverpool then in front of 32,000. In the last minute, Graham Shaw was clean through in a one-on-one with the keeper. In true Stoke fashion he sent the ball wide. Peter Beardsley's winner in the replay at Anfield would see the ball confuse Peter Fox after hitting a divot but it was the injustice of the result in that first game that had one old punter complaining to the police. As the crowd crammed down Boothen Road, he could be heard pleading, 'Officer, officer, quick, down here.' A policeman followed the old man with urgency. 'Hurry up,' the old gent implored, winding in and out of the crowd that was now stopping to see the cause of this drama. The policeman ran to keep up. The old man stopped at the main entrance by the dressing rooms and pointed to the doors.

'Officer, I want you to go in there and arrest Kenny Dalglish for robbery.'

'You what?'

The crowd was howling in laughter.

'I want you to arrest Kenny Dalglish for robbery.'

The policeman, fuming, threatened the old man with arrest.

The aftermath of the match was much the same as Man City the week before: huge mobs patrolling the dark streets and attacking one another by mistake. At the replay on the Tuesday, about sixty Stoke went to the Blue House to meet Liverpool. Both sets of lads were drinking in the pub until it went off in a pool room. The same sixty Stoke were involved in scuffles along the route to Anfield, where they joined 8,000 travelling Stoke fans. After the match several hundred Stoke went searching for Liverpool but couldn't find them anywhere.

★

Four weeks after the home encounter with Villa, Stoke played Arsenal at Highbury in the fifth round of the League Cup. A couple of fifteen-year-olds could not bear to miss out and so skived school, hiding in a bush while waiting for the bus to Stoke so as not to be seen by anyone driving past who knew their parents, only to find nobody knocking about town and no-one at the train station either. They had been under the impression that there'd be a mob leaving for London on the 11am train and moaned as kids do when they don't get what they want: 'Stoke are wank. They get a chance to have a pop at Arsenal and there's no fucker about. That's it. I'm not coming again.'

As they moped across the Kings Hall car park, a car in a convoy of four pulled up. The window slowly wound down. It was one of Stoke's top boys. 'Hey lads, you going to the match?'

'Er, yeah. Is anyone going on the train?'

The lad jumped out of the car and shouted to the driver at the back of the convoy. 'Hey Butch, you got room for two littluns in your car?'

'Yeah. Jump in lads.'

The two youngsters were not familiar with these characters and it was not until the first stop at a service station that they realised they were with twelve of the Naughty Forty. These youngsters thought they had made it. They'd have been happy to hitch back right then just to tell all the lads in Stafford who were sitting through double maths.

They arrived in London at 2pm, parking near Highbury and taking the tube to Piccadilly. The youngsters were ridiculously nervous; they knew there was no way of avoiding aggro if it came in the present company. This little firm contained some of the gamest lads in the country. It was everything the youngsters dreamed of; they were travelling on the tube with proper football hooligans. What made it twice as exciting was the subtle interest expressed in them from the other passengers. It felt good to be noticed by the people of a city otherwise so indifferent.

After a drink in the empty Cockney Pride in Piccadilly, the group ventured into Soho and spent the next few hours in an illegal drinking den/brothel. This was not because of a predilection for sleaze or mugpunter northern voyeurism in the big smoke, but because the pubs shut between 3pm and 6pm. This first-floor shebeen was accessed by a narrow staircase no more than the width of one person. It was dark and sold cans and bottles only. The chairs were of orange plastic. Upstairs were a number of rooms used by prostitutes, though this became apparent only when ten older lads appeared. These were stalwarts from the Seventies who never failed to take a van no matter where Stoke played. These guys were not casuals but wore a hotchpotch of apparel: brown leather jackets, sheepskin coats, tracksuit bottoms worn with pit boots, the occasional moustache and Tom Jones haircut. All they were interested in was boozing and mayhem. The initial mob had been discreet but this lot were just mad. On occasions they were known to drink moonshine whisky in their van. At a pub in Ipswich, one of them had to be tied to a chair with belts to prevent him attacking fellow supporters. This lamb-chop-sideburned character would be seen home and away without fail drinking two pints of Guinness simultaneously.

It was not long before they were running into the 'bar' from upstairs with objects flying over their heads and cockney hags shouting abuse at them. The two youngsters sat in the corner next to an open sluice window, which provided the only release from must and cheap air freshener, and were as good as invisible, cherishing the bottles of Holsten Pils that one of Stoke's top boys had bought them. Occasionally they would look at each other, shaking their heads and giggling as the show unfolded before them. They were only distracted when *Grange Hill* came on the old television set in the corner; to them, perhaps, *Grange Hill* was more real than the situation they were in, a potentially very dangerous situation at that.

Their reverie was interrupted when a full bottle of beer went through the screen. That was the television smashed, closely followed by the jukebox, an outburst of mayhem sparked by the extortionate bar prices. The landlord was trapped in the doorway trying to appease ever more angry hags. Out into Soho spilled the lads, twenty-strong. It was a different London now. The streets were dark and packed with people on their way home and those who had just crawled from beneath a stone. Filled with drunken bravado, the crew mooched through the narrow streets and alleys, pinching girls' arses and exchanging banter with the various freakish elements that abound in those parts. There were several cockneys with them now, lads from various London clubs who had connections with Stoke. Their knowledge was often invaluable.

An off-licence was raided on the way to the pubs. The youngsters felt invisible and were generally ignored by all. There were priceless little touches of acknowledgement though. One of the top lads or a Londoner would pass them a bottle of stolen wine to swig out of, as if it were taken for granted that they were part of the firm. The alcohol and bonhomie only partially alleviated a nagging anxiety. From all the stories they had heard about London clubs, turning up at Highbury twenty-strong would offer no security, no matter how high-calibre the personnel. They returned to the Cockney Pride, which that afternoon had been a small, empty, basement boozer. It was now transformed to something of night-club proportions. A wall had been opened, revealing a large wooden dance floor. Within were familiar faces; about 100 Stoke lads babbled in drunken groups around this floor. The Seventies stalwarts lost no time in treating everybody to a spectacle of crazy Northern Soul dancing. The tempo was lifting. The youngsters, more relaxed now, knew they could blend in and that the odds of being forced into a kamikaze fight was gone.

About 120 lads marched down Piccadilly. There is an unforgettable atmosphere about London at that time of the evening: the screeching of double decker brakes and taxis, the smell of petrol and the luminous galleries of shop window displays. Everybody else is an isolated individual; you're the only gang in town. Suddenly though, they weren't. On the opposite pavement, spilling out into the road about forty yards ahead was another mob about seventy strong. They turned out to be Stoke too, and approximately 200 mad Potters leapt over the turnstiles at a tube station and filled the escalators, a good few walking down the metal partitions. Michael Jackson's 'BAD' had not long been out and it was amusing to see blokes with beer bellies just clearing the turnstiles and shouting, 'Who's BAD?'

The tubes were packed with office workers, who were obviously made extremely uncomfortable by the beer-stinking firm. It could be argued that these situations are more uncomfortable for those lads who genuinely want to keep their antics between consenting participants. They are made uncomfortable by the discomfort their culture inadvertently imposes upon others. The turnstiles were again evaded at Finsbury Park. Stoke had quick drinks in a couple of pubs and arrived at Highbury about fifteen minutes before kick-off. They marched down the street at the back of the East Stand. Any Arsenal boys that might have been targets did not loiter for long. You could see heads here and there bobbing away at speed through the red hats of the Arsenal crowd.

About fifty Stoke had gone on ahead and run a gathering of Arsenal at the North Bank. The Arsenal scarf fans were well deflated. Even supporters who are not involved in trouble don't like opponents taking the piss. Arsenal were powerless that night. It happens to everybody at sometime or another. Some blokes were driven to the desperate measures of imploring the police to sort Stoke out. One was yelling up at a mounted cop, 'Cam on lads, sort 'em aht. They're taking the piss.' To Arsenal, a Tuesday night League Cup clash against Second Division opposition meant little, but to Stoke, having spent the last three seasons playing teams like Shrewsbury and Reading, it was a big occasion. Stoke also had a score to settle after the Gooners had the better of them at the Victoria Ground in 1985.

In 1990 Stoke played Arsenal in the third round of the FA cup. They brought a well-dressed firm (some in smart overcoats) numbering no more than fifty. They were mingled in with Stoke fans outside the away enclosure and down Boothen Road and there were skirmishes between the two sets, though it would be impossible to determine who got the better of who overall. After the game a large mob of Arsenal succeeded in running a mixture of fans and lads back down Boothen Road. They were assisted in this by the police concentrating on dispersing the Stoke fans while Arsenal had *carte blanche*. In spite of this, Stoke did manage to drive Arsenal back towards the Stoke End. In all of this there was probably only a few seconds of brawling.

chapter fourteen

Playing Away

IT WAS AROUND the time of the Arsenal away game in 1987 that the Under-Fives developed a fetish about Shrewsbury. Everybody claimed they went there for the ruck but it probably had more to do with getting to see the casually dressed girls who hung about with their little firm. On New Year's Day 1987, half a dozen Stafford Under-Fives travelled on the same train from Stoke as a dozen Shrewsbury lads who were several years older. After a few sideways glances the two groups got talking. Shrewsbury seemed to have plenty to say about the casual scene, talking more about other teams they had travelled with than their own. That was fair enough; after all, the Under-Fives from Stafford didn't follow Stafford Rangers. Shrewsbury certainly talked the talk, though their farm boy accents seemed a little incongruous.

As the train approached Stafford, Shrewsbury gave the Under-Fives a hint of the county town sliminess that would motivate the Under-Fives over the coming seasons. A plump girl with a tight, black, wet-look perm, bedecked in Burberry and sovereign rings, was with the Shrewsbury lads. She was the sort of bird you expect to see working on a 'hook-a-duck' stand at the fair. Anyway, as the Stafford lads were getting ready to leave the train, the toilet door opened and Shrewsbury's very own Aphrodite beckoned one of the youngsters with her index finger. As the excited lad reached the door, she swiped the striped ski hat from his head before locking herself in. The hat had been a Christmas present and for purely sentimental reasons the lad started kicking the loo door in to recover it. The train was on the platform by now and the rest of the lads had disembarked, howling at the pathetic desperado. As time ran out he made a final polite plea through the door before his frustration erupted. He went back into the Shrewsbury carriage shouting, 'Fucking come on.' If his hat had been stolen by West

Ham he would have worn the fact as a badge of honour but not by a girl from Shrewsbury.

As he got off the train, Shrewsbury came off further along the platform and steamed into the Mad Hatless with a stick and a flurry of handbag punches. The other Under-Fives came steaming back, throwing a billboard into Shrewsbury, who then backed off into the train. To be fair, only half had got off in the first place, making the numbers equal, but they still had the advantage of age difference. As the train left the platform, Shrewsbury were in an excited, babbling huddle at the centre of their carriage.

Now the Under-Fives had a sizeable mob, they decided to avenge the ski hat and selected Shrewsbury as the venue for their first excursion away from home as their own firm. Fifteen youngsters from Stafford met up with about forty others at Stoke station on a November morning; fifty-odd fifteen- to seventeen-year-olds donning gloves and scarves to protect themselves from the frosty air. They were like a class when the teacher has left the room. Usually they were inhibited among the older lads but now though they were free to express themselves and determine events rather than be swept along by them. Only when among their peers could the youngsters distinguish themselves by their various qualities and develop their own hierarchy of influence.

They reached Shrewsbury at 10am and headed out of town until the pubs opened so as not to be picked up by the police. Each took it in turn to run off ahead and view the spectacle of their mob. The highlight of the next hour was fifty Under-Fives spread out in a line across a ring road suspension bridge, half jumping up and down so that the others could enjoy the sensation of falling as it moved. Some of them were still at school, don't forget, and these episodes served as great bonding exercises. The shared experience helped to acquaint groups of lads who otherwise only knew one another by sight at home games and to integrate the mob for future games. The better acquainted everybody became, the more excited they got.

On the outskirts of the town centre, those at the front spotted a small group of casuals huddled around an amusement game in a chip shop. The older Stoke lads would have sent a couple in to tell them to get their boys, but this mob of amateurs were too eager. The several who flew straight into the chippy and piled into the game players probably didn't expect the other fifty to pile in after them. Most of the aggro went on outside the chip shop with the Under-Fives fighting one another to get in through the door. It was out of order but no one wanted to miss out.

Who knows what would have happened to the Shrewsbury had the white-overalled proprietor not leapt over the counter with a huge knife. Now the Under-Fives were getting stuck into one another to get out. As they piled onto the street, a riot van hurtled into the mob. Everybody scattered, each for himself. The police picked up half a dozen and took them straight to the ground. It was only 11am and these six, along with a few others, had to spend four hours in the shed of an away end at Gay Meadow before the game kicked off. The police gave them a football to play with on the terracing but this was no consolation. The only exception was Bakes, who seemed delighted. He was insatiable with that football, running around like an excited toddler with his first balloon. Among the others interned were the victim of the ski hat theft that pre-empted the whole affair and the lad who had organised the excursion. They were gutted.

On the other side of the river from Gay Meadow is a castle atop a steep hill. Around this castle are walkways and a path down to the embankment. Every fifteen minutes or so, the lads on the terracing could see a mob of Shrewsbuy running down these paths or along the embankment, pursued by handfuls of Under-Fives. Every time the Shrewsbury lads ran past again the numbers chasing them were fewer and fewer, until the Under-Fives were taking it in turns to run them alone.

Kick-off reunited everyone in the ground. Those that had been running amok had 100 tales. Having been dispersed by the riot van, they had at first skulked around in ones and twos. Thirty Shewsbury lads were out hunting them, distinguishable by the number of tall, blond characters among them; it was more like being in Bavaria than Shropshire. Things had been a bit hairy. The thirty Shrewsbury were cornering those stranded on their own and these individuals had to run for it, but with the town being so small it wasn't long before they were running into fellow Under-Fives. These handfuls were less easy to run and once they moved towards Shrewsbury it was they who were backing off. It was still unnerving for those on their own. Shrewsbury knew all the cobbled lanes and alleyways, and being stuck on your own at fifteen years old and hearing them shouting to one another and not knowing which alley they are going to come down is as scary as at any ground.

Eventually everybody regrouped into a mob about forty strong, minus some who were arrested in a ruck outside McDonald's. Now it was all over for the Shrewsbury lads. The Under-Fives, though much younger than their adversaries, had the psychological advantage of having spent so much time among a proper firm. They knew how to wear a big hat. As they were escorted by dog handlers to the train station after the game, they strutted like peacocks. Shrewsbury had been a fantasy land for the youngsters, where they lived their dream of being a proper football firm.

Shrewsbury had proved to be such poor opposition that the Under-Fives had to resort to twenty-five-a-side play fights on the train home to fulfil themselves. The local metro train they had boarded was more like a tube train with seats along each side facing one another. This left plenty of room for the two mobs to charge up and down the carriage at one another. This was the liberation of going away on their own. If they had tried that stunt in the company of the older lads they would have probably been kicked to fuck and banned from Stoke games ever after. By the time they got to Crewe the police boarded the train to stop any more fun and games.

Returning to their home station, six of the Stafford Under-Fives ended up in a ruck with a similar number of fellow Staffordians on an overhead walkway between platforms. The Staffordians were pissed up and on their way for a night out in Wolverhampton. An Under-Five got bottled round the head and one of theirs had his front teeth punched out. The most memorable incident was when one of the pissheads fell down the stairs from the footbridge to the platforms. Bakes, who was making his escape down the same stairs, had an attack of bravery as the body rolled towards him. 'Fucking come on,' he roared, to bull himself up, and steamed back up the stairs, aiming his best rugby conversion kick at the guy's head. He missed. Conversations must have stopped in every pub around town at Bakes's piercing squeal as his trainer struck the concrete step, breaking every toe in his foot. The pisshead sprang up and leapt off the steps onto Bakes's back, resulting in both rolling down the stairs. As several Under-Fives went to help, the pisshead fled, leaving an apparently unconscious Bakes at the foot of the stairs. Whether he had been knocked out or had fainted through fear was unclear. Bakes was eventually carried to a taxi and sent home.

The Under-Fives would go for many more runarounds amid the Tudor buildings of Shrewsbury. Eventually though, in the early Nineties, an episode emphasised how much the Under-Fives had outgrown their rustic counterparts. By this time they were Under-Fives in name only; many were seasoned hooligans. Days out to Shrewsbury should have been behind them but it had become an amusing bad habit they couldn't break. Besides, with every year they would get word from Shrewsbury lads claiming things would be different the next time.

In February 1991, forty Under-Fives took a bus from Newcastle-under-Lyme to the centre of Shrewsbury. The bus was consumed by a green smog of cannabis smoke. When they got off at the edge of the town centre, six of the lads were deep in conversation and so lagged a short distance behind the main mob. Shortly after the mob had passed a pub, a load of local lads came out, no doubt to perform their annual ritual of making a racket only to then turn and run. Sure enough, they started shouting to the mob ahead of them, unaware of the six straggling Under-Fives behind them. It was too late. The stragglers were straight into Shrewsbury. After a few punches there were Shrewsbury lads lying on the deck and then came the big shock, something the Under-Fives were never renowned for at the match. A Shrewsbury lad had a knife plunged into his back. The whole crew, who were oblivious to the stabbing, went into the first pub they came to and before the first rounds had all been poured dozens of police filed in. They formed a line and forced the Under-Fives into a corner without any exits. It was a revelation to see just how many people were actually tooled up as lads slashed seats to conceal their weapons. One of the Newcastle fled out of a back door and threw his knife over a fence, only to be confronted by the angry police officer who had been standing on the other side and had been hit on the head. The lad, who had a nervous affliction of whistling while twitching his head, could be heard whistling like a robin as he was led away. The lads only hoped that he would not sing like a canary at the station. Others who were unsuccessful in disposing of there blades were also arrested. Each person was searched separately before being taken outside into another ring of police that served as a barrier to the baying, vengeful crowd that was congregating. It was impossible for the Under-Fives to get into these. They were taken straight into the ground and put into an enclosure all of their own and monitored by the CCTV.

The stabber decided to try his luck and leave the ground at half-time. He was arrested immediately outside. It was obvious that they knew who they were after as they arrested another lad who had swapped jackets with him near to the scene of the crime. The entire episode had been filmed on CCTV. The knifeman spent the next two years in prison and has not been to a game since.

Shrewsbury probably regret ever pinching that ski hat.

Leeds United were in Division Two for several years at the same time as Stoke. Owing to massive police operations, all-ticket restrictions and Sunday dinnertime kick-offs, nothing ever happened between the two firms at the Victoria Ground. Stoke did take a mob to Elland Road in December 1988 but the day never amounted to much. However, the two firms did confront one another occasionally on bank holiday weekends in Blackpool, when Stoke would always be overwhelmed by the sheer weight of Leeds numbers.

One of these crazy excursions occurred in the summer of 1988. It was the stag party of a lad who often went with Stoke but was also well connected with Liverpool's firm. A coachload of top lads and two vans left town on a Saturday after a raid on an off-licence. Spirits of every description were passed around amid thick smoke from joints and bongs. They only got as far as the outskirts of Blackpool town centre before mayhem erupted. The Number 3 pub had just reopened after a million-pound-plus refit and the first guests to enjoy the champagne reception were our errant knights from the Potteries. Eighty lads poured into the bar in casual clobber, with Head bags over their shoulders containing their club clothes of trousers, shirts and shoes.

The Number 3's plush furnishings were not enhanced by red-eyed football hooligans walking around in their pants as they started changing clothes in the pub. The bouncers took umbrage and began picking up bags and trying to throw people out. One of the lads from the truncheon-borrowing episode with Coventry picked up a fire extinguisher and started spraying the penguin-suited beefcakes. These bouncers were body-building professional hardmen in their mid-thirties and were not going to be easily intimidated by a bunch of lads whose average age would have been about twenty-two, no matter how many there were. About a dozen of them fought with eighty lads in a drawn-out bar brawl of Wild West proportions. Everything was flying. Within twenty minutes the spanking new bar was a blood-dappled pigsty. One very big guy was causing Stoke real problems, decking anybody who came within arm's length. It transpired that this particular character was in charge of most of the doors and bouncers in Blackpool. As the police started arriving everybody fled. A few were arrested.

People went in different directions to reduce the chances of arrest. About thirty or forty made it to the Dixieland nightclub. In the back room, about the size of two large pubs, the lads sat in the shadows constructing a joint the length of a javelin. Another mob of lads appeared out of the main room of the club. They were Leeds. There was a freeze-frame moment before fighting erupted. It was as if somebody had set a lion free in the building. Screaming girls ran in all directions to escape flying glasses and stray punches as a battle ensued through the nightclub. When the police arrived they unleashed the dogs on the fighting mobs.

★

The success of the Under-Fives in the wake of the initial Shrewsbury excursion was highlighted early in the 1988-89 season. A coach was hired for an away game at Bradford by a lad known as Ninja. Seventy-two Under-Fives crammed onto the fifty-six-seater, toiletless hulk. They decided to exhibit their 'military precision' and leave the transport on the outskirts of the city centre so as not to be detected. How were they to know the dual carriageway they had chosen to get off their coach on was the city's ring road with no immediate exit points? With seventy lads wandering around at the side of a motorway, it wasn't long before the police appeared. Again, straight to the ground. By kick-off they were joined by about eighty older lads and so there were a good 150 after the game. The Under-Fives went ahead on their own. On a small car park at the foot of a mountain of sandstone terraced streets, they came under attack from brick-throwing 'Ointment', Bradford's hooligan firm. The older lads were not far behind and had no hesitation in bouncing up the hill towards Bradford, knocking people on their arses as they ascended while dodging the shower of bricks. They were soon running Bradford all over what seemed to be a largely Asian neighbourhood. An elderly Asian lady came out of her front door and shouted, 'Why don't you go and play in your own street?' This brought much laughter from Stoke's mob.

Bradford adored throwing missiles. In 1986, twenty-five Stoke had come out of a pub in Bradford to 100-plus rivals. Those at the front of Bradford's mob were lobbing bricks. When they ran out, Stoke had them on their toes, only then to be showered with more bricks from those who had been at the back but were now at the front. They were taking it in turns to throw and then collect more missiles. Stoke had to run back into the pub in the end. One lad was collared outside though. Bradford beat him to the ground before smashing either a paving slab or a brick, possibly both, over his head. Thankfully he recovered in hospital relatively quickly for the seriousness of his injuries. Stoke went on to run mobs of Bradford everywhere on the way to the ground. They also tried entering the home end, only to have Bradford lads informing the police who they were. Bradford's mob seemed petrified of having to face a situation where they might have to physically fight Stoke without weapons. This was probably the consequence of an incident at the Victoria Ground the season before when twenty-odd Stoke battered seventy Bradford all over the snack bar of the Stoke End seats.

Anyway, back to Bradford 1988 and the Under-Fives were crammed back onto their coach and decided to stop off in Huddersfield. Huddersfield Town had not played that day but the youngsters thought they'd pay a surprise visit anyway. They headed to the town centre and a pub called The Pig In Motion. They found plenty of pigs but little motion; the place was full of scruffy beer monsters. Half the Stoke contingent drank inside while the rest wandered off somewhere. The beer monsters were not too happy and let it show, leering with contorted faces. News soon arrived that the rest of the Under-Fives were battling with locals out in the street. The youngsters rushed out with the beer monsters not far behind. This is when it really went off. Within a few minutes there were bodies littering the street and two of the locals had been glassed. There must have been 150 people battling in the road. One of the Under-Fives got hold of a yellow litterbin and climbed onto the roof of a Ford Fiesta XR2i. All around the car the battle raged as he raised the bin above his head shouting, 'We're Stoke City. Come on you fuckers.' Leaping off the car, he smashed this bin over the head of a local brute, who hit the deck unconscious. The Under-Fives' coach driver, who had parked at the end of the street, revved his engine to indicate his getaway was imminent. This split the youngsters in two, with half running to catch the coach whilst the others were preoccupied with the orgy of violence. The locals were throwing bricks, bottles and anything else to hand. All the Under-Fives were now in retreat and, as the locals pursued them, half-enders crashed through the coach windows. As sirens pierced the night air the locals dispersed into pubs and side streets.

The Under-Fives were taken along with the coach to the police station so the driver could report the damage. They had to sit outside on the pavement and wait for a replacement coach, as every window and the headlights had been put through. There was a pub opposite the police station. Before the youngsters had even considered going over for a drink, the locals were pouring out and mouthing off. Everyone leapt from the kerb and scattered them. Then came the highlight of the day. A character called Gappy had been given a yard brush at the station to clean up broken glass that had fallen from the coach. When the police came out to investigate the latest disturbance, all they saw was Gappy running down the road waving his brush and then battering one of the locals with it. It was hilarious to see a copper marching him into the station with his arm up his back while another walked alongside, broom in hand, shaking his head in disgust.

By the time the new coach arrived everybody was desperate for bed, and the thought of a two-hour journey, three to a seat, was unbearable. But this trip had confirmed that the Under-Fives were now out there and doing things; in fact they were in danger of creating more headlines than the main firm. Still, the older lads had already been through such episodes back in the early Eighties and were a lot more calm and efficient in their exploits.

chapter fifteen

Dexy's Midnight Runners

T'HE CHELSEA MATCH of 1988 was long anticipated. When the two sides had last met in 1984/85, Stoke's most reliable lads had been sidelined by the infamous mass brawl at Rothersthorpe service station. On this occasion too there would be more speculation than realization. On a drizzly Saturday in December, Stoke's large home mob never so much as saw a Chelsea fan until they got to the ground. Even then it took twenty lads to walk around the back of the Butler Street, where away fans were allocated that season, to get a punch-up with Chelsea boys at the turnstiles. One of their lads stood out because he wore ripped jeans like the band of the moment, Bros. He was bouncing in and out of Stoke throwing punches and shouting, 'Cam on Stoke, you fakkin' slags.' Eventually the horses came galloping over and unfortunately a police officer known in the neighbourhood of the Stafford youngsters was mown down by one of them. He had to retire from duty as a result of his injuries.

The away game was not until May bank holiday Monday. The Stafford lads were so impatient for the Chelsea experience that they decided to get the midnight train to London. They would go to Stoke first, have a few beers, find out what the plans were for the next day, and hopefully recruit more numbers for the midnight journey. As they hatched their plans in an estate pub, a blond version of Shaggy off *Scooby Doo* was eavesdropping at the bar. Even the cartoon Shaggy would have recoiled at the attire of his alter ego. His Armani jeans and faded denim jacket were still stained with mud and algae from when he had been thrown in the local school pond a few nights previously in a drunken prank and his Reebok trainers reeked. He had obviously been drinking right through the weekend and not gone home. Dexy was his name. He was one of the older lads and known up Stoke where he occasionally made guest appearances for the bigger games, most notably fighting against the police in the Boothen Paddock whilst on crutches during a Wolves match. This had been a particularly vicious affair, an extension of the coal miners' dispute.

Dexy's sporadic appearances at games reflected his unsettled life. He would be back in his hometown for a few weeks before disappearing to either London or Bristol, shacking up with a vicar's daughter in Wales or on the road with New Age travellers. This time he had just returned from potato picking in Jersey. His adaptability and pragmatism can be seen in the fact that though he went with Stoke, associated as it was with the north end of Stafford, he also had an Indian-inked EFC tattoo on his arm. This of course was the bastion of the south end and he had enjoyed many a fracas and shoplifting spree with both Everton and Liverpool in his time. He had been in Everton's firm the Friday night they did Chelsea at Stamford Bridge on their return to the top flight in 1984 and perhaps the chance to relive old memories was what motivated him to sidle over to the youngsters.

'You off to Chelsea lads?'

'Yeah, we're off now.'

'Fuck it. I'm coming with yer.'

He necked his flat pint of cider in one and rushed out behind the ten youngsters. On the way to the bus stop for Stoke he deployed his scally expertise in the off-licence. He was in and out in a flash, raising two bottles of Moet to the sky and chanting, 'Chelsea, Chelsea here we come.' By the time they got to Stoke, the bubbles had taken effect on top of the beer and the lads were up for anything. The only problem was there were no faces in Stoke town. Then when they got to the railway station at about 11pm, they found that the romantically named 'midnight' did not in fact leave until 2am.

Dexy was completely sozzled. When not staggering back and falling on his arse he was offering out guards on the platform. For everybody else the effect of the booze was beginning to wear off. Two or three of the lads decided to go home to Stafford, including the sticky one who had two pints of Guinness chucked over him for waking the unconscious Dexy, who had been slumped over a beer barrel in the Bull and Bush at closing time. Somebody had heard that the youngsters were getting the midnight, as a carload of Stoke appeared on the platform. The driver was Old Man Steptoe, the Birmingham fan. They said that they were driving to London and would meet the Stafford lads there.

Dexy sprung into action. Sobering up almost immediately, he ingratiated himself with Steptoe and secured a seat in the car. It transpired that Dexy was skint. In his opinion it was only right that the youngsters should repay his gift of champagne by keeping him in ale. Nobody minded; Dexy's company seemed priceless at that moment and his antics that weekend are even more priceless now.

When the train pulled in at a brightly lit Milton Keynes at 3.30am the passengers must have been a tad intimidated by the sight of Shaggy and Steptoe leaping about like chimpanzees. Dexy was splaying his arms and shouting, 'Come on Stoke, let's have it.' Steptoe claimed it made more sense to park at Milton Keynes than to navigate the London traffic. The Stafford lads suspected that his reasons had more to do with Dexy's feet. They had not long been on the train when the guard made his first appearance of the night. When the car crew asked for tickets from Milton Keynes in broad Potteries accents, he laughed and charged them from Stoke anyway – all except for Dexy, who had disappeared while Steptoe argued the toss.

Walking around London at 4am is a uniquely unsettling experience. As the dozen trudged between Euston, St Pancras and Kings Cross, a riot van kept driving ahead, moving-on groups of overweight black hookers in mini-skirts and thigh-length leather boots. The group was also being monitored by a black guy in a BMW. It was reminiscent of the mood projected in the film *Mona Lisa*. What was most striking was the absolute cacophony of the dawn chorus in one of the world's biggest cities. The clash between the ugliness of the modern city and the beauty of nature overcoming it was jarring. The birds had adapted. They belonged there. It was the young Stoke crew that didn't. Their arms were no longer swinging. They became defensive and moved in a huddle – all except Dexy, who was constantly running ahead to seek out adventure and consult with the people of the street.

When dawn broke the group were in a deserted Trafalgar Square. Coming from the Charing Cross area were five dressed lads. Dexy hailed them, hoping they would know where to get a drink. Four of them ran off. It transpired that these lads, from Middlesbrough, were on their way home from a rave and were unduly paranoid owing to the LSD they were on. The remaining lad, who spoke like he was learning to read owing to the chemicals, gave everyone a flyer for the coming night's partying. Within six months of this encounter, everybody in the group would be immersed in strobe lights and dry ice and saturated with Purple Oms and White Caps, and would be too delicate on Saturday mornings to give a shit about football matches. They had encountered a hint of the future.

Ironically, Stoke had a miserly turnout of lads at Chelsea for that very reason. There were probably about thirty of the older lads when there should have been eighty. It was also why the youngsters had seen no-one in Stoke town the night before. Many had gone to an all-nighter at Trentham Gardens and were either too mellow or too tired to bother heading for Chelsea.

At eight o'clock the youngsters went back to Euston with Dexy and Steptoe. They sat and half lay napping against Tie Rack and Knickerbox windows at the centre of the concourse. They were tired, hung over and drained after hours staggering around after Dexy whilst he jokingly kicked tramps in doorways shouting: 'Get up you lazy bastard!' or tried to burgle river barges for beer on the embankment. At nine o'clock, 500 Crystal Palace fans arrived to board trains for Manchester. They were playing City and heading for promotion. In these circumstances twelve rival fans would normally have at least hidden their faces by pretending to read magazines in John Menzies. These lads though were too knackered to care. They could feel the London grime on their faces. The fur on their teeth felt as though their fingers would sink into it, as into uncooked pastry. Every time one of the youngsters managed to nod off, a policeman would come along, kick their feet and tell them to wake up.

Stoke's modest mob arrived at about ten o'clock. Of the forty there were about twenty-five established lads and a small group of Under-Fives. The night prowlers, by now looking like urchins, tagged on to make up the fifty. Again Dexy sprang into action re-acquainting himself with faces he hadn't seen for half a decade. His energy was boundless. He ended up leading the mob around Soho looking for an early drink. He ran ahead excitedly, as he had during the early hours, in and out of pubs. He may have been first at the bar but that's as far as it ever went; he had no intention of getting a reunion round in.

Dexy came out of one pub seemingly before he had entered, pointing over his shoulder and giggling while proclaiming, 'It's full a puffs.' A camp landlord appeared in the doorway.

'You're quite welcome lads so long as you don't upset any of my customers.'

There was a bit of a murmured debate before everybody filed in gingerly. There were no vest-wearing, moustachioed Adonises; instead they found old blokes in raincoats and a six-foot-five transvestite. The latter inspired a round of giggles but nobody bothered one another. The landlord was actually a Stokie from Shelton who knew one of the lads. The two of them were deep in conversation at the bar, the landlord, chin in cup of hand, staring into Tone's eyes. None of the lads have ever been particularly comfortable when caught on their own with Tone since.

The next stop was Shakes in Victoria, a bar that featured in the seminal ICF documentary *Hooligan*. A handful never got round to buying a drink, too busy were they reading graffiti in the toilets. That familiar undercurrent of nervousness began to permeate. Now that they were in a pub with connotations, an attack felt imminent.

The mob eventually reached the Chelsea Potter on the Kings Road. Any nervousness had evolved into sheer excitement and complete confidence in one and all. This is the complacency that comes the more you drink and the longer you roam around someone else's manor without being touched. The weather was beautiful, with clear skies and temperatures into the early twenties. It must have been some sort of fever induced through tiredness that motivated these lads, and a few of the other Under-Fives, to break away from the main mob and go further up the Kings Road by bus. Dexy, of course, stayed where the drinks were flowing.

They lounged on the top deck of a double-decker smoking skunk. Not a good idea! Everyone, about fifteen in all, piled off at a stop near Stamford Bridge. The last character down the steps had a birds' eye view of the street and could see what the others could not: about twenty Chelsea heads were bouncing down the pavement towards the bus stop. By the time the last guy got off the bus most of the Under-Fives were running back down the Kings Road. Some had their dicks hanging out where they had been caught out pissing up a wall. One lad, Turtle's Head from the Man City game, was still pissing up the wall when he was set about with a brolly. Several of the Under-Fives stood screaming at the others to stand while the Chelsea lads took advantage of those who were isolated and showing panic. Those that stood had become aware of the Chelsea mob before the attack and saw that the numbers difference was minimal. The unfortunate thing for those that get taken by surprise, though, is that the initial impression is always of a larger mob. The disproportionate panic compounded by skunk paranoia caused fist-clenching frustration for those who stood.

People scarpered off down various side streets. The three who had initially stood found themselves down a typical London terrace, arguing and trying to find their bearings. Here they bumped into a cataleptic Bakes. Chelsea could smell blood and were searching the back streets, confident they would find strays. Several came round the corner. Smirking faces projected the arrogance of their success. This handful of Under-Fives weren't running though.

Cockney accents could be heard shouting to one another down the adjoining streets. These Under-Fives knew that if they didn't act they would be surrounded. They moved towards the Chelsea lads. It didn't take much to wipe the smirks from their faces. As soon as they saw this bare hint of resistance, they turned and walked away. The Stoke lads went down an adjoining street and bumped into another pair of Chelsea lads. They too apparently only knew what to do when the opposition was moving away from them. They disappeared.

The excitement was all too much for Bakes. He became hysterical and one of the lads had to slap him round the face. Everybody was nervous. In situations like that, people are looking for a confident lad to take the lead and give everybody else courage. When somebody cracks up, the likelihood is everybody else will go the same way. The lad that did the slapping later admitted that Bakes's hysteria had caused his own.

A riot van came down the street. Bakes flagged it down. Everybody called him a wanker for this but nobody refused a lift to safety. The van then cruised the streets, stopping to pick up other isolated Under-Fives. The effect of the van rescues was the hooligan equivalent of helicopter lifts in Vietnam, as depicted in *The Deer Hunter*, so shell-shocked were the lads who clambered aboard. One missed his footing and fell back into the street. Another gripping on to the handle, slid with the door and nearly ended up under the wheels. Everybody swore never to smoke skunk at the match again.

By the time the Under-Fives had got back to Euston, after the match, it had been a long twenty-four hours. Everybody was grimy and knackered. Dexy, who had not been involved in the Kings Road fiasco, now had his own crisis to tackle. The ramp down to the Stafford train was guarded by police and there was a ticket inspector on duty. Dexy, of course, had no ticket or money.

As the train left the outskirts of London, somebody commented, 'It looks like we've finally got rid of Dexy.' In the spirit of all good horror movies, though, the story was not over. There was a sudden shout of 'Oi!' Everybody jumped. From the back of the seats where the youngsters sat at tables, Dexy's head popped up. He was covered from head to toe in black oil. Not being able to get onto the correct platform, he had circumvented the police by crawling under a stationary train. He sat proud as punch, smelly feet and all, next to an unfortunate old lady.

Dexy leant into the aisle reading *Viz* magazine out loud to the youngsters sat a bit further down the carriage. Every man, woman and child roared with laughter as Dexy treated them to the exploits of Johnny Fart Pants and Biffer Bacon. It was a wonderful half hour or so, an episode that truly makes life precious. Dexy's charm managed to enchant the other passengers only temporarily, however. Soon his feet struck again. A baby cried and the old lady next to him held a hanky to her face. Soon the whole carriage was enveloped in the stench.

★

Within the space of one competitive game, the Chelsea debacle was ameliorated in the best possible way. The opening game of the 1989/90 season brought West Ham to the Victoria Ground. It was a sweltering August day and West Ham brought about 3,000 fans. A large proportion of their lads had their hair tied back in ponytails and no doubt their passions were at that time divided between football and raving. The whole country was moving inexorably into a cultural revolution that is the norm today.

The 1-1 draw later became infamous when West Ham's Frank McAvennie tried to sue Chris Kamara for breaking his leg. Though Kamara was notorious for hard play it was judged that McAvennie's injury was brought on by an awkward fall. After the match nobody seemed in any urgency to hunt for hassle. Everybody was mellowed by the sunshine. There was a big mob in the Bull and Bush, many sitting on the grass verge outside. Even so, the police were not dropping their guard. Short-sleeved shirts were about as casual as their approach would become. They were in groups on every corner near the Bull and Bush and a riot van full kept vigil.

Nearly an hour after the end of the game, the police felt confident enough to start moving back to the station. Not all left but it was so late after the game that they were not made suspicious by ones and twos leaving the pub. About fifty eventually circumvented the police this way, regrouping half a mile away on a side street in Shelton, west of the railway station. The mob was split between the main lads and the Under-Fives.

A couple of older lads appeared, beckoning the mob to follow. Off they went then through the cobbled alleyways of Shelton. First they moved north of the railway station before cutting across the neighbourhood and doubling back, ending up on the east side of the station. They had crept through the alleys as if across a landing at night, nobody saying a word. If anybody did speak the finger-to-mouth gesture was passed along the line. The irritation on the faces of the more influential lads at the merest sound kept the younger lads in order. Because nothing was said, most people were not sure where they were going.

The mob waited behind the fence of a car park parallel with the buildings opposite the railway station. The lad at the front kept popping his head round the fence to check on the police fifty yards away outside the station. Mark Bentley and Jasper carried on to the station. They aroused no suspicion as they passed the police in the foyer and slunk past West Ham's firm on the platform. At the far end were the Royal Mail sliding doors, directly

wo of our finest, Daz and Gaz Mills, in the Punch and Judy in Covent Garden. Inset: Stan (left) and Spider, one of those aumatised by the hideous prison van breakout described in Chapter 17.

oggsy (left), Miffer and Cossack at Miff's party, when he was fighting cancer. The big man left us six months later.

These four pictures show how Birmingham's Zulu Army advanced on our end at St Andrews. The so-called normal supporters in the crowd show little fear of the advancing Zulus, such was their faith in the N40 and Under-Fives lads who took to the fence to fight them off.

am convinced that the actions of those lads, against a much greater number of attackers, prevented a Hillsborough-type disaster that day by beating back the Brummies and keeping them out of our end. Yet they were hunted down through a media campaign, identified from photographs and TV footage and banned by the club.

Sat in the Borough pub in Cardiff in 2002. Where there's a will there's a way.

Finbar joined the ranks of the Naughty Forty at just fourteen, one of the youngest members to go straight to the top.

Marcus: A formative member of the Stoke Under-Fives and the co-author of the section about them in this book. Another lad who lives for the terrace culture.

The second of Stoke's three firms heads to Manchester's Victoria Station on its way to Wigan Athletic. This was perhaps our biggest-ever hooligan turnout.

Violence flares at Wigan's ground shortly after players from both teams had stood in silent tribute to Sir Stanley Matthews. Seven minutes into the match fighting broke out between rival fans in the North Stand and spilled on to the pitch. The players were led off by the referee.

Cossack contemplates another night of persecuting the countryside with his lurchers.

splinter group of Stoke's firm is rounded up and marched back to the main firm during a visit to Sheffield Wednesday in 2002.

Steaming the old bill against Cardiff City. Finbar is just about to dive through the crowd and punch a copper, for which he was later convicted and banned from the Britannia.

Older and wiser: (l to r) Cossack, Marcus, the author, Nomad and Finbar contemplate the future while Texas the Rhodesian ridgeback eyes the photographer's leg.

opposite the skulking Stoke mob outside. As the outside doors slid open, the lad at the front of the line waved everybody forward. They shuffled across the road. Again there was lots of 'shushing' and fingers to mouths. Mark Bentley stood at the slightly ajar interior slide door.

'Ready lads.'

He slid the door open. Nobody had a clue what was waiting as they roared onto the platform. All they could see was the blurred movement of 150 West Ham running away down the platform, out into the street and even across the tracks. The only resistance Stoke met was a solitary police officer. He was up for it though, standing with his legs astride and swinging his truncheon at the ensuing mob. Stoke turned and ran back out the way they had come. Now they attacked the front of the railway station, where disorientated Hammers were trying to regroup. Stoke ran them back into the station. The whole thing lasted probably no longer than a minute before Stoke again dispersed into small groups. The police barely had time to use their radios.

Everybody was buzzing. Even the older lads, who always tried to maintain an aura of inscrutability, dropped their guard; they babbled as excitedly as the youngsters. Everyone was turning round to the guy next to him, clenching their fists and hissing, 'We fucking did it.'

This was the day the youngsters, who as they approached the end of their teens were no longer so young, ceased being distinguished as a separate mob of inferiors and were acknowledged as equals. This was a big responsibility. Now they had proven themselves they could no longer hide behind the excuse of youth.

A lot of people even talked about 'retiring' on a high after West Ham. Such ideas are often toyed with by football lads: they are either going to stop because nothing ever happens and it's a waste of time, or too much has happened and they want to avoid a dawn raid and possibly prison. The problem is there's always a tantalising encounter just round the corner.

A few weeks after the West Ham game, Stoke played Wolves away. For many, early retirement had lasted no longer than a fortnight. About twenty Stoke were already in Wolverhampton at 10am. After sitting in a café they went drinking in a pub just up from the station on the corner of the main road into town. The plan was that they would gradually gather there until the numbers were respectable enough to bowl into Wolverhampton town centre. There had been a hitch though. A Wolves lad from Stafford had arrived on the same train, a friend of the Stafford Under-Fives. A Stoke lad spotted a Wolves badge on his jumper and a Stafford Under-Five, anxious no harm came to his friend, told Stoke that the Wolves fan was with them. He claimed the badge was a ruse as they intended going into the Wolves end for the off. This, as it transpired, was a big mistake for all. The Stoke lads would never have harmed him; instead they would have organised a time and a meet with Wolves' firm via him. Unfortunately he ran straight off and got a mob of twenty Wolves, themselves not properly firmed up at that time of the morning. Stoke had not been drinking long in the pub before Wolves tapped on the window. Stoke steamed straight out. Wolves were off; it must have been their younger lads. Half a dozen Stoke pursued them, throwing glass vases from a florist's, and then everybody went back into the pub laughing.

Twenty minutes later the same mob were back. Again they tapped on the window and everybody steamed out again to the same effect. They were more like kids playing knock and run than a football firm. In the meantime more Stoke had been arriving. There were about seventy in the pub by the time they came a third time. This time nobody even looked out of the window when they inevitably tapped. They tapped again. Everyone just kept on drinking. Then the window panes exploded, half brick ends landing in pint pots. Their smashing up of the pub was dramatic but destroyed any hope of a proper confrontation that day. Within minutes, police surrounded the pub. The bar was closed and Stoke taken outside. To make matters worse, another eighty Stoke appeared while there were police everywhere and so 150 lads were escorted to Molineux.

Stoke salvaged something from the afternoon. As two sides of Molineux were condemned, the old South Bank home end had been divided up and a third of the terracing allocated to away fans. An evil little genius among Stoke's firm deduced that, as it had been one big open end, there might be a makeshift barrier beneath the stand that could be overcome. Sure enough, behind a wall of corrugated iron was an entrance connecting the whole South Bank. During the first half a few of the lads stayed downstairs removing the iron fence. Groups of Stoke started making their way downstairs before half-time, when the scarf fans and police would have appeared and rumbled their plot. They piled through this hole and pushed up the steps until they were staring at the backs of the Wolves end.

'COME ON.'

The South Bank surged forwards. Faces looked with horror over their shoulders as they scrambled down the terracing to get away. Wolves fans were fighting one another to escape at either side as well. It was all over in a minute as dozens of police battled up the steps from where

Stoke had come. It seemed doors were opening all over the place for Stoke that season.

Back in the away end again, the Stafford Under-Five who had harboured the Wolves lad was getting a bollocking. The Wolves fan had not been spotted amongst the pub wreckers (though he was there) but was unmistakable stood aloft the South Bank on a crush barrier chanting abuse at the Stoke end.

That was the last of the action until Wolves visited Stoke in the new year. Forty Stoke of respectable quality bowled through town towards Liverpool Road, where they knew a Wolves firm were drinking in The Phoenix and Star pubs. As they turned into Liverpool Road, Wolves were themselves on the march. Their mob was not much bigger but they succeeded in running Stoke back up the street without even the pretence of resistance. This was unprecedented amongst Stoke's better firms. Certainly, as has been documented in this book, Stoke have been done at home, but with the exception of the Birmingham fiasco, never without a gallant stand. Indeed, even with Birmingham there were the one-man heroics of the type which epitomize Stoke's football firm. The only explanation for Wolves is that every football gang, like every football team, suffers inexplicable humiliations at some point during its campaigns.

After the match a group of ten Under-Fives were adamant they would make amends of some sort. As the Wolves escort was marched along the eastern side of the ring road towards the railway station, they took the western route to evade the police. Half way down Liverpool Road a riot van spotted them and was cruising slowly behind. As they turned east to meet the escort the van got reduced to a crawl in the post-match traffic. Their timing was perfect. As they reached the bridge that goes from the ring road to the station, half the escort was already crossing, leaving the centre exposed as all the police were at front and back. Quite a few of the Wolves lads were in this part of the escort. As soon as the Under-Fives' feet left the pavement, about 15 Wolves came bouncing straight out of the herd to them.

One of the Under-Fives, Kev, had been acutely irritated by a ginger-haired lad who had gloatingly bowled around waving a rolled-up newspaper when Stoke got ran before the game. The newspaper had been brandished in a way that suggested it conceaed a weapon. This time both groups got straight into one another but Kev was running through Wolves punches just to get at Ginger. He grabbed hold of the lad's jacket lapel and whilst pulling Ginger towards him, repeatedly landed blows with his right fist. Even though Kev was being battered from all sides he stubbornly refused to release his opponent. It was as though he were willing to die so long as he took Ginger with him. The riot van, still stuck in traffic, was impotently flashing its light and sounding its siren. As police appeared from the back of the escort, the contingents parted. Wolves receded back into the escort and the Under-Fives made their getaway.

The following season, sixty Stoke were being escorted to Molineux when 100 Wolves lads bounced towards them, only to be repeatedly chased off by dog handlers and horses. Stoke managed to break out of the escort on a flyover. They vaulted some crash barriers, which meant the horses were now powerless to follow, and charged into the Wolves mob. Like a lot of firms they weren't prepared for the ferociousness of Stoke's aggression, and by the time the police got on top again, Wolves were backing off.

At the end of April 1990, Stoke's firm behaved in a way befitting the perversity of the club. It is no surprise that a club that builds new stands for away supporters should have a firm so strange that several hundred of them travel to the south coast for a relegation party. Stoke were already down and Brighton was the last away game of the season. By nine o'clock on the Friday night before the game there were about forty lads roaming around town. They had made no attempt to conceal themselves even when only fifteen-strong in a minibus. Still, they were fifteen of the gamest lads around. Stuck in a traffic jam in Brighton, they stuck their heads out of the windows singing Stoke City songs. They parked their van on a hilly street at the back of the railway station right outside the house of the actress who played English teacher Mrs Munroe in *Grange Hill*. After telling her what the kids were plotting behind her back, which she took in good humour, they began a pub crawl. In a pub near the railway station they encountered some Irishmen who were eulogizing the IRA. It wasn't necessarily the content of their spiel that upset those who would eventually deck them but their motivations for speaking so. These guys thought they could intimidate Stoke.

Meanwhile a carload of Under-Fives reaped the wrath of Brighton for the older lads' conspicuous arrival. It had just gone dark when they were hit by a mob of Brighton as they turned a corner onto the seafront just out of the main stretch in the direction of the Grand Hotel. 'Cam on you fackin' slags,' went the shout as twenty Brighton charged. This car crew was never going to put up much resistance, consisting as it did of Bakes, the Twitching Whistler, Ski Hat Man from the Shrewsbury game and Turtle's Head. They all ran into a side street and hid behind cars except for Turtle's Head, who had the ingenious idea of running towards the sea. He saw sense at the last minute, nestling between some old people on a bench in a tram shelter so that the Brighton ran straight past.

Brighton then made the mistake of searching out the other Stoke in town. The mob from the Irish bar, now forty strong, were in a pub on the seafront while some of the Under-Fives were down on the beach skimming stones and having a joint. As a similar number of Brighton came marching down the road, Stoke bounced out of the pub. One of Stoke's top lads fired a flare that ricocheted off a lamp post and onto a pub roof, which set alight. Stoke then charged into Brighton, who hit their toes. This was the beginning of hours of confrontations between Stoke and Brighton who kept turning up only to be run again.

Later Stoke went to the Brighton Rock pub. From outside they could see one of Stoke's top boys rowing inside with a load of Brighton. Stoke immediately started trashing the windows and terrifying Brighton in the process. The Stoke lad emerged from the pub unscathed, which considering his ferociousness is no surprise. This was to continue throughout the night, with Stoke steaming into pubs searching for Brighton. In one instance a few lads battered some doormen as the rest of the mob trashed the pub.

As everybody retraced steps back to the vehicles, glass crunched underfoot and half-broken pint pots were inadvertently kicked. This was the debris of Stoke's rampage. Most of the lads had not secured anywhere to sleep and about thirty went back to a covered car park to get their heads down. Car boots were open with people lying in them; others tried to sleep on bonnets and one even on the roof of a Transit van. More tried their chances on the concrete.

After about an hour a riot van arrived on a routine patrol. They couldn't believe what they found. When they realised the lads were Stoke fans they were flabbergasted that anybody would travel that far and sleep in a car park to see a team that was already relegated. All things considered they were decent. Any other police force would probably have escorted thirty violent vagrants out of town or at least told them to move on. These officers were genuinely amused and wished everybody an enjoyable weekend as they left.

At dawn seven of the lads came to terms with the fact that they weren't going to sleep and headed down to the beach, in one car, to see the sunrise. As they climbed back onto the prom the unmistakable red van of the moonshine posse from the Seventies came rumbling down the front. They pulled up for a view of the sea. There must have been about fifteen people in that old work van and some had brought their ladies along for a luxury weekend at the seaside. Apparently they had been boozing in London all night before driving down to Brighton.

Cossack was among them. Somehow he got involved in an argument with a homeless Scottish lad who seemed to be the leader of a small gang of vagrants. He came bouncing across the road at Cossack shouting in a broad Glaswegian accent, 'Fawkken cam own ya bastart.' He was dressed in a long green dufflecoat and baseball cap. The two got stuck into one another blow for blow. The lads who had just come from the beach feeling hungover, sleepless, grimy and fragile cringed at the heavy-sounding thuds of fists on cold dawn faces. Some were so knackered they could hardly walk let alone even imagine a ruck. Thankfully the homeless guy backed off.

They had only driven off for a short distance when the homeless guy reappeared with his little gang, which included girls. They were like troglodytes appearing from their lair as they ran through a tiny fairground to throw bricks at both van and car. It was an eerie, seedy scene. The power of this image was soon replaced when they passed a street cleaner sweeping the road in a tuxedo and dicky-bow. He had a black eye and blood on his shirt. Brighton is no doubt a violent place on Friday nights, even without visiting football fans, but it was not unlikely that he had been one of Stoke's victims the night before.

Everybody congregated around a couple of cafes near the railway station until the pubs opened. Stoke lads were appearing from everywhere and one had brought a football. About 300 lads took turns to kick the ball at hotel windows; each direct hit was greeted with an evil roar. No Brighton dared appear. At about two o'clock, at least 500 Stoke marched from the seafront to the railway station and the train to Hove. In the town's narrow streets, lads could stand at the top of the road and look down on what looked like a never-ending procession of boys right down to the sea.

One and all sang Stoke songs as they dismantled the train to Hove. One mob of about sixty escaped from the police, who were waiting at Hove Station, to go in search of Brighton. As they climbed a verge onto an oblique street, a riot van came up the road to intercept them. The lads, pumped up with a concoction of beer, drugs and natural excitement, spread out across the road and charged, roaring, towards the van. Someone threw a 'Men at Work' sign at the windscreen. The van went into reverse. Within a minute, reinforcements with dogs and a group of plain-clothes CID surrounded the mob and escorted them to the ground.

Inside the ground were about 1,500 Stoke scarf fans with all sorts of inflatable objects. Most of the lads went in the seats behind the goal and those in the terracing soon joined them after Stoke's first goal. Stoke picked this of all days to score four away from home. Progressively bigger pitch invasions followed every goal. When the first went in, fifty lads managed to get past the police and onto the pitch whilst lads from the terracing were scaling the fences and climbing into the seats. By the fourth there were 500 on the pitch. At full-time the whole Stoke contingent hit the turf. The first thing they did was charge towards the home end, which duly dispersed. People sat in the centre circle soaking up the sun and skinning up. One lad lay on a giant inflatable hand smoking a joint.

After half an hour of this a copper went up to some of the lads complaining, 'Come on now boys, this is takng the piss.'

'So what do you think of Stoke then?' one of the lads asked him.

'Yeah, you're great,' he replied. 'You turn our cars over and kick our dogs. You're worse than Leeds were last week and they've just won the league.' Apparently a mob of Stoke had spotted some plain clothes in a car and tipped it over.

For about an hour nobody bothered with the pubs. Instead they wandered around the pier doing all the geeky seaside things: eating candy floss; having photographs taken with their heads stuck through cardboard cut-outs of Popeye and Olive Oil, and practising for later on the punchball machine. Once everybody resumed drinking, the madness began again. The first pub the mob went in was really big and had a basement bar. Whilst drinks were being served to 200 Stoke upstairs, another 100 were downstairs ransacking the bar. When the manager realised this, he stopped serving. The mob reacted by throwing glasses and chairs at the optics and the mirrors behind the bar. As people made their way to the next bar, objects could be heard smashing in the one they had just left. This developed into the theme for the next hour or so: quick pint, then smash up the pub. By 10pm flares lit up the sky and the mob went on the rampage. It was the same cat and mouse game with Brighton as the night before, though now ten times as many Stoke were charging through the streets.

Throughout the mayhem the police seemed indifferent. Stoke were beginning to think that Brighton was to football hooliganism what Amsterdam is to pot. By closing time, though, they were swamping the town. Arrests were being made and officers were telling Stoke lads to leave Brighton. The lads in the car crew who had been run on arrival decided it was time to go home. Driving out of the centre of Brighton, one of them requested that Turtle's Head stop for fish and chips. Bakes lay in a fetal position on the back seat under a pink blanket. He was coming down off speed and took whining exception at having to stop. Suddenly

Turtle's Head screeched the car to a halt as a mob of Brighton ran across his path, pursued by Stoke lads. He and two of his passengers leapt out to join the chase, abandoning the car in a busy thoroughfare with three doors wide open and Bakes under his blanket.

By the end of a twenty-minute rampage, they couldn't remember where they had left the car and Turtle's Head, the driver, was missing. A lad said he had seen a maroon Volkswagen Jetta chugging along at ten miles an hour, kangaroo-hopping down the seafront. This lad, who was accompanying a local girl to the beach, was shocked to hear his name called from the car. He approached to see a very pale Bakes behind the wheel.

'You don't know how to drive a car do you mate?'

The guy was a non-driver too, and besides, he had more pressing matters on his mind. Bakes had panicked, and rather than leave the safety of the car, had tried his hand at the wheel. Meanwhile Turtle's Head was languishing in a cell at Brighton police station. He was concerned about his abandoned motor and tried to explain to the police where it might be. He told them the car had been attacked by a gang of youths and that he had to flee, leaving it in the middle of the street. Eventually a cop informed him that they had arrested a man for stealing his car. Apparently the thief had aroused their attention when he drove the wrong way up a one-way street and nearly ran over the WPC trying to flag him down. It was no great shock when he heard Bakes's whining voice from the next cell. Bakes explained to Turtle's on the way home how he had nearly killed the policewoman because he didn't know how to stop the car without having time to think about it. Of all those arrested, Bakes was the only one who had to return for court.

chapter sixteen

Agony and Ecstasy

BY THE END of the 1990/91 season, Stoke had failed to even contend for promotion out of the old Division Three. That year also saw the peak of rave-related drug consumption in Stoke-on-Trent, and after the excesses of a Friday night it was always difficult to muster a firm for away games. Those that did go had to be knocked up in the morning and badgered into waiting vehicles. Convoys constantly had to pull up in lay-bys as pasty-faced zombies vomited out the back of vans or walked in circles for two minutes to get their heads together.

It was on one of these occasions that some lads who had not slept all night decided to continue their party and head down to Stoke's last away game at Reading. A convoy of cars and vans made the journey. Green smoke bellowed from windows, amphetamines were bombed and cocaine was going around the vehicles like a fly on anabolic steroids. All this was washed down with cheap cider from large plastic bottles. By Reading, everybody was smashed and all maintained that the outrageous behaviour that was to follow owed more to the cider than any of a multitude of drugs taken that weekend. The lips of one lad even turned blue. Half the lads were laughing while the others stared in horror, believing that the LSD and Ecstasy from the previous night was making a comeback. This blue lip syndrome, along with a rabid frothing mouth, was an idiosyncratic reaction to the cocaine and was to become an established party piece over the years.

A lot of the lads spent the whole afternoon in the pub. Those who made it to Reading's dilapidated ground were happy to discover quite a few of the lads had made the journey. The cider was really kicking in now. Blue Lips climbed over the billboards and zig-zagged to the centre spot, where there was a microphone stood for pre-match announcements. His Mr Bean impression – 'Heeellloooo' – reverberated around the ground. Stewards came sprinting from all directions but Blue Lips managed to conjure the amphetamine element of his bloodstream and outrun them. Back in the safety of the Stoke end, he was asked, 'What did you do you that for?' The only honest answer he could give was, 'I haven't got a fucking clue.'

The stand was wooden and fans were not allowed to smoke. At half-time some of the lads were allowed to sit on the players' bench for a fag. Messages of encouragement were left for the Stoke players on the clay surface beneath the bench, such as 'You're all fucking toss'. Outside, a couple of Stoke lads were trying to sneak into the ground; many of the walls only consisted of corrugated iron. They went into the back garden of an adjoining house where a bloke was tending to his compost heap and asked if it was okay for them to go through in order to climb the iron fence. On seeing the state of them he didn't even reply and went back to what he was doing, no doubt praying that when he looked up they'd be gone. Indeed they were, right over the fence and into the Reading end. One of these lads was notorious for his numerical illiteracy when it came to the size of football firms. To him one and 100 were all the same and it didn't matter which, he would get stuck into them regardless. He was only five foot six as well.

It wasn't long before the Stoke fans could see mayhem in the Reading end and this character emerging from it onto the pitch. He ran across the pitch for the Stoke end, where Stoke City were in the process of taking a corner. He jumped into the air and challenged for the ball along with the team. With feet back on the turf, he beckoned the Stoke fans to come onto the pitch before being chased Benny Hill-style by the police. He ran into the main stand and down one of the exits. By the time this lunatic re-emerged through another exit, further down, Stoke's mob were charging across the pitch. The drug addicts who had now graduated to cider led the firm as they scaled the rusty old fence into the home end. The poor Reading fans were scattering everywhere. Still, they'd had their fun with two Stoke lads earlier. The only ones to put up any resistance were the old men who lashed out with their transistor radios. Stoke were only content when they had run the whole end out of the ground. As the lads were trying to scramble back onto the pitch quite a few were arrested.

On the way home the remainder of the cider was guzzled before another night of Ecstasy at either Shelly's in Longton or the Freetown in Hanley, the Freetown being a bit more *laissez-faire*. Stoke have certainly made attempts to moderate their behaviour since, as cider has never been seen at the match again.

★

The summer of 1991 was spectacular. The Stoke-on-Trent rave scene centred around two clubs in Longton: Shelly's and Entropy (formerly Introspective). This was about all there was in Longton and it was amazing to see this backwater transformed into the centre of the universe on Friday nights as up to 3,000 people milled about. It was fascinating to witness the contrast between the inhibitions of the crowd before they went in, nervously anticipating what effects the latest brand of pill they had just popped would have, and the primal dancing in the car park when they left. Dozens of car doors would be wide open whilst a cacophony of beats, basslines and piano chords from stereos made a pre-emptive strike on the impending dawn chorus.

The Under-Fives and Naughty Forty had carte blanche in Entropy, a luxury they generally enjoyed without adversely affecting the rest of the clubbers, whose minds were delicately balanced between paradise and paranoia. There were occasional confrontations but the lads would argue that these coincidentally ensured that the types who would otherwise have imposed themselves to the detriment of others never got a foothold. What was special about Entropy was that it wasn't actually a nightclub but part of a leisure centre. The dance floor was an old basketball court that vibrated when the real hard-core or anthemic piano tunes came on and the place erupted. Because of its makeshift quality, Entropy achieved a spirit more in keeping with a small underground warehouse party than a nightclub. You had to descend a stairway into the court. From the top of these stairs you could survey the whole heaving mass. It was like a monster stomping there in the iridescent light of the Moonflower before disappearing in a fog of dry ice, to re-emerge in flashing strobe light as a spasmodic army of robots. Because of this perspective at the top of the stairs it became known as The Pit. On both sides of The Pit there were ledges on which lines of people danced and in the centre an elevated, tiered platform that accommodated a pyramid of waving arms.

The MC at Entropy was hilarious. Ragga was a diminutive black guy with dreadlocks. What made him special was that he never took himself too seriously yet was naturally and genuinely cool, not trying to be cool like all the other MCs who were ersatz versions of one another, descending in scale from the Limelight in New York to the fourteen-year-old impersonating his sister's Top-Buzz tapes whilst deejaying at the youth club. Testimony to humility was when he turned up at a village hall on the outskirts of Stafford to MC for some lads who had bumped into him in a record shop.

On one occasion, Ragga stopped the music and had all the lights put on. From his eyrie eight feet up, he demanded that the whole club turn and face the wall behind them. There, high up on the black surface dripping in condensation, was a solitary letter E no more than twelve inches high and cut from A4 paper.

'Now I want everybody to look up at that wall and chant that letter. Come on ravers. Repeat after Ragga: Eeeeee.' Five hundred people responded: 'Eeeeee!' This was the prelude to the lights going down and the spinning of 'I'm Your Ecstasy'. The moment seemed to bring 500 strangers together as one, similar to the bonding effect of episodes at the football only with attractive women as well. That there are similarities may indicate that it's not necessarily the violence that attracts people to the football scene but the spirit it engenders, through which people experience temporary liberation.

Ragga's indoctrination of his drug-crazed disciples was to be his downfall. For some reason the Leisure Bowl, who owned the building, had demanded that their own orthodox bouncers be used, no doubt in an attempt to regain control from drug dealers and casuals. The incongruity of their black suits, dicky bows and moustaches gave rise to anxiety among the flimsily dressed and highly sensitive ravers. Ragga and DJ Daz Willet managed to excite the doormen's ire as every week they pushed the playing of tunes a little further beyond 2 am, until one week people weren't leaving until nearer 3 am. So long as tunes were playing it was impossible for the management to remove hundreds of hypnotized ravers. Things finally came to a head when, with about ten minutes to go, several bouncers stood at the bottom of the DJ box to make sure things were wrapped up within the legal time limits.

Ragga let the tune on the decks degenerate into a slow dirge and grind to a halt, before having the lights switched on. He then flew into one of his vintage tirades. 'Ravers. Ravers. Listen to Ragga. Turn and face the management, ravers.' All eyes located and focused on the bouncers. Ragga was pointing at them from the DJ box like some biblical prophet.

'That's your enemy, ravers. Everybody after Ragga. Kill!'

What had only moments before been 500 peace-loving ravers now echoed: 'Kill!' This went on for a minute before the lights went back out, the tunes went back on and the whole place went wild. Dancing that is, not fighting. The three suits could not have looked more isolated and lonely.

That was to be Ragga's last week at Entropy. It was probably a good job. Another few weeks and he might have had his beloved ravers performing human sacrifices on the podium.

The dance network often brought people together who hadn't seen one another for years. You'd bump into people who had moved to other parts of the country or you hadn't seen since school. Once they might have been unassuming swats; now they would be gurning, semi-naked exhibitionists asking who had all the drugs. One chilling example of this was the night in Entropy when a mysterious character was dancing with a gas mask on. He grabbed one of the Stafford lads and started hugging him. Then he stood back, spreading his arms as if everyone should auto-matically know who he was. The lads were starting to get a bit concerned when he finally removed the mask. It was Dexy! Nobody had seen him in the two years since Chelsea. His hair was shoulder-length now. He explained that he was in a bail hostel in Newcastle-under-Lyme and had escaped out of a window in order to attend Entropy. The bail hostel had a 10pm curfew. Ten years before, Dexy had been absconding from a detention centre on Tuesday nights in order to attend Teenscene at the Top of the World in Stafford. Anyway, the reunion was the beginning of a bender of a weekend that ensured Dexy never returned to the hostel. By 3am on Monday morning a group of them were still high as kites when they decided to play football in the infamous graveyard near the Victoria Ground. One of the lads, who lived in a bedsit across the street, stuck his stereo speakers out of a window and set up a strobe light on one of the gravestones. Because of his shoulder-length blond hair and ecstasy-induced gullibility, the others convinced Dexy that he was former Manchester United keeper Gary Bailey. In between a pair of gravestones that served as goalposts, he leapt around like a salmon while the others hallucinated that they were Pele. Even a nasty graveyard had succumbed to a flashing rave makeover.

The next notable episode in a league short on excitement came at Bradford not long into the next season. A handful of Under-Fives, along with the lad who had come on as a substitute for Stoke at Reading, decided not to bother with the game. Instead they drank in the grounds of a hotel, not far from the ground, soaking up the sun on the grass. As usual, narcotics of every description were in abundance. Stoke's lads subscribed to the philosophy that sleep only makes your weekend go quicker so why not stay awake instead.

At half past four, a youth of about eighteen years old popped his head into the grounds. It took a while for the penny to drop that he was a Bradford scout. When it did, the half dozen decided it would be a good idea to go back to the ground and meet with the rest of the mob, numbering about fifty. On the way, a car full of Under-Fives pulled up to warn them that about forty Bradford were heading in their direction. It was good of them to give the warning but only one was chivalrous enough to get out of the car and swell the numbers to seven. The scout from the hotel was spotted bouncing around at a junction waving a traffic cone. They knew he would not be that game and that his posturing indicated the Bradford were near. Stoke knew without actually seeing them that they must be coming down the sloping street the youngster was at the foot of. The Under-Fives could have easily run off. Instead they zipped up their jackets and, on hitting the corner of the sloping street, spread out in a line and bounced into Bradford. A black lad who was swaggering at the front of the Bradford forty was spooked by this and ran off straight away. The rest were happy to bounce around but didn't enjoy the magnificent seven landing punches on them and this meagre number of Stoke held their own.

The substitute from the Reading game ran a group of Bradford into what he thought was a pub. As he carried on throwing punches inside he was dismayed to discover a policeman serving behind the 'bar' and that it was in fact an old police station used on match days. On hearing, 'Get him wit blue jumper on,' he tried to escape but was nicked. Outside the remaining Stoke lads were just as bemused when a line of police came running out of a side door and into the fracas. The six Under-Fives made off up the pavement in a huddle, using parked cars as a barricade between themselves and the Bradford firm in the road. As a gap appeared between the cars one of the Under-Fives bounced into the road clapping his hands: 'We're Stoke fuckin' City.' The six again steamed into Bradford, using the gap between the vehicles as a safe haven to back into if things came on top.

At this point the police caught up and a couple of the Under-Fives were arrested. There was much laughter later as people recollected one of the lads being chased by three coppers shouting in Yorkshire accents, 'Him, get 'im wit' yellow coat on.' He dodged a waiting policewoman like a kid playing British Bulldog in a playground and bolted off towards the ground. He then got away with a stunt unimaginable today. He turned his reversible coat inside out so that it was now purple and came back, no longer ''Im in yellow coat' but an innocent supporter on his way back from the match.

Stoke had a massive encounter with Birmingham at St Andrews during the same season, in which both teams were competing for promotion out of Division Two. The Under-Fives travelled in cars and all were recovering from the debauchery of a Friday night. They missed out on Stoke smashing up the Shakespeare Hotel and arrived not long before the kick-off of what was to be a tumultuous match. Birmingham were winning the game until the last few minutes when Stoke equalized. The Blues fans felt hard done to by the ref and there was not much football played afterwards. Hundreds of Birmimgham swarmed onto the pitch and, after assaulting the referee, charged across towards the 6,000 Stoke fans penned in the corner.

Blues were throwing advertisement boards and anything else they could get their hands on. The away end was fenced in and so Stoke were finding it difficult to get significant numbers over to have a go at Birmingham without being arrested. Birmingham got onto the fence where many Stoke, including a large number of Under-Fives, were already waiting to meet them, and the two mobs traded punches across the top. One lad later described how he had been on the fence and seen a small black dot coming across the pitch and getting bigger and bigger until it eventually punched him. Another twenty of Stoke's top lads managed to get onto the pitch from the seats, dropping down from the roof of the executive boxes. They fought toe-to-toe with huge mobs of Birmingham.

Outside, Stoke's mob ran Birmingham, though the Under-Fives did not hang around long, as they didn't want to be arrested for their antics on the fences. A lot of them were eventually arrested anyway after images of their faces were published in national newspapers. A couple of weeks after that match, a few of them suffered dawn raids and were taken down to Birmingham to be questioned, though only one was charged. He was kept in custody and taken to court next morning. Birmingham courts have their own Victorian cells beneath them, with an iron landing reached by winding stairs. The lad charged was twenty at the time and was a tad nervous. Sharing sandwiches and orange squash with a burglar who supported Villa helped calm him down a little. The burglar said he was willing to share anything with somebody who had been arrested for punching Blues fans but the Stoke lad told him it was okay as he had a girlfriend. He went 'no comment' all the way and ultimately walked out a free man.

Highlights on the pitch were few but in 1992 Stoke City won the Autoglass Trophy at Wembley after beating Peterborough away in a midweek semi-final. On the way home from the latter, a vanload of N40 and Under-Fives ended up in a bizarre ruck in a most unlikely place. Another van overtook them in the middle of nowhere on an unlit dual carriageway, and as it did there was a loud bang against their van. They presumed something must have been thrown. Bozzeye put his foot down to catch up with the transgressors. After overtaking, he pulled up at the side of the road and the other van did the same about twenty yards behind. Everyone crouched at the back doors.

'Ready lads? Let's do it.' They leapt out onto the road yelling. The other vanload were already out though they were barely visible in the black of a rural night. Silver beams seemed to be flashing in the air. It wasn't until the first of the Under-Fives into the ruck felt an unusual blow to his head that Stoke realised that the beams were in fact swinging golf clubs. Luckily it was only the stem that hit him. Nevertheless, the club snapped on impact and the heavy end whizzed off into the van, smashing another Under-Five in the face. After a valiant stand in the face of such armoury, Stoke had to run back to the van. Before they could pull off, the van was surrounded and a club went straight through the driver's window, hitting Bozzeye in the face. Stoke tried running the van straight into the golfers but this only resulted in it being smashed completely to pieces. Stoke had to accept that they had been well and truly done.

The first Under-Five out of the van, Blue Lips from the Reading game, had obviously upset somebody. As Stoke chugged off all that could be heard from outside was, 'Where's that little fucker gone?' The golfers had Stoke accents! It transpired that they were beer monsters from Trent Vale. Among them was the famous One-Eyed Finnigan, a cyclopian doppelganger for Jeremy Clarkson. It seemed then that Bozzeye had been done by One-Eye. In all the panic nobody realised that Bakes wasn't in the van until he dived out of the hedgerow a hundred yards up the road to flag it down. He had no qualms about admitting he had fled into a cornfield the moment he had seen the first golf club. The van looked like there'd been a hailstorm inside it as Bozz was driven to hospital. Next day he sheepishly returned half a van to the hire firm that, strangely enough, he has never used since.

In the following years the harmony of the Under-Fives was shattered as heroin became de rigueur for some of them, creating mistrust and suspicion among people who had spent all of their teenage years together and who relied on each other for understanding, so special were the experiences they had shared. A lot of the users continued going to matches with the firm but became a group within a group. They now had an extra experience that only fellow users could really relate to and this produced a culture of exclusion and counter-exclusion between users and non-users. Relations were particularly strained between using Under-Fives and the older lads. Under-Fives who had merely had a one-off dabble with a Kit-Kat wrapper were being ostracized by some of their seniors who were determined not to make themselves vulnerable to the theft and deception associated with the drug. These older lads had seen it before, though on a more modest scale, back in the early Eighties. Had some of the Under-Fives enjoyed the same wisdom they might not have suffered the death, imprisonment and homelessness that has afflicted a good few of them since. Still, it's a crime that anyone should end up in such desperate straits merely because they imbibe a brown powder that but for its illegality would probably be cheaper by the gramme than drinking chocolate.

In spite of everything, the phenomenon of the Under-Fives that began one September afternoon back in 1985 is still going strong. Some of those present that day still travel up and down the country with the firm. Now that they are in their thirties, there is little distinction between them and the Naughty Forty. This has been a bone of contention with many. Some love the idea of having graduated to the N40 but many don't want to give up their identity as an Under-Five. It is, after all, how they will be remembered by others: everybody they went to school with, the blokes at work, the girls they fancied and the girls they married. Like blokes who still wear Teddy Boy suits, they are stubbornly going to be Under-Fives until they die.

section four

The Lads

chapter seventeen

Hooligans to Heroes

MY INTENTION WITH this final section of the book is to relate a few of the lads' experiences over the years. As I have already said, I was abroad on and off for a number of years but eventually returned to Stoke as the rave scene was heading towards its peak. It frustrated me: I was one of those who bemoaned the fact that it took lads away from the match and the rivalries we had so enjoyed. There seemed to be a definite dip in terrace activity but it never went away completely – like it or not, it never will.

Stoke City versus Crewe Alexandra does not leap out as one of football's bitterest rivalries. Nevertheless that fixture in March 1991 was the catalyst for an insane journey that has been left engraved on the memories of six young men from Alsager.

Stoke's steady decline during the late Eighties and early Nineties pitched them against smaller clubs they may have met only once in a cup game or pre-season friendly in decades. Crewe were one of these, so this fixture was not deemed to be a derby game despite the proximity of the two towns – more of a new rivalry. Stockport County were another team that, for a couple of seasons, became bitter rivals, with a number of serious clashes between players on the pitch and supporters off it.

Dario Gradi had instilled self-belief and spirit into his young Crewe team and their results showed they were capable of finishing in the top three, a position we longed for ourselves. The local press hyped it up all week, saying the Railwaymen were coming and had snapped up their allocated 5,000 tickets. It was a Potter short of a full house and a great atmosphere; the Boothen was on song, and the Crewies bellowed to the sound of a hunting horn. The game ended in stalemate and 21,000 subdued supporters headed into a crisp March night. The usual gathering outside the away end lasted minutes, if that, as most of the lads headed straight for the bars. A couple gazed back every couple of yards but did not expect to see any Crewe lads making an attempt to get through the segregation railings and onto the street. Everybody had the same idea. *Fuck it, let's have a pint.*

The Alsager lads didn't want a pint. They had a train to catch, and fifteen youngsters aged between fifteen and twenty piled into the back of a white Transit van. They had a nine-mile journey and fifteen minutes to get to the station. From there it is less than six minutes and you're on the platform at Crewe, a journey taken daily by several of these young men, as some worked for Rolls-Royce and others for the railway itself, lunching every day with Crewies who supported Liverpool and Man Utd and who scoffed at them over the *Daily Sport*, mocking Stoke's 14,000 attendances. Bitterness spilled over to Sunday mornings, as youths half-cut from the night before played Sunday league football against work colleagues in the other team. For the Alsager lads, this was not a no-mark fixture. Crewe had been buzzing about the game and had sold out their ticket allocation. All those wankers who followed Man U were going for the piss-up.

Alsager station was the dividing line between Alsager and the Linley area of the town. On one side was the Alsager Arms, noted for its fine ales and food and its hostile locals. On the other side of the railroad tracks was the Yeoman public house, which could be equally lively when filled to the rafters. The safety barriers had started to come down as the van drew level with the Alsager Arms. They had missed their chance to park at the Yeoman and get onto the northbound platform to pile onto the train. All three carriages were full to the brim with lads from Crewe, Sandbach and Nantwich. It was not a heavily organised mob but they looked like they were up for a tear-up.

The lads had missed their opportunity to get some hand to hand action, but as far as they were concerned no fat Manc was going to sit laughing into his brew at work tomorrow. The Crewe lads spotted the white Transit before its occupants had spilled out and into the shadowed platform. The train was about to pull away when the doors flew open, a roar went up and for a brief moment it looked like Crewe were going to come over the tracks. A house brick was grabbed in haste and a young hand prepared to let fly.

'Yah, wankers.'

The Crewe lads gave the gesture and climbed back inside. It was a blag; they had seen the age of their assailants and underestimated the situation. The young hand unleashed the full house brick into the closing door. It smashed through the window, shattering glass into the faces of the frozen antagonists. A dozen more missiles were launched into the side of the train, several hitting innocent bystanders. The emergency handle was pulled, leaving one carriage left on the platform. The train emptied and furious Crewe charged to the narrow exit. It took four transport policemen smashing into them with their sticks to hold them back, at least for a couple of minutes until more police arrived on both sides of the barriers.

Most of the Alsager lads jumped down onto the lines and headed off into the darkness. The remaining six crossed the road to the Arms car park. The train was going nowhere, and the sound of sirens and barking dogs gave them little option than to split up and call it a night.

'See you on the train in the morning.'

'Night mate.'

Four, five, six, she counted in her head as she scribbled down their names on the back of a beer mat. She had been the landlady for about six weeks and had barred most of the local lads and turned the pub into a students' gaff. She handed the list to the British Transport Police, and four days later the Alsager Six were arrested at dawn, most at their parents' homes, handcuffed and driven to Crewe. They were placed in holding cells and interviewed individually. There were no witnesses to the crime, other than the landlady placing them at the incident. They all held firm in their denials – bar one, who was eighteen and lost his bottle. After fourteen hours in custody, all six were charged with violent disorder.

Simon Davies is the least offensive of men, a wisp, slight in build, deep in his make-up and astute in thought. He was the ginger-haired one of the firm, pale, with red freckles, dry skin and green eyes that protruded slightly in Gerard Houllier fashion. At the age of eight, he set fire to the warehouses at the back of Twyfords railway sidings. Witnesses reported seeing a red-headed boy scale a fence, run across the railway tracks and hide inside a disused railcart. Others claimed to have seen the child laughing as he left the area and climbing a tree like a spider to observe his handiwork. That was the only time 'Spider' had been on the wrong side of the law – until now.

The lads were left with no option but a straight guilty plea and they were finally given a crown court date to be heard at Knutsford – and a chance of appearing before the dreaded Judge Robin David QC. The clerk to the court called out six names and six young men nervously stood to order. It was explained that they would be appearing before one of three judges this day, and hopefully by the time they,d had a final chat with their representation, they would be given an allocation.

Spider was in way over his head and felt intimidated by his surroundings. Nervously he watched other equally frightened men with nail-biting girlfriends. One had even 'borrowed' a cousin's child for effect, hoping for sympathy from the judge. Policemen strolled along the corridors, going over their notebooks with that 'don't let him make me bite' look. Press men darted in and out of court rooms, taking notes and speaking into Dictaphones. *Hope they don't write anything about me.*

He hardly had time to answer himself. 'Simon Davies' was the first of six names to be called and the six young men this time stood up together. *Court one! Shit, it's Judge David lads.* Their solicitor tutted; it wasn't good. They already knew they were going to serve time but with this man it was a question of how long? Judge Robin David served with the Royal Air Force during the War and fought gallantly in the Battle of Britain over the skies of London. He was awarded commendations for bravery and didn't suffer fools gladly. He believed in prison and passed out sentences to each of them ranging from twenty-eight days to six months.

The prison officers joked with the lads and made light of the situation. One by one they emptied their personal belongings into snap bags and signed where they were told. They each were given a brief visit with loved ones via a telephone link across small glass screens. This was the moment it hit home. Spider placed his hand against the window. He knew he must dig deep. He smiled at his parents, whispered he was sorry and left the room. There was no point mulling it over and getting upset; he had feared the worst for months and was actually pleased that the uncertainty was over. Twenty-eight days, to keep his mouth shut, do his bird and get out.

He wasn't short of people to call on for advice, and over the past few weeks he had spent time with a number of friends who had already endured Her Majesty's Pleasure. They discussed things he might come across and types of currency he could use to buy his necessities. To some degree, he was prepared. Cuffed left hand to right, he was led out of the holding cells with sixteen other inmates, walking two abreast and stopping and starting as the guards placed them in their designated seats.

Nothing anybody could have said could have prepared Spider and his young friends for the nightmare journey they were about to embark on. There were a number of fresh inmates on this journey who were in for a variety of things, mainly petty crimes and motoring offences. The numbers were made up, however, by four desperate criminals who had spent several months on remand awaiting sentencing for serious armed robberies. They had each received twelve-year sentences and Robin David had gone home a contented judge.

Their coach was a standard fifty-three-seater contracted from a local firm. The driver was a balding man in his late fifties whose last drop had probably been a party of schoolkids at the local swimming pool. Spider watched him joking nervously with the last of the screws as they boarded.

'Why so many of you today?'

The driver received a non-committal answer and two nervous heads looked round. Spider caught their glance and turned to see a wild-look-ing character, the only con who was cuffed to a guard. He was unkempt, with black, shoulder-length hair and a dark growth around his face and neck. Spider caught his eye in the window reflection and glanced away sharpish. The man's eyes burned.

The journey from Knutsford to Liverpool's Walton Prison is a relatively short one. The cons had little to say and the guards sat quiet too; they had a job to do and it wasn't a particularly pleasant one. Most of the younger cons had been paired off and seated near the rear of the coach, placed alternately on either side of the aisle. A guard would then sit in the seats that separated them. The older cons and the four who had received the twelve-year sentences were near the front, about four rows in. This was where most of the guards sat, with one standing on the steps beside the driver.

There was no signal, there was no sign, it just happened. The dark-haired con reached for a metal ballpoint and lunged out of his seat, grabbing an unsuspecting guard in a headlock. He had made his target the screw stood chatting to the driver. In one sudden surge, he had pulled two fellow cons and the screw he was cuffed to over a set of seats, grabbed his victim and fallen back onto an empty seat, his choking prey beneath him. In a scene that resembled a B-movie prison bust-out, the three other cons leapt from their seats, screaming and punching at anything in uniform. Spider was out of his seat too and being pulled into the nightmare.

The driver kept on going but was now being directed by a tall, skinny lad of Middle Eastern origin, who would continue to throw punches into the guards who were desperately trying to save their colleague. Spider stared down into the crush. The wild-eyed con was squeezing the life out of his victim's throat and the pen was embedded deep beneath his chin. Blow after blow piled into the con's ribs and his fingers were bent back past snapping point but still he refused to let go. In one final lunge, his three partners in crime steamed the guards and brought their pal some space. Spider glanced out of the window. They had just passed Sale in Greater Manchester and were heading the wrong way.

The con was now upright on his seat, holding the guard's face up and explaining what his demands were. His request for the keys fell on deaf ears, so without hesitation and without placing his aim, he plunged the ballpoint savagely into the guard's face several times, showering Spider with blood. One of the guards charged to his friend's aid, but received a sickening headbutt that rendered him unconscious. Again demands for the keys were screamed, but this time he stabbed as he yelled.

The keys were handed over and the guards were cuffed together and sat in the first six rows. Spider had managed to crawl back into his seat and watched as the guards were relieved of their belongings and cash. Spider realised for the first time that he was shaking, and so were the rest of the cons who were all now uncuffed and free to move to where they wanted to. The hijackers approached the youngsters and asked if they were all okay. Each one nodded and said, 'Yes mate.'

Guards were now being singled out by each of the four men and all received punishment. The sight of one having his cheek sliced with a piece of glass was gut-wrenching and some of the guards started pleading with them to calm down. It became apparent that this had been a desperate escape bid made on the spur of the moment and nobody knew what was going on as the coach circled a roundabout for the third time. The driver was terrified and added to the panic by saying that he must follow his route to the prison. He received two blows to his back and a barrage of abuse.

'Keep fucking driving, you cunt. Head for Sale. Head for fucking Sale now.'

All Spider could do was gasp as the driver's grey cardigan turned black with blood oozing from two puncture wounds below his left shoulder. This was insane; how could anyone stab the driver of the bus they were travelling on?

'You don't fucking like it when the cuffs are on you, do you, eh?'

The guard who had been cut became the target again. His blood was seeping through his fingers, and on the window were the splash marks from the initial strike. After what seemed a lifetime, the coach pulled off the motorway for the last time and headed into Sale Water Park. It was late afternoon and the picnic site was deserted, bar a courting couple. They were mauled apart and dragged from their seats. 'Out. Now, out, out. If any of you want to come, let's go.' The con was an awesome sight, pumped up and frothing from his mouth.

'We've only got a month. Go mate.'

A horror scene was left behind. Nobody could speak. All that could be heard was the sound of the engine running. The smell of human waste lingered in the air. 'Somebody get the keys, who's seen the keys?' Despite the panic in his voice, the rookie decided to act. He had been cuffed to Steve Yates and together they headed to the park exit and attempted to flag down a vehicle. Both con and screw waved frantically as a couple returning home from the supermarket veered onto the grass verge. The sight that greeted them as they pulled into the layby beggared belief.

All the guards were off the coach and on the grass bank. Some sat up, others had been placed in the recovery position by the remaining prisoners. They were all in a mess and still cuffed. Washing-up liquid and shampoo were commandeered from the couple's shopping bags and Spider and the lads applied it to the bruised and swollen wrists in an attempt to slide the cuffs off. Eventually all of the emergency services arrived together, and the pieces began to be picked up. Medics attended to the wounded, cuffs were removed by the fire brigade, and the police collected the remaining prisoners and gave a head count. They were taken to Stretford police station, where a number of the lads were treated for shock before being given a brew and a hot meal.

They spent the night at Stretford police station and in the morning were shipped out to Hindley young offenders institution near Wigan. Here Spider got his first taste of prison life. The first night was not too bad. He was padded up with a couple of lads from Merseyside. They had a lump of pot stashed in their cell and after lights out Spider lay on his bunk trying to figure it all out. Nothing would stay in his thoughts long enough for him to analyze before another flashback took him back into his seat on the nightmare coach. He remembered the advice he had recieved off one of the lads in the weeks leading up to the trial: 'Close your eyes and think of the Boothen filled to capacity on a red hot sunny day.' Spider smiled and got stoned with the scousers.

Exactly seven days later, six cell doors were unlocked and six young men were escorted out of the prison gates. They were taken in a civilian minibus by a number of the guards present on the day of the escape. At Knutsford Crown Court, they sat nervously in the dock that a week before had seen them sentenced. Judge Robin David QC listened intently to the prison guards' stories of being over-powered and of how some of their colleagues would never work as guards again. He also listened as each of the men pointed to the lads in the dock and spoke of their roles in assisting with the first aid.

Judge David commended the prison officers for their bravery that day and awarded each of the Alsager Six a full pardon, with a recommendation that each pay £20 to British Rail for the damage they had done to the train. The young men punched the air and hugged each other. Spider left the court as quietly as he had entered it. He had one thing on his mind: a half-filled application form that needed completing. Six months later, he and his best mate Mickey Rodriguez emigrated to Sydney, Australia.

chapter eighteen

The Freetown

MY LIFE WAS nowhere in particular in the early Nineties. I was back hanging around in Stoke again, mainly for match. Even the team was languishing in the lower divisions. Nights out in Hanley were vibrant and drug abuse amongst the locals was rife. I started working the doors, a precarious occupation but somebody had to do it. It was there that I got to know the Freetown – and Ged.

GED: *I knew of Jasper before I had met him, by reputation and the fact that we had many mutual friends. We'd see each other around and say hello. We first met properly working on the door of a mate's club. I'd been working there every Friday and this particular time Jasper and Wilson were helping out. I had never been involved in football; my only experience of casuals was of the ones I used to fight with in clubs and at gigs.*

I had lived in other cities but it was instantly noticeable that the N40 were an integral part of the pub and club life. Many lads I was drinking with were involved. I had grown up mostly on my own, an only son raised by my mam. The previous four years I had spent living and working with a band. They and their following were tightly knit and loyalty was important to all of us. I was impressed by the loyalty the lads in Stoke showed each other and that it was more far-reaching than knowing someone would stand in a row.

Jasper and I would swap stories, mine from gigs, his from football. Jasper's got a lot of charm, he's a charismatic character, and he's also a right moody cunt at times. Given the fact that he wears his emotions on his face, this can make for an amusing show. Those of us that love him and know him well find it especially entertaining when he's not being paid enough attention. The stormy frown can quickly turn into a rogue's grin as he realises we are laughing at him. If he calls you a friend his expectations are rigid and high. He knows his own mind and what he expects from each of his mates, and it differs depending upon the person. One thing is guaranteed: whatever his expectations, reciprocation is without question.

There were three key moments in the first two years that I knew Jasper. One of the first matches I went to was a home game and about 200 of our lot waited outside the away end.

'Gedi, I don't like it when it's big numbers like this, let's you and me slip down one of these side streets. See if we can't have a little guerrilla attack on about five or six of them.'

We didn't find any but I'd been bitten by the bug and was well and truly infected. Around this time we were working on the door of the Freetown Club most nights and spending a lot of time together. One afternoon we were drinking in Minstrels. Jasp was talking about his tour of duty in Northern Ireland and made a comment about 'Fenians'. It was time to approach a potentially touchy subject. I asked if I could have a word with him outside.

'Jasp, I like you and I respect you, I think you and me could be really good mates. But there's something we need to get out of the way. I'm a Fenian. I'm a Catholic boy from a mixed family in a Protestant town just outside Belfast. I came over here when I was a lad but I'm a Mick, mate, and me heart's emerald green.'

His heavy brow got a touch heavier and he stroked the top of his head. I thought to myself, I'm either all right or I'm going to be fighting like fuck here.

'You've got no idea how much I respect you for bringing me out here and telling me that, mate,' he said. 'Let's get inside and get a drink in us.'

The weekend the Good Friday Agreement was signed, he called me and we shared the hope of peace. I spent the summer of 1991 in Ibiza and I came back in quite a bit of bother. I'd had a nervous breakdown brought on by my activities and excessive drug and alcohol abuse. When I got back to Stoke, I spent two days in a chair at Brunty's flat saying fuck-all. Brunty and Stanner talked me into going up to Left Bank to see the lads.

As I walked into the bar, Jasper was straight up to me, full grin on and hand outstretched. He shook my hand and gave me a hug. There was a £20 note in his hand. He whispered in my ear.

'Get a round in and keep your head up.'

It was one small thing but at the time it was like being given a new spine. We now live at opposite ends of the country, but each knows that, when needed, the other on the end of the phone is guaranteed.

The Freetown represented different things to different people. Affectionately known by some as Free-for-alls and to others as the bar in Star Wars where the scum of the galaxy hung out, for a couple of years it was home to us. We had gone there before when it was a gay club called the Excalibur; friends of ours had done acid house nights there. When it first opened, the doorstaff were me and Jasper. The people that opened it had previously run an arts club; unfortunately they thought they were still running an arts club. They decided Friday night was reggae night and began booking bands that had played their previous venue, great acts like African Headcharge.

The first night we were on the door when five rastas from Cobridge came in. They said they weren't paying to get into a reggae night. We told them they were paying or leaving. They left. In an effort at diplomacy we spoke to them outside and told them that we knew they were the boys in their part of town but this was our club and if they wanted to be treated with respect, they had to show it first. The lads had not started frequenting the club yet and this small incident plagued us until the club was shut down nearly two years later.

The lads began using the place Fridays and Saturdays so we got to increase the doorstaff: the two of us were joined by Tyrone, Rocky, Stanner, Andy and Hutch from Liverpool. As well as our lot and assorted business-men of our acquaintance from various parts of the city (and various criminal backgrounds), we had bikers, rastas, students, prostitutes, drug dealers, thieves, leg-breakers, young villains, old villains, general nutters and virtu-ally every estate or local hardman: basically everyone that was barred from everywhere else.

The club had three self-contained bars and a dancefloor. We only really had one door rule: if you could walk through the door, you were in. One night some old villains were rowing with me and Rocky. The old bill arrived and said that we had all the shit of the city in our club and they thought we were doing a good job. The clientele were outcasts everywhere else but respected us because we showed them respect but never took shit. As the club became our second home, we would go in on a Thursday and leave on a Monday. Me and Jasper would be back Monday afternoon so Brunty, who had taken over the kitchen, could practise his chef's skills and we had at least one good meal a week.

The Freetown was a place we will never be able to repeat or forget, even though we can't remember half the nights we had there. There wasn't an area of the club that the lads didn't have carnal knowledge or at the very least a moment of pure sleaze in. The original owners were sidelined and friends of ours took the reins but a combination of a race war that wasn't and certain elements of the police top brass meant it was closed less than two years after it opened. For those too young to have gone through its doors, it is a local legend, the club Lucifer went to on his nights off. For those of us that lived it and loved it, it always brings a smile and that kind of laugh that starts a bit dirty and ends up somewhere in your past.

The Freetown was an incredible learning curve. I averaged at least three or four individual fights a night, and that was without the major disorder, when it was all hands on deck. In such situations you rely on your instincts and the support of a flanking wing forward; on one occasion, in a part of the club's darkest history and during a terrifying night of racial tension, my back was covered by a young pool hustler called Slugger Smith. Slugger was a young lad from LA (Longton area) who resembled a mixture of Brad Pitt and Shaggy off *Scooby Doo*. Slugger may have echoed their animation but pound for pound he could more than punch his weight. He became an integral part of the Freetown and its legend.

We were surprised at its high profile and popularity and could feel a desire for our turf building among a certain element on the other side of town. I don't think it was ever a racial thing on either behalf. The fact was that we had a lucrative club in the heart of the city and the local gang-sters – who happened to be black – wanted it. It was as simple as that. Only thing was, this was a football club run by football lads; no fucker was getting anything.

Tensions had been developing for a couple months. We had kept the door policy the same – if you could walk in, you were in – and the usual faces were of all races. Slugger was the first to point it out but I hadn't half seen a lot of new black faces, that tended to lurk about rather than party. For weeks we stood solid on our door in anticipation of some form of a takeover bid. Nobody knew what form it would take, but needless to say, we didn't expect it through the post.

Tense is the word to describe the early stages of the night that it came to a climax. It began with several early black and white encounters in different areas of the club and it was plain to see that this night was a tick-ing bomb ready to explode. By 9.30 p.m. I was well over my usual quota of fist fights. Over the previous weeks, several of our lads had been victims of knife attacks, as running battles had erupted throughout the city centre between the two factions. This night, as I noted the lack of numbers working the door, I couldn't help wondering how long it would be before I was on the sharp end.

For a number of reasons, the door security this evening was depleted. Shelley's was another club in Longton that had become very popular with out-of-towners, and the previous week a firm from the Castle Bromwich area of Birmingham had gone there and butchered some of our lads with machetes and axes. They were expected back so most of our lot had gone to defend Shelley's, leaving myself and Slugger to work the Freetown, with the added bonus of Mark Bentley and twenty-five lads from the match.

Mark Bentley came from a military family. The son of a major in the

Grenadier Guards, he served with them too, standing in full ceremonial uniform outside Buckingham Palace – though unfortunately tripping on acid at the time. Like myself, he was a social misfit who found contentment among the followers of Stoke City. Mark was quite soft-spoken but in a fight he would grab his victims, maul them, bite their noses and then snap them, leaving them discarded on the floor. He was a big gun to us and we relied on him heavily at times.

This night dragged on. No word came back up from Shelley's and the two messengers we had sent there failed to return. You know when you get that feeling, that no matter what the script is the final chapter is left open to the mind of a schizophrenic author. It could have gone any way at any moment. It felt like we'd got a war on two fronts, and the communication lines had been severed. No strategy, just waiting.

Slugger, all nine stone of him, stood beside me staring out of the double-panelled windows of the club door. It was 12.30 a.m. Little was said as we strained our eyes into the neon haze of the adjoining car park, from which any attacking force would come. Reflected in the glass door I could see the eyes of the man stood next to me for no other reason than loyalty. He was chewing his tongue in anticipation. Noticing my stare, he smiled back.

In the words of Slugger:

As you can well imagine, after catching Jasp's glance in that reflection, my palms were feeling mancky, but I was ready to face whatever was about to happen. Jasper and I were facing the glass doors oblivious to anything that might be happening inside, such was our concern for whatever may manifest itself from the night. When they first appeared over the top of the inclined car park, it resembled a scene from a zombie movie. Silhouetted dreadlocks swayed to the motions of men with a mission. They numbered thirty, and we had roughly twenty seconds to make our decision. I resumed my position, chin in, mouth shut. As they got closer, it was immediately apparent that they had come tooled up.

Luck had it that two of the Deets brothers were leaving one level of the club to reach another. They passed us and got the immediate call to arms going as they headed to the Groove Bar and Bentley. They had chosen a match day to bring it on, and the lads were already on the ball.

Two oversized black lads pushed their way inside the doors.

'What do you want?' said Jasper, as cool as ever.

Their reply was simple and direct: 'Where's Wilson? Where's me man Wilson?'

With Wilson nowhere about, I knew that the next best thing for them would be me and Jasper. Almost together, without acknowledging each other, we let out a roar and charged the two men back out of the door with all our might. As we surged forward, moving them towards the street, the mob outside crammed into the doorway to meet us.

The weapons thrust inside the club varied from machetes to potato peelers, and they had come to use them. In a brief moment of fear, Jasper and I realised the massive danger. A stool used by the cloakroom attendant was quickly obtained and launched into the doorway as we clambered to push the doors shut. This we managed to do, for a brief moment, as reinforcements from within the club surged to our aid. The mob outside stepped back to let one of their own launch a huge slab of concrete into the glass, which held firm, holding the slab suspended inches from our faces.

'COME ON.'

Stoke's firm exited the club in a tsunami of aggression and ran headlong into the knife-wielding cut-throats. We numbered twenty-seven and in the first few moments were reduced to twenty-five as two of our number went down. It was difficult to gain any ground and push them back towards the car park; as determined as the Stoke lads were, they now had to stave off the rasta men and somehow get the injured back through the doors into the club. As the fight continued without let-up, fifty-odd men used whatever they could to batter their enemies. Retreat or submission wasn't on either agenda. It wasn't a pretty sight and most of the blood spilt was ours.

Cue the man-giant himself, Mark Bentley. Mark had left the club from the Groove Bar at the rear, had run down a set of fire stairs onto a car park, and strode into view carrying half a pool cue. Seeing Bentley filling the huge gap to the left of me was the tonic I needed, and the squaring up ended with a sweet punch that I landed on the jaw of a bearded rasta, dropping him to the floor.

Bentley, in his usual ambling manner, walked into the middle of the debris-littered street, and without saying a word raised the thick end of his pool cue high above his six foot six frame and crashed it down with all the might his twenty-two-stone body could deliver over the head of one of their men, who was in the throes of taking a second swipe across the back of Boomer's head with a knife. The man collapsed in a crumpled heap. Bentley casually walked amongst the feud, picking targets and delivering the same swift punishment. He resembled a toddler hammering pegs into a board as each of his victims disappeared on impact. He had the edge now, as little or no interest was shown in him by any of the black firm. They were fighting for their lives.

Not for the first time in our history, Mark Bentley had turned the tide, rotating a serious threat to a full-on COME ON THEN CUNT YOU

FUCKIN WANT IT DO YOU? The fight was being pummelled out of them, and those that could, fled. A bit of a sad way to end an era really. The Freetown was loved by everyone sober enough to make the two steps from entrance to foyer unaided. But after that final battle, the place was closed down, leaving the social misfits from our town with nowhere to call home.

Life did go on without the Freetown, and within weeks we had found our new HQ, a terraced back street pub called the Stoke Inn. To the single or estranged lads among our firm, there was always room at the Inn, with Carter and Slugger taking up residence immediately. It was a home from home, with a quality Gentleman's Evening every Thursday. Sadly for me, it was the last Stoke-on-Trent address I would ever live at. Stoke was my home, and my 'family' were football hooligans with an unhealthy liking for unruliness at the match and uptown, and a festering cocaine habit. I awaited one last crown court trial, before making my move.

Not guilty! Relieved and tired, I took the jury's decision as my last chance, my final reprieve. I left Stoke in 1994, after spending the best part of a decade living in lawless animation. I was tired of it all, and slipped away unnoticed to another town. It was not hard to figure out: stay in this life you've chosen, and end up in prison, or even the morgue, or say goodbye one last time. If you feel I exaggerate, the following chapter is devoted to three immortal characters who did not make it.

chapter nineteen

Legends

T'ALKE PITTS IS a stone's throw from the lush suburb of Alsager, with its affluence and two-car families. A couple of miles as the crow flies but galaxies apart in essence. Alsager with Twyfords and Radway Green, the country's second largest ordnance factory, did have one small council estate built to facilitate these two local employers, but as estates go, it wasn't rough. In fact it probably had the best Grand National any of us kids would ever run in: loads of neat little gardens with trimmed hedges and conifers. Twelve or fifteen of us little bastards would enter, line up silently under starter's orders, then race from one end of the street to the other as house lights came on and dogs start barking, diving over and sometimes through the hedges, desperate not only to win the race but to get out of that bottom garden before the furious neighbours caught up.

Lippo had it much different. Talke Pitts was elevated and cold, the first peak of the Peak District, a mining area with grey terraced streets and pre-fabs, corner pubs and women with tattoos. He came from a good, steady family, with two brothers either side. His parents owned an oatcake shop, which Lippo burnt to the ground. This was the problem; it was never a case of not being wanted, just that Lippo was uncontrollable, a renegade child of fourteen and a known pyromaniac.

The only option was to place him in care. Time and again, the authorities would find Lippo a suitable home, and time and again Lippo would abscond and find himself drinking in the back bar of the Queens public house, dancing his way around the pool table taking pound notes off the old boys with his trick shots and seven-ball breaks. Lippo was at home. Even if the coppers had dared to enter the place, he would never have been given up. It was not their way. He fast became an apprentice, and a cheeky one at that, always associating with men ten or fifteen years his senior. He was a likeable little urchin, the kind you could chase on the school fields at dinnertime and though you could never catch him, you'd carry on the chase for the entertainment and out of curiosity at what he would do next. But while the rest of us attended the local comprehensive or secondary modern, Lippo was a pupil at the academy for young offenders and excelling at most subjects.

In the Seventies, the Talke Pitts lads were into Stoke City FC and Northern Soul. Wigan Casino was an hour's drive up the M6, and a couple of miles across the city in Tunstall was an all-nighter called the Torch. Combining the football, the all-nighters, and the drugs that went with them, the Talke lads were an active little unit with some unscrupulous characters. One of these was Brian 'Coddy' Hughes.

Coddy was the brother of Trevor Hughes, the corporal I had befriended in the Army. He was big and menacing, a butcher by trade and a butcher by nature. He was known all over the city, and particularly at the match, standing five foot ten and weighing over 200 pounds. He used his intimidating stature to effect. Coddy saw in Lippo what Fagin saw in the Artful Dodger and, with his huge, tattooed hands clasped around the neck of his young understudy, would stand at the turnstiles of many a football ground cadging the entrance money. Other Stokies would inevitably dig deep for a man and his 'son' who had travelled all that way on the off-chance of a glimpse of their heroes.

Lippo had just finished a short stint on the young offenders wing at Risley Remand Centre near Warrington. Grisly Risley had been Lippo's home on numerous occasions. He was placed with a foster family in Congleton, south Cheshire, and for a time he became quite settled, but it was summer and he was living in the countryside and there were fields to set alight. As the smoke cleared, Lippo was once again a fugitive, and back at the Queens.

August arrived and the new season. It was 1978 and an early fixture away to Ipswich had the Talke lads buzzing. The van was parked at the back of the Skylark pub. It was Friday and the fifteen or so lads intending to travel were sat, shirts off, on a wall waiting for Lippo to get back from the fruit and veg shop, where he had been sent to get as many fruit boxes as he could carry. It was a long way to Suffolk in the back of a Transit, and unless you were up front or hard enough to grab the wheel arch, it was left to you to make your journey comfortable.

The trip down was the usual mix of banter, tales of sexual conquests, who had been nicked and what he was up for. They arrived in the Suffolk town early in the morning and drove round the streets looking for a café, or somewhere they could put their feet up for an hour. The van was cramped and stank of stale farts and bad breath. They found what they were looking for and fell out the back door before the vehicle had come to a stop, and with a new wind piled into the café.

Coddy went in search of the nearest telephone box. Twenty miles away was the garrison town of Colchester. Based here were some of the spearhead battalions, usually on forty-eight-hour standby. Among these was the 1st Staffordshire Regiment, nicknamed the Black Staffords, a name awarded during their stint in the Transvaal for some of the ungentlemanly conduct they got up to with the locals. Coddy's older brother Trevor was a corporal in the regimental police. He too was Stoke-mad, along with two-thirds of the serving Staffords, the rest being from the West Midlands, Wolves and West Brom. This fixture was all the more poignant as the Staffords were to begin an eighteen-month tour of Londonderry the following Monday. Trevor, as I've already described, was a big bruiser and a handful, though to his credit he was a fair disciplinarian and carried out his duties by the book, occasionally overlooking the odd misdemeanour. He was no stranger to the glasshouse himself and was sixteen years into a twenty-five-year career. You could say he had been around the block a few times.

Trev arranged to meet Coddy and the rest of the lads just off the main drag up a little side street. Ipswich was littered with cobbled streets, thatched roofs and untold boozers, the perfect place for a piss-up. By two o'clock the lads were steaming and in high spirits. They neared Portman Road and found another place to drink. The afternoon sun was bright and warm, and the thirty or so squaddies took centre stage among the travelling potters and pit men. The atmosphere was a bit special. Stoke fans congregated around the Staffords, joining in with their rendition of 'She Wore A Yellow Ribbon' and listening as the Staffords added their own words to the chorus. There was a feeling of intense pride among the travelling army.

Coddy left with his protégé and headed towards the Portman Road turnstiles. There was a good twenty minutes of blagging to do, and with pockets full of coins Lippo went in on his hands and knees as Coddy fumbled at the turnstile, demanding the attendant exchange his pocket of pennies for pound notes. Distracting them from Lippo's commando-style entrance, Coddy sneered to himself as he rolled up a bunch of green notes, and with a belch he entered the stand.

Two of the Longton lads, Dalton and his mate Henry, entered the Ipswich enclosure to the left of us on the other side of a sectioned-off piece of terracing made firm with fencing and wire mesh to the roof, a precaution taken at many of the clubs during this period to keep out darts and home-made kung fu stars. The ball had hardly touched the boot of the first player when the Ipswich fans surged forward to expel these two northern invaders, who had waited for the Stoke players to come onto the field before making a two-man assault on the enclosure.

It was important for the players to have witnessed this somewhat misguided loyalty to the club. As far as Dalton and his mate were concerned, they had travelled all this way and were prepared to fight for what they believed in, *so get stuck in and win this match for us, 'cause we've just taken a kicking for you!* The pair were being pulled back into the seething mob as they tried to get onto the pitch. They decided to launch one last attack, and jumped back in among the local yokels. Again they disappeared, though the Ipswich mob probably caused more damage to each as they punched and kicked. After what seemed an age, stewards and the local constabulary hauled the friends out of the terracing, onto the pitch and over to their own end. Dalton hung on the fence, red-faced and out of breath, before swinging over, dropping the four feet or so to safety, and acknowledging a round of applause and cheers. Arms around each other, the pair laughed and headed up the steps to the back of the end and the rest of the Stoke mob. Henry looked and smiled at Dalton's first words to the rest of the lads: 'Eh, they've got some big lads in there.'

Newly promoted to the First Division, our aspirations took an early dent with a 3–0 defeat, with Alan Brazil and Paul Mariner playing blinders. Nonetheless the atmosphere was top notch. Red stripes had been placed on the ball for the first time, bringing chants of 'beach ball' from the Stoke end. Jimmy Hill and *Match Of The Day* had turned up as well. The thought of a TV appearance would help relieve the monotony of the long journey home; after all, that's why we stood behind the goal.

The Talke lads left Ipswich with the promise of a good piss-up in Colchester and a barrack room bunk for the night. Army hospitality is second to none. Coddy was thirty-four, an estranged husband and father of four. He was a keen amateur boxer and was given his nickname for his passion for swimming as a schoolkid. Tamla Motown and Northern Soul were his other passion. He loved the music and the all-night dancing and would work out on the dance floor, preceding a back flip with a couple of casual sit-ups. His love for Northern Soul proved fateful this night.

Colchester is no different to any other garrison town: loose women, squaddie-bashers, military policemen and untold pubs. One pub in particular was a local to a lot of the Staffordshire men. The Robin Hood was owned by Ansells brewery, which supplied most of the pubs in the Midlands. Dating back to the eighteenth century, it was a white building on a corner plot along the main drag. Saturdays was disco night and a good place to pull. The lads got in the front bar early, found a spot in the corner and plotted up. A few played cards, others supped ale and checked their Pools coupons.

Lippo found some entertainment of his own, persistently asking the DJ if he could be of any assistance as he set up his deck and twin sets of red and green flashing lights. The DJ said he was OK but agreed to let Lippo flick threw his singles cases.

'See if he's got any soul, Lippo.'

Coddy was with Trev at the bar, watching the apprentice in the mirrored optics. The flicking soon became rummaging, met by, 'Oi, in a min.'

Lippo stopped and grinned. 'As't got any mar, mate?'

'If I have I'll stick it on. I'll have a look in a min.' The DJ didn't like Lippo. He retrieved his box of music and stuck his headphones on.

The night was pleasant and some of the lads had taken to the pavement outside. A few tokes on a spliff and a shufti at a mammoth set of double-D cups had them following the unsuspecting recipient of a classic, 'Dust want an 'and with them, duck?' The pub was now in full swing. People jostled to get served at the bar while others formed a ring in the middle of the room, which had been set aside as a dancefloor. An array of Essex girls strutted their stuff while the apprentice eyed up their halves of lager being guarded by an overweight lady eating chips out of last night's paper as she moved her head slowly to the music.

Lippo's minesweeping was blown from the water by a broadside from Coddy, as he stormed through the disco dancers, fixed on the unsuspecting DJ.

'Lippo, is he gonna play some soul or not?'

The site of Coddy with his finger up the DJ's nose meant one thing: it was going to go off. A glance at the bar told him it was already on top. A young man behind the bar was jostling in a doorway which led to the upstairs accommodation. With him was the landlord. A glance back at Coddy and the situation was getting worse; he and the DJ were in a death roll over the decks and Terry Jack's 'Seasons In The Sun' was like a rap song. As the lights came on and the music stopped, several women started screaming; others ran for the door while men threw tables and chairs in front of themselves while backing away towards the windows.

Coddy released the DJ as his senses told him he was no longer the hunter but the hunted. He turned sharply and went into his southpaw stance, chin tucked in and tattooed knuckles ready to be read. The landlord smiled at the boxer and Coddy's guts sank; his opponent brandished a cutlass inches from his face. Common sense prevailed and a relieved barman guided his sword-wielding boss up the stairs.

The show did go on but the now half-empty pub seemed to divide into locals on one side and the Staffords and Talke lads in an alcove on the other. The girl with the chips burped as she finished off Lippo's planned minesweep and her mates took back to the dance floor. The lads started to laugh as they enacted Lippo's look on seeing the cutlass. Nobody mentioned Coddy's face. Trev and a couple of the lads ordered another round and it turned out the young barman was actually the landlord's son. They bought him a drink and he assured them everything was sweet. He wished them a safe tour of Derry and proceeded to serve the girl with the double-Ds. *Sorted, let's get minging.*

'Are they fucking smooching?'

Coddy was well pissed off. Lost 3–1, had a sword shoved in his face and this cunt still hadn't played any soul. Three days on the piss on top of that and he was ready to blow. He had not even reached the DJ before the landlord charged up to the pumps.

'Fucking come on!'

The first barrel tore into the ceiling, blowing chunks out of the plaster, the fluorescent lights showering the room in glass and white powder. The squaddies stood to, then backed cautiously to the door, wary of this seriously disturbed and enraged character who had now jumped up onto the bar and was looking down both barrels as he bid them farewell.

'Come on lads, we're off.' Coddy gathered the remaining Talke lads and, like a shepherd, steered them towards the street and safety. He turned once to see that his apprentice was out of the pub before him. His arm enveloped Lippo's shoulder. Just as his big hand pulled him in close, the second barrel hit Coddy full in the body. The blast lifted the two Stokies clean in the air and in a second they crashed onto the pavement.

Everything from then on was in slow motion. Pinned to the floor, Lippo could taste the flesh blown from Coddy's body but could not move to remove it from his mouth. His eyes filled up as Mally rolled Coddy off and blew into his already blue lips. Coddy was lifeless. As the first pint pot hit Mally in the head, the lads returned the empties which had been discarded earlier on. Lippo bounced to his feet. *Fuck me, they're glassing us.* He ducked down from a flying glass ashtray and sprawled over his mate, who was still frantically trying to revive the man who had brought him through the ranks as well.

The scene now was one of complete carnage. The Staffords had gone berserk. The fighting became sporadic as lads from other regiments joined in and sorted their differences. Glass-throwing continued from the pub and stools and chairs were traded through frameless windows. Trevor, in a one-man assault, stormed the pub door. He did not see or feel a thing; it was blind rage. As he vaulted the bar, the door to the cellar slammed shut. All that stood between him and that door was the landlord's doberman, which snarled and went down into its defensive stance. Trevor snarled back, and the two did battle.

'It's OK Trev, it's OK mate.'

A friendly hand fell on his shoulder, and the two military policemen nodded. 'Trev, let it go mate.' Trevor trembled and his arms felt weak. He whispered 'sorry' gently under his breath, released his grip on the lifeless animal's neck, and carefully handed the dead animal over.

Mally tried to keep his friend alive until the ambulances arrived, but Brian 'Coddy' Hughes had lost too much blood and was pronounced dead on arrival. The subsequent trial lasted ten days and ended with an acquittal. The landlord was rumoured to be part of an East End gang and, on punching the air, jumped into a Roller and headed for the Costa. The lads had lost another mate, and Lippo became a patient on the secure children's wing of a psychiatric ward. Coddy had danced his last all-nighter.

Miffer has already been mentioned many times in these pages. As we entered the new millennium, Miff was diagnosed with cancer. He fought it with typical spirit but eventually passed away in 2001. These words of tribute are from Cossack, one of our lads who was particularly close to the big man:

Mark 'Miffer' Smith was a big, bull-necked, rough-looking lad even at the age of seventeen. I first met him when I was sixteen. I had a chat with him about his recent rucks with Stoke city. His deep voice was scary enough, let alone his one-hit leashes. I could not stop looking at his tattoos on both arms and fingers. I was looking at a man who undoubtedly knew what he was on about. From then on I was going down Stoke, proud, cocky and with a man who was one of our top boys. Before I met Miff I knew a bit about the scene but this man put me on the road to Stoke's firm.

He made a lasting impression. I remember when we had come home from a game against Everton and all descended on the Wheatsheaf pub. As I looked out of the window I saw Miff: deerstalker, Lacoste polo neck, Pringle jumper. I can still see him now. Game as fuck and scared of no-one, he loved being outnumbered, his deep voice bellowing, 'Here they are, stand Stoke.' Then he would bowl straight into their firm, not giving a fuck what might happen.

We always had it mad at Luton; they must have loved Stoke going to their place. One year we took three coaches, were in their pub early, nice quiet

drink, then off to the ground for a row. As we walked, Miff said, 'He's here.'
Now I knew straight away, and as we confronted Luton, there he was: a tall,
black lad, well-dressed. As their eyes met, they clashed, then it was going off
everywhere. In the end Luton ran right up the road. Miff had met this lad
on every one of his outings to Luton and they always had it. I'd like to meet
this lad to exchange his views on Miff.

Before Miff was into Stoke he was a big fisherman – he loved it and
would go fishing all year round. We would take the piss out of him but he
never batted an eyelid. He played a big part in the lives of us Trent Vale lads.
He cared about us, like a big dad, and would be there for us, never letting
anyone tread on our toes. We owe him a lot.

When Miff was diagnosed with cancer the firm was gutted to see a man
built like a brick wall go to nothing, but he was well looked after by his
family. They went to hell and back but did a terrific job under the circumstances. Wigan away was going to be his last rowing match. Stoke's firm was
massive that day and the old bill couldn't control us. There was about 200
boys in the ground and still about 200 on Wigan Pier. As Stoke's firm was
coming in their ground, I knew they'd had it off; I could see it in Miffer's
eyes. Fifteen of them had had it with forty Wigan; both steamed each other
but Stoke well did them.

The big man is no longer with us but plays a big part in this book. We
all miss him and so does his family, especially his daughter. The day of his
funeral was hard for everyone. As I turned the corner it was like Reservoir
Dogs: all our firm turned up, shades, bald heads, like a gangsters' conven-
tion. There were a lot of flowers and a lot of Stoke City wreaths. We had a
big one that was laid out the full stretch of a window in the hearse: 'Naughty
Forty' in red and white. He must have been looking down on us and saying,
'Nice one lads.' He's got three sisters and a daughter who sadly miss him but
never forget him. I loved Miff, like so many others, but we'll meet again up
in the big blue sky.

'Berserk soccer thugs fight running battles' was the local news headline
after an infamous cup clash between Stoke City and Newcastle United at
the Victoria Ground. Newcastle have possibly the most passionate following in the country, and the first of their 6,000 supporters began to arrive
in the city as early as 10 a.m. for this evening fixture. It was going to be
a long day.

Stoke-on-Trent had received an influx of north-eastern families
during the mining revolution. Many settled in the Potteries but maintained family links with the north. So that day different gangs travelled
down in vans and cars and arrived at numerous locations and times, many

stopping off for a drink with Uncle Ebenezer and cousin Sharon before heading into Stoke town itself. It was a bit of a get-together.

The whole of Stoke was aware of the impending invasion, and by eleven o'clock the pubs around the town centre were beginning to fill with shirt boys and casuals alike. The expectant air was heightened for us by the sight of the normally non-participating shirters patrolling the streets in small mobs and scanning out of pub windows for any sign of a van or coach of 'boys' that might have taken a wrong turning.

Throughout the afternoon, hundreds of Newcastle fans entered the town wearing their team colours. They came in good spirits and were left undisturbed. There was no sign of any of their lads, though. Stories flew around all day – fifty in the Pig Pen in Hanley, others drinking outside the Market Tavern – but nothing was substantiated until Deadly Darren arrived in the Wheatsheaf, out of breath and in the usual rush to tell his tale. Darren was one of Tony's lads off the Battle Wagon, a local taxi driver who had gone to school in Alsager a few years above me. I had first met this tall, lean, compulsive storyteller during the punk heyday of the late Seventies at some of the village hall gigs we had urinated and vomited all over. He was the self-proclaimed Punk Poet of Punk-on-Trent, and called himself Nasty Dog. After a night of pogo-ing, believe me, he smelt like one. Darren's stories normally fell on deaf ears with most of the lads, but this day his sincerity was noted of by all.

'You won't believe what those Geordie bastards have done. Glassed a little girl!'

I found that hard to believe, as did most of the other lads. However, Darren was adamant, and not even he could make up a story that bad and hope to get away with it. There was still disbelief as people began to question where he had got such information.

'Signal Fucking radio, man, Signal Radio. I had it on in my cab on the way down. A vanload of Geordies have kicked it off in a pub on the outskirts of town, it's gone full-bore with some local lads, and a kid's been hurt.'

Within minutes, Darren's story was confirmed as phones went off and radios went on. The local bulletin confirmed the sickening attack and Stoke town centre went up like a furnace as the story spread from pub to pub. There were still five hours to kick-off and suddenly any Geordie about to enter Stoke town was going to get burnt. All reasoning went out of the window. Latecomers were turning up in the pubs straight from work, seething about the awful story they had heard on the car radio, not bothering to go home and get changed for the match. Everyone began hunting the Geordies.

By six o'clock the atmosphere was one of the most evil I had witnessed in all the years I'd been going to the match. A riot was imminent, and both police and the Geordies could see it. By seven o'clock, most of the Newcastle following had supped up and taken sanctuary in the Stoke End Stand. The normally exuberant Geordies stood in a subdued throng, with no hint of a rendition of 'The Blaydon Races'. It was near impossible anyway for anything to be heard above the lawless roar outside, as hundreds of Stoke fans charged at police lines in an attempt to break into the Stoke End turnstiles.

It is not acceptable under any circumstances to attack a 'civilian' supporter, whether he is wearing a shirt or a scarf, and ninety per cent of Stoke fans adhere to that unwritten rule. Unfortunately that code went up in smoke this night, and anyone who looked physically capable of defending himself – bar women, kids and the elderly – was attacked. Most of what I witnessed turned my guts, but I could understand the local reaction to the crime that had taken place earlier in the day.

While mayhem reigned around the ground, not all of the lads were convinced that Newcastle's boys had failed to make the effort. Seventy of the older N40 remained in the town in the back bar of Charlie's. Lee Carter, for one, couldn't keep still. Hanging about on the chance of a decent row when all hell was breaking loose at the ground had tipped him over, and he took his frustration out on the spindled staircase, sending everyone diving for cover from the flying splinters. He punched another three through before turning to Gina, our much-loved landlady, and ordering her a large one.

'I'm not having this. The Geordies are game as fuck. Where are they?'

Carter's question was answered immediately when the face of Bert the Meerkat, our top scout, appeared from nowhere.

'Roebuck, a hundred of them, big lads. They've got the EBF with them.'

'Nice one Berty baby.' Carter cupped the face of the young scout and planted a big wet one on his cheek. The EBF were the English Border Front, the hooligan mob that followed Shrewsbury Town. They were friendly with Newcastle's Gremlins. All the better as far as we were concerned.

'C'mon lads, keep it tight, the Geordies have got Shrewsbury with them, we're really in trouble now,' said Carter sarcastically. He was hysterical as he left the pub with Mad Barry, his life-long accomplice. The sight of them falling through the pub door and punching and kicking each other as they made for the train station had the lads falling into a jog behind. The tomfoolery stopped and not a word was spoken for the next six minutes.

If you have never had the pleasure of sampling our fine city, I'll give you a very brief description of the station and its vicinity. Horrible. Certainly not a place to be on a match day, but the Geordies had found it to their liking and had filled the Roebuck pub 300 yards along from the station. The area is dimly lit and terraced, and as you approach the pub at a crossroads you head down under a railway bridge, through a dark tunnel and over the D-road into Stoke itself. This was the approach the lads took, dark, restricted, uphill and right to the door.

'Right Baz, have this.'

Carter punched his mate clean on the jaw and Baz sent one straight back. With that, and the sight of the pub doors appearing as they headed up out of the tunnel, the Stoke mob fanned out across the junction, spotting several of the Geordies' vans hidden on the post office car park opposite.

'Let's torch those fuckers later, Baz.'

Baz chuckled and nodded towards the pub. 'Here we go mate, they're coming out.'

Estimated numbers of the joint Newcastle/Shrewsbury firm touched 100 and they steamed out of the Roebuck and charged down into the waiting Stoke. They came out to fight and had brought no tools. This delighted Carter and his mad mate, as they stood firm in line with the rest of the lads and let them come.

'Keep it tight. Keep it fucking tight.'

The charging mob roared down the hill with no hesitation. The Stoke lads tucked their chins in and prepared to start windmilling. Carter could already see his coming, a stocky bald lad carrying a screwdriver and screaming, 'E, E, EBF.' Now, having guests from other firms is one thing, but when they start shouting the odds, that's another entirely. This was Newcastle and Stoke's issue, and it pissed Carter off; not the fact that he was about to plunge a screwdriver into him, but that he knew this lad hadn't the bollocks to come into Stoke with just the EBF and have a go. *Don't get loud just because you've got the Geordies to carry the weight for you.*

'Wanker,' Carter shouted as the screwdriver tore up through his jacket, ripping his shirt and puncturing his skin under the arm.

Their front rank had arrived and Stoke held tight across the road, exchanging punches. Carter let the big lad follow through in motion and caught him with a sickening combination on either side of his jaw, dropping him instantly. It was time for the off immediately as the roar of the SPG police vans sounded the retreat.

'Carter, come on mate, you'll get nicked.' Baz was pulling on his mate's arm.

'Hang on Baz.' Carter leaned down into the face of the man sprawled out on the floor below him. 'Oi, dick. We're Stoke City and we're fuckin' mental.'

Carter stood back, simulated a drop-kick and ran off with Baz, laughing while Mr EBF lay on the floor screaming.

Events around the ground were degenerating into widespread disorder and the police were stretched to the limit. Hundreds of ticketless and banned supporters hid in darkened alleyways and gardens and ambushed vans carrying Newcastle's lads. Others laid a continual onslaught on the turnstiles of the Stoke End. Ambulances turned up in numbers to ferry injured Geordies up to the North Staffs Royal Infirmary, three being detained with serious head and face wounds. Inside the ground was much the same as the Stoke End faced a continual barrage of coins, ripped-up seats and abuse. It was relentless throughout the ninety minutes.

Fifteen minutes into the second half, another attempt was made to breach the police lines and get into the Stoke End when 200 Stokies left several town centre pubs and descended on Campbell Road. They watched from the shadows, getting more psyched up by the atmosphere inside the stadium. Sick of waiting, thirty of the lads decided to climb onto the flat roof of the police observation room between the Boothen Paddock and the Stoke End, run across it and make the six-foot leap across to the floodlight stanchion, from where they could climb across and jump down into the Newcastle end. This they did, and after making a human ladder several of the lads got onto the roof and ran across it as planned. A roar went up from the Butler Street Paddock as the lads caught sight of their mad mates making their attack. The Stoke lads all jumped simultaneously, landing precariously on the floodlight girders and beckoning the Geordies to come and fight as they climbed towards them. One thirty-one-year-old Stoke fan lost his footing and fell thirty feet to the concrete below, badly injuring both his legs and spine. Again police struggled to restore order.

'We are Stoke, we are Stoke, we are Stoke.' It was loud, aggressive and hate-filled. Even if we had won this cup tie, the atmosphere amongst the Stoke fans would have been no different, and an army of thousands waited outside the gates of the away end. A garden wall was demolished in a nearby street and bricks were lobbed into the seated top tier of the Stoke End. Most of the Geordies had to take cover down below in the tea bars and toilets.

For twenty minutes more the police endured attack, until finally the Stoke mob, still in its thousands, returned to town and other ambush points. For a while order was restored and the visiting fans were allowed to leave the ground and make their way back to their transport – but their vehicles had already been spotted and noted during the game. Six thousand Geordies now filled the streets and once more were hunted as hundreds of Stoke fans left their hiding places and rampaged through the narrow lanes, turning over vans and pelting the police with house bricks.

Fighting became sporadic once again as small groups of Stoke stalked an escort of 1,000 Newcastle, nibbling away at them as they approached the town centre. Here they came under a heavier, more coordinated attack, as several hundred Stoke hiding in the open-air market stormed into view, attacking the Newcastle escort directly in the middle, splitting them in two and causing chaos. Seconds later, Carter and thirty others made their move from inside the graveyard on the opposite side of the road, jumping out at the Geordie frontrunners. Stoke struggled badly on this attack and were beaten back over the wall and into the darkness.

Carter was incensed. 'Let's go again. Come on, let's go again.'

The lads wanted to wait and try another attack by the Glebe but Carter had made his mind up. He jumped the wall of the graveyard back into the street and ran punching into the front of the Geordies' lines, being smashed in the face with a haymaker immediately. He was lucky that police reinforcements were yards away and wading in with batons. Carter received a couple more sturdy blows from the crowd and was unceremoniously dumped back over into the graveyard, where he was dragged to safety. Those lads who threw him back definitely kept Carter out of the cells that night.

Once the police had managed to get the Newcastle fans through the town centre and past the Glebe, they could gain control again due to the land layout. The bridge and then tunnel were secured at both ends before the Geordies were allowed to proceed, stopping and starting every 100 yards or so. It must have been an eerie feeling for the Geordies as they crossed over the bridge and headed through the dark tunnel. All that could be heard by the 100 Stoke fans lying in wait in the post office car park on Leek Road was the loud echoes of hooves and the distortion of police radios.

'Shhh, they're here now.'

The Stoke fans let the first three or four hundred appear and walk past them. They were only on the other side of the road, yet still sat in silence, watching from between the cars.

'Keep waiting.'

As the first of the Newcastle escort reached the relative safety of the station entrance, out of relief they let out a chant of, 'Newcastle, Newcastle, Newcastle.' That was what the Stoke lads had been waiting on.

Once again mayhem ruled as 100 Stoke charged out of their hiding places, some running over car roofs and bonnets, and slammed into the retreating Geordies. They didn't back off for long, as survival alerted their instincts to stand in the face of the enemy or suffer the crush. It was toe-to-toe again for a few minutes until police reinforcements pressed home. For another hour, police fought running battles with stone-throwing men. Only eighteen Stoke fans were arrested throughout the day, a sure sign of how stretched the police manpower had been.

Stoke's shirt boys are renowned for being crazy. We have seen them perform for no reason, being set off by whatever it is that sets them off. It is not surprising; after all, nobody in Stoke has anything, it's a rundown place with poor mental health and the odd explosion in a group situation is always on the cards. This was one of those nights. Everybody fed off each other, culminating in primeval behaviour. The little girl being attacked may have started it, but there were people throwing bricks and fighting who had never had a fight before. It was a social message from the downtrodden people of Stoke-on-Trent, saying, *all right, we put up with it, and get on the best we can, but just beware, every now and then there is a chance that someone is going to light that fuse, and if it's long enough the whole city is going to go up with it.* The lads, however, hardly ever mention that night. A lot of innocent people were terrorized and we are not particularly proud of it.

If you remember the *Loony Tunes* cartoons of the Seventies, and the character called the Tasmanian Devil, well that was Lee Carter. You either liked Lee or you hated him. I prefer to think that those who hated him were too scared to risk getting to know the lad. Carter was from the Biddulph Moor area of Stoke, a rugged and wild place, like the man himself. As a youngster he was the apprentice of Philler the Beast, and through him, joined the ranks of the N40.

It wasn't long after his induction that the teenager was sat among older, more prominent members of the firm, charming them with his wit and humour and astounding them in battle with his quick-thinking and audacity under pressure. Lee Carter could have been a purpose-built football hooligan and cemented his place as a prominent, committed member at an early age. His dedication to the firm was matched only by the amount he showed Claire and his three boys, Liam, Jakey and Ryan. They were his world and he was fiercely proud of them; such was his love, he would have died for them.

For most of his early twenties, Carter lived his life on the edge, earning his money by whatever means was the most lucrative and least consequential. His family never went short, though Claire longed for a bit more stability and security as the boys grew and became more aware of their surroundings and their dad's goings-on. Lee realised this, and although he didn't like the early morning starts, or being told what to do by anyone he considered to be a 'dick' (his favourite expression when referring to someone not from our life, delivered in a broad Potteries accent), he knuckled down and took employment fitting airducts into factories, and lodged away with some of the single lads from down the match.

Working away and having the crack with the lads suited Carter, and the money was good too. Claire had found some stability; the only thing now was to get her family off the Sneyd Green estate and away from the marauding gangs and discarded syringes. The family moved to Biddulph, back to where Lee had grown up and close to his family. Claire had finally got what she wanted.

Carter didn't change any, his love for his other family only deepened as time went on, and his Saturday outings were as eventful as ever. At five foot eight and a deadringer for a 1960s Rod Stewart, Carter was wiry and lively. No opponent, except probably Wilson, fazed him at all; he could fight, and I should know. During one of my many justified tantrums, I ended up taking a left jab right on the button from him; not a KO punch, after all we loved each other, but enough to have me hopping on one leg and shaking my head as I listened to that universal tone and fought to regain my vision.

Family life in Biddulph was secure. Claire loved her new house and the boys went to a decent school. While taking them there she became familiar with the other mums. One mother told of her anxiety over neighbours who had recently moved in and kept unusual hours, with streams of visitors to the door. In no time at all, other parents were complaining too, saying how frightened they were to allow their children out with this influx of visitors to the area. Claire shared their concern; after all, one of the main reasons they had left Sneyd Green was to get the boys away from drugs. She told Lee and his decision was instant. *Dirty smackheads. Hate 'em.*

The mothers had devised a plan: *Why don't all our men get together and get them off the estate.* Lee was working down in Leicester at the time but arranged to meet six vigilante dads after tea on Friday when he got home. Who knows what was going through Carter's head but he didn't approach the football firm for any help. Maybe he saw it as a civil matter, but he chose to go it alone with a bunch of blokes he had never met. He did know the person whose house he was going to, and he was fully aware of how dangerous this man was. Chris Taylor was a sad loner from

Newcastle who we had first met during the drug scene of the late
Eighties. Taylor hadn't moved on from it. He looked like Virgil from
Thunderbirds, only on smack. He had been run out of town once before
after giving Ged thirty-seven stitches in his face and neck (hence the roll-
neck). Taylor had gone for a one-on-one straightener with the neck of a
Grolsch bottle hidden in his hands and Ged fought on unaware of the
appalling injuries being inflicted on him. Taylor was a cutthroat and a
nasty piece of work.

Carter met the six men and wasted no time. He said they would kick
the door in, batter the bastard and drag him out onto the street. No problem, they were up for it. It was tea-time on a Friday night and Carter
accepted the word of the men as gospel. They headed off. Along the way,
sat in a bus stop, was a fifteen-year-old apprentice hooligan who recognized Carter as being N40 and could see he was walking with purpose.
He crossed the road and offered his services. Lee told him that they were
getting smackheads off the estate and they entered the garden of a
Seventies-style semi. The youngster watched as Carter psyched up the
dads for the imminent adrenalin rush.

The door went through first hit and Carter burst into the hallway
screaming, 'Smackheads!' The other dads froze at the garden gate. Their
bottle had left them, and they had left Lee. Not the apprentice though; he
arrived in the lounge doorway as Carter was in mid-flight. Taylor was sat
skinning up after his tea, watching *Fifteen To One*. Carter nearly kicked his
head clean off, then landed a sequence of kidney punches into the sad
smackhead. Taylor's woman was in the kitchen washing the pots, and
came flying into the room carrying a sixteen-inch hunting knife. She
pointed it at Carter, who was stamping on Taylor's head stuck down the
side of the settee. The woman was hysterical and lunged at Carter, screaming for him to back off. The apprentice watched as Carter raised his arms
and backed away, trying to reason with her.

Like some demonic manifestation, Taylor rose from the settee, grabbed
the knife from his partner's hand and, with the full weight of a man in
motion, plunged the blade through Carter's abdomen, lifting him off the
floor with the sheer power that a drug addict has when he has lost the
plot. Carter slid down the blade as it protruded through his back.

Taylor removed the knife and, with a huge upward motion, brought
the blade through Carter's neck, slicing his jugular. Falling backwards he
hit the wall and started to slide down it, until he was propped up by a
radiator. Taylor plunged the knife back into Carter's face, choosing the eye
socket; the blade exited behind his ear. Carter fell face-up onto the floor
and Taylor's final blow went into his chest, plunging the knife through the

breastbone and into the floorboards. Such were the severity of Carter's wounds that one paramedic knelt with both knees on his chest to try to stem the blood flow, to no avail. Lee died from his injuries and we lost a legend.

The young apprentice who witnessed the horror remained with his choice of lifestyle and became a firm member. We all knew that friends his own age would find it hard to console him through his trauma, and although even we could barely imagine what it had been like, the lad was brought in close and carefully nurtured for a while. As for Taylor, after nine months on remand he was sentenced to four years in prison. The judged ruled that Carter had entered Taylor's house to cause harm and Taylor was within his rights to defend himself, although not to such excess. He served less than eighteen months and then disappeared, probably skulking around on some housing estate near you. To the six brave vigilante dads: shame on you.

Lee Carter had a traditional Naughty Forty send-off. The turnout was huge, and hundreds of family and close friends crammed into Carmount Crematorium. Outside, several hundred more football casuals of all ages listened together as the service was relayed through speakers. Lee's coffin disappeared to the sound of 'Wish You Were Here', his favourite Pink Floyd song. Sadness was etched on every face and the thought *why did he go it alone?* went through scores of tortured minds.

The family wake was followed by an N40 wake at the Talbot Hotel. It was an emotional night that went on into the following day. At eleven o'clock that Saturday morning, Cossack, Finbar, Stan and Billy Burton moved on to the Kings Arms at opening time. Every football supporter I know has a ritual that they abide by on a match day. Some wear a certain pair of boxer shorts, others have a certain breakfast. Carter's was a first pint in the Kings, where he would put his favorite song on the jukebox and have a quiet moment before joining the lads down at Charlie's.

The lads scored their pints and sat in the alcove in the front window of the pub. The sun spread its light inside and warmed the four friends after their marathon session, which none of them wanted to end. Going home and facing reality, alone and hungover, didn't bear thinking about. They needed each other. It was out of season and the pub was quiet but for a couple of old drinkers and the sound of bottles chinking as the landlord stocked his shelves. The silence was broken by the sound of the jukebox selecting a track. Amazement filled the faces of the grieving friends when the sound of Floyd's 'Wish You Were Here' gently filled the room. They recognised it from the previous day, and a chill went through them.

Cossack called to the man behind the bar and asked who had put the jukebox on. He was informed that it came on every so often when not being played and chose a track at random. Their jaws hit the floor as he went on to tell them that the only time he ever heard that record was when Stoke were at home, when a short fella would come in at opening time and play it while supping a pint, sat in the very window where the friends were huddled.

Typical Carter, there to the end, never missing a party, with a loyalty that never wavered. He is sadly missed.

chapter twenty

The Lads

T'ONY THE AXE Man was born in Newcastle-under-Lyme in 1953, the youngest of four children, and grew up in Chesterton, a pit village. His father worked at the two local pits, Oldditch and Parkhouse, until he was tragically killed in a roof fall in February 1955. Tony's mother took over the role as provider and travelled to work at Woods pot bank in Burslem, over five miles away across the city. Her three young boys were left in the sole care of her eldest child, so Tony's fourteen-year-old sister became 'mum', running the house while their mother went to work and seeing to the needs of the boys before her own.

Tony loved the outdoors, and would rush home from school every day, change into his scruffs and head for the local ponds with his fishing rods. Though not a big lad, he soon became known as a bit of a handful among the kids in this hard mining area. He took no shit or lip off anybody, though to his credit remained a polite and respectable boy. His sister at least gave him some guidance and he was a likeable rogue.

Tony was only eight when he and his schoolmate Trevor Hughes found their way to the Victoria Ground and the terraces of the Boothen End. He was soon a regular, and impressionable. September 1965 saw the visit of Leeds United. The Chesterton lads had taken their spot at the back of the Boothen. Leeds was always a big game and the lads were excited. They had sat around the ponds every night that week speaking of little else.

'Leeds Saturday, Tone. Do you think they'll come in the Boothen?'

'They're mad enough, all right. But if they do come in, they won't take it.' Tony spoke confidently, not once raising his stare from his bobbing float, and the other kids somehow believed what he told them.

As expected, right on kick-off the Leeds mob entered the Boothen, walking up a steep set of steps and onto the highest gangway in the ground. Twenty of them walked into the middle of Stoke's mob. This small gang of Yorkshiremen were mad enough and men enough, and strolled along the gangway in front of Tony and his lads. They made no attempt to hide their scarves.

'Eh ar, this is them!'

The kids surged forward, crushing against the safety barrier before them. Their high-pitched roar alerted the rest of the Boothen End – and the nearby bobbies. Two of the gamer Leeds lads reached up, and pulled themselves level with the juveniles, and started trading punches. Age meant nothing to either side: it was going off and the Leeds mob knew it would not be long before they were hopelessly outnumbered. This was what they had come in for. It was now or never.

The fight was just seconds old when the brawlers were joined by three policemen, who piled in without caution. They dragged the Leeds fans down off the safety barrier above them and hurled each one back down the stairs. Both police and Leeds now came under attack from all sides. Tony was alive and buzzing; this was his first real taste of the action and he didn't want it to stop.

'Get the copper!'

As the last of the Leeds lads were ejected through the exit, the police turned their attention to the Stoke fans battling to get down the stairs and finish off their chase. Batons were drawn and a handful of bobbies were beating back the attack, pulling themselves up on the barrier where the Leeds lads had staged their attack. One bobby leant over too far and failed to land a blow on Tony's head. His balance went and he was dragged over into the mob of kids. All of a sudden the twelve-year-old took it person-ally. Tony took a quick step back, and let loose his winkle-picker, straight into the lawman's eye socket. The attack was witnessed by all, and true to fashion the crowd swallowed up the youngster and aided his flight.

He had done it; he had got stuck in and played his part in defending the Boothen End. Tony had been blooded at the age of twelve. For the next thirty-eight years of his life he would be a stalwart, one of the most violent members of Stoke's small hooligan following.

Nine years on, and Ajax in 1974. Stoke in Europe for the second year running saw a twenty-one-year-old Tony searching for his passport. A one-all draw at home left us needing a win in Amsterdam to progress into the second round of the UEFA Cup. Ajax were a form team in Europe and the likes of Johan Neeskins and the master Cruyff made it a daunt-ing but exciting prospect. Over 1,000 Stoke fans made the journey in more than thirty coaches. Tony paid £21 for his ticket with Co-op Travel. He was with one of his many fighting partners, Minstrel from Leek, in a little mob of twenty good drinkers and fighters, and all in the mood for both. They travelled overnight, Dover to Calais, and up through Belgium, appearing slightly worse for wear mid-morning in Dam Square. It was the first time abroad for most of them, let alone Amsterdam, with all its sugar and spice. By mid-afternoon most had satisfied their curiosity and slipped back into the 'boozy Brit abroad' syndrome, swigging wine from two-gilder flagons and belching appropriately.

Over 300 Stoke lads gathered round two huge statues of lions, which they draped in flags. Tony had carried his flag all the way from home, a huge, eight-foot by four-foot union flag on a six-foot pole. He had spent every night for a week lovingly painting 'Stoke City' in white across the middle. He scaled the back of the lion's mane and stood atop the beast's head, with both feet on its ears. This was Tony in his element, taking centre stage as he waved his flag from side to side.

> We'll be with you, be with you, be with you.
> Every step along the way.
> We'll be with you, be with you, be with you,
> By your sides we'll always stay.
> CITY, CITY.
> Tell the lads in red and white everything will be all right.
> CITY, CITY.
> You're the pride of all of us today.
> We'll be with you, be with you, be with you.

Stoke City in Europe and the lads were loving it. These lads in the square had all more or less jumped off their coaches at the first available moment, many out of the back exit at a set of traffic lights. None had any luggage or spare clothes, and the only bags they carried contained Duty Free. This was a major all-dayer. It was asked several times if anyone remembered where the coaches would be parked, but it was sunny and no-one really gave a fuck.

The game had switched venues from Ajax's ground to the magnificent Olympic Stadium, causing slight confusion with the Dutch fans as well. The Stoke transport had all been put aside in one street, to make their exit from the city more controllable. The Dutch FA, however, obviously had not liaised with the police and had put Stoke fans at the opposite end of the ground to their transport.

Late afternoon saw the square empty as the small army of flag-waving Stokies split up into groups of twenty, each from their own area or from a certain pub. They had all agreed it would be more effective if they turned up at the stadium at the same time but at different parts of the ground. That way they would definitely catch the Ajax mob, and whichever group was lucky enough to get the first bite of the apple knew it wouldn't be long before the roar brought the other lads piling in from all directions. Within minutes Ajax would be in total confusion.

The Leek lads were the first to arrive. The first thing on their minds was to find their coach. They were delighted to find it parked outside the Ajax end. It was already busy at the stadium. Fans milled round shouting out for spare tickets while scarf sellers and pickpockets watched with keen eyes for business. It was not moody, just a little unfamiliar to men who normally only ventured as far as Blackpool twice a year.

'Eh ar lads, lets have a look through these turnstiles.'

The twenty lads followed Tony and Minstrel to a double set of turn-stiles. There were no police on duty and no stewards to help with directions. Tony presumed this was their entrance, until he saw three younger Stoke lads who had travelled with the Longton mob hurdling the turnstile from the inside.

'Eh ar, these are ours. Get 'em out.'

The three youngsters were pulled to safety.

'What's up lads?'

'Ay up, Tone. Fuck all mate, just this big youth at the top of them steps.'

The lads looked up inside the concourse that separated the perimeter from the ground itself. There were two ways in, you could either trudge up the massive flight of stairs and have a grandstand view from the top of the open end, or walk through a small tunnel that would place you at the bottom right behind the goal. Tony eyed up the options.

'Why, what's up with this big youth?' Tony asked, still staring at the tunnel.

'The twat pulled a blade on us, and told us we could only stay in that end if we'd come in to fight. He said he was going to cut us up.'

'How many of them?' Minstrel was quick with his question.

'Not many, thirty tops. But he's a right big fucker, with a big black leather bomber jacket, and he pulled out this big …'

'Right, if this is the wrong end, that means we're in the right place.' Tony was in mid-flight as he disappeared into the ground, his flag going in first. 'Fucking Dutch, let's give it 'em.'

The young Longton lads were thrown back in and everyone piled over into the concourse. It was packed inside with gruff-voiced orangemen singing, drinking and sounding horns. All wore red and white flat caps, and compulsory curly 'taches. The Dutch fans were so drunk and so loud that the Stoke lads slipped in unnoticed and walked along the tunnel towards the goal.

Tony had made up his mind. 'Hang on here for a couple of minutes till we get together, we're right opposite the Stoke fans so they'll get a bird's eye view of us storming this end.'

The lads looked at each other. 'Er, yeah, all right Tone.'

'What's he look like, young 'un?' Tony was unfurling his union flag as he spoke.

'Tall. Dark curly hair.'

'That'll do.' Tony was off. The end was not yet full and he didn't need the youngsters to point out the mob in question – he could see them. He chuckled. 'We can only stay in here if we've come to fight, eh lads?'

Tony raised aloft his flag and waved it from side to side as he zig-zagged up through the crowd. Two other union flags followed suit and the sight for the Stoke fans at the other side of the ground must have resembled something from the pages of a Sharpe novel.

Tony's eyes locked onto the big Dutchman simulating a knife-pulling motion inside his jacket. The giant laughed at the sight of this little man and his big flag. As soon as the Dutchman smiled, Tony saw his target. Two more steps and BANG, Tony turned his six-foot-long pole into a lance and lowered it as would a Plantagenet. In one almighty lunge, he put his eight stone behind the pole and plunged it into the man's face, catching him between his top lip and nose.

The man's lip split in half, revealing an over-sized set of tar-stained teeth, and his nostrils were ripped away. Covered in blood, the big Ajax fan turned screaming and ran towards a small hole in the wire fence. This was the Dutch mob's only means of escape and they could only get through one at a time. Time for a turn in Tony's character. As violent as he was, he liked to intimidate as well. He had got his power and violence in one massive hit. That was over. Now it was time for the psychological attack. The sight of those sad Ajax fans queuing to go through the fence to safety was the ultimate victory to Tony; not only had he splattered the main man, he had stripped his boys of their dignity as well. And then he stripped them of their flags, hats and a tin horn. Each of the Dutchmen handed them over as gifts before making their humiliating escape. Tony had never been a materialistic man and monetary value meant nothing to him. For that reason the Ajax fans were not robbed of their wallets and valuables. To Tony it was all just a bit of fun.

By the time the match kicked off, the lads had made it over to the Stoke section. The mood was victorious as the conquering heroes found their spot.

'It looked mad, that did Tone, we could all see you marching up the hill waving your flags. Brilliant.'

'It looked better from where I was standing mate. You should have seen that youth's face bust open. Fucking blade boy. He's lucky I hadn't brought my axe.' Tony wasn't joking either.

The experience was memorable but a 0–0 draw saw Ajax through to the next round and Stoke go out at the first attempt for the second time. All because of that killer away goal. The ground emptied in minutes. To Tony, the Ajax fans were on their toes.

'These lot are shitting it. Look at 'em. Come on Stoke, let's get together and walk back to the coaches. If these lot have got anything about them, they'll have a go there.'

The result was banished as the crowd jumped together and became one huge mob as they entered the street. 'City, City, City.' Nearly all the Stoke fighters wore light tan bush jackets bought from the Army and Navy stores in Hanley and sewn with huge patches on the backs and arms: 'Stoke City Boothen Enders' in red and white. There was no attempt made to hide your team's colours in the Seventies. The lads who wanted to fight always knew who they were fighting. You just knew.

Tony was right, the Dutch hadn't all gone home. Several thousand of them had gathered around the Stoke fans' coaches. The noise was deafening; what a send off they were giving us. As the approaching Stoke fans drew level, one solitary missile, a pop bottle full of urine, came from within the Dutch lines and showered the first couple of rows of Stokies.

'Dirty bastards! Come on.'

That was all it took, and hell broke loose for the second time that night. Not all of these Dutchmen were there for the fight, and big gaps opened up in front of Tony and the Stoke mob.

'Get in space.'

That was all Tony needed, enough space to start swinging his flagpole. As the Dutch backed off and the gap got bigger, Stoke got braver and ran in among the Ajax fans. The Dutch backed off again. Most of those who were not there to fight moved away to the sides, leaving what was left to take their pleasure.

The Dutch had now got it together and a good chunky mob of sixty were gaining some ground. Tony got trapped and fell well behind their lines. He could feel himself being dragged away and feared a blade. He had to act fast. He clasped his stolen tin horn in his hand and jerked it backwards over his shoulder, into the face of his big bald attacker. The attacker let go and clasped his face as he went down in agony.

'Do you want it as well?'

Tony crashed his flagpole down over the man's head, splitting it down the middle. He wanted to admire his accuracy but was off and back into the safety of the crowd once again. He loved inflicting harm on people, especially the big ones. The fight carried on for no more than a minute before the police gained control. Tony had one thing on his mind as he climbed onto the bus.

'Pull that back seat up.'

The seat was upturned, and Tony stashed his coat, horn and flag. The lads sat waiting for the coaches to leave. They were uneasy; none of them liked sitting around on a coach parked next to a massive brawl. People had been injured and it didn't feel right.

'What's holding these coaches up?'

'Not sure but the police aren't letting any of us go yet. Ay up, there's dogs coming now.'

Immediately the lads knew something was up. The police concentrated at the door of their coach. Tony had been spotted and they were waiting for the injured man to be brought to the coach to identify him. The man appeared minutes later, escorted aboard by two officers, one with a dog. He was pale and visibly shaken, wearing a blood-stained towel around his head.

'That is the man.'

He pointed to the rear of the coach, and Tony was escorted off. Four policemen took him to the local station and threw him in a small holding cell. A number of Stoke people came to his aid along the way but their pleas fell on deaf ears. Not one of these officers could speak English. Tony leant against the door of his cell. 'Can't bloody understand a word they've said to me. Foreigners.'

His half hour in the cell felt like half a day, until the sound of footsteps and a key turning in the lock brought him to his feet. In the doorway was a six-foot-odd inspector who stooped as he entered the cell. He looked extremely upset and his broken English accent was deep and powerful.

'Do you know what you have done to that man?' Each word accompanied a stinging slap across either side of the prisoner's face. 'He has had to have fourteen stitches in that wound on his head. However, the man has left the hospital without leaving a proper name and address. This will make it very difficult for us to contact him regarding your case. We could charge you in his absence, and you will go to jail.'

The slaps got harder and his voice bellowed.

'But, you too much trouble, we fuck you off home!'

Tony was on his way. No apology, he had a ferry to catch. He was met at the reception desk by six Staffordshire policemen who had come over to help their Dutch colleagues. They were all in civilian clothes and one of them held Tony's flag. They had brought it with them as evidence. It was explained to them that he was to be released with a caution and a strong recommendation that he never attend a football match again in the Netherlands. They also made it clear that Tony was to travel with their coach to Calais, and on to the ferry, where he could rejoin his party.

Tony knew exactly where the lads would be on the ferry, and headed straight for the bar on the top deck. It was packed and smoky.

'Yeah! Here he is, ay up Tone. Still got your flag then mate?'

Tony lifted it aloft for all to see and the room exploded in cheers. Tony and Minstrel walked together through the customs at Dover, with the six-foot pole resting across their shoulders. Rolled up inside was enough tobacco to pay for both their trips. Tony loved his flag.

Not every lifelong Stoke City fan comes from the Potteries. Some of our most loyal supporters have had to endure a life-time of travelling endless motorways and train lines, enduring traffic jams and missed connections and dreaded nights on cold, windswept platforms, all for the love of their team. For these men, every Stoke fixture is an away game. Towns like Ipswich, Liverpool, and South London are all places that have produced loyal Stokies. This story is about one of them.

Born in Nottingham in 1965, Millsy was brought up in the rough back-to-back terraced streets of the Meadows area, a stone's throw from Meadow Lane, home of Notts County football club. Millsy was the second son of three boys whose parents were both hard-working and upstanding citizens amongst their community. His mother was a machinist in a nearby factory, and although she worked long hours she always made sure that all three boys came home to a loving home and a hearty tea. Being mother was her most important and fulfilling role. Her husband, a heating engineer, strove hard to provide for his young family, and went on to take the boys into the business with him. Millsy had a disciplined, loving and happy family environment, right in the heart of our glorious country.

Millsy was no different to any other young lad of his age. He loved football. The back of his house faced over the huge open away terrace of Meadow Lane, a perfect view for the three young brothers, who would squeeze out of the attic window, sit precariously on the tiled roof and watch Notts County's home games. For ninety minutes every other Saturday, the house was peaceful.

At the age of nine, Millsy sat on his hot slate roof staring down at a sea of red and white. Ten thousand Sunderland fans had invaded the city; it was the first time he had ever seen such a travelling army. He was alone this day and had his perch and his thoughts to himself. *Wow!* He was entranced by the sight of two Sunderland fans who climbed out of the away end minutes before kick-off, ran to the centre circle, unfolded a huge red and white flag and planted it in the ground. The applause was thunderous. Millsy found himself slowly edging his way forward along the tiles. He might have had the best seat and view in the house but it wasn't enough any more. His long-distance spectating days had come to an end; the kid was itching to get down there amongst it and feel it properly.

Millsy did just that and within minutes was on the street below. Everything now had a different perspective. No longer was he looking down on his street scene; now he was looking up at the faces of support- ers of both teams rushing to take their places in the ground. Turned-up jeans and ox-blood boots were all about and the youngster was in a spin looking for a space that he could move into. His heart was pounding and he felt anxious.

'Have ya got the time, marrer?'

The strange dialect had the youngster turning to see what type of person spoke in such a way. He saw five long-haired Sunderland fans and five local lads, all decked out in red and white and black and white scarfs, proceed to knock lumps out of each other. The local lads, all in their mid- teens, had been waiting for such an opportunity to come along, and bang on cue the north-eastern lads, teenagers themselves, provided the rush. Neither side gave an inch. Millsy was frozen to his spot and was coming close to getting hurt by a stray boot.

'Come on nipper, on your way.'

Millsy was weightless and petrified as he was scooped up by a huge northerner and lobbed out of harm's way, literally landing on the seat of his pants in the middle of the street. He then watched the big man launch a decisive volley into the ribs of his victim, who let go of his grip on an opponent and crumbled to the floor screaming. Millsy had been thrown from the frying pan into the fire as the sound of screeching brakes had him staring up into the shocked driver's face. Fortunately the driver had spotted the disturbance seconds before and already started to brake. The sight of the small boy being thrown in the air and landing in front of his bonnet had the man shaking and holding his ashen face in his hands at the thought of what might have been.

Millsy was unperturbed. Still sat in the middle of the street, he had an ant's-eye view of what was by now a nasty little affair, with two men rolling across the stopped car's bonnet and disappearing on the other side. He could not believe what he was watching and, what's more, how he was feeling. He had never been as scared yet in the same pump of a pulse had never felt as thrilled. He could have sat there all day.

'Come on son, let's get you to your mam.'

The old sergeant lifted the boy and placed him back on his feet as the battle raged on. Both sets of supporters were tiring now as he watched the last punch and kick find their targets. It was over as the police van's doors flew open and the fighting fans were dragged and thrown into a heap. The van's door slid shut.

'Where do you live, son? I'll take you home.'

Millsy was put out that the policemen had come along and ruined his excitement. He shuffled along with his head down and mumbled to himself, 'I was only looking.' The nine-year-old had taken a ride on an emotional rollercoaster. He had never seen anything like it, and he wanted to feel and see it again. Soon. That two-minute wonder drug had him hooked.

For the next four years, the youngster strove to recapture that feeling, never missing a home fixture. Often he sat alone on the steps of the away end, his eyes scouring the throngs of visitors, watching changing fashions come and go and feasting on dozens of punch-ups. Nothing, however, compared to the Sunderland match until the first game of the 1978/79 season. Millsy had to travel to Mansfield to taste it.

Tony was his oldest brother and a budding goalkeeper. His childhood hero had been the legendary Gordon Banks and that was his reason for following Stoke City. Tony, only a young teenager himself, watched Stoke home and away all through school, making every journey alone to marvel at the likes of Dennis Viollet, George Eastham and Terry Conroy. Not only were Stoke marvellous on the pitch but Tony would stand in awe with countless others as the Axe Man and Mark Bentley put in fantastic performances themselves to give vocal support to the team. Proper enter-tainment value. Tony loved all of it with a passion. He was hooked.

'What's it like at the Stoke matches? Why do you always go there Tone?'

'It's nothing like you've ever seen, our kid.'

'So what's it like that I've never seen then?'

'Look if you stop pestering me and do my dishes for a week, I'll show you what it's like. Promise.'

Tony kept his pledge to his younger brother and three months later newly promoted Mansfield Town played host to freshly-relegated Stoke City at the Field Mill stadium, less than twenty miles from Millsy's bedroom.

'How long now, Tone? It's miles, this.'

'Listen our kid, we've only been on the train ten minutes. Two more stops and we'll be there. Jesus.'

Two more stops could have meant anything to the thirteen-year-old, who had never been on a train before, let alone left Nottingham. He felt sick with anticipation.

The brothers arrived in Mansfield at twelve o'clock. The town was already busy with supporters, who were basking topless in the summer sunshine and downing large amounts of warm ale. Millsy noticed that the large group of Stoke fans sat outside a public house on Quarry Road, a stone's throw from the ground, were particularly scary. Both brothers stopped to observe their behaviour.

'That's some of the Stoke nutters there, our kid.'

Millsy said hardly a word as he stared at what he thought were cave-men, with long hair and beards, grunting and shouting at each other and hanging up flags on the railings around the pub as if in some significant tribal decoration.

'Why are they all skinny and milk-bottle white, Tone?'

'Don't know, that's just what they all look like in Stoke. Come on, let's go and queue up to get in or we won't be able to see a thing.'

Mansfield Town had reached their highest-ever league position in entering the Second Division. It was a momentous day in their history and a large crowd was expected. Stoke had slipped, but their 4,500 following was resolute as ever and made for a great atmosphere. The brothers stood in a long line for over half an hour before taking their place on the terracing behind the goal. All the while Millsy had stood in wonder at some of the sights falling off a Bassetts of Titensor coach.

'These Bassetts lads are mental, our kid.'

Millsy had never met anybody from Stoke-on-Trent before this day and it left a lasting impression. *How could they all look so menacing and aggressive, yet look to be having a great time?* He puzzled at the way a growled explosion vented at somebody would be met by collective high-pitched laughter, which the aggressor would immediately fall into. He couldn't make out if these people were falling out with each other or not. One thing he did notice was the way they were dressed. A little shabby, to tell the truth. Long hair, T-shirts, denim jackets, flared trousers, steel-toe-capped boots and scarves that needed washing. Then there were the tattooed hands; they all had hands covered in ink and it unnerved him as they took up their position behind the goal.

'COME ON YOU RE-EDS. COME ON YOU RE-EDS.'

'YEAH! CITY, CITY, CITY.'

The boy was pinned. His whole body imploded with emotion, as he looked to his brother for permission to join in. Tony was already going berserk and the youngster let loose.

'BRING ON THE CHAMPIONS. BRING ON THE CHAMPI-ONS.'

'I fuckin' told you, our kid, eh? I fuckin' told yer. Mental. Come on City, come on City.'

Minutes from kick-off and space was growing sparse for the youngster now clinging on to his brother's back to stay on his feet.

'You just hang on there our kid, you won't fall over, and if you do you'll get picked up. Everybody always gets picked up.'

Millsy held on tighter. The atmosphere was all the more special for the much-anticipated appearance of our new goalkeeper, Peter Shilton, bought from Leicester City. Millsy's view of the playing surface was nil as he was rammed in so tightly he could barely see over his brother's shoulder. However he could see the nutters off the Bassetts bus climbing up and standing on their mates' shoulders, and trying to start off songs before toppling backwards and falling into the arms of their brothers They were paralytic, and you could smell it. Beer everywhere, along with the combined smells of stale pasties and rivers of piss.

'Fucking hell, these are like a bunch of Vikings.'

He was in shock and awe, and glad he was with Tony. Tony was glad he had come. This was the older sibling's first chance to share this mad world he had found all through the love of being a goalkeeper.

'STOKIE AGGRO, STOKIE AGGRO, AGGRO AGGRO.'

Millsy had never heard that song before but it was the loudest so far. The whole end began to shake and move forward.

'GET IN TO 'EM. GET IN TO 'EM. GET INTO 'EM.'

Millsy could hardly breathe as he and Tony disappeared beneath the crush. The daylight disappeared and all became muffled. He began to panic. He thought he was going to suffocate and Tony's frantic movements confirmed it. *Oh my God, oh my God.*

'Up you come, young 'un.'

Tattooed fingers grasped the boy's wrist and pulled him up into the toothless face of one of the Bassetts lads.

'You'll miss all the fun down there, ma mate.'

With that the man was gone. Millsy had been pulled free, and with him his brother.

'Phew. Never been in one as bad as that before. You OK our kid?'

Millsy was fine. He just wanted to know what was going on and most of all why were the Stoke fans were climbing over onto the pitch in their hundreds.

'Look our kid, Stokies are in the Mansfield End. Climb up here and see.'

Millsy joined his brother on the crash barrier and looked in complete amazement. It was going to be at least another ten years before he met Mark Bentley but this was the day he saw him in action for the first time. He was awesome. Bentley was huge but to Millsy he looked like a broncing bull coming out of the gate, determined to beat that eight-second intrusion on his back. The man was going berserk as he led the invasion onto the pitch, his face purple and slather all round his mouth. He looked rabid.

The reason for this massive change in the atmosphere was simple. Stoke's attempt at taking Mansfield's end was looking increasingly desperate for the thirty or so who had attempted it and were now being beaten badly as they fought a retreat across the terracing towards the corner flag. It was a painful sight. The Mansfield mob was 100-plus and growing. They had the hill and the momentum. Millsy wanted to be sick.

The Stoke mob covered the pitch like swarming bees and sounded like charging elephants as they headed over the fences of the Mansfield end and up onto the terraces. Millsy dared not blink. Mansfield's lads had been game all day and continued to defend their territory with valour, until Bentley came crashing among them from the side, his shirt being pulled over his head as they made their retreat. Millsy could see; everybody in the ground could see: not one of the Mansfield fighters wanted to mix it with the big man. Mark had caused mayhem. They were in complete panic and fought with each other as they retreated back up the steps and to the exits at the back of the home end.

Pockets of Mansfield who had been quite happy to dish it out beforehand were being hunted as they tried to blend in with other supporters. It was going off everywhere. The Stokies were not going to stop until they had chased their adversaries out of their own end, and they carried the fight down into the tea bars and turnstiles. There was a lot of punishment being given out; the lads had not enjoyed watching their mates get battered and everyone wanted their ten bob's worth. Over 200 Mansfield were run out of the end, and most of them headed for the same four turnstiles. Tony the Axeman and six of his mates were queuing at one to come in and have a go themselves. Tony was knocked flying and badly crushed against a wall as the turnstiles were hurdled by this fleeing steeplechase of screaming bootboys.

'Tone, is it always like this?'

'Usually, yeah. But it's even madder when someone tries to take the Boothen. That's real tense. And mobs like West Ham and Wolves always have a good go at taking it.'

'Will you take me on the Boothen, Tone?'

'We'll see.'

Huge applause met the appearance of the conquering heroes' return. Millsy watched captivated again as 300 tiny figures flooded down the terraces, dancing a victory jig on the steps.

'WE'RE PROUD OF YOU, WE'RE PROUD OF YOU, WE'RE PROUD OF YOU, WE'RE PROUD …'

The whole end joined in the salute in a feeling of utmost pride and togetherness. The young Nottingham boy felt touched. He had never seen the people that came from his area rally over such appalling behaviour; all he remembered at Notts was loud boos and slow hand-clapping at any sign of crowd trouble. It wasn't tolerated at all. In this case however, it felt like one of the highlights of their day. Small kids to elderly gentlemen stood side by side and clapped. His brother was right; to these people it meant everything. Many had spent the past five days of their lives half a mile underground or slipping out in a pot bank. They had thought of nothing else all week.

Back at the other end the dancing continued a little longer as the lads savoured their moment before ambling back across the pitch. Nobody was in a rush; being on someone else's pitch and not being challenged is another victory in itself. Men embraced other men, with huge hugs followed by aggressive roars and then hysterical laughter. The boy took it all in. He couldn't think of anything that had happened in his life so far that had gripped him so intently for so long. He was hooked too.

Standing room was sparse and the smell of sweat and beer once again filled the boy's nostrils. He was the only youngster of his age among the whole Stoke following he had seen that day – hardly any kids and not a single woman. He doubted his right to be there and, for the first time, wished he wasn't. He looked for his brother's reassurance, which he got immediately.

'What's up little 'un?' Tony ruffled his hair.

Millsy leaned in and whispered in his brother's ear. 'Tone, what if they find out, that we don't come from Stoke? What if they think that we're Mansfield fans?'

'YEAHHH.'

The reception the Stoke players received as they ran onto the pitch was deafening, and once again Millsy was hurled from one emotion to the next.

'Yeah! I've told you our kid, they're really friendly people. Don't worry about anything. Do you really think I'd bring you here if I thought you'd get turned on?' Tony carried on cheering, and his brother just watched. Everybody.

Within a couple of minutes, he witnessed the second pitch invasion of the day. Peter Shilton had taken his position in goal at the Stoke end of the ground and continued to warm up. Without warning or reason, 100 nutters behind the goal piled back over the fences and onto the pitch. Millsy feared what might happen next, until the sight of Peter Shilton being lifted aloft and paraded around the pitch. The whole Stoke end was in uproar, with waves of belly laughter and tears. Shilton was laughing too as he looked down at his adoring subjects. The atmosphere had taken a turn once again at the drop of a pin. Millsy joined in the laughter. He was having a good day again now.

The day ended for the two brothers at the final whistle. Tony had told his mum he was taking his younger brother to the park, and they had got a mad dash on to get back to the train station to catch the five-fifteen to Nottingham. Tea was at six on Saturdays, after their old man had checked his coupon. If they were lucky they would get away with it.

The boys could hear the sound of battle in the streets behind them as they headed off, and although they both desperately wanted to hang around and watch, both brothers were happy as the train pulled away to the sound of tired wood creaking and metal rolling on metal. Millsy relaxed. Neither spoke a word as they stared out of opposite windows. They didn't have to speak; they were thinking the same thing.

Millsy thought of nothing else for weeks. He kept his day out a secret, telling only a handful of close schoolmates. He had made his mind up the minute he walked past the Lord Byron pub and saw the flags being raised. Millsy was a Stoke City fan, and thought nothing of the alienation he might face from schoolmates. It was his decision as a thirteen year old, and one that never wavered. Tony too continued to follow Stoke but only took his brother to a couple of games every now and again. Tony was old enough to get in the pubs, and was starting to get into his own adventures. Millsy would have to bide his time until he came of age.

Over the next three years he attended three fixtures, all at the Victoria Ground. He stood on the Boothen each time and loved it; it was even better than his brother had told him – if there are words to describe 15,000 Stoke fans at full cry under the same roof. Man United and Wolverhampton Wanderers twice were the teams that he saw play. United rioted in the town centre before the match, but Wolves came looking for it in the ground. Both brothers stood in the bottom left-hand corner of the Boothen each time against Wolves, a perfect view of the Boothen Paddock, where thirty of the Wolves Subway Army fought with the same number of Stokies in a confined space for over five minutes. It was one of the most sustained battles a lot of the lads had ever fought in, and is talked about to this day.

On his sixteenth birthday, Tony asked his coming-of-age brother if he would like a season ticket to stand with him on the Boothen End. Millsy was thrilled.

'A season ticket for Stoke? Nice one Tone. Erm, would it be OK if mine was for the Boothen Paddock instead?'

Tony grinned. 'No probs, our kid, I fancied a change anyway.' Tony knew where his brother was heading, he could see it in his eyes, it was just a case of not letting him get hurt in any way. You could get no guarantees of that, standing in the Paddock in the early Eighties.

To continue the story on through the Nineties and beyond, I will introduce a few of the lads who were still being bitten by the bug and continued, in all honesty, to blight the name of our football club. I don't think there's one of us who is not secretly ashamed of the black name we have painted our club with. Indeed, I think we're all in agreement that a contributing factor to the uprooting of our ancestral home, the Victoria Ground, to the cold Britannia Stadium on the hill, is partly due to our appalling behaviour in the back streets of Stoke. For this I am deeply sorry. I look at a picture of a packed-out Boothen and sometimes cry at the thought of all those childhood memories and the agony of never being able to set foot in my only true home, ever again.

But just because I have repented my sins does not mean everybody has, and certainly does not mean hooliganism is going to go away. The stories that follow were contributed by the lads. I have placed them in roughly chronological order to reflect the changing nature of our firm.

First up is Spoon, original N40 and a well-known face to the lads and the law. The kind who knows virtually everyone at Stoke, he had been a diehard and followed his team through thick, and mostly thin, for over twenty-five years. He spends most of the pre/post-match time catching up with dozens of lads he has got to know. He is never a leader by choice but 100 per cent reliable when your back's to the wall. One of Stoke's typical 'older and balder' crew, he also has a heart of gold. He once got £5,000 redundancy and spent half buying drinks for mates worse off than himself. Tragically, he lost his brother a few years back, but found it inside himself to bounce back, something lesser men would not have done. Hard working and as hard as they come, his 'Phil Mitchell' appearance belies his qualities as a generous and intelligent bloke.

Getting Started (Spoon)

I started to watch Stoke City in 1973, at a time when, walking down Lonsdale Street, you could see all the shop windows boarded up on match days. The Stoke End was a big open away end with no segregation, no police in the ground, no riot vans, dogs or helicopters. There were no groups hanging around on street corners back then, speaking shadily into mobile phones, but it was hooligan heaven. Everyone was a hooligan back then. Every match involved a fight and for a young lad games could be a bit frightening.

I never got caught up in any violence until Arsenal away in 1975, when I was nine years old and some cockneys wanted to give my family a kicking. Stoke never hit kids or scarfers; it always has been and always will be that way. But in 1978, I had to run on the pitch with the fifty Stoke fans at West Ham, where there was no segregation. A copper told me and my family, as he desperately tried to hold back a seething mob of some hundreds of skinheads, 'If they get through, make a break for it onto the pitch.' They promptly did when Stoke equalised, and we escaped for safety. They even had female skinheads, complete with braces, who looked as hard as their men. It seemed like the whole end wanted to kill us. I walked with my dad back to the car thinking, *I'm going to die here at this match*. At Millwall I had my scarf nicked by some neanderthals but I wanted to carry on watching my team and never gave up.

The worst violence I've ever seen was at Bolton in the Seventies. They had just built a new wall and there was rubble everywhere. All through the game, people were getting stretchered to hospital, with bricks flying everywhere. It was the first time I had sat in the stand at a game and I was glad I had. Even in relative safety, part of a pushbike flew inches past my head. It was rough as fuck.

From 1979 to 81, virtually all the home games had trouble: Wolves at home battling in the Paddock, Leeds trying to take the Boothen End, West Ham getting kicked all the way out of the Boothen into the Paddock and back out again. Villa ran onto the pitch the year they won the league, but didn't stay there for long. In those days the railings were spiked, and the Paddock and Boothen End came on and kicked fuck out of them. In the rush to escape, one Villa lad impaled himself.

There weren't any casuals back then, at least not at Stoke. It was mostly long hair or skinheads and most people looked like they had just finished work. There wasn't the organised police intelligence or observation such as CCTV, video cameras, undercover officers and riot squads. We were beginning to get organised. The top boys were organising travel and certain pubs would house the hooligan lads getting it together. And at Stoke, if there weren't any away fans to have it with, they used to fight regularly at the back of the Boothen End; for example, Longton and Newcastle would have a set-to to ease the boredom. The buzz came when you went out of the ground. It would kick off straight away, and in those days Stoke got crowds of 20-30,000 so the numbers involved were high. Fights usually erupted from the ground all the way back to the station.

Birmingham are a side I have always hated. In 1979, I got hit walking back to the car and in 1982, when we played them again, I twatted the first Blue I set eyes on. In 1985, when we were relegated, Rich and I went to Tottenham on the official coaches. There were few casuals there, and Tottenham were in our enclosure with the other forty or so Stoke fans. We were embarrassing, and it was enough to put anyone off the scene. They even attacked us through the lines of police on the walk back to the coach.

I had decided by that time that instead of quitting Stoke, I'd become one of the lads – if you can't beat 'em, join 'em. The first away match with the boys was Chelsea. I was seventeen and cocky in my Pringle sweater, tidy jeans and Adidas trainers. We only made it as far as Northampton services when it went off with Man City, we all got nicked (the first of many times for me) but most of us got off without being charged. I was hooked from then on.

A couple of times I've stopped going with the lads because I was getting nicked too often, but I'm still here, a bit wiser but still loving the buzz when I'm with the lads and a big game means it's likely to go off. At fourteen I watched, at seventeen I took part, at thirty-six I still do. I'm Stoke and, like other lads my age, it's in my blood, like a drug.

Leeds mid-Seventies (Pecker)

Somewhere between the ages of sixteen and eighteen I began to understand the need to go with all the lads, as I'd had a few escapes, being legged down the road when only a couple of us were present. I had never considered myself one of the lads; my only priority was to see the Potters whenever possible, but it was a safer way of travelling – and the quickest way then was by train.

We were top of Division One and took two special trains to Leeds. In those days you might have a few cans and maybe a small bottle of spirits and when you left the train you were marched to the ground by the old bill. The attire of the day was twenty-four-inch bottle-green cords with fuck-off side pockets, which made you look like Lurch from *The Addams Family*. I bought these from Gladrags, which used to be the old Co-op building down Hope Street in Hanley. There were no fancy signs up; you went in and there was a counter and shelves behind with a few bits of clobber like cord and tweed bomber jackets and trousers. Some of the lads would visit the shop and all they could hear was the machinists knocking up the clobber in the back. On a few occasions nobody would come to serve them – I think they could not hear anybody entering the shop because of the noise – so they helped themselves and made a few bob selling what they had acquired from behind the counter, which would go to fund away days.

The shoes, fuck me, I can't believe I wore the offending items. They were bought from either Dolcis or Freeman Hardy Willis and had like a crepe wedged sole and a dead shiney top which used to peel off. The jumper was a V-necked plain woollen one bought from either Dorothy Perkins or Chelsea Girl; yeah, that's right, before you take the piss that's how small I was in them days. The shirt was a pyjama-collared one from Haydens, the jacket was from Chawners in Hope Street (I can't believe I wore all this bollocks), a 'budgie' jacket: these were like a tapered bomber jacket which had a four-inch zip at the bottom of each arm, a massive butterfly collar and two zipped side pockets. I must have looked a right cunt.

As we came out of the railway station, there were still Stoke lads coming over the railway flyover; that's how many there were that day. I heard a bit of a roar and saw the Stoke lads chasing fifty Leeds lads down the road. There were some massive advertising boards beside us and the Leeds lads were running across some spare ground which was covered in red ash. When I got to the boards the Leeds lads had stopped on this spare ground and started tossing pieces of red ash. I popped my head from behind the boards and could see the Stoke lads dropping like ninepins.

The old bill sorted it out and marched us up to the ground. It seemed about a three-mile march. All I remember on the way was demolished houses and a few Leeds lads mouthing off. I was a bit relieved to get to the ground but at that stage scores were about even and I was not too worried about the march back to the station with the police in tow. How wrong I was.

We lost the match 2–1 and a young Stoke prospect called Kevin Sheldon broke his leg with some help from future Stoke manager Joe Jordan, then a toothless forward for Leeds. By the end of the day I wished I had been carried out of the ground with Kevin Sheldon on that stretcher. Ten minutes from the end it was already dark. The gates had just been opened when some Leeds lads came in behind us. The first I knew about it was when I heard some northern accent say, 'I'm having his shoes,' followed by one of his mates saying, 'I'm having his trousers.' Before you could get your head around what was going on, the brawl had begun. Fair play to the Leeds lads, they were hugely outnumbered again but really up for it. Stoke waded in and legged them out of the ground, only to be confronted by the police.

Now it was the begining of a long walk – no, not a walk, a run, trot, dodge, whatever it took to get back to the station in one piece. It was a three-mile nightmare. Everything was OK for the first minute or two, until we crossed the point where the home supporters exited the ground. Next thing, they were mingling in with us at the back. One Stoke lad – who many of the lads know and who later went to work in Hong Kong – was a couple of years older than me and wore a trendy black leather trench coat. I did not see him on the way back but he must have been close to me a few times, as I kept hearing the line, 'I want the fucker's leather coat.'

All the way back to the station we were getting slaps. Most of the lads in the escort were divided by the Leeds lads mingling in and were being picked off at will. Even walking with the police meat wagon was not a wise move; you would see a group of Stokies walking quickly behind a meat wagon, but as soon as there was an off down the road, the wagon was gone and the Stokies got a slapping. This happened on several occasions.

The platform was a nightmare of bloodied snotters and ripped clothes. A few lads were moaning that they would have to go home and get changed when they arrived back into Stoke, as they would not get in the Kingspin (Kings Hall) dance in that state. The Kings was a regular Saturday night do. I'm glad to say the only thing I had suffered was a ripped V-necked jumper.

It was one of those days that even thirty years on I can remember like last week.

Liverpool Away (Dyer)

It was the 1980-81 season and I was sixteen. Word had gone round that a coach was leaving the Roman Candle in Hanley, they were out for mischief in Scouseland and only game lads would be allowed on. I'd been out around Longton all day with Sutto, he'd thrown a sickie from his training scheme and was fast blowing his £23.50 wages. We met up with

Kieran, Ginger Billy from Goms Mill and the Cotterill brothers, Beege and Bange from Dresden. Would we be deemed game enough to get on? When we arrived at the meeting place every face was familiar: Trent Vale, Trentham, Blythe Bridge, Cobridge, Shelton, Newcastle, nearly everyone recognised each other from previous rumbles at home.

The match was being played on a Friday night to avoid clashing with the Grand National the following day. I was as nervous as hell at the thought of one coachload taking on Liverpool in their backyard. That it was a night match added to the fear. All of my mates were older but I'm sure even they had butterflies. The talk on the way was *hit fast and hit hard*; the element of surprise could work if we all stood our ground. I was not so convinced.

As we neared the ground, I felt more and more ill at ease. Thousands thronged the streets. We were on our feet straining to see out of the windows, and catcalls and two-fingered gestures came from every street corner. Some of their boys started to follow our bus as it was slowly guided to a line of other coaches parked at the side of Stanley Park. This famous Merseyside landmark had its own reputation and seeing it for the first time in fading light, with scousers everywhere – phew!

The two lads that had organised the outing clenched their fists and looked back at us all. 'Stick together, no one runs.' We piled off, adrenalin flowing like the Trent. Our group of fifty or so seemed like a lot more once we were off and I stayed as close as possible to Kieran Delaney. He was a Stokie of Irish descent who lived on Blurton, close to both Sutto and myself. I had been knocking around with him for a while as we both shared an interest in Punk, New Wave and now New Romantic. Kieran was game as fuck, as were others with me that night. Me? Well I just tagged along; I had done a bit but not as much as the older lads.

The open space between our crew and the Anfield floodlights was full of still bodies in the blackness; all Merseyside eyes trained on the outsiders in their midst. A shout went up: 'Come on!' Our front ranks went into a jog and then a sprint as forty Liverpudlians stood before us. They did not stand for long as we engulfed them, punching and kicking. As one group of Ken Dodd men dispersed, their early runners and battered standers regrouped further ahead, calling all and sundry to their aid. They probably outnumbered us three or four to one in different groups but each time we ran at them they were on their toes; only the bravest stood for a twatting. Our firm was now about eighty-strong, as other late-arriving Stokies attached themselves to us. The element of surprise had worked and, before the game at least, the coach from the Roman Candle had run the Scousers on their own territory.

The police finally rounded us up with the use of horses, dogs and drawn truncheons. It was they who now cracked the whip: 'Get in line you fucking woollybacks, you won't be so brave after the match.' We were crammed together like cockles in a jar, not daring to fall out of line for fear of an alsatian bite or getting trampled by Red Rum's mates. The recipients of our kickings in the park watched as we were marched the short distance to the turnstiles.

Each one of us had our own tales to tell the other Stoke lads already in the ground. There weren't many either, only about 600 in a crowd of 33,000. I didn't fancy being one of the few who had come on the train; some lads spent the entire duration of the game trying to fix up a lift on one of the buses. They had run the gauntlet from Lime Street before the match, had the cuts and bruises to prove it and after what we'd just done on Stanley Park the Liverpool boys would be after blood.

The football didn't offer us much excitement, Stoke were under the cosh and we spent the ninety minutes taunting the Scousers to our right. We were separated by a fence with high meshing to combat missiles, five yards of empty terracing containing old bill and then another fence. 'One job between ya, there's only one job between ya,' and, 'Where were you on Stanley Park?' The Merseysiders responded eerily with, 'La la la la la, slash slash, slash slash,' and made knife-slashing movements with their hands.

By the time the whistle went, the Potters had gone down 3-0. We poured into the street at the back of the Annie Road End almost glued together in expectancy; there were many more of us now, knowing that if we split we would be lambs to the slaughter. A strong police line blocked the street to our left, separating us from the home fans spilling out at the same time. Again there were dogs and horses but it didn't look like we were having an escort. We began to walk quickly, then jog, surveying all around us as we filled the road. Sporadic fights broke out up ahead, with groups of the enemy waiting on the sides of the road and on corners. They had been having a go at the first Stokies out of the ground but now we were here.

The odd copper tried to stand in the way of the inevitable but the sight of fisticuffs twenty yards ahead provoked us into full charge mode again. As we reached the trouble spots we fired into any Scouser there. Some stopped to fight and others disappeared into the dark. More police with dogs appeared and forced us onto the buses. My heart was thumping as I took my seat – we had taken the piss. As our coach pulled away there was much backslapping and laughing. The tension gave way to relief. I saw much larger mobs of Liverpool fans knocking about as we were leaving the vicinity; the police had obviously kept them away from us. I again felt sorry for anyone on the walk back to Lime Street. As our bus picked up speed, we began to settle down.

Missiles hitting our windows shattered the peace. Several found their target but none came through. We shouted at the driver to stop, he pulled over and everyone spilled out again into the night. We ran back up the road towards a big pub on the corner where the ambush had been orchestrated. As we got closer I could see Scousers clambering to get back in and the bouncers frantically trying to bolt the doors. Faces appeared at the windows, frightened faces that soon disappeared as bricks, bottles and anything else we could lay our hands on rained on the hostelry. I don't think there was a pane of glass left. Some boys tried to get in at them but the doors held firm and sirens filled the air. We legged it back to our transport.

I couldn't wait for the next one.

Naughty by Nature? (Rich)

Any individual who can claim to know the exact date he 'joined' a firm should be dismissed from credibility immediately. It's not like you pay a subscription or receive a membership card. Nor is there any ritual to go through like other 'underground' organisations such as the Freemasons or the Mafia. I, like many hundreds of others, just drifted into the culture and from then on saw it evolve, grow and shrink for many different reasons.

Stoke is and always has been a working class, tough city. Young men have to be streetwise, hard-working and able to look after themselves and their own. There's a strong drug culture and a thriving black economy, which helps people to survive. A visitor to our city doesn't need football to find violence: go looking for trouble and you can find it in dozens of clubs, bars and streets, where a word out of order can put you on your arse before you know what's hit you. Wages are low, as are social expectations. Opportunities are limited and this simmering environment has bred a culture of violence and self-protection in and around our football club that has been maintained for over four decades.

People can talk about the social and psychological aspects of the football hooligan 'tribe' as long as they want. In my own opinion, there is no such thing as a 'firm' of Stoke lads, or for that matter the Naughty Forty. Even the police, who spend hundreds of thousands of pounds and time and resources beyond belief gathering evidence, could not define or list exactly who belongs to Stoke's firm at any precise point in time, or what they view as the hierarchy of hooligans. Nor is there a line of command, or a system of underground communication. For instance, our mass turnout of lads at Wigan in 2000 was a natural act. Word was out, everyone was up for it and for that reason only we took so many animals to Wigan. Nobody orchestrated it or planned it.

All that exists is a loose, amorphous association of blokes who support Stoke City, but more importantly, have an even stronger bond with each other than with their football club. In the past few years that bond has got even stronger, as the club the lads love bans them, helps punish them and as a result drives them closer together. Rejected by their football club, who through the police and local media make it known publicly that they do not welcome the custom of our kind, the lads continue the bond. We aren't talking about a sporting experience here. Match day isn't about ninety minutes of football, it's about much more than that. Even lads who are not banned have stopped going to the games these days, preferring to spend less money than the price of admission on a few beers with their mates. In fact, many lads have turned towards hating the club for their continued failure, poor management and self-publicised hatred of our culture.

Why, on a typical home match day, would banned lads travel up to twenty-five miles into Stoke to drink with their mates? Onlookers might say that they attend in the faint hope of a street fight or confrontation with the police. That's wrong, plain and simple, because the chance of a ruck at Stoke has become so small that it would be a waste of their time and money. They drink together because the strongest pull of the Stoke culture is our mutual bond and respect amongst our own kind. A nod and a wink, or a chat at the bar with someone who you've stood shoulder to shoulder with in a brawl in the name of Stoke City means more than anything else in the culture we know and love. You might not know their name, where they're from or what they do for a living, but the bond remains. That mutual respect is like gold dust and is the very glue that holds our culture together.

My drift into the scene came at about sixteen years of age when the casual culture had just started, emerging mainly in London, Manchester and Liverpool. Being influenced by the latter two cities due to geographical proximity, Stoke lads were fairly quick to adopt the casual appearance, though there has never been any real clothing snobbery at Stoke. We never have been particularly bothered about the trivia of the rarest imported trainers, most technical fibres used in obscure Italian tailoring, or if the cut of a lad's jeans is in or out of fashion. We're a working-class club in a working-class city and fuck anyone who wants to look down on us because of our fashion sense. If a lad is scruffy as a tramp but respected and well known, he'll be treated as good as any other. Plus you rarely see anyone in the old 'black boots and donkey jacket' attire any more. Casual clothing is now more of a 'uniform' of sorts, a way of identifying that you're a lad and up for a ruck. Sure, it's easy for anyone to go into an expensive clothes shop and pick out fairly standard pieces of clothing and come out instantly looking like an archetypal hooli-thug, but the vast range of styles make this more complicated. You can usually tell the real lads by their attitude rather than what they wear.

In a working-class city like Stoke, expensive clothing was one way to stand out, making a statement that, despite low wages or a mundane job, you could get your smartest, most expensive gear out of the wardrobe on a Saturday and feel like a king. That was the attitude I think most Stoke lads took, even way back before the days of £700 Stone Island jackets. From leaving high school in 1984, I had three or four part-time jobs at any period over the next two college years (where I met Spoon, who was to become a mate for life) and ninety-five per cent of the money went on clothes, drinking and football.

At Stoke, the mid-Eighties was the point where casual clothing emerged properly. I remember a pre-season friendly at Crewe. Gathered on Stoke station that morning was a firm of about 120 good lads and it looked like a fashion show. It was clear that summer that everyone had been out buying some tasty clothing and rather than a rent-a-mob dressed in similar clothes, there was a fair range of styles and attitudes. Before that point, a mob of Stoke lads would consist of a mix of casuals, semi-casuals, scruffs and complete nutters. After that point, if there was trouble and Stoke lads were involved, the vast majority were casuals and clearly out for trouble. It's a bit bizarre, but nowadays 'normal' Stoke fans rant on about the Burberry/Stone Island-clad 'thugs' yet in reality the casual soccer thug has been around football at Stoke for over twenty years. Have these dimwits taken a few years to cotton on to the casual scene, or are these the complaints of the 'Johnny-Come-Lately', post-Euro 96 new boys, who can't remember the appalling treatment, fences and overflowing toilets of the old football grounds before Sky television?

It would have been easy for me to remain a scarf-wearing shirter, which in 1982 I was. I could have accepted the normality of standing with other shirters, making friends at home and away matches. Instead I was drawn to the 'dark side' of designer clothing, avoiding police attention, risking arrest or a good beating, plotting away matches, turning up at the matches that mattered, and being a face amongst many hundreds of others over the years. There have been times when I turned my back on the scene. The rave years were a distraction, and like many Stoke lads I got hooked on the pills, thrills and earache of the local rave scene. This was an exciting time of new music, a new culture and making friends from all over the country through music, clubs and drugs. This was before the club/dance scene got tired and bloated, at a time when many lads were making good money from running clubs or their own shady drug deals. Or before that, just after my marriage, when my American cousin died of cancer aged seventeen, leaving me devastated and in a fucked-up mental state. I ended up like a virtual recluse for a while. Other times, money became scarce (mainly due to a hefty mortgage) and rather than risk my marriage, time out was taken. At other times, I thought my job and career were more important than being part of the Stoke scene. But like most of the other lads, I always came bouncing back.

Social drinking has been another main aspect of the culture, with groups of lads coming into town from wide areas. Each had their own ritual of meeting up, perhaps at their own local then getting a taxi or bus to Stoke. Plenty of pubs have been used as meeting places but the main gathering point has always stayed within half a mile of the centre of the town. There's a certain degree of 'follow the leader' as some lads want to be seen at the 'in place' where the top lads drink, especially when lads are trying to be seen as regulars or a part of the scene. There's also been less point in trying to evade police attention for a few reasons, but mainly because (1) there's rarely any trouble in the town centre any more, and (2) the police already have everyone's details and pictures so there's little point trying to hide from them.

In fact nowadays the lads don't care if they are photographed going into and coming out of their regular pub. It has become a part of life on match day. We're all mindless thugs who should be treated like scum, right, and who would listen if we complained? Even our own local media, forthright in its criticism and condemnation of our activities, would dismiss this as the complaints of the guilty. Human rights goes out of the window. Our left-wing local press goes the last hurdle to help the police and football club, putting names and faces of wanted thugs on its front page, and using any opportunity to brand Stoke City as a club with a huge and troublesome hooliganism problem.

An observer would be surprised at the down-to-earth nature of our lads. The sense of humour is incredible and anyone who takes himself too seriously is shot down quickly. A trip to an away game with Stoke's mob is sure to be one crazy and potentially violent trip but also as funny as hell. Anyone describing us as mindless cannot know the lads I have met over the years. Also, contrary to outside opinion of Stoke being a highly racist, right-wing firm, our coloured lads are well respected and drink side by side with everyone else. There may be some extreme personal opinions held but they would never be openly expressed at the cost of dividing our lads, due to mutual respect.

Most of the lads I know got into the scene at about the same time. They are mainly from the Newcastle area, from where a large number of Stoke's lads have always come. These lads are mainly from areas like May Bank, Pool Dam, Clayton, Hartshill and others. Newcastle is a market town and historically has always been violent. Even today, bank holiday carnivals can erupt in outbreaks of alcohol-fuelled mob warfare which goes back to medieval times, when locals fought outsiders to have the best market stall sites and to ensure their fair share of the local female population. Lads usually put local rivalries aside on match days and factions have rarely troubled each other at the match. It should be no surprise that Newcastle lads were drawn to the match-day scene, as any wayward young man would be attracted to the scent of football, mob culture, violence and alcohol. Also, in the early Eighties Stoke City was a First Division club and entertained all the big teams. Street battles involving hundreds a side were common, so the chance of getting involved was much higher, with the price of being caught much less than nowadays.

My match-day ritual was born out of Friday night drinking around town, amid a background of pub fights, the occasional glassing, and before the era of the mobile phone. A quick chat at the bar would usually involve arrangements for the home or away match, and you could guarantee that most of the lads who said they would be at Stoke station at 9am the next day, would be (barring arrest or hospitalisation). Over time the circle of contacts widened, and before long it was easy to recognise and get to know lads from across the whole Borough of Newcastle and further afield.

I have met lads from London, Oswestry, Cheshire, Yorkshire, Shropshire, Manchester and other areas, all drawn to Stoke by that common bond. You would be surprised at the reception someone gets when they walk into one of our pubs after being away from the scene for a while. It is like they have never been away. I have lived in South Wales and Devon but always felt the need to get back home regularly because of family, local roots, but mainly the common bond of Stoke City. You can try to 'adopt' another club but the passion and excitement is faked. It's not in the blood. A local derby match of Plymouth versus Exeter (with respect to their local rivalry) is hardly going to set the pulse racing like a 25,000 crowd at Stoke versus Wolves, with passionate fans, mutual verbal abuse and the scent of violence hanging in the air.

My view is that the lads who make up the huge hooligan following of Stoke City are just wayward, disorderly types who live on the edge and want a bit more from life than a weekend of shopping, a takeaway and an early night. They're naughty for sure, but they just can't help being naughty by nature. That is why year after year they remain with us, or come back from 'retirement', and younger lads are attracted to the culture that this book aims to explain.

The Scouse Scallies (Rich)

I've never been particularly fond of scousers. Maybe that's because the first slapping I received at football came from a sneaky pair of scallies. This was in the 1983/84 season at our place. Before the match two mates and I were walking through town. A gang of scallies had raided Bourne Sports and nicked loads of casual clothes. We walked away from Church Street and a scally flashed the longest bread knife you've ever seen at us. We didn't fancy this one bit so walked briskly away.

Inside the ground, we were in the Boothen Paddock with about eighty lads, and sitting above us were most of Liverpool's scallies. They started throwing cups of coffee and beer down at us, and after a while this really did piss us off. A few scallies in the Paddock got battered and run right out of the doors. Then right at the end of the game the Scousers opened a door that led down the stairs to our part of the ground, and we met on the stairway. It went berserk for a few minutes and you could see trainers left on the ground where lads had been kicking at each other.

This carried on just outside the ground and honours were pretty much even, despite a huge Liverpool following. I was keen for a bit more so went up to the station. The escort had got a bit mixed up by then, and outside the station was a set of lads who were clearly going to get at each other. I was outside the North Stafford Hotel when one scally tapped me on the shoulder from behind and another one smacked me right in the mouth. It was one hell of a punch and in seconds my new white Tacchini top was covered in blood. Worse than that, when I got home I would have the dubious pleasure of explaining to my mum and girlfriend why it was covered in claret.

The sore mouth soon healed and didn't deter me from seeking further pugilistic excitement in the years to come. Had I received a chopping from that bread knife, I might never have gone to another football match. My thirst for revenge would be quenched the season after, again at home. We had a good crowd and more than the usual number of lads out after the game. Word was out that everyone was heading for the station, and we got ahead of them as the police held them back in the ground. We gathered near the station in our hundreds. Everyone got bricked up or grabbed bottles. Eventually, in the gathering darkness, the scousers' escort could be heard. They were being forced under the railway bridge, and there were thousands of them, but they didn't fancy meeting us head on, that was clear. The police had to force them round the corner as they received a barrage of bricks and bottles. Our lads got stuck into them at the front and they backed off even further. The police were battering them from behind, and we were going full tilt at the front. You could see them going down from bricks or punches and I took great delight in fronting loads of them and landing a few sweet kicks and punches in glorious revenge. Eventually they had no choice but to turn the corner and when they did, in their hundreds, a full-on row erupted. We had run out of ammo by then but a ruck carried on for a couple of minutes before the coppers got heavy and laid into anything they could see.

Man City on the Park (Millsy)

Most of the Stoke lads travelled by train. Ours left at 11 a.m. with about 200 lads on board, not all 'top-notch' but it was a tidy firm. We avoided Piccadilly Station and carried on to Oxford Road, where we were met by half of Greater Manchester Police, with horses, dogs, video cameras and riot cops. This was a bit of a letdown. A lot of lads piled into the nearest pub to the station but for the dedicated among us this was a no-no.

We managed to get into another pub just around the corner, thirty or forty-handed but the police were all over both pubs. After an hour or so, word got around to leave in dribs and drabs and try to get into another boozer further down the road. Seventeen of us managed to give the old bill the slip and met up in a wine bar. We could see from there that the police had started to escort some of the Stoke mob of 2-300 towards Maine Road. We decided to drink up and follow but at a distance of 200 yards. I must say the escort did look long and impressive. During this walk, which was a fair old one, we stopped at the back of some buildings to take a leak. Two nosey old coppers cottoned on to us. No-one spoke to them and they didn't speak to us, they just kept tailing us.

We came to a big open park, entered it and walked along a pathway. There was five yards of grass to our left and the open park on our right. As we walked along we noticed a pub in the distance. Outside were Man City fans watching the Stoke escort pass. They were easily 300 yards from the escorted line and 200 yards away from us. As we got nearer, you could see that one or two had turned their attention to us and were starting to point, as if to say, 'Who are these fuckers?' but they knew who we were.

They crossed the road and entered the park on the same path as us. At first they were walking but soon they were running fast, straight towards us. Anyone remember a certain someone saying, 'Right, get your breathing right lads, nice and calm'? – surreal. We walked casually and straight ahead, no deviation, with Man City still running full pelt. As they approached they slowed. I rolled up a newspaper in my hand as they got closer. Suddenly they unleashed all the bottles and pint glasses they had at us. They whizzed by our heads, mostly hitting arms that were up protecting faces. As Man City got closer I hurled my newspaper; as the paper unravelled and scattered, several of them ducked. God knows what they thought was in the paper but we laughed about it later.

Man City let out a roar and we were put on our back foot. You could feel the fuckers trying to trip you up as you were retreating. We ran for about fifty yards when the call went up: 'Stand, stand.' All of us got our bearings. Man City were about twenty yards from us as we turned, seventeen of us facing at least sixty. We looked about: no kids on either side. We started to bounce and let out a roar in unison, then all seventeen piled into the on-coming Mancs. They were now weaponless and had to stand and fight.

Both mobs went into it among the flowerbeds, with the two nosey cops trying to part us. As the seconds passed it was obvious who was up for it. The Mancs became scattered, a number lying out on the grass. One last roar and they were on their toes. We chased them off the park and down some dodgy side street, then got everyone together before the riot vans appeared. I overheard one of the two nosey coppers say to the other, 'Say it wasn't our fault and we were attacked.' This made me breathe a little easier, as I thought nickings were on the cards.

As we were escorted to Maine Road, the Mancs we had been battling with were walking back in two and threes, their heads bowed. It had been a cracking row with uneven numbers: quality not quantity was the lesson.

The Smell Of Grimsby (Ridgers)

No matter how notorious, organised or, in our case, brutally violent a firm you are, there will be places and incidents that come as a surprise. Over on the bleak east coast of our cherished island lies the hole that calls itself Grimsby. Grim by name and grim by nature, a coastal town that could not be blamed for throwing itself into the sea. Just another run-of-the-mill away match for us, or so we thought.

A day out there in the late Eighties had the usual agenda of lager and offs, with the sea air to clear the buzzing head from the previous night at Introspective. *Oh, the Ecstasy!* During this period our firm adopted an almost paramilitary attitude towards organisation, with independent area cells wreaking havoc wherever possible before combining later with devastating effect. Whether it was Podge, Rich, Cossack and the Trent Vale Game Casuals, or Harvey, Weston and the Blurton loons, anyone who came across a Stoke firm was guaranteed a battle. At Grimsby it was time for the Trentham lads to do their bit.

Before bowling into town like we owned the place, it was usual to drive around any likely-looking back streets in the hope of finding lads who were up for a row away from prying and spoiling eyes. The back streets were our home from home, reminding us of familiar territory. There were two cars on this day, containing Slammy, Tay, Ant, Mick, Hoss and Nidge, six lads from middle-class Trentham, products of solid family backgrounds but nevertheless still having that different chromosome to 'normal people' that brings out the dark side. We were already pissed from drinking Anton's home brew on the way there.

No sooner had we arrived but some lads on a street corner were giving us the once over as we crawled by, half looking for mither, half looking to park up for mither. Mick was wearing some daft scarf, like Yasser Arafat, and the Grimsby lads took the piss. Predictably Mick was out the window telling them to follow us away from the main road. We moved on another fifty or so yards so we could park and kick it off.

The numbers changed when the cars split up looking to park but *no problem*, we thought, give it two minutes and we would all be together. As soon as Ant parked we saw the same six Grimsby coming towards us but we were only four. This was the buzz, the drug we craved every Saturday. Mick, Slammy, Ant and Tay thrived on situations like this, a tight four against six codheads who thought they were game. We clashed immediately around a group of parked cars and gave no quarter. They struggled to understand our overwhelming arrogance despite being outnumbered. This is Stoke.

Everything went our way for a while as we stood, fought and won, with one of the codheads running off up the street with his blade in hand, not having had the bottle to do anything other than wave it. The situation took a turn when another four or five sprang out of a garden on our right, though by now Nidge and Hoss had made our numbers up to six. The problem was that their newcomers had come equipped with the contents of a garden shed and were tooled up with just about anything that didn't need plugging in.

Credit where due, these lads were already game but now they were game and tooled-up. We battled like always and still gave no quarter but the numbers and tools became a problem. There was no danger of backing off but we knew there would be casualties. As Slammy was rowing behind a parked car, he found himself with one of these lads either side of him. The one behind had a large pair of garden shears and, as Slammy fought the one in front, the one behind brought the shears crashing down onto his skull, splitting his scalp down the middle to cause a gaping wound. Mick looked across anxiously to see blood pouring down Slammy's neck and realised the seriousness of the situation. He'd got Mick's leather jacket on!

The old bill arrived to end what must have been a good five minutes of action. Hoss volunteered to take Slammy up to the local accident unit and he emerged hours later looking like a tennis ball with a seam down the middle of his head. And Mick was gutted about the stains on his jacket.

One or two seasons later, Stoke returned to Grimsby in force. The Trentham lads saw a mass of boys outside a big boozer and immediately went to look into things. As they got there Stoke stormed the pub, which was full of Grimsby's boys. The pub seemed to empty totally, and what must have been 200 lads clashed in the middle of the main road. The traffic stood still as well-dressed thugs traded blows between, around and on top of the trapped vehicles. There was even a cavalry charge of mounted police right through the middle, though it was the dogs that finally dispersed the fighters.

At the ground the mayhem continued, with disgusted shoppers looking on at the violent strangers who had come to town this day, though it wasn't a town that needed much spoiling. The fever pitch was temporarily halted by a game of football, though this did nothing to detract from the single-minded aim of one and all. The match came and went, which is about all you can say for a game against Grimsby. But then …

We were in a poxy stand behind one of the goals, with Grimsby having boys high to our right and the paddock low to our left. Once the match finished, Grimsby came onto the pitch and, fancying their chances, started to throw the usual coins at us. We poured forward to the fence and tried to storm the police and stewards. The safety gate burst open under a barrage of kicks and Stoke poured through and over the fence. Grimsby were flapping. This was vintage Seventies hooliganism but without sideburns and flares (apart from Tony the Axe Man) as we ragged Grimsby from one end of the pitch to the other. We were fighting as far as the opoosite penalty box, where the corner flags came in handy. Grimsby had nowhere to go other than the paddock mentioned earlier, so this was where they headed.

The final insult saw Grimsby flee down the paddock and out of the ground. This was now a Stoke ground and no pretenders were welcome. Being game is one thing, but the relentless desire to be number one takes you onto a different plane. And for any of you reading out of curiousity or trying to understand our mentality, please ask youselves, did anybody enter that pitch to fight who wasn't willing? Some are just more able, and they usually have an ST postcode.

On the way home, the final satisfaction was listening to Radio Humber, which portrayed us as violent thugs on the rampage. This may have been accurate but the circumstances required firm action, and at Stoke we have the firm.

The Wurzels (Spoon)

In the 1988/89 season at the Victoria Ground, the Stoke casuals had a trick that they used at most home games. Away fans were allocated standing room at the Stoke End and part of a section of seating above that. This was also used to accommodate home fans, and was convenient for the Stoke lads to gain access to this area, close to away fans and near enough to bait them, throw coins and celebrate Stoke goals in an effort to incite their opponents.

The police did little at the time to stop any trouble. This was before CCTV and handheld digital video recorders. The authorities would make themselves known to the lads, but most home games seemed to be a free-for-all. If you got stuck in, the only risk of grief would be if an over-zealous copper grabbed you. There was a sense of one-upmanship at the time as well. The seating was more expensive than the terracing, and the Stoke lads got a sense of superiority by occupying the more expensive seats. Jobs and money have always been hard to come by in Staffordshire, but these lads were lording it up. They wore the best clothes they could get their hands on, often purchased on trips to Manchester or London. The 100 to 150 casuals of mixed ages who regularly took to the Stoke End seats thought they were the cream of the casual scene.

The trick was to spread out and sit down to enjoy the game, giving the team plenty of vocal encouragement, then at half-time, as the fans from both clubs went to use the toilets or the tea bars, they would get mixed up in the walkway below the stand. The police would usually lose interest at this point, as there was no way of identifying who was who.

Someone would kick it off and then all the Stoke lads would get stuck in, with plenty of room to fight with their opponents and the usual array of rubbish bins at hand for chucking.

During the 1988-89 season alone, Stoke kicked it off with Blackburn, Portsmouth, Hull, Bradford, Oldham, Leicester and Barnsley using exactly the same tactics. Only the fully segregated games against Chelsea and Man City escaped without incident inside the ground itself. The Man City game saw them bring about 12,000 fans all in fancy dress and huge pitched battles outside the ground, but that is another story. We must also mention the bizarre sight of a twenty-stone skinhead Mancunian dressed as a pink fairy fighting hand to hand with an eager young Stoke casual from Stafford. That was the kind of Boxing Days we had back then!

The next season followed the same pattern: good rucks with Hull, Oldham, Bradford, Leicester, Barnsley and Portsmouth, all in the same manner. Good results were had against all of these, other than Leicester, who at the time were always tasty and gave as good as they got, while Pompey brought very few, older well-dressed lads who dished it back out to us. The 6.57 were well rated at the time.

The season had been a bit tasty for Stoke, starting with West Ham at home, and there had been some good battling in the streets around the ground after that game. The ICF brought about 200 lads who got a good reception committee to meet them about 200 yards from the ground. One Stoke lad suffered a broken leg in the melee, which seemed to be an even result after a couple of minutes' combat. We were happy with that, as the ICF of that time had a top-notch reputation. The younger, newer and rawer Stoke youth firm were still working on our reputation.

In the January we played Arsenal at home in the FA Cup. They brought a good few hundred lads. After the game, which Stoke lost 1-0, the majority of Stoke lads emptied out from the paddock area. Arsenal had been allocated the entire Stoke End, so our plan was to steam straight in at them. About 300 lads of all sorts moved onto the street, with more coming down the road from the 12,000-capacity Boothen End. We had a bit of a shock when about 400 game-as-fuck Gooners steamed us back into the paddock, helped by the old bill laying into us. We had nothing else to do but fight back. This lasted for just a few seconds when the rest of the assembled Stoke nutters – casuals, scruffs, old blokes in donkey jackets – joined us and drove the masses of Gooners back up the road. I remember everybody shouting, 'Where's Denton, the big black bastard?' as he was singled out as their top lad. The police managed to get on top of things by sheer numbers and brute force, and things calmed down.

On Saturday, March 17, we were due to play Plymouth Argyle at home. Argyle were not expected to bring much of a following up to us that year – they were performing poorly in the league and after years in this division they were about ready for the drop, plus we'd had no incidents with them in the previous few years. The pubs were a bit quiet before the game and there was no word on the wires of any Argyle lads in town. The Stoke lads made their way to the ground numbering about fifty – far less than usual. At the turnstiles about half the firm went in to the ground, leaving a few of us outside. We stood around trying to cadge cheap tickets off punters who wanted to sell theirs. Rich continues the story from here:

Just before kick off, I felt a right smack on the back of my head and Argyle were there right by us. They had walked into the fenced-off enclosure behind the ground and straight up to us, and one cheeky bloke had dished a good strong but sly punch out to me. I turned round and about thirty Argyle lads had almost walked past us, the one big lump catching me unawares.

I heard this lad say in his West Country drawl, 'Come on Stoke, we're Argyle, let's have it then.' This lad looked a real hillbilly. He had thick blond frizzy hair and was the size of a brick shithouse. His wild eyes stared at me like he had been on the cider all the way up the motorway. 'The Thing' continued to stare at me, as all around me the lads fronted up to this grizzy assembly of casuals and half-men, half-monsters. This huge lump had got one over on me but I waited to see what happened. I didn't fancy losing my teeth to a yeti.

Suddenly a dozen police hit the scene and split the two small firms apart. One of our younger lads shouted, 'Where are you parked? We'll have you later, you fucking bumpkins.' They gestured towards the gate at the front of the ground. This didn't give us a clue but we wanted it with them. No-one turned up without getting the respective amount of grief from the Stoke lads, and even with just fifty in total all aged under twenty-three, this was our manor. Our evolving reputation meant there were standards to keep up to, and those absent from our ranks wouldn't let us forget if Argyle had one over on us. We would have no end of grief from older Stoke lads if we got run.

We went into the ground and the police kept a close eye on things, the now fairly quiet Argyle lads going into the terracing. This prevented us using our usual battle plan in the seats, so after a fairly uneventful 0–0 draw we hung around for a few minutes then went out of the ground. The police ushered us away from the enclosure, so we mingled with the home fans making their way towards the town, keeping one close eye on the Argyle escort. We doubled back round towards where we thought they would go and as the crowds thinned out, we walked quietly towards the target area just off Cambell Road.

As we rounded a corner, we saw them, the same bunch as before, all big and ugly looking, heading for a large box van parked in a narrow street about 300 yards from the ground. The shout went up and the remaining forty of us youth lads walked towards them. They didn't seem too troubled by this, which should have warned us of something. As we got closer, we saw they had lifted the back of the van and out came an assortment of beer bottles which they launched at us. We had to keep our distance, and about forty feet separated the two factions. We stood our ground but couldn't get near them; no-one wanted to take the chance of getting hit on the bonce. After a minute or so, we got so wound up that some of our younger youth members took it to the Argyle lads, facing up within punching distance and then getting stuck in to them.

My earlier reservations proved right – this was a grizzly bunch and as more of our lot faced up we realised they weren't budging. Sporadic stand-offs followed with a bit of hand-to-hand but we could not budge them. These West Country lads were here for business. The old bill arrived in small numbers and it was only when an unmarked car arrived and the officers drew coshes and batons that the two sides parted. Both sides backed off and Stoke were pushed back up the road away from the van. The Argyle lads would have a long five hours' drive home, buzzing at the thought of their antics against an up-and-coming football firm.

Forest (Skinny)

Nottingham Forest were one of the top scalps for our young firm to take but on this day we took them and came of age. Fifteen of us went in a minibus accompanied by a car with six of the older Trentham lads. We were all sixteen to nineteen and priveleged to have with us the likes of Podge, Neil, Rich, Hoss, Hilly, Nidge and Whito, older lads who had been all over the country and done it. We got to Nottingham and went straight to a boozer just off the station, a small, compact place. We drank in there with some other lads who had come on the train – there was about thirty of us by now.

Suddenly one of the lads came running in and said Forest's lads were coming down the road. We backed into a small back room and fifty Forest came into the boozer. Their top lads stood round us as the atmosphere went quiet.

'What's up Stoke, why are you so quiet? Nothing's going to happen,' said one.

Wilmot, who looked like Mick Hucknall, said, 'You're all right Stoke,' and started humming 'Silent Night', taking the piss. I was eating a pie and was scared, to be honest, but thought, *if it goes off I want to smash one of the cocky cunts in the face.*

Sure enough, as he hummed, Podge said, 'Fucking quiet,' and smashed him over the head with a stool. That was all we needed to go berserk. Forest's cockiness turned to giving it toes as we took the upper hand. Their fatal weakness was underestimating their opponents. Our tight, tidy mob backed them out of the boozer. The old bill arrived not long after and videoed us one by one as we left. We got escorted to the ground and won the match 3–2 (Stein scored two and Regis one). It had been a top day but it got even better.

If you heard that twenty Stoke (fifteen of them young casuals) faced fifty main-firm Forest, your money would be on Forest. Well, after the game they came at us like zulus on the train station car park. We had no old bill around and no other lads, we had to stand or give it toes as they came steaming across. Five of the lads, me included, jumped over a wall as if to run but one of the older lads said, 'You run now and you're fucked in Stoke.' Adrenalin pumped through me and we jumped back and all ran at Forest.

I still remember the look on the face of the lad I ran into – as if to say, *what the fuck?* We all stood. One lad got nicked but we had it toe-to-toe with one of the best firms in the land and got a right result until the old bill came. If we had broken our line and run we would have had it but we stood. As Forest were being seen off by the old bill, Podge shouted over, 'You've been done Forest, by a bunch of kids as well.'

One of the lads in our van that day was another who would eventually commit suicide. Ricky Johnson R.I.P.

The First Battle of Bolton, 1990/91 (Rich)

Six of us were drinking in a pub on the outskirts of Bolton. It was around 1.30pm when we heard a massive roar. We legged it out and onto a busy main road and my first sight was a bad one – Stoke being run. It was equal numbers, about 100 lads each side. I joined at the back of Stoke's firm. Wilson was alongside me shouting, 'Fucking stand, you're Stoke City.'

Gradually we started to pull up and firm up – right outside a pub full of around another fifty Bolton. They came out throwing bottles, glasses and stools. Stoke stood firm but now we were well and truly outnumbered. We needed someone to do something quickly.

Mark Bentley steamed into the middle of the stand-off area outside the pub and picked up one of the bar stools thrown at us only moments before. He walked up to the pub and threw the stool back through the front window. This gave us the moment we needed and the Stoke boys followed his lead by throwing anything we could get our hands on through the front windows of the pub. That was enough for that little firm; they locked themselves inside.

Wilson then took the lead again but this time against an even bigger firm of Bolton lads. He went straight into them, going toe-to-toe with boys at the front of their firm. Stoke, on a high after doing the pub, followed Wilson's lead and steamed in. It was Bolton that were now on their toes. We legged them back up the main road, occasionally stopping to fight when Bolton tried to re-group but the sheer number of Stoke and the gameness of Wilson at the front was too much for them. After what seemed like hours but was probably only twenty minutes, the old bill took some kind of control. It was Stoke's day, with Mr Wilson and Mr Bentley turning things round.

The Second Battle of Bolton (Spoon)

In the early Nineties we took a firm of about 150 good lads by train to Bolton and headed straight for a pub called the Albion, which ended up rammed full of our lads on the piss. A good two and a half hours passed before we decided to hit the road and marched down a long street towards Burnden Park. We had not heard a squeak from Bolton, and had drunk merrily in their town unhindered.

As we approached the bottom of a bank close to the shopping area, we heard a loud roar, and Bolton emptied from our left onto the street from a pub called Trotters. We still numbered 150 and they had roughly the same. It was bizarre, as there were no police about at all. Each firm fronted up the other and after a few seconds we were led into battle, with Mark Bentley at the very front. We had some big grizzlers with us that day and soon enough it turned into a complete pitched battle in the middle of the street.

Things turned ugly as bottles, glasses, tables and chairs were lobbed at us by the Bolton. At one stage a black umbrella was going to and fro and if it hadn't opened up mid-flight, the fucker could have taken somebody's eye out. We were holding it together well and charged Bolton back into

Trotters, lobbing everything they used back at them. The window went in and yet more tables and chairs came out at us. We backed off to get it together again and they belted back out at us, tooled-up again with more missiles. The street was awash with debris from this battle and still no police.

At this stage Bolton ran us back down the street about forty yards, where we played holy fuck with some of our lot who had failed to get stuck in. On the retreat we had seen one big geezer in a black coat lying on the road, having received a KO punch and a hearty kicking from our 'Sporting Hero'. This time we pulled back together and virtually the entire firm ran screaming at Bolton, who backed off before more heavy-duty hand-to-hand combat kicked in. A double-decker bus pulled up and the astonished Christmas shoppers watched the pitched battle around them.

Missiles were still whipping through the air in both directions and you had to have your wits about you. One coloured Bolton lad fronted a few Stoke up and pulled out a blade. Three Stoke lads clocked each other as if to say 'fuck it' and ran at him. The guy ran round the side of the parked bus, where he met a couple more Stoke who laid into him and he took it from both sides.

This chaos went on for about twenty minutes unhindered by the police. A few prone bodies lay around the streets and everywhere you looked there was glass and debris. Trotters was like a bombsite, with tables and chairs at funny angles outside. We continued to have an almighty and ferocious fistfight with Bolton until we got pissed off with it and really went berserk. Mark B once more led the charge, along with the Sporting Hero, and screaming and shouting we steamrollered Bolton past Trotters. A few of them got stuck on the way and were slapped silly.

The police finally arrived, and we found out later that they had got stuck in the awful Christmas shopping traffic. Overall we got the upper hand but Bolton will always be highly respected for that row, and some of their older lads have complimented Stoke in the same way via the internet.

Man City (Daz Mills)

Last home game of the 1997/98 season. Stoke were already relegated for this game, while if other results went their way, Man City had a chance to stay up. Most neutral hooligan observers thought the Manchester giants would converge on Stoke-on-Trent and take over the ground and parts of the city – how wrong they would be. The game was a 1.30pm kick off so pubs opened early and lads filled them early. At about 10.30am a large, handy firm of Stoke had massed in the Vic Hotel opposite the site of the old Victoria Ground.

Now Stoke-on-Trent is not Manchester, it is a small town centre, but though Manchester City had sold nearly 5,000 tickets not one blue shirt or lad had been seen. Stoke's firm started to move nearer the ground, down to the Gardeners Retreat and Uncle Tom's Cabin. Still no sign of Man City.

I entered the ground with some younger elements of our mob. As soon as I put my arse on my seat, BANG, 1–0 to Man City. The first three rows of our block in the Sentinel Stand jumped to life: Mancs, and lads as well, they did not turn and fight, or carry on cheering, they ran for the away end, they ran for their lives, fist fights were breaking out all over the ground, there were certainly a lot of Mancs all over the ground, but it was not the invasion we were threatened with. The Man City who were jumping up were getting punched back down, we didn't know which way to turn, there was so much choice of who to punch, as Mancs were getting dragged around the pitch, even the normal fans were getting stuck in over the barriers. Some of us didn't think the game was going to finish, there were that many beatings being dished out. Every time Manchester scored (and they knocked in five that day) a few more Mancs would be rooted out.

After the game, a Stoke firm of around 200 left the Sentinel Stand and up the path towards the away end, some lads trying to pull the fences down around the away enclosure. Being at the front of this mob, I turned at the top of the path to see the firm and was overawed by the sheer numbers, this firm looked the business.

A few Mancs had got over-confident and came out of the away enclosure, only to be ragged back in. The bulk of the Man City firm, which had been elusive all day was also having second thoughts about coming out and mixing it with the Stoke; when stewards and police got a control of sorts of the situation, the verbals began through the fence. I joined a tidy firm of fifteen on the car park behind the McEwans Stand. There were little 'one-on-ones' all over the place, with the police just separating people, they had totally lost control of the situation. We were waiting for and offering on a similar-sized group of Mancs, led by a tall black lad in a denim jacket. They made a couple of attempts to come out of the enclosure, all sunglasses and palms outstretched, but were kicked and punched straight back in. Disappointed, we left the area and headed away from the ground and across the bridge. We heard a roar go up and we were amazed to see this group of lads coming down to the bridge, looking like they wanted to take on all comers. Myself, Dave, Nidge, Neil, Woody, Warbo and the rest of the lads steamed at them but they again did the off, with two dedicated coppers and a dog running through the Mancs and into us. One copper offered me CS gas or the truncheon. 'Neither please, I'm off to the pub officer!'

Over the coming months, more than seventy Stoke lads were arrested for events at the ground that day and so were us lads from the bridge. I was convicted of affray, fined £400, banned from Stoke for two years, received a life ban from the club itself (though they still send me application forms for a season ticket!), a ban from England for two years and was subsequently kicked out of the England Travel Club.

The incident on the bridge took place fifty-four minutes after the end of the game. Another six minutes and it would not have been classed as football-related because of the timescale. Typical.

The Battle of Hanley (Podge)

One Saturday night in the mid-Eighties I was sitting in the French Horn with Rich and Cockney Darren when in walked a Port Vale fan who was making a bit of a name for himself up there. Rich took exception to him straight away and kicked off. Fair play to the lad, he got stuck in even though he was on his own and the pair of them brawled around the pub until Darren had had enough, gave the lad a big left hook and told him to fuck off. Off he went, a bit bruised and shouting he'd have his revenge.

We were kicked out of the pub and walked round to Leadbellys, our haunt in those days. We had been in there ten minutes when in walked some old mates from Trentham. They had been drinking in their local, the Trentham Hotel, when in walked two vans of Derby on their way back from Everton. The Derby lads had asked where was the best place to go for a row and were told to get up Hanley.

Unfortunately, and unusually, there was only eight of us, including the Trentham lads. However, the juices were flowing so we decided to go and welcome them. I suggested their first stop would be Heaths wine bar, so off we went. Heaths had two entrances round the corner from each other. Darren and I walked in first and could just make out some lads going out of the other door. We followed them out, but because the pub was packed the others didn't see where we went, so Darren and I ended up outside with about twenty of them.

Darren was never one for messing about. 'Are you Derby?'

'Yes.'

'Wait here, I'll get my lads.'

Darren went inside to get the others. For some reason they had not sussed me, so I mingled in and awaited my chance. As our lot steamed out, I twatted the biggest lad I could. Unfortunately they couldn't get out of the door, so I was chased up the street. Coming down towards me were two more lads and I thought I was fucked, but they were two Stoke who had heard the roar.

The three of us ran the ones chasing me back to the pub, where our lot had finally managed to fight their way out. There's a crossroads there and it went back and forth with both sides temporarily gaining the upper hand. On one occasion they were backing off and one of their lads screamed, 'Look how many of them there are!' This went on for five minutes and still no police. I up-ended a bin, always a good place to find something to throw, and out came a big metal bin-liner. I hefted it up, ran straight in and bonged it on someone's head.

That was it – they were off. 'Walk,' we shouted as we went after them, me with my lucky bin-liner. I wondered why they kept legging it down the street and as we got to the bottom I could see why – all the rest of their lads were outside the Black Lion. Still, we were full of confidence. They gathered outside the pub, facing us. We steamed straight in as they came at us. I threw my bin and was then surrounded by them as they momentarily backed the lads off. I got a right kicking, including a broken nose. Seeing me getting mullered, the lads waded back in and got me to my feet. We backed them into the pub doorway just as the old bill arrived in numbers. Amazingly none of us got nicked.

Derby versus Stoke (Penfold)

Derby upped the stakes for this game when about fifty of them returned from a game at Everton and went into a Hanley pub to find twelve good Stoke lads, some with birds. A vicious fight ensued. So when we played Derby at their place, revenge was high on the list; in fact revenge was the only thing on the list.

About 120 Stoke arrived by train, trying to give the old bill the slip and to get into the town. After about forty minutes the police restored order and got us into a pub called Strutts, next to a roundabout near the town centre. Derby had been telling one of our main young lads to come to a pub called the Grange but nobody knew where it was. About 2pm we decided to take matters into our own hands, kicking open the fire exit and sneaking out of the back. We crossed the road and into a shopping precinct. We were well ahead of the old bill and slapped anybody who looked like a boy. Our target was PJ Peppers, a Derby pub we knew. A big advertising board which displayed the meal deals promptly went through the window. Lads went inside but found no opposition. Next stop was a clothes shop Derby lads frequented. The window went in there as well, a bit unnecessary but Stoke were in a naughty mood. Some Stoke faces actually shopped there and Fat Craig told me he saw his twenty per cent discount special disappear along with the window.

Stoke predictably lost the game 3–0. About fifty of us left the game before the final whistle to be stopped by the old bill, when all of a sudden, shirt boys started giving it the old bill, big style, allowing us to search for Derby and this elusive Grange pub. We doubled back around the ground, punching anybody who looked like a boy. For forty-five minutes we went looking for this pub with not a copper in sight. Just when we were all but giving up, we spotted it on a corner down a road. We walked down coolly and confidently, let the lads outside it know we were Stoke and punched them back inside. Not many came back out. Everything was put through the windows – bricks, bottles, alarm clocks and manhole covers.

We decided to fuck off before the old bill came. Derby came out about twenty-handed with pool cues and bottles but we steamed them back in to the pub with little resistance. Again the pub was attacked. With few windows left, people began to smash the frames. When we left this time, nobody came back out. The pub resembled a bombsite. Near the train station we encountered a mob of about seventy Derby who we informed, over the shoulder of the plod, that we had just air-conditioned their pub.

Memories of a Bucknall Red (Mozzer)

I've followed Stoke for over twenty years and have seen a few good days on and off the pitch. One was when stoke played Oldham in the late Nineties. We had a good firm of about 150 lads and decided we would give Stockport County a visit on the way. Stockport have had a bit of rivalry with Stoke but not a long, on-going thing; it only went back to about 1993, when we were both battling for promotion to Division One. We also met them in a Wembley final for the Autoglass Trophy. Anyway, the decision was made to renew acquaintances, but as the train pulled in we were met by a line of police stopping us getting off, so on to Manchester Piccadilly it was.

Any teams from south of Manchester will know that once you get to Piccadilly, it's a walk across Manchester city centre to Victoria to continue your journey to Oldham. This walk often allows a quick pint and the chance of bumping into an opposing firm playing one of the Manchester clubs. This day City were at home to Spurs, and as our front lads went down the ramp at Piccadilly they spotted the Spurs firm, about thirty in total. Of course the odds were stacked against the cockneys but not much, as most of our boys were still fannying about in the concourse buying tinnies and the like and were not yet out of the doors. Stoke waded in with a vicious assault and to their credit the Spurs gave as good as they got until more started to back-up our front line, causing Spurs to retreat down the road as the old bill arrived. So the day was off to a flyer: 10.30am and already an unexpected meet.

We arrived in Oldham at 11.30 and were met by a couple of Oldham's lads. They explained how they were camped in a certain boozer and the police had installed cameras above a few shops in the street to capture any trouble, so it was a no-show day. We marched up the high street and saw their boys in the said boozer, so we camped a bit higher up the road in Yates's. A few of the lads had a wicked skirmish in the back streets up by the market area. One Oldham lad was knocked unconscious and a few took severe kickings. Some of the lads evaded the old bill by hiding in a boozer full of Stoke and swapping clothes to escape detection.

Nothing else really happened before, during or on the journey back to Victoria, but once at Victoria, oh my giddy bollocks, all hell broke loose. Five of the lads had gone straight back to Victoria while the main firm stopped for a pint in Oldham. When we arrived at Victoria en masse, a police cordon was stretched across the station to keep us together. About ten of us got away, and as we crossed a large car park outside the station we were met by the five Stoke who travelled earlier. They came running over in terror. They had gone into the Mitre pub around the corner and been chased out by Stockport, whose game had been called off. Nobody asked if we should front them, we just did, no hesitation, steaming in the direction of the pub to be met by about forty handy-looking lads, tooled up for a sustained war.

They unleashed a barrage of flares, glasses and rocks which had Stoke on the back foot, but soon as the ammo ran out the lads were straight at them. They backed off around to the pub, where a few more lads joined them. Stoke retreated to see if any one else had been able to get away from the station. We decided to go around the front to a big square in front of the boozer, which was better lit and where we could hopefully back away some of the less-up-for-it lads and so cause some panic in their firm.

The opposing mob were now all out of the Mitre and coming at us. At first they looked a handy mob but you could see that although they had more than us, not all of them wanted it, whereas Stoke's tightly knit unit consisted of lads that thought this was a good bit of fun. Both sides clashed in the middle of the square in a free-for-all that lasted a good five minutes, which seems more like two hours at the time. The battle raged, with Stoke getting the upper hand, then the opposition gaining ground.

A gap between the two sides opened up as people tired. The brawl then turned into a missile war, with bins and bottles used. Scattered around was the odd victim, debris from the missile attacks, terrified yet nosey shoppers who although tell you how frightened they were, can still not drag themselves away from the area, people still brawling one on one, but gradually fading, Stoke not backing off, the opposition not backing off, although their uncertain few retreated back in to the boozer.

The old bill arrived but had no numbers to control it, so it carried on until the dogs appeared. They rounded us up and lined us against the rear wall of the Arndale shopping centre, under a tunnel. We were quite pleased about this as it was pissing it down. They made us wait here for ten minutes while the lads at the station were escorted up our way to make our journey over to Piccadilly. Not one Stoke lad was arrested.

However, on the journey across Manchester the plod gave us a torrid time, viciously manhandling our lads, taking them into doorways for a 'friendly chat' and sneaky smack. I think this was due to Stoke ruining their carefully laid plans. On the train home the old bill informed us that the firm we had encountered was in fact Oldham, not Stockport; a good mob of Stockport had been waiting in Manchester but their boozer had been sealed off until we were away. We also found out about how Oldham had hatched their plan, how they had got taxis after the game and travelled to Manchester for the off, as they had a good turnout before the game and fancied their chances. Oldham pulled the stops out and took the battle to Stoke, although it should be pointed out that had that firm on the station been together on that car park, there would have only been one outcome. Still, Stoke gained a lot of respect that day for Oldham's small but game firm.

Back home we went. Now at Stoke there are three lines through the station, and as we pulled in we noticed a train on the middle line. Through its windows we could see a large firm of lads on the opposite platform. This turned out to be Wolves; they had played Port Vale earlier in the day and had stopped off at a pub called the Terrace, a pokey student tip just down the road from the station. Rumour had it that it was being run by one of the older Wolves lads who used to be a face in their firm.

As Stoke got off the train, the four police there tried to get us off the station. The lads were having none of it. Wolves started to taunt Stoke and Stoke retaliated. Now there were four police on top of our stair, four on top of theirs and four on the platform. Stoke went straight across the track, around the middle train, onto their platform and into them. They were slightly outnumbered but still had enough to come out on top if they wanted it bad enough. Stoke unleashed a barrage of stones and steamed them on the platform, with Wolves backing away. Stoke launched a charge followed by a flurry of blows and kicks aimed at their lads at the front.

At this point the police cavalry arrived and pushed Stoke back across the tracks, off the platform and out the station. They then sealed the road in front of the station. As Stoke were being led away the Wolves lads started again to taunt, so the lads went down the road and over the other side of the station, where they broke down two huge metal gates and steamed Wolves from the other side. What a picture: fifty Stoke lads running 200 feet up the track to confront the opposing firm. They expected an inter-city and all they got was a Stoke City going full-steam ahead.

The following Saturday we were at home to Wolves and a few of their boys spoke of the station incident, saying how it had been the talk of Wolves firm. They also said how they call Stoke the Ninety Percenters, as there is always a ninety per cent chance that it will go off when they play us.

A memorable day out: one Saturday, three firms and three rows.

The Biggest-ever Stoke Turnout (Spoon)

Cross Stoke and revenge will be sweet. Wigan can testify to that. They turned up in Hanley for one fixture, coming up against a smaller mob of Stoke, and for once we lost the edge. Wigan gained a result with a tight bunch of mainly older lads who meant business. Whatever our excuses, they had the upper hand.

Revenge had been planned for some time, so the next away game at their new stadium was the perfect opportunity. We were riding high in the league with a good run of form and it was also the first match following Sir Stanley Matthews's death. We had been given the luxury of a large away allocation of 4,800 tickets, highly unusual in the second division, and almost everyone in Stoke, young, old, retired or active, had been talking about this game for months.

At Stoke Station, the scene was incredible. The entire station and platform was filled with lads. Every face from present to years ago was there.

One train arrived and it was filled with about 500 lads. People were standing in the bogs and you had to fight for air and elbow room. The remaining 200 had to follow on the next train. We had been told that the Crewe train had left with another 100 lads from Crewe, Alsager and Stafford. The numbers were so silly you just knew what kind of day it would be.

We got off at Manchester Piccadilly and the trail of lads on the walk to Victoria was hundreds of yards long. Some Man City scouts saw us and did a swift runner. Some of our lads had a beer at Victoria Station, then we got on a series of three small trains to Wigan. These were like drug runs as joints, pills and powders were consumed.

The old bill herded us together and took us down to the Wigan Pier pub, but no sooner had they got hold of one train-full than another lot turned up. We overheard conversations where the match co-ordinators thought they had got hold of our main troublemakers, only for another radio call to say they were gathered somewhere else. There were in total three different mobs arriving at different times, as well as forty lads who managed to get away into the town centre for a beer. They would later have the better of a toe-to-toe with Wigan in town while the game was being played.

We had a quick one in the Pier then made off for the Ship, where the landlord hospitably left his cellar door unlocked. The Newcastle lads helped themselves to a few crates of lager and passed the time outside in the sunshine. Some spoke to a few police who were tasked with monitoring us, discussing the relevance of our 'No Surrender' flag hanging from the wall. They told us that the Wigan firm were drinking in town and the senior officer on duty had advised them to fuck off, as there was no way they could take on the Stoke numbers, and told them, there was no offer of protection if it turned ugly. Prior to this, the only trouble occurred when a small mob of Wigan came in to the Pier to see off the few Stoke lads left there and, outnumbering them, they got the upper hand. They clearly didn't fancy a walk down to the Ship.

At half past two, we decided to make our way to the ground, and with the police attempting pitifully to escort us, we went on the run down an industrial estate. Greater Manchester Police could barely contain us until we got to a metal footbridge over the canal. There were so many lads running riot that we just hopped over the fences at one side and strolled across toward the home end. A few lads had got round to the home stand and two Wigan lads lay sparked out on the tarmac. It was swamped with Stoke around the ground, and the police were struggling to contain us. Some lads without tickets managed to smash past the stewards through a big side gate.

The away end was crammed top to bottom with almost 5,000 Stoke fans. The front of the stand was a flat concrete walkway and even that was standing room only; obviously they were the overflow who had gate-crashed the party. The atmosphere was white hot and instead of the usual mix of fans, parents and children and lads it was pretty much all lads and blokes.

The teams came on to the pitch and there was then a minute's silence for Sir Stanley Matthews. This was impeccably observed by everyone, other than near the end when one big-mouthed Wigan fool shouted something. The Stoke following went berserk and the intense abuse started from there. As well as the emotion of the day, beer had a large part to play in later events as a lot of lads were bladdered after nearly three hours of heavy drinking.

Shortly into the first half, some Stoke fans (including one woman) who could not get tickets for the away end came into the stand on our right. At that point a huge 'Delilah' went up from the Stoke following and, just as it kicked in, some Wigan lads stood up behind the Stoke fans and started kicking off with them. There was only about a dozen Stokies, and about three times as many Wigan, and as soon as it kicked off our lads started pouring onto the pitch at the corner. Whether it was loyalty, misguided protection towards their own kind, or whatever, a few managed to exchange blows with some of the Wigan. Hundreds more behind them got on the pitch or to the front of the walkway, where they had it with the stewards and riot police. More Robocops came to the front of the stand, trying to contain an imminent pitch invasion. It was berserk, as lads from the middle and back of the stand tried to force their way down to the front, dozens of lads trying to lay into anyone who was getting in their way. Dozens were either thrown out or arrested. Play was suspended for about fifteen minutes as the authorities tried to restore order among the Stoke following. Even old blokes were shouting and screaming for blood. In our stand stewards were threatened and if they didn't heed the advice to 'fuck off' they were attacked, even by shirt-wearing Stokies.

The atmosphere was truly ugly, the ugliest most of us may have seen at a match. The infamous England chant of 'No Surrender' could be heard throughout the game. Most Stoke fans were going mental and the riot police just about managed to restore order at the front. Half-time came and went, with us winning 2-1 courtesy of a cracking goal. Towards the end of the game the riot police came into the stands and placed them-selves on duty at each exit to the concourse, with more at the stairwells and turnstiles.

At the end of the game, the Stoke following poured out of the seats down the exits and one spark lit the whole thing off. In one corner a man with his young son got hit on the head with a truncheon. He went mad and this kicked it all off. Within seconds, the concourse was a sea of bodies as lads battled with riot police. They had helmets, sticks, gas masks, Kevlar body armour, the works, but the unarmed Stoke lads were laying into them all through the concourse. At some points they backed off in small groups and then laid into our heads with batons, but we retaliated and you could see their glass visors getting punched. Heads were being cracked and you couldn't help but get pushed into the melee. It was a case of unarmed self-defence or get a crack on the head. Some fans tried to evade the chaos by going down the stairs, only to be driven back up by the armed officers. They got to the top only to be told to get back down again, followed by another crack on the skull. Meanwhile up on the concourse, two Stoke lads grabbed a big bin and between them lobbed it right into the faces of some riot police.

It was chaos, and at many points the tooled-up officers came off second best due to the sheer aggression of the Stoke lads. One lad stood on his own, inches away from a burly officer's visor and, screaming, proceeded to punch it with both fists. This kicked off another holy row as everyone laid in to help him as he got beaten over the head. Coming outside the ground, some officers on the car park were trying to arrest some of the older lads, but the youth mob kept running up to them and laying into them, letting our lads go free in the process. Everyone was keeping it tight and there was no way ground would be conceded to these thugs in uniform.

Anyone who has seen the police video of this incident will testify to the fact that Stoke were mad that day, enough to warrant dozens of lads being arrested and subsequently banned for their part in the crowd violence. It has been proven in the latter part of the 1990s and early 2000 that only three firms are mad enough and have enough numbers to go berserk in such style, and that is Stoke, Cardiff and Millwall. Some people claim that the days of organised football violence are drawing to a close. If that is true, these three firms can claim to be going out in style.

A hot day in Oldham (Mozzer)

A day that Stoke's N40 made the news was when we played Oldham away in the 2001 season. It came the week after an old white war veteran had been badly beaten by a group of young Asians on a council estate on the edge of Oldham's town centre. All week long the news-papers and television had shown footage of this harmless old chap lying battered and bruised in his hospital bed. Lancashire Police had tried hard to play down the story and the racial angle but newspapers and local media showed signs warning white people to stay out of this predominately Asian area. These stories combined with tales and rumours that were emanating from this part of the country fuelled much conversation and further rumour mongering on the journey north. The events that followed were blamed by some as the spark that ignited the Oldham riots in 2001. This is one account of what happened, although it is not a complete picture, as Stoke had split into three groups numbering roughly 150 each and each group was involved in different acts of lawlessness.

Stoke's firm met on the station at 9.30am, a good following of about 400. The old bill were out in force, videoing and photographing the lads. History dictated it was going to go off somewhere during the day, either with Oldham's small but game firm or in Manchester before or after the game. We travelled to Piccadilly and made the walk over to Victoria to get our connection. We were slowly surrounded by the boys in blue and it was at this point that a few of the better known faces decided to 'do one', blending into the surroundings to disappear from the plod. Another train was due in with a smaller firm of lads, so phone calls were made telling them of the situation at Victoria and where we were now holed up having a drink.

Eventually everyone met up and caught the train to Oldham. As it drew into the station, it was clear that the police had no reception committee waiting and we were on our own. One of the boys knew an Oldham lad from England games and was being continually phoned to tell us their firm was on the outskirts of town in a pub called the Centurion. Nobody knew where this pub was, and the directions given over the phone were not the clearest, so off Stoke set to track them.

A large roar was heard and Stoke's lads charged up the road to be met with flying glass and bottles, and to be surrounded by old bill, who then marched the mob straight to the pub from where the charge was head-ing. It was met with large cheers and claps from the defenders of the pub, who turned out to be the Stoke firm that had been earlier rounded up at Victoria and who had mistaken us for Oldham. The roar that provoked the charge was caused by elderly locals who had felt safe enough with the gathered firm to exact a touch of revenge by kicking a few Asians as they passed their bus stop.

Stoke drank until 2 p.m. before flooding out of the police containment and marching straight up the high street towards the shopping centre. A left at the top of the road, a short walk on and another left led into the open-air market. All the time the mob chanted the name of Walter Chamberlain, the O.A.P. who had been attacked the week before. The numbers continued to swell as local people joined the throng; it had turned from a football escort to a political march within seconds as local white people of all ages took the chance to chant and cause waves. As the mob went forward it ragged the stalls of the Asian traders, gaining momentum as it moved on. Though hundreds finally exited the market, the police had enough numbers to get things under control. They decided to split the mob with a baton charge.

Three groups of lads went in different directions. One went to the right and into a housing area. After a few minutes they came across the Centurion pub. They kicked in the door panel but Oldham refused to come out and within minutes the old bill had moved them further into the terraced streets. They were then confronted by a firm of Asians, who fired fireworks and building debris in their direction. Stoke charged but again were baton-charged by the police, resulting in Stoke being pursued by the police and the Asians.

The second group ran down a bank onto the estate near where the old guy had been attacked. A large group of police followed, mostly in vehicles. Halfway down, the road was cordoned off with concrete bollards so they could not follow without leaving their vehicles. At this point Stoke's lads and some locals started to attack anything ethnic: businesses, taxis, houses. Local residents were even standing on their doorsteps pointing out neighbours who were Asian. A local bobby tried to make a solitary arrest but was manhandled to the floor by the surrounding mob and had second thoughts as his hat was kicked down the road by his escaping prisoner.

This pattern of events followed the crowd all the way to the football stadium. Now, I am not trying to excuse Stoke's behaviour on this day, but the media later put the blame at Stoke's feet, saying it had been pre-planned and organised with far-right organisations and that the final touches were put together on the train journey in to Oldham. They even made a TV documentary about it in the 'Hooligan' series on BBC television with an undercover reporter. What a load of bollocks. Stoke went there to meet Oldham with the intentions of a bit of a footy row, not to cause mass disorder. That was the result of a spontaneous chain of events that, yes, did involve Stoke but not in the way the media portrayed.

As the group arrived at the ground, Stoke's marauding fans were put into the stadium. Local people actually applauded them as they left to watch the game. The third mob were stewarded to the ground by a sparse police presence; this spelled disaster as groups broke away to confront the local footy hoolies and the now baying Asian groups, who were getting themselves organised into a defence force.

Stoke filled the Chadderton Lane End of the ground. Not a ticket remained, as Stoke needed the points for the play-offs. About 4000 were inside with 200 locked out. The racist chanting continued throughout the game with Stoke winning and collecting the needed points. At the end of the game Stoke exited the stadium to be met with a wall of riot police who corralled everyone for the walk back to the station; they must have drafted them in from as far away as they could because there were three to every fan. The main Stoke firm hit the front and, with the pressure of the crowd surging forward, burst through the lines. Talk was spreading fast that the police knew of a problem up ahead.

Within five minutes, that problem became apparent as the 400-strong Stoke firm were met by a small army of angry, chanting Asians tooled up for a mini war. Stoke surged forward, bouncing up the road as they tried to meet this accommodating opposition, only to endure a shower of petrol bombs and rocks. The firm spread across the road to be met with brutal police tactics. Stoke had been the aggressors before the game but were now an unarmed crowd walking along a police-designated route and being attacked with Molotov cocktails, yet the police ignored the throwers and baton-charged Stoke, beating and pushing as they went. Everyone had to walk past the throwing mob, dodging rocks. Protests were lodged with the police but all met the same reply: 'Orders mate,' or, 'We were told to clear you lot to diffuse the situation, hopefully the Asians will just go home now. The orders came from the top, complain to them not us.' The situation did not defuse. That night gangs of Asian and whites clashed around Oldham, with thousands of pounds' worth of damage done to property and businesses.

As the lads waited at the station for their train, phones were going mad as people all around the country rang to see what had happened and lads gave their version of events and the role in the disorder they had taken. They were then put on trains, given massive escorts across Manchester and bundled back to Stoke-on-Trent. Manchester City had been at home that day and their firm had rung Stoke to try to organise a bit of an off. They claimed to have good numbers around the city centre and were awaiting our return. What a scene must have greeted them as Stoke returned to Manchester, hundreds of lads marching through their city centre but enough old bill to outnumber both mobs.

Why do we do it? (Cossack)

Good question. People say things like, 'Thugs, shame on you,' but we only fight people who want to fight us. It doesn't matter what your background – lawyers, builder, accountant – you will be what you will be.

My father died when I was two. I'm not asking for sympathy, I'm just telling you how it is. If he had been alive when I was bang at it, I wouldn't have been what I became. I am an only son, and brother of four sisters, and if my mum could see me now she'd turn in her grave. Sorry mum.

But there's no better feeling than when you are in someone else's manor, budging nowhere, smirking, laughing, outnumbered four to one – and I've been there many times. Steaming straight into each other, the opposition are thinking, *here, these boys don't give a fuck, they're budging nowhere.*

I have had some good days out with Stoke, some up, some down, but we are a family and we care about each other. When you are walking down the road with Stoke you feel proud, special, with your Stone Island coat or Lacoste jacket on, like this is your platoon and look how well-dressed we are. The older generation don't understand why we spend so much on clothes but when you have got a top match, you want to be looking the top bollocks.

Stoke have had a hooligan element as far back as I can remember, and a bad reputation, but have always been fair to the opposition when it matters. I know innocent people get caught in the mayhem but there's been trouble at away matches with our shirtboys and we've come to their assistance many times – but that's never recognised.

It was Everton at home and I went down Stoke with Miffer. Bear in mind I was sixteen at the time. Miffer looked after me all day, buying me beer and some food, but that was Miffer doing his fatherly thing. We left the ground and gathered at the hotdog stand outside the Stoke End. Somebody said Everton were waiting at Booth Street. Miffer's words were, 'Stay on the outskirts.' I was young and cocky but still respected his wishes.

At Booth Street it went mad. Both sets of fans clashed and I had never seen anything like it in my life. It was very scary for a young lad. Half of me was mystified and the other half intrigued as to what these two sets of fans got out of it. But as it went on I saw the buzz they got and I knew I wanted a piece of that cake.

My life with the N40 has no regrets. I've loved every minute of it, though I would like to say a big sorry for the hassle I have caused my dear wife Sam. She knew what I was like when she met me but she ended up putting a ring on my finger anyway.

I'm thirty-seven now, married with two boys, and have settled down, but still love the buzz, whether it's on television or at Stoke. It never leaves you.

Cardiff Away (Hoss)

One game that always raises a smile is Cardiff away in January 2002, not for mob violence but for psychological and bonding reasons among the lads. Cardiff have a big firm and possibly an even bigger reputation. This was seen in 2000 when we had last played them at their place. At the time there was little interest among the lads. It was a night match and we had no scores to settle with Cardiff, as we had not played each other for years. Despite this, Stoke took about twenty lads who, by all accounts, had a torrid time against a group of between sixty and seventy Taffs before the game, and half the Valleys afterwards.

Fast forward to 2002. By now we had certainly met Cardiff, with their reputation, like ours, growing at a rate of knots. This included the incredibly hyped (by Cardiff) 'Battle of Britain' in 2001, which was actually no more than two groups of lads attacking the record number of old bill at the Britannia Stadium, resulting in a lot of arrests and bans for each side. This time we were determined to leave our mark. Coaches and trains were dismissed, as there was a high possibility of getting pulled by the police. At just after 9am, eighty of Stoke's dedicated hardcore hooligans set off on the long journey to Cardiff in private transport.

After a couple of service stops and a beer break, we parked by an out-of-town train station and took a train into the city centre. It was three o'clock in the afternoon, almost five hours before kick-off, deliberately chosen as the time the twenty lads had arrived in the city centre two years before. Throughout the short train journey the talk was of violence, past and future. As we arrived, raised voices were heard: 'OK, this is it, we know what we're here for,' and, 'Keep it tight.' The usual stuff.

We bowled off the train ticketless and went straight through the waiting ticket collectors and onto the Cardiff streets. Our target was the Prince of Wales, a massive Wetherspoons boozer just past the bus station; the scene of the crime in 2000. We had come for a row, but no-one knew what lay ahead. Cardiff knew we were coming. *Would the whole of the Valleys be awaiting our arrival?* We were prepared for whatever was there.

Jack-hammers ceased, buses and taxis stopped and shoppers halted in their tracks to watch our now 100-strong group, showing gritted teeth and frowned faces, ready for the fight.

'It's here.'

'OK, keep it tight.'

'This is their boozer.'

We were only a few yards from the target. Millsy was first in, closely followed by Jasp and then me. Despite the long, long build-up, we found fifteen Cardiff and a few office workers listening to Nat King Cole. We left them alone. What's the point in 100 destroying fifteen? We let them know we were there and told them to get their firm together. No punches, no tables thrown. It was not worth fucking up the rest of the day.

We went back onto the streets. Unfortunately the cries of 'let's go through the whole town' were unheeded as the alcoholics pulled us towards the Borough, apparently another of Cardiff's pubs, opposite Wetherspoons. Two of the lads stayed in Wetherspoons and witnessed the aftermath as the fifteen Taffs made fifteen frantic calls to their mates. Before long the whole of Cardiff would learn of our presence, be it via mobile phone message, word of mouth or BBC Wales, who were to soon take up residence outside the Borough, alongside ranks of riot police.

All we could do was drink and try to make contact with the Soul Crew by mobile phone. A few Cardiff walked past the windows, applauding our actions, although a certain Sam Hamman was less than complimentary as he stood outside the doors, between the pub and the old bill, laughing at us and mouthing, 'Is this all you've brought?' Cheeky foreign bastard! Inside the pub everyone was getting more excited as the alcohol flowed. Discussions were had with bouncers about the Soul Crew, with their comments on our inadequate numbers being roundly jeered. A Welsh flag behind the bar was soon also to become a target for abuse and following a cry of 'burn the fucker' it was felt best to station one of the bouncers beside it.

At 7pm we left and were swooped upon by the riot police, whose numbers had swollen ridiculously. Jackets, scarves, caps and hoods were pulled over faces as cameras followed us at close quarters on our march to the ground. We had hoped that Cardiff would come out of Wetherspoons at the same time but only a few got out. Maybe that was all they had, despite the four hours to prepare. Or did they have something planned further along the route? This was the famous Soul Crew after all. Surely we would meet some time before the game? That was the reason we had left our beds at 8am.

Normal supporters who were either walking or standing in pub doorways on the route to the ground once again stopped and stared. The back streets of Cardiff had obviously not often seen what they were now witnessing. But where were the Soul Crew? We eventually arrived at Ninian Park. The expected attacks had not materialised, although there were a lot of riot police preventing any confrontations.

We were in the ground by 7.30 and placed in a cage, with a narrow caged walkway segregating us from their supporters. These were not the Soul Crew, or at least I hope they weren't, but they were still an aggressive crowd of anti-English Cardiff fans who had most likely terrorized numerous other clubs. We aren't 'another club'. We had come for a meet with the Soul Crew and were still buzzing with anticipation. Will they come onto the pitch as with Leeds in the FA Cup? Will they climb the fences? What lay in store? *Fuck this waiting lark, let's attack them.* The Cardiff in the adjacent paddock had not seen this before as forty nutters attacked the fences. They soon withdrew as the police came into our end. Various arrests were made, with lads charged with racial incitement against the Welsh. Funny how the old bill ignored the constant anti-English jibes aimed at us throughout the game.

Lost the game, but so what. No pitch invasions, nothing. We were kept in the ground as Cardiff left the area. The funniest moment of the day was seeing a twelve-year-old Stoke fan throw part of a burger stand over the gates at passing Taffs, in full view of the police. We were again forced to take matters into our own hands and steamed the gates, eventually managing to get them open. Unfortunately, our path was barred by more riot police, who also lined the route back to the nearest train station. From here we were put on our way back to our transport. Surely they would have sussed where we had parked up? By now though, this was more in hope than expectation. We had already been let down too much today. Ever the optimists though, we got our 'heads' back on and were back onto the streets of Cardiff.

Again we came across no opposition so retired to the pub where we stayed until last orders, unfortunately having to watch the game again on Welsh TV. Despite a few requests from the more intoxicated of the lads to go back into the city centre, at about 11.30 we headed home, content that we had achieved our aim of showing Cardiff that we were there, in their city centre and spoiling for a fight.

Outnumbered in Bristol (Rich)

At the end of the 2001/02 season, we had chucked away our chances of automatic promotion and were struggling for form to catch the play-offs. In May we played Bristol City away, and plans were being hatched to get into the city centre with the minimum of fuss. Some older lads had stayed over on the Friday night, being invited for a dance outside by a few CSF (Bristol City's hooligan firm). The invite was declined, as it would spoil an otherwise pleasant social event. Why get greedy on the starter when there is a perfectly decent main course to be had?

On the Saturday, a good group of forty lads met in Bath just after dinnertime, a mix of youth and older Stoke, Newcastle and Stafford. After a few pints in a dirty local boozer, and some quality South American fighting powder, a bus was hailed to get us into Bristol. The driver was a top bloke and took us all the way into town, his passengers being forty casual football hooligans and a couple of OAPs going home from their weekly shopping. Such are the logistics required to evade the forces of law and order.

As we got into town, we could see police stationed outside every pub and bar, scanning the streets for rogue-like characters. None of them saw the bus roll past containing top-class lads. We jumped off at the last stop before the bus station and went straight into a pub. After a quick pint we were on the move again, getting closer to the city centre all the time, and after one more port of call we met up with more of our lads on the main street. A round was had and then it became obvious that the old bill were getting closer to us, as two officers were outside the pub. Instead of the usual Stoke trick of setting the pub on fire, we left through the fire exit and went for a stroll round the back streets of Bristol. We were on the phone to their lads, who were trying to direct us to where they were, but it all went tits up and before long we were collared by the law and split in different directions for a pint, some to head towards the ground.

On the way to the match, a few lads were taken out by bigger numbers of Bristol, mainly whilst walking through the park. Four Stoke lads from Hartshill and Penkhull were dropped off by taxi, and the driver helpfully advised them to get a beer in their top boozer. In they strolled and got clocked straight away. Being Stella'd up, they wandered out to be followed by a bigger mob of Bristol, who tried tackling them. The Stella kicked in and the four lads stood proud, one lad dodging the ruck whilst having a piss. One Bristol lad was knocked clean out once the lucky gent finished his piss with a punch that was praised by a police officer who broke up the row. Stoke had got into their city before the game, gone walkabout, and tried to take it to them, but sly ambushes were their order of the day. As the away end filled up there were a few stories of similar scams by Bristol lads, and this riled the 350 lads who were spread out in the away end amongst a healthy following of about 3,000 Stokies.

We came out at the end and weren't really sure where to head. The natural course was to go for the home end. We turned right, down a main street, and heard one hell of a roar further down the road. It transpired that a mob of Bristol had met one of the first lot of Stoke fans to come out of the ground and as they headed to their coach the bigger Bristol mob had taken it to a bunch of genuine shirt-wearing supporters. This is not in the rulebook. As we got closer to the Stoke lads, a couple of them had very bad head wounds and one was on the floor bleeding heavily. The Bristol lads were further up the road but still in sight so we offered it to them.

The police split us up quickly, but a few wiser heads managed to evade them and went under the roadway towards the Bristol. We were about thirty-strong, older Alsager, East Midlands, Newcastle and Stafford lads and about half youth but these lads were well up to anything. We had all seen Stoke blood spilled on the road and feelings were running high.

The Bristol lads were above us on a roadway, about fifty-strong. More joined them as they started lobbing rocks down on us, so we ran forward to join the walkway down from the road. They had twice the numbers and came running down at us, with height advantage. They were a mixture of scruffy older lads and youth, and as they steamed down one lad pulled CS gas out and sprayed it about wafting down at us, but as he was higher up than us it went into the air above. Another young lad in a pale blue tracksuit top pulled a small blade out from his sleeve and waved it about. Still the rocks came at us.

Both firms laid into each other and we backed them up the walkway about thirty yards. They stood right at the top looking down at us. We bounced at them and stood firm, waiting for them to make the next move. They came back down at us, backing us off almost from the walk-way but pulling it back together we steamed back into them. One older Newcastle lad grabbed a big fuck-off rock that they had lobbed over and from just inches away his side of the barrier threatened Bristol lads with it. Seeing the fist-sized rock they backed off and this allowed more Stoke to get in at them. At that point a well-known Alsager lad picked up the rock that the lad had thrown and wellied it right into one of their bigger lads' face. Blood pissed down his shirt and some lads laid the boot into him. We now had them on the back foot and as they backed off one Bristol older lad was grabbed and kicked to the ground. Another was grabbed and had his scruffy jacket ripped off his shoulders. The rest backed off and left the older lad on the ground to endure about forty-five seconds of a good kicking. One older Newcastle lad stood right at the front making huge wanker signs at them as all they could do was continue to chuck rocks the size of bricks at us.

After a while they managed to muster up enough bottle to charge at us again, and we once more held our own, again outnumbered two to one. It was only when we heard sirens that we backed off, with Bristol coming at us saying we had been run! We moved further up the road, but at that point the odds became even sillier. The same 60 from before moved round the side of us, with a few more coming from the other side. We moved up to a wide dual carriageway and then in front of us about another 80 or so Bristol came running across from the parkway.

Now it sounds like a pisstake, but if you've seen *Zulu* you can imagine how we felt. There was 30 of us, mixed ages, fucked from battling the other lot, now faced with about 160 lads coming from every direction, still dodging flying rocks. A couple of our top lads pulled us all together and we stood firm in the middle of the road, stopping traffic and bouncing up and down at them. Still they came but we fronted them all the way across the road. It was completely fucking mental – we were all buzzing our tits off. Not one single Stoke lad was running away, our bottle held and we felt completely untouchable. We were outnumbered five to one and they couldn't touch us, even with numbers, blades, gas and rocks. The old bill moved in heavily cracking a few heads and legs and we were moved to one side of the road, and to be fair to the CSF their mob doubled in size as they started lobbing all sorts at the police who were by now all round us, but when it came to fists and street brawling, we were well on top.

Defying the Law (Rich)

February 8, 2003. A day to make a statement. We were playing away at Grimsby, not a big deal even after our ding-dongs in the early Nineties, though a place never to be underestimated. This was the match where Stoke's new True Supporter ID card was being introduced, amid a fanfare of support from our local press. We had known for weeks that a firm would be put together, because we had to make a point. We had to show how loyal, how stubborn, how passionate we were. We are Stoke and year after year the authorities struggle to contain us, prevent our growth and work out ways of beating us, yet only succeeding in driving us underground and tighter still.

A coachload of lads gathered at a rendezvous kept secret from any travellers until the night before. This was mainly older lads but with some top quality younger lads aboard. There was no way any of these known faces would ever get an ID card, in fact the authorities would fall over in amazement if any of us even bothered applying. We all knew we were risking arrest just by travelling without a card. We were in for an interesting day.

We had a quiet trip up there and arrived undetected by the law at about 10.20. A handful of Grimsby youth saw our coach pull up and within seconds mobiles were out as they contacted their superiors. Now most of us older lads will admit to getting a bit large in the jeans size these days, and anyone will tell you that amongst other pleasures a Stoke lad likes his ale and grub. It was only right and proper that we headed straight for a local café and the nearest McDonald's to refuel. We watched from just yards away as a few more Grimsby youth roamed the streets, scratching their heads trying to figure out where we had gone.

We were stuck in the Submarine boozer and left to sup our ale. Grimsby had pulled their lads together and they knew we were here and were drinking pretty close to us, but lines of riot police made any effort to meet impossible. After a while we were told by the top plod that we were to get on the coach or risk arrest. It was a fair deal, after all who can blame them for being pissed off? We were handed a flyer explaining why we were being removed from the area and were banned from the whole county of Lincolnshire. Stoke had got a firm up, no tickets, no ID cards, and arrived in town before Grimsby or the law had even supped their first cuppa of the day or read the morning headlines.

Even as we were escorted out of town, a few lads who had travelled by car had it with Grimsby. There was about a dozen of them and forty Grimsby had tried to attack the pub they were in. They gave a very good account of themselves, to the extent that one Town lad had his head caned with a pool cue for his troubles. Word was that he was hospitalised but later turned out to be OK.

The way back was bizarre, with us having a sizeable police escort all the way home, exchanging forces at each county as we crossed borders. We stopped for a piss break and those getting off the coach were met by a mob of riot coppers headed to us, batons raised ready to quell the beasts from the Potteries. What were we going to do? Rampage through the hard shoulder calling it on with passing motorists? They even watched as we pissed, with one dumpy, short arse female officer staring at our exposed cocks until I wafted my yellowy, Guinness-drenched piss in her direction and she looked away disgusted. This happened again, handled by another county force, who this time let us go as far as the woods fifteen yards away, but for what it was worth we might as well have been manacled death-row inmates marching through the heat and sweltering humidity of the Mississippi swamplands.

As we crossed the Stoke city limits we got the driver to stop and did one quickly, as the harassed car of two Staffs coppers tried to reason with us to stay on the coach. No way – if you ask me they were taking us straight to Stoke nick for 'processing' and we made the right choice in doing one. Eventually everyone made their way to Newcastle, and there was a hint of irony in the fact that we supped our first pint back home just before the match at Grimsby kicked off. The town was full of a grizzled-up firm of top quality Stoke and we had an afternoon and night on the lash. By tea-time everyone was wasted and I remember walking into Yates's to be met by a sea of nasty faces, everyone off their heads.

We had once again achieved something; continuing the notoriety of Stoke City by blatantly breaching the rules of the law via the ID card scheme. We had told them, very publicly, to FUCK OFF with the scheme. A good tight little firm of Stoke had risen early once again, got it together and some of the lads even had a row. That firm did as much as any other battle, any gathering of Stoke's firm or any other event to continue our reputation of defying authority and of rewriting the rule book.

And the breakfast was quality too.

Crystal Palace Away 2003: The Future? (Spoon)

This was the first game for Stoke, unofficially, where ID cards were abandoned, because Crystal Palace had decided to sell anyone a ticket on the day. Word was out, and everyone was looking forward to the day. A draw and we were safe from relegation. Stoke really look forward to a good day out in London. You never know who you'll bump into.

Trains left at 6.30 a.m. from Stafford, 6.30 from Stoke and 8.10 from Stoke. Each one had a grizzly collection of lads aboard. At 7 a.m. the ale was opened, the first of a long, long day of drinking. At 11 a.m. we met up at the Blackbird in Earls Court, numbering eighty good lads. At Victoria the numbers have risen to 100, with others scattered about all over.

No trouble before the game and after a few drinks in Norwood with some friendly shirt-wearing Palace fans we had about 200 lads in the ground. The atmosphere was pretty evil and the usual chants of 'No Surrender' go up. About half the away support of 1,400 are singing it. A hooligan minority? Hmmm.

Back on the train, out of Victoria, we're across the road to the Shakespeare. Surely Chelsea are there waiting for us. The buzz comes on strong ... yes, there's lads outside the door. It's gonna go mental. No, it's a pub full of Stoke.

The phones are buzzing to Chelsea and Millwall, but nobody wants to come out to play. We get the 7.30 train home rammed full of bladdered Stoke. More ale. Drugs. Racist chanting. No surrEnder. It's a proper horrible scene. Three coppers stand watching in the doorway of our carriage, shaking their heads in dismay. Somebody offers them a bottle of poppers. We're pissed, angry and doped-up.

Palace away was probably a snapshot of future games for us.

Closing Words

DID I REALLY live and buzz off such a lifestyle for all those years? As I sat and wrote this book, I found myself on numerous occasions searching for words other than mayhem, crazed or chaos. Yeah, chaos. What sort of a word is that to describe somebody's lifetime of achievements? Am I embarrassed? No not really, nor am I ashamed. The fact is it wasn't just about the fighting or the don't-give-a-fuck attitude; it boiled down to a needing to feel loved, to be wanted. Accepted for the person you are.

I left Stoke for good in 1994. It was a necessity, both for my liberty and my sanity. Leaving the bricks and mortar behind came as easily as ever, but leaving behind the hearts of the people I had grown to love and respect plummeted me to an all-time low. Such was my addiction to cocaine and football violence that I was left with no other choice but to place myself in complete isolation. For the next four years I became a hermit, living alone with no methods of communication. Cossack and Finbar were the only two friends who I couldn't possibly live without, and twice, maybe three times a year, they would travel up to see me. I was a shadow of the man I had been and their sadness was plain to see.

As time elapsed, I started to walk upright again and the cheeky grin returned. Within days I was running and punching the air with delight: it was definite, the attraction was mutual, and the brightly coloured butterfly that had left me in the back bar of the Alsager Arms all those years ago had me mesmerized as she floated into my one-track life. Katie was the most beautiful creature that I had ever set eyes on. And not only that, she fancied me for being me.

Kate knew nothing about my other life. I told her a bit about how my Nan had raised me, and that I in turn had come to look after her out of respect for all she had done for me. Other than that, as always I kept it tight. Katie came from what I would call a proper traditional family – in fact she had a fantastic family, though meeting them was the first hurdle that we had to cross together. Me go to dinner? Meet the family? Sit round a table? I lost my bottle and refused point blank.

The day I finally met Mike and Pauline was one of the hardest things I've ever had to do. They were friendly and made me very welcome, but I made sure that I was continuously in Katie's presence. The thought of Mike, the concerned father, asking me anything about my education or career had me sweating profusely. Blagging the fella would have been the easiest option – that comes natural to me – but I actually started to have feelings for his daughter, and decided instead to avoid the man as politely as possible. Show me a father who would want his daughter to end up with one of the worst football hooligans in the country.

The honeymoon period came and went and the inevitable questions appeared. 'Why don't you have a TV? Haven't you got a mobile? Where are your friends?' The bombshell. How could I introduce her to Finbar, whose first words would be, 'Who do you support? Have they got a firm?' The idea of taking Kate to Stoke was inconceivable.

But the lads loved Kate and she loved them from the off. I had been wrong to underestimate her, and she showed a frank and open approach to this new world that she was being introduced to. Her perception of a football hooligan before meeting them was the usual bootboy, skinhead image, the type that beat up old ladies for their purses. Katie also had a good look at me in my own environment. She could see, and told me, how special was this bond that a group of men held for each other. I was relieved, and we planned a life together. This was a first for me.

It was important having the lads back in my life. I had missed them. My retirement from the football was readily acknowledged by everyone now. Gone were the pressure and expectancy, although attending a match was too much like tempting fate. Ask any junkie who has cleaned himself up and is then faced with a hit for the first time in years. I was happy with just the banter, and the reminiscing.

Being back in the fold opened my eyes to a new breed of young men that had attached themselves to the N40. Some of them I already knew. I had watched the likes of Bud growing up on his brother Nomad's shoulders. Staring down at us from his vantage point, I could see in his eyes when he was seven where he was going. Now Bud was a strapping young man, battle-hardened and blooded. Through him I was introduced to over 100 youngsters whose ages shocked me, as the scars they carried showed more life than their fourteen years should have. It was a new generation of disenchanted youngsters who could barely remember life without closed-circuit television and held an unhealthy disrespect for law and order. Behind the fluffy little fingers that protruded below the sleeve of oversized Stone Island jackets and the four-day-old bum fluff on their chins lay a tight-knit bunch of violent criminals whose loyalty and respect seemed to be given only to the senior members of the Naughty Forty.

My life had become evenly balanced for the first time ever, a loving home life, and a newfound social life back at home with the lads. The thought of the front door coming off its hinges was a distant memory. I was happy.

I have never been an avid book reader; in fact the only book I had completed from start to finish was *Bury My Heart At Wounded Knee* by Dee Brown, in which she chronicled the persecution and demise of the Native American Indian. Finishing her book was the only time in my life that I look at the White American Cowboy and his ruthless greed with disdain. The only other book that had provoked such an immediate feeling was *Guvnors*, the Manchester City football hooligan memoir. It was this publication that fuelled, not only in me but the lads as well, renewed undercurrents in our disdain for Manchester City football club and its hooligan following. None of us bothered to read it but copies were picked up and flicked through and the account of our clash at Rothersthorpe services station was brought to everybody's attention. We were horrified. Not only did three of them grass us up on the day, but years later they write about it, as if it were some kind of a screenplay, where their hero warriors take on an overwhelming force of *Deliverance*-style hillbillies who were so inbred that they would hardly be able to read it and set the record straight.

This was foremost in my mind when publisher Peter Walsh, whose company had published *Guvnors*, offered me the opportunity to write this story.

Cardiff City's Soul Crew had just completed their own book for the same company and the authors Dave and Tony were holding their book launch on the last day of the season in one of their colourful little watering holes just off the city centre. Stoke had been invited. Six of us travelled down by train: myself, Bobby, Marcus, Finbar, Chelly and Nobby 'Steelez'. We were excited at the thought of a day out, and not knowing if they would turn on us had us buzzing. I hadn't felt like this for years. And as we sat supping warm lager from cans, I felt myself slipping back inside my old skin … *Remember Barnsley away in the cup, night match, went off by the level crossing* … and so the day continued.

All Stoke lads from the Eighties know Hugh. He was from Port Talbot, and Soul Crew through and through, but spent time living in the Potteries and became a close friend of Nobby and the Castle lads. I remembered him well, and it was in his trust that we placed our safety.

Hugh met us at Cardiff Central with the Wasp, another known face in their firm. We were then taken to a small quiet pub, where we were to be introduced to Cardiff's older top lads. On the short journey, I re-examined my situation. *Why, after all those years away from it, are you now walking into a boozer to meet the top boys of a firm that your lads are having an on-going feud with?* That just added to the excitement. Shaking hands with another leading figure, and looking into his eyes for the first time, lasts seconds but is a massive moment and can set the stage for the rest of the day. The handshakes were firm and eye contact strong and genuine. Although never 100 per cent certain, my gut feeling told me that the Cardiff lads were as inquisitive about us as we were about them. We sat down and chatted about the old days, neither side mentioning the day that they had been to Stoke the previous season and rioted. It was diplomacy of the highest order and again placed a certain easiness on the day.

The launch party was in the afternoon in a basement nightclub in the city centre. With our hosts, we six N40 entered a claustrophobic venue rammed with the Soul Crew. Cue massive adrenalin buzz. Marcus, being the pain he is, immediately headed for the authors and publisher. They were sat in an alcove, signing their books. Marcus, as familiar as ever, bought one, got it signed, introduced himself and sat down.

Standing around looking out of place wasn't my thing either, so I headed to the bar, got my back against it, and paused for thought. From where I stood, I had the advantage of being able to see everything. Finbar was chewing the Wasp's ear with incessant questioning: 'How many lads have you got on a big day? I've been nicked against Swansea!' I smiled at the sight; although I couldn't hear a word, I knew what he was saying. The Wasp answered back with as much enthusiasm, so they were happy.

Next were the little huddles and discreet nods as I clocked some of the Cardiff younger element pointing out the visitors to each other. I surmised that it was a precarious situation, but the Cardiff lads were full of respect, so I ordered another vodka and tonic and chatted to the lads that had been the subject of a recent TV documentary. Marcus came over after twenty minutes or so and, frothing at the mouth as always, proceeded to tell me that he'd been doing Pete Walsh's head in.

'I've kept telling Pete Walsh you're over here and you're pissed off about that *Guvnors* book.'

I didn't need that. Unbeknown to any of our lot, I had met up with some of Blackpool's boys in a nightclub six months previously. They had heard I was Stoke and came over for a chat. They were good lads and I enjoyed their company for a while until H informed me that he knew a publisher that had worked on the *Guvnors* book. My reply was, 'Tell your fucking mate if he's going to write books on football hooliganism, to get his fucking facts straight, especially when it involves us.' The atmosphere fell flat, and no doubt my comments would have been conveyed.

'Marcus, for fuck's sake, not in here mate. Where is he? I'll have a chat.'

I didn't know what Peter would be thinking. He didn't know me from Adam, so I approached his table with a smile and introduced myself in an easy, open manner. I wasn't intent on making an issue about anything, so we chatted briefly about the *Soul Crew* book and his expectations of it. That was when he made comparisons with *Guvnors*. The subject had been opened and I had my say. Peter took my reaction as his opportunity to offer me a contract to write my own book, and if I felt that anything needed to be said, that would be my opportunity to do it. We swapped cards, and I said I'd think about it.

I did give it a lot of thought, almost to the point of asking myself, *is it revenge and is that petty?* But it wasn't really about that. I had to think of the lads and what would they want me to do. Discussions at home left me with no doubt what Kate wanted me to do; she had confidence in me. So I made a call to Cossack and put the plan to him. His reaction was as I expected, and a meeting was called for a fortnight later.

I travelled to Stoke not knowing if I was doing the right thing at all. Cossack had put the word out to a certain few that I wanted to speak to people of prominence from the different eras of Stoke's following. I was made up, and my mind was as well, when thirty serious geezers greeted me in the pub. They didn't half look a tidy firm and I warmed all over. Home!

It was a unanimous decision: 'Yeah, do it Jasp. We've earned this.' They meant it, and they were right, we did deserve it. Only thing was, it was me that was going to have to write it. Their answer to that was, 'There's only you that can do this for us, J, you'll do us proud mate.' I didn't make any remark to that comment. Instead I remained on a stool at the bar and looked into all those hardened faces staring back at me with united approval.

'What about the book cover, J?' Finbar brought me round from my deep contemplation and I just told them there and then.

'Book cover? It's dead simple. It's us. We've never run from anything in our lives, so why run from this? Let's front it up, big time.'

The approval was rapturous. We sang the house down. Truth and honesty was only ever going to be our approach. Nobody failed in their promise to be at the end of a phone if I needed them, and as for putting their faces on the front of a book, well it's not as if the police needed telling who any of them were.

So I set to work, knowing the enormity of chronicling such an intense subject that spanned decades. I found it difficult to know where to start, or who to start with. So I decided to use my story as the spine; that way I would be able to give 100 per cent to the lads, and although not everyone would get a big mention, at least I could give the reader some humanity, which is lacking in a lot of the books written on this subject.

In the initial stages of writing, I relied on telephone conversations and interviews. That was a great way of collecting information that I may have forgotten over the years, and the notes began to pile up – and pile up. And that's all I did have: loads of notes, loads of photographs and loads of ideas, but unfortunately no desire to put pen to paper. I'm not a writer and I'd got the block before I had even penned the title. I needed some inspiration.

It was my decision to get back down the match with the lads. After much thought, my plan was to research the subject all over again, right from its grassroots. This would enable me to get the feeling back in me and hopefully it would show through in my writing. Within a week, I was in a convoy of Renault Espace people carriers, leaving Stoke at 8am for a fixture at Burnley, a journey that takes a little over an hour. This early start was an effort to get off the roads and into Burnley before the police had started to deploy their officers along the routes into town. *Same old tactics but the transport's improved since my day*, I thought. The van I was in contained lads from the Castle area. They were called the May Bank Casuals and, along with other youngsters from the Penkhull and Longton areas, formed the main nucleus for the new breed of Stoke's hooligans. They were all very relaxed around me and I saw no bravado. Their pleasure at having one of Stoke's old faces with them was more than apparent. And to be honest, I enjoyed the attention. It felt good to be back, and so I went on with my old stories of Stoke being ripped off the fences in the Longside End of Burnley's ground way back when I was a schoolboy in the Seventies, and my audience of seven young men were captivated.

Designer clothes, designer scars. All as it used to be, but with the bonus of the new fashion accessory of the modern day 'football casual' – the mobile phone. Minutes after arriving in the outskirts of Burnley and finding a couple of cafes, the continual tones of the mobile took precedence, and within an hour the small firm I had travelled up with had grown to over 100 young casuals, with the older lads minutes behind them. This was new, but I liked it. That day out had all the thrills of the funfair. Police chases. Running battles in the seats between the Young Casual Element and police. Skirmishes with Burnley's Suicide Squad after the game. I returned back home that night wired, wasted and wanting more. The rot had begun to set in.

The early signs were the singing in the bath. Not the usual 'Rhinestone Cowboy'; now it was, 'Will ya come? Will ya come? Will ya come to Stoke-on-Trent? Will ya come to Stoke-on-Trent?' And it was loud. For the first time in over a decade, I had a fixture list, and studied it ritually every day. I was now attending every away game, even Brighton on a Tuesday night.

Still kidding myself that I was researching for the book, I made plans to travel with the lads to Portsmouth. I left home at 4am and drove to Stoke, the texts off all the excited lads started coming through at about 5am, and it was plain to see, I hadn't been the only one who couldn't get to sleep that night. I played the UK Subs at full volume, and put my foot down. It was an appalling December morning, and at Stafford Station 160 of the N40 boarded the 7am train to Portsmouth. The lads filled three carriages, and in each as I walked along, inspecting the quality, was a different party, most were still drunk from last night, and all were drinking now.

The train made good speed to Birmingham New Street, and with no visible coppers on board the lads all thought that they'd pulled off another successful swerve of the police. There were no other firms on New Street, it was far to early, and only two transport police officers were present, and they stayed on the platform. Result, we're on our way now lads. The train left New Street and remained at one drab speed all the way down to Oxford. It took over two hours to make the journey; the train was deliberately late by forty minutes, and we all knew why. The police were preparing a welcoming committee, at the other end. This soured the mood, and a few of the older heads started grumbling. 'Fuckin' said we should have gone in vans. We're fucked now.'

At Reading the train was boarded by a dozen Thames Valley Transport Police, all donning their riot smocks and balaclavas. They looked very impressive. They already knew the layout of the train, and where each individual was placed. They entered our carriage and approached the table I was at. They made no attempt to crowd us at all, in fact the tall sergeant was quite courteous as he spoke in my general direction.

'Morning, lads. I'd just like to ask you all a few questions.'

'OK.'

'You made a block booking for two hundred seats over a month ago, Only a hundred and sixty of you have travelled today. Where are the other forty?'

The reply came in the form of a question: 'If we're right with you, will you be right with us?'

The sergeant agreed.

'This what's on the train is what we've got mate, honest. What's going to happen to us at Pompey?'

The sergeant accepted our answer and informed us that the Hampshire police would be waiting for us at Fratton Station. Where they would take us, he didn't know; he presumed a pub by the ground or even the ground itself. The lads knew they had to act fast or the day would be ruined. They politely thanked the sergeant for his information and civil manner, and watched the officers return to their positions at either end of the train.

There was a slight chance, but highly unlikely, that the police hadn't placed their cordon as far out as Havant, as that was the next stop and the last one before capture. Under the watchful eye of the Thames Valley police, whispers went through three carriages.

'Wait for Havant. Don't get out of your seats because of the timing device on the locks, let the busies think we're staying on, and once all entering passengers have taken their seats, calmly get up and walk off with no noise. If the platform is full of police, just leg it anyway.'

When the train pulled into Havant at eleven-thirty, the platform was completely empty. The N40 had pulled it off, and in less than a minute the long line of taxis outside the station was being filled, with shouts of, 'Pompey town centre mate. Anywhere will do.' The nine-mile drive into Pompey felt like your first ride on the Ferris Wheel, everyone was buzzing as the speeding convoy of taxis took passengers to their uncertain destination. I was buzzing myself just listening to the four lads I was with ringing their mates back in Stoke and screaming to them what a mad day out they were missing. I was getting severely caught up in this emotion and I too began ringing people: 'It's mad down here, Stoke are berserk, these young 'uns don't give a fuck.'

Stoke had evaded capture by the police, who were still waiting at Fratton, and were heading into Portsmouth from all directions in small pockets of experienced football casuals, all on a roll. The potential was massive. Gone was the 160-strong firm with its relative safety in numbers. Stoke could easily go from hunter to hunted as soon as they stepped onto the 6.57's streets.

Within minutes, ten of Stoke's older lads found the Raven Pub in Somerstown. They knew immediately it was a Pompey pub by the paraphernalia on the walls. Even so it was empty bar a few regulars. Out of respect to the establishment, the landlady was asked for. It was explained to her who we were and what we were, and that although there were only ten of us at that moment, the pub would soon be full of Stoke fans who would inevitably bring the attention of the police. The lady thanked us for our frankness, and raised her fresh large gin and tonic with a smile of approval. We'd made it. Mission accomplished, we settled into a good drinking session with the luxury of the landlady's blessing. Gone are the days of roaming your opponents' streets, looking for continual encounters; these days, this is as good as it gets. Now it was in the hands of the 6.57.

The police duly arrived with their cameras, and after speaking to the landlady, left us to drink on, quite happy to pose for the odd Section 60 interview. The police concentrated their attention on the 100 or so Stoke lads that they had contained in the Raven pub, unaware that in the next street to us, under cover of the Registry pub, were thirty unaccounted for and very lively N40 of mixed ages and experience. From a safe distance, these lads tailed the huge police escort that began a two-mile walk to Fratton Park.

We could tell by the reaction of the locals who lined the streets and left cafes and hair salons to see what the fuss was all about, that this wasn't the norm for a match day in Pompey. Stoke numbered about 120, and were surrounded by twice as many policemen, with horses and dogs. The police linked arms and shepherded us at their pace towards the ground. I was in the middle of this mob and also knew that we were being tailed. As we approached within 500 yards of the away end, it was plain to see that the fun and games were about to begin, as the little side streets we were about to pass were full of the 6.57. Stoke roared and charged into the police lines, trying to break the escort and get into Pompey's boys. This went backwards and forwards for a couple of minutes. Nobody managed to get near the local lads, it was just mischief. I looked into the eyes of a guy of similar age as myself who was watching from a side street. He was an old-school football lad, I could tell, and for a brief moment as Stoke staged another breakout attempt, I saw him smile and wink at me, as if to say, *Go on mate. I know.*

Seeing all the commotion, the thirty Stoke lads that had been tailing us saw their opportunity to get past us and through the police lines in front, behind which a tidy mob of the 6.57 were waiting. The lads in the escort saw their move and charged, feigning an attack, to draw police attention away. It worked, and they got through, screaming into Pompey's unsuspecting firm. Stoke had turned up and had made their intentions clear.

The confusion ended with the entire Stoke mob penned into the street outside the away end. I have to say that the Hampshire police were the best we have ever come across, and it was because of their friendly, non-aggressive approach that we all consented to be searched and videoed.

This done, the commanding officer said on his loudhailer, 'Right lads, get your tickets ready, we're allowing you to enter the ground.'

Not one person moved. The police were surprised at the lack of movement and started saying, 'Come on lads, you've already missed the first ten minutes, what's up with you?'

'We're all banned, mate,' replied Rezin.

The old bill were dumbfounded. They had spent the last hour and a half walking us through their city, under the continual threat of attack, and not one of us had a ticket. They were forced to stand there as a large group of men laughed, joked, telephoned friends and generally had a good time. At the interval, Stoke's ticketless fans were escorted to Fratton Station, where they were all given another Section 60 for good measure, and were packed off to Reading, where Thames Valley Police could have us back.

Ten minutes before the end of the game, twelve of Stoke's lads that had got in the game came under attack as they walked along a dark street on their way to the station. It was a tough little encounter that went slightly in Pompey's favour, even though the numbers were the same on each side. As the fight drew to a close, more of Portsmouth's lads came bounding onto the scene, taking their numbers to over thirty. Stoke huddled tight and prepared to make a stand. It didn't look good at all – until one of the local lads shouted up, 'Oi, oi, these lads are game, leave 'em be.' The same gesture that I would hope our lot would produce in a similar situation at our place. Stoke had shown Pompey that they were game, and had come to fight, and they had come second best, despite handing out a broken nose to one of their lads. That was in a fight with even numbers, so why batter them again with a larger number? The gesture was appreciated, and we all headed back up north.

Weeks later, Stoke City football club introduced a new ID scheme, making away travel for any convicted fan almost impossible. The crime carries up to a six-month prison sentence. Our reply to this was: 'Bollocks. Ban us.'

In a short period of time, I had become completely immersed in the world of the new-breed football hooligan. This was much more than research; I was beginning to live it once again and inevitably my home life was going to bear the brunt. Being caught fronting myself up in the bedroom mirror, pulling hideous faces and brandishing a rolled-up magazine, was the cause of the first puzzled look. Fronting up a gang of foul-mouthed youths just because they were trying to emulate the football look without, in my eyes, earning the right, was a further shock. I was becoming more volatile each day, and obviously less attractive to Kate.

The sad thing about it was my 'what do I care, I've got the lads and the firm' attitude, which would make any women feel second best, and unloved.

After several months of bewilderment, the aggression that was part of daily life now as I sifted through piles of photographs and chatted about violence over the phone with people I had hardly spoken to in six years, finally sent a huge crack through the relationship. Katie didn't know the man she was living with any more. With five months to our wedding, all plans were shelved, the wedding cancelled and she moved back home to her parents.

Alone in a cold empty house, I looked around me. The sunshine had left, and I was sat surrounded by dozens of news clippings and photographs, with the continual tones of my mobile and landline battering my head as more lunatics queued to add their fuel to the fire. The lads were back in my life but they had come at a price. I proceeded to write this story with my head completely up my arse.

What does the future hold for the Naughty Forty? Difficult to say. More life bans from the club for the people involved with the writing of this book? Fair enough, that's to be expected. Where, I would like to know, do the club and police think they are banning these people to? They are not just going to disappear into thin air, problem solved. They are just pushing them further underground and adding more of a stigma to an already rich reputation of disgrace.

In my short time back with the firm, the most noticeable thing was the resurgence of old-school football heads coming out of 'retirement' after a sixteen-year failed marriage, with the kids grown up and gone. These are the disenchanted men that have given it all up only to have it thrown back in their faces. You can't blame them for seeking out that old feeling and having the comfort of being with dozens of old friends. Isn't the thought of stepping out of your mundane nine-to-five life, and catapulting yourself back to your youth every now and again, attractive, even just for a few hours on a Saturday afternoon? That's what the majority of thirtysomething hooligans, who are reappearing all over the country, are doing at the moment. Not just at Stoke, everywhere.

Football violence is definitely on the increase. The difference with the Stoke lads is the magnitude of the 'youth policy' surrounding Stoke's young hooligan following, and their surge up the league of infamy. It makes an attractive day out for an old, semi-retired Eighties head, who can now don his designer clothes, travel to a big game with all the excitement of the old days, and watch a load of crazed youngsters re-enacting his youth for him. And these youngsters are getting more confidence and bigger stages to perform on, in front of people who were their own schoolyard heroes, the people that they wanted to be like when they grew up. Sound familiar? You tell me where it's going.

As for me, well I've got a butterfly to go and catch.

Blind Rage: A Poem

If you don't want it, don't bring it on. That's what you say, that's what you
   live by.
So why the rage? Why every so often do you lose the plot?
If you don't bring it on, how can you justify that outburst, that anger? Hurting
   loved ones that hurt for you?
Feeling sorry for yourself? Don't bother. Your choice, mate. How many times do
   you have to do it? Who is it you're really angry at?
Feeling let down? You really need to take a good look at yourself.
Do you like people looking at you? No! Then why give them the opportunity,
   it only makes it worse? Scrutiny, who fuckin' needs it?
'Nice guy, but he's a mad cunt.' Have a nice night.
Ever walked in a room … and how many times have you asked yourself,
   have they stopped laughing? Is he saying something? Never takes you
   long to find a seat, does it.
So you keep on traveling along your track, getting off every now and then.
Funny how it's easier at first. That charm, your cheeky grin. The ladies love it!
   And the men notice it.
This is where you're best, isn't it mate? This is your ground, you're strong now.
Is this the only role you know? Is this as good as it gets?
Never takes long though does it? Sharing something, then being let down.
   Feeling unwanted.
Tantrum at first, just to let them know. You gain more ground that way.
But for what? What's your game mate? You're all right just being you.
Haunted? Can't remember? Blind rage was it, mate? Or something personal
   that you've managed to bottle up since you were a child.
So what's that got to do with any of these people? Can you not love
   anybody?
Why can't you let them touch you? Isn't that what you've always wanted?
What happens inside? Why do you cower? You're supposed to be hard,
   aren't you?
Is it better just wanting it, does it keep you going? How can wanting be all
   you want?
Feel it! It's here now, your time has come. Let down no longer, c'mon man,
   this makes you stronger.
Put this to bed; let it all be said.
Remember my friend, you're a long time dead.